Xi'an Relics Essence_Gold and Silver Vessels

초판인쇄 2015년 7월 10일
초판발행 2015년 7월 10일

엮은이 시안시문물보호고고학연구소
옮긴이 중국문물전문번역팀
펴낸이 채종준
진 행 박능원
기 획 지성영
편 집 박선경 · 이정수
디자인 조은아
마케팅 황영주

펴낸곳 한국학술정보(주)
주 소 경기도 파주시 회동길 230(문발동513-5)
전 화 031-908-3181(대표)
팩 스 031-908-3189
홈페이지 http://ebook.kstudy.com
E-mail 출판사업부 publish@kstudy.com
등 록 제일산-115호(2000. 6. 19)

ISBN 978-89-268-6988-8 94910
      978-89-268-6263-6 (전11권)

 한국학술정보(주)의 학술 분야 출판 브랜드입니다.

中國 西安(長安)의 문화유산

금은기

金
銀
器

시안시문물보호고고학연구소 엮음
중국문물전문번역팀 옮김

한눈에 보는 중국 시안(西安, 長安)의 문화유산

시안(西安, 長安)은 중국 고대문명의 발상지로 역사상 13왕조의 왕도인바 중국 전통문화의 산실이라고 할 수 있다. 주(周)·진(秦)·한(漢)·당(唐)나라 등의 수도로서 청동기(靑銅器)를 비롯한 각종 옥기(玉器)와 금은기(金銀器), 불교 조각상(佛敎彫刻像), 당삼채(唐三彩), 도용(陶俑), 자기(瓷器), 회화(繪畵), 서예(書藝) 등 수많은 문화유산을 남기고 있다. 그러나 이러한 문화유산은 여러 박물관이나 문화재연구소에서 분산 소장하고 있어 한눈에 감상할 수가 없다.

시안을 답사했을 때 중국의 지역연구기관으로서 시안 지역의 유적·왕릉·건축물 등 역사문화유적의 보호와 연구를 담당하고 있는 시안시문물보호고고소(西安市文物保護考古所)에서 정리하고, 세계도서출판시안공사(世界圖書出判西安公司)에서 발행한 『西安文物精華(시안문물정화)』를 접한 바 있다. 이번에 출간된 『中國 西安(長安)의 문화유산』 시리즈는 이를 번역·출판한 것으로, 이를 통하여 시안의 문화유산을 한눈에 감상할 수 있게 되었다. 이 책은 전문가들이 몇 년간에 걸쳐 시안의 문화유산 가운데 에센스를 선정, 회화·금은기·옥기·당삼채·불교조 각상·자기·청동거울·도용·청동기·서예·도장(圖章) 등으로 분류하여 집대성한 것이다. 중국어를 해득하지 못하는 이들을 위해 각종 문화유산에 대한 상세한 해설을 실어 이해를 돕고 있으며, 화질이 좋아 원서보다도 선명하게 문화유산을 접할 수 있게 되었다.

특히 회화편은 원서보다도 화질이 선명하여 그림의 색감이 더 살아나며, 청동기와 동경(銅鏡)도 세밀한 부분이 더 입체적으로 드러나고 있다. 회화편의 경우, 그림을 보고 있노라면 한국화의 주제나 기법이 어디서 영향을 받았는 지를 확연하게 알 수 있어 한국의 회화를 이해하는 데도 많은 도움이 될 것이다. 청동기와 동경의 경우, 한국의 그것과 공통점과 차이점을 비교해보는 재미를 느낄 수 있으며, 불교조각상과 자기의 경우에도 중국과 한국의 공통점과 차이점을 한눈에 살펴볼 수 있다. 이와 같이 『中國 西安(長安)의 문화유산』 시리즈는 중국의 문화유산을 감상하고 이해하는 것뿐만 아니라 한국의 문화유산과의 비교를 통하여 두 전통문화 간의 공통점과 차이점을 느낄 수 있다.

실크로드의 기점인 시안은 중국뿐만 아니라 서역의 많은 문화유산을 소장하고 있으나 이곳의 문화유산을 감상하려면 박물관이나 미술관에 직접 가야만 하고, 중요한 유물을 모두 보기 위해선 여러 번 발품을 팔아야 한다. 이에 『中國 西安(長安)의 문화유산』 시리즈는 한눈에 중국의 우수한 문화유산을 감상하면서 눈의 호사를 누리고, 중국의 전통문화를 제대로 이해하는 계기가 될 것이다.

2015년
前 문화체육관광부 장관
現 고려대학교 한국사학과 교수
최광식

중국 시안(西安, 長安)의 유구한 역사를 보여주다

시안(西安, 長安)은 중국의 역사에서 다양한 별명을 갖고 있다. 중화문명의 발상지, 중화민족의 요람, 가장 오래된 도시, 실크로드의 출발지 등이 그것이다. 시안의 6천 년 역사 가운데 왕도(王都, 혹은 皇都)의 역사가 1200년이었다는 사실도 시안을 일컫는 또 다른 이름이 될 수 있다. 즉, 시안은 남전원인(藍田原人)의 선사시대부터 당(唐) 시기 세계 최대의 도시 단계를 거쳐 근대에 이르기까지 중화의 역사, 종교, 군사, 경제, 문화, 학예 등 분야 전반에 걸쳐 가히 대륙의 중심에 서 있어 왔다고 할 수 있다. 그만큼 시안은 역사의 자취가 황토 고원의 두께만큼 두껍고, 황하의 흐름만큼 길다고 할 것이다.

시안시문물보호고고소(西安市文物保護考古所)에서 엮은 『西安文物精華(시안문물정화)』 도록 전집은 이와 같은 시안의 유구한 역사와 그 문화사적인 의미를 잘 보여주고 있다. 첫째, 발굴 및 전수되어 온 문화재들이 병마용(兵馬俑), 자기(瓷器), 인장(印章), 서법(書法), 옥기(玉器), 동경(銅鏡), 청동기(靑銅器), 회화(繪畵), 불상(佛像), 금은기물(金銀器物) 등 다양할 뿐 아니라, 시안만이 가지는 역사 배경의 특징을 심도 있게 관찰할 수 있는 분야의 문화재가 집중적으로 수록되어 있다. 각 권의 머리말에서 밝히고 있듯이 이 문화재의 일부는 시안 지역의 특징을 이루는 것들을 포함하면서 다른 일부, 예컨대 자기는 당시 전국의 물품들이 집합되어 있어 그 시기 중국 전체의 면모를 보여주기도 한다는 것이다. 둘째, 당 이후 중국 역사의 주된 무대는 강남(江南)으로 옮겨갔다고 할 수 있는데, 이 문화재들은 시안이 여전히 역사와 문화의 중심축에서 크게 벗어나지 않고 있음을 보여준다. 문인 취향의 서법, 인장 및 자기들이 이를 말해준다고 할 수 있다. 셋째, 이 문화재들은 병마용의 경우처럼 대부분이 해당 예술사에서 주로 다루어질 수준의 것들이지만 다른 일부, 예컨대 회화 같은 경우는 그러한 수준에서 다소 벗어난 작품들로 보이기도 한다. 그러나 이 경우 이 문화재들은 해당 예술사 분야에서 대표성을 갖는 작품들이 일류 작가의 범작(凡作)들과 이류 작가의 다른 주제와 기법을 통하여 어떻게 조형적 가치와 대표성을 가질 수 있는가를 되비쳐줌과 동시에 중국적인 조형 의식의 심층을 엿볼 수 있게 한다는 사료적 가치가 있다고 평가할 수 있다.

이러한 시안의 방대하고 의미 있는 문화재를 선명한 화상과 상세한 전문적 설명을 덧붙여 발간한 것을 한국학술정보(주)에서 한국어 번역본으로 출간, 한국의 관련 연구자와 문화 애호가들에게 시의적절하게 제공하게 된 것은 매우 다행스럽고 보람된 일이라 생각한다. 향후 이를 토대로 심도 있는 연구가 진행되고, 이웃 문화권에 대한 일반 독자들의 이해가 깊어질 수 있기를 기대하면서 감상과 섭렵을 적극적으로 추천하는 바이다.

2015년 관악산 자락에서
서울대학교 미학과 교수
박낙규

　　시안시(西安市)문물보호고고학연구소에서 편저하고, 쑨푸시(孫福喜) 박사가 엮은 『中國 西安(長安)의 문화유산_ 금은기(金銀器)』(원제: 西安文物精華_金銀器)가 드디어 독자들과 만나게 되었다. 본서는 시안(西安, 長安)에서 출토된 역대 금은기[류(鎏): 도금(鍍金), 착(錯): 금은입사(金銀入絲) 포함] 2백여 점의 유물 모음집으로 시안문물정화 시리즈 대형도록의 중요한 역작으로 학술적 · 예술적 가치가 높다.

　　시안시가 소장하고 있는 역대 금은기는 그 수량이 많을 뿐만 아니라 종류 또한 풍부하고 다채로운데, 특히 황실 용품으로 많이 사용되었던 당대(唐代) 금은기는 수준이 높을 뿐만 아니라 공예 또한 정교하다. 일반적으로 시안 허지아촌(河家村) 가마터, 산시성(陝西省) 푸펑현(扶風縣) 법문사지궁(法門寺地宮), 장수성(江蘇省) 양저우시(揚州市) 딩정마오(丁卯橋) 가마터에서 출토된 당대 금은기가 알려져 있다. 시안시에서 소장하고 있는 당대 금은기는 비록 양이 많지는 않지만 역대 출토품을 모아 놓고 보면 그야말로 장관이며, 그 중요성 또한 말할 나위가 없다. 예를 들어 도관칠국육판은합(都管七國六瓣銀盒), 쌍어문만초화은반[雙魚紋蔓草花銀盤, 이면(李勉)이 진상한 것임], 무금무풍해당형은반(撫琴舞風海棠形銀盤), 쌍봉함수대문오곡은합(雙鳳衘綬帶紋五曲銀盒) 등은 모두 높은 역사적 · 예술적 가치를 지니고 있다. 당대 금은기의 대표작으로 손꼽히는 금비룡(金飛龍), 도금주룡(鍍金走龍), 금난봉(金鸞鳳), 금압(金鴨) 등은 형상이 다양하여 보는 이로 하여금 찬탄을 금치 못하게 한다. 시안시 소장품은 당대 금은기의 연구와 감상에 없어서는 안 될 중요한 역할을 한다.

　　시안은 국제적인 문물도시로 소장품의 가치는 성급(省級) 문물과 견줄 만하다. 오랫동안 주목받지 못한 진귀한 유물을 선보인 본서의 출판은 학술계와 독자에게 매우 뜻 깊은 일이다.

　　『中國 西安(長安)의 문화유산_금은기(金銀器)』 저자는 학문 연구에 있어 실사구시적인 태도를 견지해 본서의 설명은 상세하고 정확하다. 또한 아름다운 디자인, 선명한 사진, 글 등을 함께 실어 다채로움을 더했다. 필자는 본서를 통해 많은 수확을 얻었는데 독자 여러분 역시 다를 바 없으리라 믿는다.

2011년 11월
유윈후이(劉雲輝)

由西安市文物保护考古所编着，孙福喜博士主编的《西安文物精华·金银器》一书要与读者见面了，该书匯集了西安地区出土的歷代二百余件组金银器（包括鎏金，错金银器）。这是西安文物精华系列大型图录的又一重要力作，具有极高的学术价值和艺术欣赏价值。

西安市收藏的歷代金银器，不仅数量多，而且种类也丰富多彩，尤其是唐代金银器等级高，工艺精湛，不少属皇家用品。世人多知西安何家村窖藏，陕西扶风法门寺地宫、江苏扬州丁卯桥窖藏出土的唐代金银器。但西安市收藏的唐代金银器虽多是零星出土物，而将歷年出土品匯集在一起也是洋洋大观，这些金银器的重要性是不言而喻的。如都管七国六瓣银盒、"李勉奉进"双鱼纹蔓草花银盘，扶琴舞凤海棠形银盘，双凤衔绶带纹五曲银盒等唐代金银器，均具有极高的歷史价值和艺术价值；金飞龙，鎏金走龙，金鸞凤，金鸭，其造型极富神采，令人赞嘆不已，而视为唐代金银器中的代表作。研究和鉴赏唐代金银器，西安市的藏品已经成为不可或缺的重要组成部分。

西安是具有国际影响力的文物大市，其文物藏品完全可以与省级文物收藏单位媲美，将这些尘封多年的文物珍品集结出版，是一件十分有意义的好事，对学术界和广大读者是一大福音。

《西安文物精华·金银器》的作者，坚持实事求是的严谨治学作风，文字说明详细而准确，反映了作者具有深厚扎实的学术功底。笔者先睹为快，已获益匪浅，相信广大读者会有同感，此书设计版式美观，照片清晰逼真，图文并茂是一本难得的好书。

2011年11月

刘云辉

Quintessence of xi'an Cultural-Gold and Silver Wares, a book edited by Xi'an Relics Preservation and archaeology Institute with Dr. Sun Fuxi as the chief editor will be published. This book collected more than 200 pieces(sets) gold and silver wares(including gilt bronze and inlaying gold and silver wares) of different dynasties unearthed in Xi'an. It is another masterpiece of the grand antique catalog Series of Cultural Relics Prime in Xi'an, and is of high academic value and artistic value.

The gold and silver wares of different dynasties collected in Xi'an are not only large in amount, but also of great variety, especially those of Tang Dynasty, which are high in rank, meticulous in craftsmanship and many of which belonged to the royal family. A lot of people in the world know the Tang Dynasty gold and silver wares from Hejiacun Village in Xi'an, the underground palace of Famen Temple, Fufeng, Shaanxi, and Dingmaoqiao, Yangzhou, Jiangsu Province. Though most of the Tang Dynasty gold and silver wares collected in Xi'an are sparsely unearthed, it's very spectacular if they are collected together, so their importance is quite evident. The Tang Dynasty wares like the followings all have very high historical and artistic value: Duguan Seven-state six-petal silver case, "blation by Li Mian" double-fish grass flower silver plate, Fuqin and Dancing phoenix crab-apple-shaped silver plate, Double-phoenix with ribbon held in the mouth five-curling silver case. The very vividly made golden flying dragon, gilt bronze walking dragon, golden phoenix and golden duck have gained great admiration, therefore, they are regarded as the masterpiece of Tang Dynasty gold and silver wares. To study and appreciate Tang gold and silver wares, the relics collected in Xi'an are an indispensable part.

As an important city of relics, Xi'an has profound international influence. Its relics can absolutely rival with any provincial relics unit. To publish these dust-laden relics treasures is of great significance and is also good news to the academic circle and the readers.

The editors of the book are exact and practical about their editing, and the illustrations are detailed and accurate, showing their solid academic grounding. It's a pleasure for me to be among the first to read, and I have gained to the eye, and has very clear pictures, the pictures and their accompanying essays are both excellent, therefore, it's really a hard-won book.

Nov. 2011
Liu Yunhui

　西安市文化財保護考古所で編集され、孫福喜博士が編集主幹となっている「西安文化財の精華－金銀器」という本は、いよいよ出版されることとなる。この本には西安地区から出土された歴代の二百件余りの金銀器(鎏金、針金象眼銀器を含む)が収録されている。これは、西安文化財精華シリーズ大型写真録のもう一つの重要な力作であり、きわめて高い学術価値と芸術観賞価値がある。

　西安市で収蔵されている歴代の金銀器は、数量が多いし、種類も豊富多彩である。特に唐代の金銀器は等級が高く、工法が完璧であり、その多くは皇室用品である。西安何家村の穴蔵、陝西扶風法門寺の地宮、江蘇省揚州丁卯橋の穴蔵から出土された唐代の金銀器が世間の多くの人々から知られている。西安市で収蔵されている当代金銀器の多くはまとまりがなく出土されたものであるが、これまでの出土品を集めると、やはりすごいものになる。これらの金銀器の重要性はいうまでもない。たとえば、都管七国六かけらの銀ケースや「李勉奉進」雙魚紋蔓草花銀皿や撫琴舞鳳カイドウ形の銀皿や雙鳳銜綬帯紋五曲銀ケースなどの唐代の金銀器はすべてきわめて高い歴史的な価値と芸術価値がある。金飛龍、鎏金走龍、金鸞鳳、金鴨は、形が巧妙で、全く感心させられ、唐代の金銀器の中の代表作とされている。唐代の金銀器を研究？鑑賞するにあたって、西安市の収蔵品はすでに不可欠の重要な一部となっている。

　西安は国際的な影響力のある文化財の大きい都市であり、その文化財の収蔵品は、省レベルの文化財収蔵団体と肩を並べることができる。これらの長期的に埋蔵された文化財の珍品を収録して出版することは、非常に意義がある良いことであり、学術界と読者の皆様にとって一大朗報だと思う。

　「西安文化財の精華－金銀器」の作者は、事実に基づいて真実を求める厳しい学問研究作風を堅持し、説明が詳細で的確であり、作者のしっかりとした学術基礎が現れている。私は先に読んで非常に勉強になっており、読者の皆様も同感するだろうと信じている。この本は設計判型がきれいで、写真がはっきりと見え、挿絵が多く、文章も優れており、得難い良い本であると思う。

2011年11月

刘云辉

관중평원(關中平原)에 자리 잡은 시안(西安, 長安)은 서북과 서남으로 통하는 교통요충지로 한대(漢代)부터 당대(唐代)에 이르기까지 13개 왕조의 도읍지였고 실크로드가 시작된 지점이다. 국제적 대도시였던 창안성(長安城)은 동서양 경제 및 문화의 중심지로서 세계의 경제와 문화에 거대한 영향을 미쳤다. 오늘날 시안은 풍부한 유물로 역사의 발자취를 보여 주고 있으며 조상의 창의성과 지혜, 동서양 문화 교류의 성과를 보여 주고 있다.

시안지역의 풍부한 문화유물 가운데 가장 독특한 금은기(金銀器)는 시안시문물보호고고학연구소 소장품의 주를 이루고 있다. 여기에는 순금은(純金銀) 제품뿐만 아니라 동(銅)에 도금(鍍金)한 금기(金器)나 상감한 금은입사기(金銀入絲器)도 포함된다. 고대 중국인들은 금과 은에 대해 잘 알고 있었다. 『산해경(山海經)』「오장산경(五藏山經)」에는 중국에 분포된 89가지 광물자원 산지에 관한 기록이 있다. 그중 황금 산지는 19곳, 은산지는 20곳이다. 금속 광물자원은 시안 일대의 잉산(英山), 태창산(泰昌山), 수리산[數曆山, 지금의 치안양현(千陽縣) 경내], 롱서우산(龍首山), 양허산[陽虛山, 루오난현(洛南縣) 경내], 양후아산(陽華山), 치산(岐山), 선산[申山, 지금의 안사이현(安塞縣) 경내] 등지에 분포되어 있으며, 은광은 주로 다이시산[大時山, 지금의 메이시안(眉縣) 경내]과 수리산 등지에 분포되어 있었다. 이 밖에 란톈베이산(藍田北山)의 음지에는 대량의 금이 매장되어 있다는 기록이 있다. 중국은 금은 등 광물자원이 풍부하여 일찍이 상주(商周)시대부터 금은기물이 나타났다. 후베이(湖北) 하오청(嵩城) 유적지와 인수(殷墟)에서 상대(商代)와 주대(周代)의 '황금덩이 및 금엽(金葉) 조각', 시안 북부의 네이멍구(內蒙古) 항진치(杭錦旗) 아루차이덩(阿魯柴登), 준거얼치(准格尔旗) 시고우판(西溝畔)과 산시(陝西) 선무나춘가오투(神木納村高兔) 등 흉노족의 무덤에서 춘추시대 금은기가 대량 출토되었다. 그중 매 모양의 금관정(金冠頂), 금관대(金冠帶), 동물 모양 장식, 사슴 모양의 괴수 등과 같이 동물 형태로 된 것이 가장 많다. 이러한 금은기는 기법이 복잡하고 형태가 다양하며 조형 또한 생동감이 있다. 시안(西安), 바오지(寶鷄), 시안양(咸陽) 등지에서도 비교적 많이 출토되었다. 용청(雍城) 유적지의 용수번룡금대구(龍首蟠龍金帶鉤), 금이수(金異獸) 장식물, 금압취대구(金鴨嘴帶鉤), 금절약(金節約), 금수면(金獸面), 금포(金泡) 등 진대(秦代) 금은기가 가장 대표적으로 진대 문화의 발전수준을 보여 주는 좋은 예이다. 당시 열국의 분쟁으로 패권을 잡았던 제왕들이 시시때때로 바뀌는 가운데 서쪽에 위치한 진나라가 동쪽 열국과 패권 지위를 다투었다. 진나라의 도읍이었던 용청 근처의 별궁 및 종묘와 묘지에서도 대량의 금제기물 및 마구(馬具), 장식품, 병기도 함께 출토되었다. 그중 금병철검(金柄鐵劍) 자루는 투각된 변형반리문(變形蟠螭紋)에 녹송석(綠松石)을 박아넣었다. 그 후 세력이 커진 진나라는 동쪽으로 세력을 확장하여 통일을 이룩함으로써 경제의 번영 및 수공업의 발전을 가져오게 되었다. 특히 수공업 발전을 드러내는 금은입사공예와 도금공예 등이 크게 발전해 기법 또한 매우 뛰어났다. 바오지시 평시양현(鳳翔縣)에서 출토되어 시안시문물보호고고학연구소에서 소장한 누공회수금와호(鏤空回首金臥虎)와 금호부(金虎符)는 조형과 공예 특징이 비교적 뚜렷한 작품이다. 누공회수금와호는 용청 유적지에서 출토된 춘추시대의 용수번룡금대구(龍首蟠龍金帶鉤, 평시양현박물관 소장)와 풍격이 같으며 머리 모양이 비슷하다. 금호부는 바오지시 치엔허웨이지아야(千河魏家崖)에서 출토된 금호[金虎, 천창구(陳倉區)박물관 소장], 시안에서 출토된 유금은대구(鎏金銀帶鉤), 유금감패동대구(鎏金嵌貝銅帶鉤), 착은삼선문대구(錯銀三蟬紋帶鉤), 은입사대(銀入絲鐓), 착금은통형차식(錯金銀筒形車飾) 등과 풍격상 비슷하다. 그 밖에 창 자루집의 장식품에 속하는 착은구비모(錯銀鳩秘冒)도 동일한 풍격을 띠는데, 은입사무늬가 새겨져 있는 비둘기의 몸 옆에는 명문(銘文), "卄三年服工□治古, 三十八(입삼년복공□치고, 삼십팔)" 11글자가 음각되어 있다. 이로부터 금은입사한 도금기가 전국시대에 보편적으로 사용되었음을 알 수 있다. 춘추전국시대의 사회변혁은 경제, 문화 및 수공업 생산에 중대한 변화를 가져왔으며 전통적인 청동 예기(禮器)가 내리막길을 걷는 한편 새로운 기형(器形)과 공예의 발전이 두드러졌다. 금은기의 참신하고 화려한 장식은 새롭고 활기찬 당시 사회 모습을 보여 준다. 진시황(秦始皇)의 중국 통일은 사회 발전에 튼튼한 토대를 마련하였을 뿐만 아니라 수공업의 발전을 견인하였다. 『사기(史記)』 「진본기(秦本紀)」에는 "여산(驪山)의 진시황릉에는 부장품인 황금 물오리와 기러기가 있다"라는 기록이 있다. 진시황릉의 용갱(俑坑)에서는 대금포(大金泡), 2호 동거마(銅車馬)에서는 금은기물이 출토되었는데 이를 통해 금은기 제작 면에서 거둔 성과를 알 수 있다. 한대에 와서는 국력이 강성해졌다. 『사기』에서도 "한왕조는 대량의 금은과 금은기를 보유하였다"라고 기록되어 있다. 예를 들어, 『한서(漢書)』 「공우전(貢禹傳)」에는 다금왕조(多金王朝)라고 불리는 "촉한(蜀漢)에서는 금은기를 제작하는 데 드는 1년의 인건비가 각각 5백만에 달했다"라는 기록이 있으며, 서한 황제가 신하한테 백여 차례나 황금을 하사하였다고 나와 있다. 『사서(史書)』 「평준서(平准書)」에는 "대장군 표기(驃騎) 장군의 영솔하에 오랑캐와 대대적으로 전투를 벌여 포획하거나 죽인 적군이 총 8~9만이었는데, 공을 세운 장수에게 금 50만 냥을 하사했다"라고 기록되어 있으며, 『사기(史記)』 「양효왕세가(梁孝王世家)」에는 "양효왕(梁孝王)은 살아생전 그 재산이 헤아릴 수 없을 정도로 많았다. 그가 죽은 뒤에도 부고(府庫)에는 황금 40여만 근이 남아 있었다"라고 기록되어 있다. 그 밖에 금은광산 및 제련에 관한 기록도 있다. 『염철론(鹽鐵論)』에는 "형주(荊州), 양주(揚州)의 동쪽에는 동광이 매장되어 있고", "단양(丹陽)과 장산(章山)에는 풍부한 금과 동이 매장되어 있다"라고 기록되어 있으며, 『수경주(水經注)』 「약수(若水)」에는 "난창(蘭倉)의 물에서 사금이 나는데 월인(越人)들은 모래를 일어 금을 얻었다"라고 기록되어 있으며, 『사기(史記)』 「화식열전(貨殖列傳)」에는 "강남(江南)에서는 금과 석(錫)이 나고", "예장(豫章)에서는 황금이 난다"라고 기록되어 있으며, 『화양국지(華陽國志)』에는 부현(涪縣)에서는 "잔산(屛山)의 잔수(屛水)에서 나는 금은광을 세척하여 불로 녹이면 금은이 된다"라는 내용들이 기록되어 있다. 또한, 진서우현(晉壽縣), 보난현(博南縣) 등지에도 금은광과 금사(金沙)가 매장되어 있다. 『태평광기(太平廣記)』에는 광무(光武) 황제의 동생 곽황(郭況)이 "수억 재산과 가동(家僮) 400명뿐만 아니라 금으로 만든 기물도 사용했는데 그 제련하는 소리가 온 나라에 울려퍼졌다"라고 기록되어 있다. 이로부터 금은 작업장의 규모가 매우 컸음을 알 수 있다. 현재 시안시문물보호고고학연구소에서 소장하고 있는 금병(金餠)은 1999년 11월 시안시(西安市) 웨이양구(未央區) 탄지아향(譚家鄕) 베이시리보둥촌(北十里鋪東村) 벽돌, 기와공장에서 출토된 것이다. 모두 219점이 출토되었는데 하나의 무게가 227.6~254.5g이고, 대부분 도장[戳記]이 찍혀 있었다. 문물을 쌓아둔 모습에서 농민봉기나 망조(亡朝) 위기에 직면한 화폐 소유자가 도망하기 전에 지하에 서둘러 숨긴 것으로 추정된다. 금병은 당시 귀중한 금속화폐였다. 이 밖에 한대 무덤에서 출토된 금은봉조진(金銀鳳鳥鎭), 도금 은입사(銀入絲) 와호형진(臥虎形鎭), 도금 응형준(鷹形鐏) 등도 소장되어 있다. 이로부터 귀족들이 소유했던 황금의 양이 상당하였음을 알 수 있다. 한대에는 금은기 제작기법 면에서 비교적 큰 혁신을 가져왔다. 이전의 부조(浮雕)나 입조(立雕) 기법을 탈피해 소박하면서도 거친 풍격을 보이던 전통적인 청동공예 기법에서 벗어나 점차 자신의 풍격을 만들어 갔다. 한대에는 성형 시 추엽(錘揲), 용접 등의 방법을 사용하고 범주(范鑄)하는 경우는 드물었다. 표면을 장식할 때 먼저 두드려 얇게 부조하거나 입조한 다음에 세부적인 부분을 다시 조각한다. 그 외에 세선세공, 용접, 금주(金珠) 등의 기법도 함께 사용한다. 1966년 시안시 베이지아오루자커우촌(北郊盧家口村)에서 출토된 금조(金竈)는 제작이 매우 정교하다. 금조에는 금주(金珠), 상감 기술 외에도 용접하거나 세선세공하는 등의 기법으로 선이 교차하는 구름무늬에 녹송석(綠松石, 지금은 떨어지고 없다)을 상감하였다. 금조 안에는 쌀이 가득 담긴 모양으로 밥을 짓고 있는 듯하게 만들고, 바닥에는 "日利(일리)"두 글자를 새겨 넣었다. 1972년 시안시 제2기 벽돌공장에서 출토된 도금 응형준(鷹形鐏)은 표면에 전체적으로 금을 입히고 요주(料珠)를 상감하였는데 요주 다수가 완전히 보존되어 있다. 한대에 실크로드가 개통되자 한왕조와 서방 사이의 경제문화교류가 활발히 진행되었다. 외래문화가 중국에 유입되면서 금은기도 잇달아 전해졌다. 광저우(廣州)의 서한(西漢) 남월(南越) 왕 무덤에서 출토된 은합은 추엽(錘揲) 기법으로 만들어진 것이다. 고고학 전문가들은 입체적인 효과를 나타내는 물방울 모양의 꽃잎무늬로부터 이 은합을 실크로드를 통해 중국에 전해진 페르시아 또는 로마지역의 은제기물로 추정하고 있다. 상술한 금조(金竈)에 사용된 제작기법은 외국으로부터 전해진 것으로 이러한 기법을 이용한 금은기들이 그 뒤로 속속 출토되었다.

복잡하면서도 섬세한 금은기 제작기법은 뛰어난 아름다움을 만들어냈다. 구체적으로 범주(範鑄), 추엽(錘揲), 도금, 용접, 세선세공, 금박을 입히거나 금은입사(金銀入絲)를 상감하거나 금주를 용접하는 등의 기법이 있다. 범주는 동기(銅器) 공예와 흡사한데 금을 1,063℃(은은 960℃)까지 가열하여 액체로 용해한 뒤 거푸집 안에 부어 넣어 냉각시켜 형태를 만드는 것을 가리킨다. 추엽(錘揲)은 금은의 전성(두들겨 펴지기 쉬운 성질)과 연성(잡아 늘이기 쉬운 성질)의 특징을 이용하여 평평한 모양으로 두드린 다음에 물이나 모형을 이용하여 누르거나 두드려 모양을 내는 것을 가리킨다. 용접은 금은기와 금은 장식물이 맞닿은 부분에 금속 액체를 부은 뒤 냉각시켜 견고하게 맞붙게 하는 것이다. 도금은 일명 '화도금(火鍍金)', '홍도금(汞鍍金)'이라고도 불린다. 이는 황금덩이나 황금조각을 400℃의 온도까지 가열하고 일정한 비율의 수은을 넣어 용해시킨 뒤, 냉각시켜 '이금(泥金, 흙 모양의 고체)'을 만들어 기물의 표면에 바른 다음에 불에 구워 수은을 증발시키고 황금만 남게 하는 공예기법이다. 이 도금기술은 전국시대에 세계 최초로 발명되었다. 참화(鏨花)는 조각도로 금은기의 표면에 여러 가지 도안을 새기는 것을 가리킨다. 장인들의 숙련된 솜씨로 유려한 도안들이 생동감 있게 각종 기물을 통해 연출되었다. 상감은 금은기 표면에 녹송석, 수정, 진주, 보석 등을 상감하여 기물의 화려함과 고풍스러움을 한층 더 두드러지게 하는 것을 말한다. 금은착(金銀錯)이라고도 불리는 금은입사(金銀入絲)는 일찍 전국시대에 성숙되었다. 동기(銅器)나 은기(銀器)의 모형을 주조하고 금은입사로 오목 새김한 뒤에 금은사(金銀絲)를 오목한 부분에 박아 넣어 표면을 매끄럽게 하여 여러 가지 무늬를 만듦으로써 화려함을 더해주는 공예기법이다. 세선세공과 한철금주(焊綴金珠) 기법은 두드려서 얻은 얇은 금은 조각을 가늘게 자른 다음에 실[絲, 편전사(片剪絲, 가위 같은 도구로 잘라낸 실)와 발제사(拔制絲, 틀을 이용하여 뽑아낸 실)로 나뉜다]로 비벼 꼬아 도안을 만드는 것을 가리킨다. 한철금주 기법은 금실을 가열하여 구슬 모양으로 만들거나 금실의 한쪽만 가열하여 녹으면서 동그란 진주 모양을 얻는 기법이다. 세선세공하거나 한철금주한 도안에는 보석을 상감하는 경우도 있다.

위진남북조(魏晉南北朝)시대에는 사회의 혼란으로 말미암아 경제가 파괴된 반면 민족이 서로 융합되고 대외경제문화교류가 활성화되었다. 외래의 불교 및 예술이 유입되어 이 시대 문화예술의 발전을 촉진하였다. 당시 상대적으로 발전한 금은기는 조형 및 문양 면에서 전통문화와 외래문화가 융합된 특징을 그대로 보여 주었다. 당시 금은기의 제작 및 사용이 줄어들었는데 이에 대해 한 학자가 고고학 자료를 연구한 데 기초하여 "황금과 백은의 생산량이 줄어들어 기물을 제작할 수 있는 여건이 마련되지 않았을 뿐만 아니라 불교의 흥성으로 말미암아 불상을 제작하는 데 대량의 금은을 사용하였다"라고 밝힌 바가 있다. 금은기는 주로 상류사회에서 유행하였다. 조조(曹操)의『상헌제기물표(上獻帝器物表)』와『상잡물소(上雜物疎)』에서는 석가모니입상을 제작할 때, "순금 10만 근, 황금 6백 근이 사용되었다"라고 기록되어 있다. 그 외에 순금향로, 타호(唾壺), 순은향로, 쟁반 등과 같은 금은기를 제작할 때 순금, 순은 재료를 사용하도록 규정되어 있었다.『낙양가람기(洛陽伽藍記)』에는 북위(北魏) 때, 새 기르기를 좋아하는 하간

(河間) 사람 왕원침(王元琛)은 금병(金甁), 은항아리 100여 개 외에도 수많은 금은제 식기와 주구(酒具)를 갖고 있었는데 말의 구유를 은으로 만들고 말뚝에 단 고리도 금으로 만들었다는 기록이 있다. 이 밖에도 금은기를 선물하거나 하사하거나 공납하거나 훔치거나 수색하는 등 다양한 내용들이 기록되어 있다. 위진남북조시대 창안청(長安城)은 불교의 중심지였기 때문에 시안지역에서 도금불상이 다수 출토되었다. 창안구(長安區) 황리양향(黃良鄕) 석불사(石佛寺)에서 출토된 '법로문(法盧文)'이 새겨진 금동좌불(金銅坐佛), 시안 베이지아오(北郊)에서 출토된 천화(天和) 5년 금동입불(金銅立佛) 등이 그 예이다. 2002년 린퉁구(臨潼區) 다이왕(代王)에서 출토된 양수금패식(羊首金牌飾) 4점은 북방 소수민족의 복식 장식물로 당시 소수민족들이 중원지역으로 이주해온 증거이다. 시안시문물보호고고학연구소에서는 동로마제국(비잔틴제국)의 금화 여러 점을 소장하고 있는데, 이는 북조시대 문물의 수량과 맞먹는다. 이로부터 서방국가들이 실크로드를 통해 창안과 통상무역을 진행했음을 알 수 있다.

　금은기의 제작 및 사용에 있어서 황금시대였던 당대(唐代) 금은기는 그 양이 가장 많고 종류가 다양하며 제작이 정교하여 금은기 제작공예의 절정기에 이르렀다. 시안시문물보호고고학연구소는 수많은 당대 금은기를 소장하고 있는데 구체적인 출토지점은 지안꿔루(建國路), 사포촌(沙坡村), 추지앙치(曲江池), 산자오촌(三兆村), 시베이공업대학, 싱칭꿍(興慶宮) 유적지, 신주자오위안춘꿔(新築棗園村國), 시안 기차역, 창안구(長安區) 쭈촌(祝村), 대명궁향(大明宮鄕) 마치자이(馬旗寨), 시안 벽돌공장, 판지아촌(潘家村) 도시건설국에서 넘겨받은 문물이 포함된다. 산시성(陝西省)박물관에도 시안에서 출토된 금은기가 다량 소장되어 있는데 난지아오(南郊) 허지아촌(何家村)에서 출토된 270여 점이 바로 그 예이다. 금은기는 당대(唐代) 귀족들이 사용했던 기물로서『당률소의(唐律疏議)』의 가옥과 의복, 기물에 관한 부분에서는 "일품(一品) 아래의 관리들은 순금(純金), 순옥(純玉)으로 만든 그릇을 사용하지 못하고",『당회요(唐會要)』잡록에는 "신룡(神龍) 2년(706년) 9월에 반포된 의제령(儀制令)에서는 일품 이하의 관리들은 제련하지 않은 금과 옥으로 만든 그릇을 사용하지 못하며, 육품(六品) 이하 관리들은 제련하지 않은 은을 사용하지 못 한다"라고 규정되어 있다. 상층귀족들은 수많은 고관대작들을 시시때때로 불러 연회를 열었는데 잔칫상에서 가장 눈에 뜨이는 것이 금은기였다. 당시(唐詩)에서는 "그 누가 술을 가져와 금산에 따르며, 화려한 연회에 가인더러 춤을 추게 하리오."라고 읊조렸고, 왕건(王建)의『궁중 시가 100편』에서 "똑같은 금쟁반 5천 개에, 산해진미가 홍모란마냥 담겨 있네"라는 시구가 눈에 띈다. 문헌을 살펴보면, "회남(淮南) 절도사 왕보(王播)가 황제에게 금은기를 세 번에 걸쳐 공납한 양이 무려 5,900여 개에 달했다"는 내용이 기록되어 있다. 여기서 당시 금은기 사용 상황 및 사회, 정치, 경제, 문화 수준을 엿볼 수 있다. 당대(唐代) 경제와 문화가 번영하고 실크로드가 연장되어 중국의 대외경제문화교류가 더욱 빈번해졌다. 당대(唐代) 중국인들은 서양의 영향을 받아 외래의 기물을 숭상하면서 외래의 기물들을 사용하는 것이 일종의 유행이 되었는데 특히 금은기 사용이 더욱 그러했다. 위진(魏晉)부터 수대(隋代)까지 상류사회에서 유통되는 금은기들은 주로 외국에서 수입한 것이었다. 당대에 와서는 수입과 함께 국내생산, 제작규모를 확대하였다. 황실 및 귀족들은 금은기를 사용하는 데에 전통적이면서도 신비스런 관념을 갖고 있었다. 이를테면,『태평어람(太平御覽)』진정부(珍定部)에는 "금은으로 만든 그릇을 사용하면 장생불로한다"라고 기록되어 있다. 문헌과 고고학 자료를 비추어 보면, 금은기가 고급 실용기물로 사용되었을 뿐만 아니라 하사, 선물, 대외교류 등에 사용되었음을 알 수 있다. 금은기의 종류는 풍부하고 다채로워 사발, 쟁반, 접시, 잔 등의 식기, 컵, 이배(耳杯), 주전자, 찻잔 등의 음기(飮器), 은합(차를 저장하는 데 사용), 다사(茶篩), 은염대(銀鹽臺), 은단지, 은솥, 은숟가락, 은잔, 차맷돌 등의 찻그릇과 용기, 연단기석류관(煉丹器石榴罐), 금은솥, 제량관(提梁罐), 당(檔) 등의 약품기구, 향주머니, 향로, 타호 등의 위생

용품, 잠(簪), 채(釵), 빗, 떨잠, 목걸이, 팔찌[手鐲], 팔찌[臂釧] 등의 장신구, 조상(造像), 보함(寶涵), 관 등의 종교기구, 은자물쇠, 경첩, 주주(酒籌), 주령구(酒令具) 등의 잡품도 있었다. 기물 표면의 무늬는 매우 다채로우며 풍부한 문화적 함의가 담겨 있다. 용, 봉황, 원앙, 기러기, 꿀벌, 나비, 천마(天馬), 천록(天鹿), 사자, 곰, 거북이, 원숭이, 마갈(摩羯) 등 동물문양과 전지화(纏枝花), 단화(團花), 보상화(寶相花), 절지화(折枝花) 및 여러 가지 인물문양도 있다. 전반적으로 시대적 특징을 나타내며 웅위할 뿐더러 생기와 자신감이 넘쳐 보인다. 동물과 화훼문양은 현실을 바탕으로 발전된 것이다. 특히 단화, 절지화, 전지화 무늬에서 그 특징이 더욱 돋보인다. 풍만하며 우아하고 생명력이 넘치는 인물 도안은 현실생활을 소재로 하였는데 기악(伎樂), 주연(酒宴), 수렵, 사녀(仕女)들의 생활 등을 묘사하였으며, 이전의 장식과 달리 경사, 길상, 아름다움을 표현했다. 무늬장식은 통속적이면서도 오색찬란한 형태로 발전했다.

당대의 역사는 300년에 이른다. 당대 이전의 금은기는 주로 외국에서 유입되었지만 당대에 와서는 사회가 발전하면서 금은기의 전례 없는 발전을 가져왔다. 출토자료 및 기물의 조형과 문양의 발전, 변화에 따라서 금은기의 발전단계를 크게 당대 초기로부터 고종(高宗, 618~683년), 무측천 때로부터 현종(玄宗, 684~755년), 숙종(肅宗)부터 헌종(憲宗, 756~820년), 목종(穆宗)부터 애제(哀帝, 821~907년)까지의 네 단계로 나눌 수 있다. 일부 학자들은 셋이나 여섯 단계로 나누기도 하는데 이는 그리 중요치 않다. 금은기의 발전단계를 살펴보면 초기에는 외부의 영향이 크고 풍격이 점차 중국화되었음을 알 수 있다. 공예기법은 추엽(錘揲) 기법을 사용하여 요철 모양의 윤곽을 만든 후에 세부적으로 무늬를 새겼다. 일반적으로 안정감 있게 만들고 표면에 금을 입혔다. 당대(唐代) 장인들은 서방의 기법과 제작기술을 익혀 중국인들의 사용과 감상 취미에 맞게 제작함으로써 금은기의 질적인 도약을 이루었다. 당대 중ㆍ후기는 금은기가 보다 성숙되고 널리 보급되었던 시기였다. 소박했던 사발, 쟁반, 합 등은 형태상의 변화가 생기고 굽다리가 높은 잔이나 손잡이가 달린 잔은 보기 드물었으며, 다구(茶具), 주통(籌筒), 받침대, 깔때기, 취사도구 등이 나타났다. 문양들은 보다 다양해졌으며 짙은 민간생활의 정취를 풍긴다. 시안시문물보호고고학연구소의 소장품, 시안 시지아오(西郊)에서 출토된 인동문규형은완(忍冬紋葵形銀碗)과 사포촌(沙坡村)에서 출토된 녹문은완(鹿紋銀碗)은 소그디아나(Sogdiana, 중앙아시아의 샤라프샨 하천과 카슈카 다리아 유역 지방의 옛 이름) 은기의 풍격이 짙어 모두 제1기의 기물로 추정된다. 시안 추지앙치춘(曲江池村)에서 출토된 철삼족은반(凸三足銀盤), 절지단화삼족은반(折枝團花三足銀盤) 3점은 뚜렷한 중국 공예 특징을 지닌 그릇들로 제2기 기물에 속한다. 시안 시베이공업대학에서 출토된 쌍리어보상연판은반(雙鯉魚寶相蓮瓣銀盤), 황리절지화은반(黃鸝折枝花銀盤), 쌍홍안문은완(雙鴻雁紋銀碗), 원앙홍안절지화은완(鴛鴦鴻雁折枝花銀碗), 석류절지화은완(石榴折枝花銀碗) 등 그릇은 제3기 기물이다. 이와 같은 기물들의 조형은 물론이고 문양에서도 중국적인 특징을 지니고 있다. 시안교통대학에서 출토된 도관칠국육판은합(都管七國六瓣銀盒), 앵무문해당형권족은합(鸚鵡紋海棠形圈足銀盒), 구배문은합(龜背紋銀盒)은 제4기 기물에 속한다. 이 시기의 기물은 조형이 다양하고 사용 범위가 보다 확대되어 황족뿐만 아니라 지방관원 및 부유한 백성들도 사용하였다. 금은을 채굴하고 제련하는 데 관한 내용은 사서에 구체적으로 기록되어 있다. 『신당서(新唐書)』「지리지(地理志)」, 『통전(通典)』, 『당육전(唐六典)』, 『원화군현도지(元和郡縣圖志)』 등을 예로 들 수 있다. 채광경영은 관부(官府)채광과 개인채광으로 나뉘며 두 방식은 상호 보충작용을 했다. 『구당서(舊唐書)』「직관지(職官志)」에는 "무릇 사적으로 동과 철을 채굴하는 자는 관청에 상응한 세금을 바쳐야 한다"라는 기록이 있다. 당대에는 개인의 금은 채굴을 허용하였을 뿐더러 민간에서의 채굴도 권장하여 세금을 거두었다. 채굴한 금은광석은 보존하거나 휴대가 편리하도록 제련하여 일정한 양식에 따라 정(鋌), 병(餠), 정(錠) 등으로 만들어졌다. 관부에서는 세금으로 거두어들이

거나 매입하는 방식으로 전국 각지에서 생산된 금은의 대부분을 황실 및 관청으로 집중시켜 기물을 제작하는 데 사용하였다. 시안시문물보호고고학연구소에서 소장한 당대(唐代) 창안청(長安城)에서 출토된 '요주공금(姚州貢金)' 금정(金鋌), '요주증성(饒州證聖) 원년' 은정(銀鋌), '건부(乾符) 6년' 은정, '영남도(岭南道)' 진공은정(進貢銀鋌), 다리 모양의 은정 등이 대표적인 예이다. 금은기의 제작도 중앙관부 작업장, 지방관부 작업장 및 민간 작업장으로 나뉘었다. 중앙관부 작업장에 속하는 소부감(少府監)과 장작감(將作監)은 황실과 중앙관부에 속한 수공업 관리기구로 장치서(掌治署), 좌상서(左尙署), 중상서(中尙署) 직속의 금은작방원(金銀作坊院)이 있었다. 성당(盛唐) 이후 황제는 지방관료에게 금은제 기물들을 공물로 바치라는 칙령을 내렸다. 선종(宣宗, 847~858년) 때에는 황실 전용 금은기 제작 전문기구인 '문사원(文思院)'을 설치하였다. 법문사(法門寺)에서 출토된 여러 금은제 기물들에는 "文思院制造(문사원에서 제작하였음)"이라는 명문이 새겨져 있다. 이 밖에 사서 및 출토된 금은기를 보면 중앙 및 지방 고급관원들이 금은기를 진상하는 것이 이미 하나의 사회적 풍조가 되었음을 알 수 있다. 시안시문물보호고고학연구소에서 소장한 1975년 시베이공업대학의 가마터에서 출토된 '이면봉진(李勉奉進)' 쌍리문만초화은반(雙鯉紋蔓草花銀盤)에는 "進奉器[진상품]"이란 명문이 새겨져 있다. 이면은 숙종(肅宗), 대종(代宗), 덕종(德宗) 세 왕조의 종실 재상으로 사서에는 "청렴하고 소박하여 종신들의 본이다"라고 기록되어 있으나 명문에는 그가 홍주자사(洪州刺史)로 있을 때 황제에게 은쟁반을 진상하였다는 내용이 담겨 있다. 이는 당시 진상하는 풍조가 얼마나 성행하였는가를 보여 준다. 지방관부 작업장은 일찍 초당, 성당 시기에 이미 출현하였으며 중당, 만당 시기에 흥성하였다. 고고 발굴을 통하여 출토된 금은기에 새겨진 명문을 보면, 지방관부 작업장은 지앙난(江南) 둥다오(東道)의 월주[越州, 지금의 저장성 시아오흥(紹興)], 지앙난 시다오(西道)의 홍저우[洪州, 지금의 지앙시 난창(南昌)], 선저우[宣州, 지금의 안후이성(安徽省) 수안저우(宣州)], 저시다오(浙西道) 룬저우[潤州, 지금의 지앙시(江西) 전지앙(鎭江)] 등 남방지역에 위치하였음을 알 수 있다. 저시다오(浙西道)에서 주조한 금은기는 산시의 야오현(耀縣), 푸펑(扶風) 법문사(法門寺) 등지에서 출토되었다. 민간 작업장은 중기 이후에 발전하였는데 이는 남방의 금은 채굴량이 많아 원료가 풍부하고, 정부가 수공업에 대하여 '납자대역(納資代役)', '화고(和雇)' 등 새로운 정책을 실시한 것과도 밀접하게 연관된다. 시안 난지아오(南郊) 허지아촌(何家村) 가마터에서 출토된 고족배(高足杯)에는 "馬舍(마사)", 산시 야오현(耀縣) 리우린베이인촌(柳林背陰村)에서 출토된 각화사곡은완(刻花四曲銀碗)과 오곡은반(五曲銀盤)에는 "馬馬明(마마명)", "朱口(주구)"라는 명문이 새겨져 있는데, 이는 모두 민간 작업장에서 생산하였음을 뜻한다. 민간 금은 작업장에 관한 사서의 기록을 살펴보면, 조직적인 민간작업연맹, 즉 행회(行會)가 이미 형성되었음을 알 수 있다. 행회의 수령은 일명 행수(行首) 또는 행두(行頭)라고 한다. 금은행(金銀行)은 관부의 허가를 받은 조직으로 관부의 사무에 협조한다. 지방관부와 개인 작업장의 발전은 당대 금은기 제조업의 성과를 그대로 보여 주고 있다.

송대(宋代)에 이르러 상품경제의 발전과 도시의 번영은 금은기의 흥성을 불러일으켰다. 이 시대의 황족, 왕공대신, 부유한 상인뿐만 아니라 중농과 부유한 백성들도 사용하였다. 금은기는 고분(古墳), 탑기(塔基), 가마터에서 모두 출토된 바 있는데, 가히 한 시대를 풍미하였다고 할 수 있다. 송대 금은기는 흔히 복식장식물로 사용되었다. 통계에 따르면, 태종(太宗)부터 도종(度宗)에 이르기까지 23회에 걸쳐 금은기 장식품의 금지에 관한 영을 내렸지만 뿌리를 뽑을 수는 없었다. 송대에는 당대의 풍격을 기반으로 혁신을 거쳐 시대적 특징을 지닌 새로운 금은기를 선보였다. 당대의 풍만하고 화려하며 기세가 넘치는 등의 특징들이 사라지고 우아하고 독특하며 참신한 풍격이 나타났다. 요금대(遼金代)의 금은기는 제작기술 및 형태 면에서 지방의 민족적 색채가 짙어졌으며, 원대(元代) 금은기는 송대

(宋代)의 것과 비슷하면서 일용품과 진열품이 늘어났다. 송원대(宋元代)의 문양은 사회생활을 소재로 하여 다양한 내용들이 표현되고 보다 세속화되었다. 화훼나 과일과 같은 식물문양이나 날짐승, 길짐승무늬를 막론하고 사녀(仕女)와 같은 인물문양을 포함해서 모두 건강, 장수, 부 등 길함을 뜻하는 상징적 의미를 부여하여 율동감 있게 표현하였다. 중국 봉건사회 말기인 명청시대에 나타난 금은기는 시대적 풍격을 드러내는데 질박한 명대 금은기와 달리 화려하며 정교하다. 명청시대의 황제, 황실, 공후(公侯) 등 상류계층이 사용한 금은기는 조형과 무늬가 모두 정교하고 화려하다. 여러 가지 색상의 보석을 상감한 것도 있어 금은기와 보석이 어우러진 아름다움을 유감없이 표현하였다. 민간에서 사용했던 금은기와 장신구들도 풍부하고 다채로운 공예기술과 장인들의 뛰어난 기예를 선보였다. 시안시 문물보호고고학연구소에서 소장한 금잠(金簪), 금반지, 금팔찌 등 장신구에서도 이러한 공예기술을 엿볼 수 있다.

금은기의 발전사는 중국문화발전사의 한 부분으로서 각 시기의 예술적 풍격을 보여 주는 지침서라고 할 수 있다. 이러한 풍격은 당시의 미의식과 정신적 면모를 보여 준다. 금은기의 발전은 문화역사의 발전을 담고 있다. 시안시문 물보호고고학연구소에서 소장하고 있는 수많은 금은기들은 귀중한 문화재로서 인류역사에서 중국이 이룩한 휘황찬란한 성과를 보여 준다.

2010년 11월
왕창치(王長啓)

西安位于关中平塬，是通往西北，西南的交通要道，曾是汉唐等十叁个王朝的国都，是丝绸之路的起点。在歷史上长安城曾是国际大都市，是东西方经济文化的中心，对世界的经济文化产生了巨大影响。今天的西安地上，地下文化遗存极其丰富，记录着歷史进程，闪耀着歷史光辉，展示着人们创造与智慧，东西文化相互交流的成果。

西安地区丰富的文化遗存中，金银器最具特征，在西安市文物保护考古所藏品中属大类，这里所指的金银器，除了纯金银制品外还包括铜鎏金器及错金银器。我国古代先民对金银早已认识，《山海经·五藏山经》就记载我国分布各地的89种矿藏的地点，其中出产黄金的地方有19处，白银的地方20处，在西安地区周围，金矿藏有英山，泰昌山，数歷山（今千阳县境内）、龙首山、阳虚山（洛南县境内），阳华山、岐山、申山（今安塞县境内）等地。银矿主要分布在大时山（今眉县境内）和数歷山等，还载蓝田北山"其阴多金"。由于金银矿藏丰富，金银器件早在商周就出现，河北蒿城遗址和殷墟有黄金制品出土，发现"黄金块及小片金叶。"春秋战国时期西安北部内蒙古杭锦旗阿鲁柴登，准格尔旗西沟畔和陕西神木纳村高兎等匈奴墓藏曾出土大批金银器，有鹰形金冠顶、金冠带、动物饰片等，还有金鹿形怪兽，在金饰中动物形象极为常见，工艺復杂，形态各异，造型生动。在西安，宝鷄，咸阳等地出土也较为丰富，特别是秦国金银器，有雍城遗址的龙首蟠龙金带钩，金异兽饰件，金鸭嘴带钩，金节约，金兽面，金泡等。从中可以看到秦文化的发展。当时列国纷争，霸主更迭不已，地处西陲的秦国励精图治与东方列国竞争霸主地位。雍城曾是秦国的都城，在它的附近有离宫，宗庙及墓地陵区，曾出土大批金器，除上述介绍外，还有马具，装饰品及兵器等，其中金柄铁剑的金柄装饰为镂空变形蟠螭纹，上嵌绿松石。此后秦国实力得到加强，进一步东扩直到秦统一，经济繁荣，手工业发达，特别是错金银工艺和鎏金工艺得到大发展，它是这个时期手工业发展的标志，其工艺手法復杂，技艺高超。西安市文物保护考古所藏有镂空回首金卧虎，金虎符，塬均出土于宝鷄市凤翔县，造型与工艺特征比较明显。回首金卧虎与凤翔县博物馆藏雍城遗址出土的春秋时期龙首蟠龙金带钩首形相似，风格相同。金虎符与宝鷄市陈仓区博物馆藏千河魏家崖出土金虎相似，还有西安出土的鎏金银带钩、鎏金嵌贝铜带钩、错银叁蝉纹带钩、错银镦、错金银筒形车饰等等，还有错银鸠秘冒，秘冒整体鸠鸟形，回首长尾，错银为纹饰，座侧阴刻"廿叁年服工口治古，叁十八"八字铭文，为戈柄上的装饰。从这里可以看出错金银与鎏金器在战国时期普遍应用。说明春秋战国时期社会变革带来经济，文化及手工业生产的重大变化，传统的青铜礼器礼崩乐坏，走向下坡，新的器形新的工艺得到发展。金银造型新颖，装饰华丽，反映当时整个社会呈现崭新活泼的面貌。秦始皇统一为社会的发展奠定了基础，手工业同样也得到发展。

《史记·秦本纪》载："秦始皇葬骊山，以黄金为凫雁。"秦始皇陵的俑坑中曾出土了大金泡，在二号铜车马上亦发现金银制附件，可见金银器的制作取得很大成就。到了汉王朝时期国力强盛，史书记载汉代拥有大量的金银与金银器。例如：《汉书·贡禹传》记载："蜀广汉主金银器，岁各用五百万，"被称为多金王朝。又记载西汉皇帝对臣下赐赏黄金约一百多次。《史书·平淮书》记："大将军，骠骑大出击胡，得首虏八九万级，赏赐五十万金。"《史书·梁孝王世家》："梁孝王未死时，财以巨万计，不可胜数。及死，藏府黄金尚四十余万斤。"还记有金银矿藏及冶炼，《盐铁论》：荆、扬"左陵阳之金。""丹、章有金铜之山。"《水经注·若水》："兰仓水出金沙，越人收以为黄金。"《史

记·货殖列传》载："江南出……金，锡……"，"豫章出黄金。"《华阳国志》记，涪县"屠水出屠山，其源出金银矿，洗取，火融合之为金银。"还有晋寿县、博南县等有金银矿或金沙。据《太平广记》记载光武皇后之弟郭况，"累金数亿，家僮四百人，以金为器皿，冶铸之声，彻于都鄙。"这里描写的金银作坊规模之大。西安市文物保护考古所藏1999年11月在西安市未央区潭家乡北十里铺东村塼瓦厂出土窖藏金餅219枚，每枚重量254.5克至227.6克，绝大多数有戳记，从出土堆放情况看是属恩忙埋藏，可能是遇到农民起义或本朝将要灭亡逃亡前埋入地下的，这是当时贵重金属货币。还藏有汉墓出土的鎏金银凤鸟镇，鎏金错银卧虎形镇，鎏金鹰形鐏等等，可见贵族拥有黄金之多。汉代的金银器制造工艺技术有了较大的改造，不是以前主要采用浮彫或立彫的形式，改变古朴粗放风格，其工艺脱离了青铜工艺的传统技术，逐渐走上独立发展的道路。汉代多锤揲、焊接法成型，范铸成型者减少，图案加工一般是先锤打呈立彫和浅浮彫后再镌刻处理细部，此外还应用掐丝镶嵌、焊接、金珠等工艺。1966年在西安市北郊卢家口村出土金鬵，形体不大，制作精巧，工艺手法在鬵壁的周围以掐丝焊接、金珠、镶嵌手法饰金线交错的云纹嵌绿松石，锅内盛满米，如正在做饭（塬嵌绿松石脱落），底刻"日利"两字。1972年西安市第二机塼厂出土鎏金鹰形鐏，通体鎏金，上嵌料珠，多数料珠完好。汉代丝绸之路已开通，汉王朝与西方在经济文化方面往来增多，外来文化传入中国，金银器也相继传入。广州西汉南越王墓出土银盒，采用锤揲技术制成，上有浮彫水滴状花瓣纹饰具有立体效果，据考古文物专家认为它是通过丝绸之路传入中国的波斯或罗马地区的银器。上述金鬵上的制作工艺，就是由外国传入中国的技术制作，以后这类工艺的金银器多有发现。

金银器工艺復杂精细，有很高技艺。它的工艺具体分为范铸、锤揲、鎏金、焊接、镶嵌错金银、包金、掐丝、焊缀金珠等：范铸同铜器工艺相似，金要加热至1063℃熔化金液浇入模范内，冷却成形，而银溶化温度960℃。锤揲，利用金银的延展性，用锤打成片状，再置于器物或模具挤压捶打成形。焊接是在金银器和金银装饰之间的接触点上烧灌金属液体，使之冷却牢固结合一起。鎏金，或称"火镀金"、"汞镀金"，它是用黄金块或碎黄金片在400℃的温度下按比例加入水银，使之熔化于水银中，冷却成泥状固体，俗称"金泥"，然后涂于器物表面，用火温烤，使水银蒸发，黄金就固留于器表，这项鎏金技术是战国时期发明的，是世界上最早使用这种技术的国家。錾花，用錾刀在金银器表面刻錾刻各种图案，由于能熟练掌握技能，錾刻的图案生动流畅。镶嵌，在金银器表面嵌饰绿松石、水晶、珍珠、宝石等，以增加器物的华丽富贵程度，提高器物美观，更显艳丽。错金银，也称金银错，战国时期已成熟，它是在铸铜或银器的范模上，设计并做出错金银的凹饰，再把金银丝嵌于铜银器表面凹槽纹样内，打磨平齐，呈现各种纹样，更加华丽。掐丝和焊缀金珠工艺，将捶打得极薄的金银片，剪成细条，扭搓成丝，（从出土的金丝看，有片剪丝与拔制丝。）编成图案。焊缀金珠工艺是把金丝加热熔聚成粒，也可将金丝的一端加热熔化而落下圆珠。掐丝图案与金珠焊接器物上装饰，有的内嵌宝石等。

魏晋南北朝时期，社会动乱，经济遭到了一定破坏，另外各民族长期共同生活，相互融合，对外经济文化交流活跃，佛教及其艺术的传入促使这一时期文化艺术的发展，金银器相对发展，而形制和纹样明显带有这一时期文化艺术特征，即传统文化与外来文化的结合。关于这一时期生产制造和使用金银器相对减少，有学者从考古资料中经研究提出其塬因，黄金和白银产量减少，器物制作受到一定限制，加之

佛教兴盛耗费大量金银造佛像。当时金银器的制作有所提高，主要在上层社会流行。曹操《上献帝器物表》和《上杂物疏》中提到造释迦立像时"用赤金十万斤，黄金六百斤"。还有纯金香炉、唾壶、纯银香炉、盘等，制作金银器要求纯金、纯银。《洛阳伽蓝记》记：北魏河间王元琛好鸟，其喂马用银槽，拴马用金锁环，所藏金瓶、银瓮100多口，还有很多金银餐具、酒具等。关于馈赠、赏赐、贡献、偷盗、查抄金银器的记载相当多。长安城在魏晋南北朝时期已是佛教中心，佛教兴盛传播很广，在西安地区出土鎏金佛造像较丰富，例如长安区黄良乡石佛寺出土刻"法卢文"鎏金铜坐佛、西安北郊出土天和五年鎏金铜立佛等、2002年在临潼区代王出土四件羊首金牌饰，是带有北方少数民族的服饰物，反映当时少数民族内迁中原地区的例证。西安市文物保护考古所还藏东罗马帝国(又称拜占庭帝国)金币数枚，相当北朝时期，反映西方国家经过丝绸之路与长安通商贸易的情况。

唐代是金银器制作和使用的鼎盛时期，期数量大，种类多，制作精美，是中国古代金银工艺达到了顶峰，西安地区出土极为丰富。西安文物保护考古所藏了一大批的唐代金银器，具体地点有建国路、沙坡村、曲江池、叁兆村、西北工业大学、兴庆宫遗址、新筑枣园村国、西安火车站、长安区祝村、大明宫乡马旗寨、西安博长、潘家村，还有城建局上交等。陕西省博物馆也藏有西安出土的金银器，数量也丰富，南郊何家村出土270余件就是一例。金银器是唐代贵族使用的器具，据《唐律疏议》舍宅与服器物条载："器物者，一品以下，食器不得用纯金、纯玉。"《唐会要》杂录记："神龙二年（706年）九月，仪制令诸一品以下，食器不得用浑金玉，六品以下，不得用浑银。"在上层权贵中，多喜豪宴，动辄宴请上百公卿大巨，多用金银器，正如唐诗所述："谁能载酒开金盏，换取佳人舞绣筵。"王建《宫词一百首》中"一样金盘五千面，红酥点出牡丹花。"文献又记淮南节度使王播曾叁次向皇帝进奉金银器多达5900余件。从这里可以看到当时使用金银器的盛况，同时它反映当时社会政治文化的一个层面。唐代经济文化繁荣，丝绸之路进一步畅通，中国与国外的经济文化交往更加频繁，更加发达。唐人受西方影响对外来的器物崇尚，应用外来物品在社会上成为一种时髦，对金银器表现更为明显。在魏晋至隋代，由于金银器皿华贵在上层社会就有使用，主要是外国输入，而唐代继承前朝，金银器皿除外来品外，生产制造增大。皇家与贵族对使用金银器有传统神秘观念。"金银为食器可得不死"，能延年益寿，正如《太平御览》珍定部所载，从文献与考古资料看金银器不但是高档的使用器，更多地运用于赏赐、馈赠，对外交往等活动。金银器的种类丰富多彩，主要有碗、盘、碟、盏等食器；杯、耳杯、壶、茶盏等饮器；银盒（贮茶用）、茶罗子、银盐臺、银坛子、银锅、银匙、银杯、茶碾子等茶具与容具；炼丹器石榴罐、金或银锅、提梁罐、档等药具；香囊、熏炉、渣斗等卫生用具；簪、钗、梳、步摇、项链、手镯、臂钏等饰件；造像、宝涵、法器、棺椁等宗教器；银锁、合页、酒筹、酒令等杂品，其上面的纹饰多彩多样，有着极其丰富的文化内涵，具体纹样有龙凤、鸾鸟、鸿雁、蜂、蝶、天马、天鹿、狮子、熊、龟、猴、摩羯等动物纹，缠枝花、团花、宝相花、折枝花等，还有各类人物纹等。从总体看展现了时代特征与气息，浑圆饱满，大度雄伟，生机勃勃，充满自信。其动物与花卉纹以现实为基础进行演变，特别是团花、折枝花、缠枝花最为突出，丰腴典雅，富有生命力人物图案取材于现实生活，有伎乐、宴饮、狩猎、仕女生活等，与前朝的装饰大大不同，带有喜庆，吉祥，美好，趋向于世俗，五彩缤纷，蓬勃向上。

唐代歷时近300年，金银器在唐代以前主要是外来传入，进入唐代随着社会的进步发展也得到发展。根据考古发掘资料与器型纹饰演变为四期：初唐到高宗时期，（公元618~683年）；武则天到玄宗时期（公元684~755年）；肃宗到宪宗时期（公元756~820年）；穆宗到哀帝时期（公元821~907年）。有的学者还分为叁期，也有分为六期，总之从金银器分期可以看出早期金银器受外来影响比较明显，同时金银器皿的风格已开始中国化，工艺手法多数采用锤揲技术，在锤出凹凸变化的纹样轮廓上再錾刻细部纹样，一般比较厚重，许多银器通体鎏金。这都是唐代工匠学习西方技艺与并掌握制造，使之更适合中国人使用和观赏，是一个大发展时期。中后期，金银器属成熟，普及多样化时期，一般的碗，盘，盒的形制都有变化，高足杯，带把杯等少见，茶具，筹筒，支架，渣斗，竈具等出现。纹样更加丰富多样，具有浓厚的民间生活气息。从西安市文物保护考古所藏品看：西安西郊出土的八出忍冬纹葵形银碗与沙坡村出土鹿纹银碗，具有浓厚的粟物银器风格，应属第一期的器物；二期，西安曲江池村发现的凸叁足银盘，折枝团花叁足银盘共叁件，明显是中国工艺特征的器皿。叁期，西安西北工业大学出土的双鲤鱼宝相莲瓣银盘，黄鹂折枝花银盘，双鸿雁纹银碗，鸳鸯鸿雁折枝花银碗，石榴折枝花银碗。这类器物不论造型与纹饰均具中国特征。第四期有西安交通大学出土的都管七国六瓣银盒，鹦鹉纹海棠形圈足银盒，龟背纹银盒。这时期造型繁杂多样，使用的范围广大，除了皇族贵亲外，地方官员与富裕的百姓也使用。金银源料开采与冶炼，在史书资料均有记载，并且描述得非常具体，例如《新唐书·地理志》，《通典》，《唐六典》，《元和郡县图志》等。其采矿的经营分为两大系统，即官府开采和私人开采，两种方式互为补充。《旧唐书·职官志》载："凡天下出铜铁府，听人私采，官收其税。"唐朝允许私人采矿，并鼓励民间开采金银，从税收中获益。金银矿开采和冶炼后，为便于保存和携带，通常是按一定的样式冶铸或捶打成铤，饼，锭等，通过税收及收购的方式，使全国各地生产的大部分金银都被集中到皇室及官府，它们不在普通市面流通，而成为皇室与官府制作器物的源料。西安文物保护考古所藏唐长安城出土的"姚州贡金"金铤，"铙州证圣元年"银铤，"乾符六年"银铤，"岭南道"进贡银铤，还有桥形银铤等，这些实物可为例证。制作金银器同样分为中央官府作坊，地方官府作坊与私营作坊，中央官府作坊是少府监和将作监，为皇室和中央官府服务的手工业管理机构，主要机构有掌冶署，左尚署和中尚署司下的金银作坊院。盛唐以后，皇帝时常下诏向地方官僚"宣索"金银器。在宣宗时期（847~858年）还增设专门为皇室打造金银器的"文思院"，法门寺出土的多件金银器，明确刻铭属文思院制造。另外，从史料与出土金银器中，可以看到中央与地方高级官员进奉金银器，进奉金银器已成风气，西安市文物保护考古所藏1975年西北工业大学窖藏出土的"李勉奉进"双鲤鱼宝相莲瓣纹银盘，上刻铭文记为进奉器，李勉为肃宗，代宗，德宗叁期宗室宰相，史书记载："清廉简易，为宗臣之表"的清官，但铭文记他在洪州刺史任内，向皇帝进奉的银盘，可见当时进奉之风之烈。地方官府作坊早在初唐，盛唐已出现，兴盛于中晚唐时，从考古发掘出土金银器的铭刻看，地方官府作坊在南方，江南东道的越州（今浙江绍兴），江南西道的洪州（今江西南昌）与宣州（今安徽宣州），浙江道润州（今江西镇江）等是金银器的主要制造地。浙西道制造的金银器在陕西的耀县，扶风法门寺等地均有发现。私营作坊在中期以后得到发展，当时特别是南方，金银的开采量大，源料充足，加之政府在手工业中逐渐推行"纳资代役"与"和雇"等新政策，私营金银手工业得到发展。西安南郊何家村窖藏出土的高足杯

上有"马舍"，陕西耀县柳林背阴村出土刻花四曲银碗与五曲银盘上刻"马马明"，"朱口"是私营作坊生产。私营金银作坊据史料记载，已形成了有组织的民间私人作坊联盟，即行会，其头领称为行首或行头，金银行组织为官府认可，还协助官府处理事务，地方官府和私人作坊的发展说明唐代金银制造业呈现的成就。

宋代商品经济发展，城镇繁荣，促使金银业的兴盛。当时不仅皇亲贵戚，王公大臣，富商大贾享用金银器，而一般中户农家与富裕市民也使用，在墓葬，塔基与窖藏均有出土，金银器可谓风靡一时。宋代金银器的制作使用，特别是用于服饰方面大大增加。由于金银器饰使用广泛，从太宗到度宗期，据不完全统计，共发了23次严申禁断金银器饰的诏命，但屡禁不止。宋代在唐代基础上不断创新，形成了具有鲜明时代特色的新风貌。唐代那种丰腴富丽，气势博大的特征消失了，而呈现出典雅秀美，奇巧新颖的风格。辽，金的金银器的做工与形制带有浓郁的地方民族特色。元代金银器与宋代相近似，日用器与陈设品增多。宋元时期的纹饰题材源于社会生活，表现内容更为广阔，更为世俗化，不论是花卉瓜果的植物纹，还是飞禽走兽动物纹，包括人物仕女其形象刻画生动活泼，充满生机，均隐喻着健康，长寿和富有的吉祥用语。明清时期是中国封建社会的后期，在金银器上呈现出不同时代风格，明代仍具古朴风格，而清代却工整华丽，细腻精工。在明清帝王，皇家，公侯，上层人物使用的金银器，造型与纹饰均精美华贵。有的还镶嵌各色宝石，交相辉映，可谓奢华艳丽，但在民间使用的金银器与饰品也较普遍，其工艺丰富多彩，技艺精湛，从西安市文物保护考古所藏的小件金簪，金戒与金镯首饰也能看到它的工艺技能。

金银器的发展史，是我们中华民族发展史的组成部分，从中可以了解到各个时期艺术风格，这种风格既是那个时代审美意识的反映，亦展示出那个时代的精神风貌。它的发展演变，记录着文化歷史的发展，西安市文物保护考古所收藏的金银器是一批巨大的文化财富，五彩缤纷，色彩斑斓，它呈现着中华民族在人类歷史上创建的丰功伟绩。

2010年11月

王长启

As a vital communications line to the northwest and southwest of China, located at Guanzhong Plain, Xi'an City is an ancient capital of 13 dynasties such as Han Dynasty and Tang Dynasty, and the starting point of the Silk Road. Xi'an City has great influence on the economy and culture of the world as an international metropolis and economic and cultural center between the east and the west in the history. At present, Xi'an City is rich in the aboveground and underground cultural relics. With historical glory, they record the historical progress and display the achievements of creation, wisdom and exchange of the eastern and western culture.

Of the rich cultural relics in Xi'an City, the gold and silver wares are typical and have large proportion in collections of Xi'an Cultural Relic Protection and Archaeology Institute, including pure gold and silver articles, gilt bronze wares and metal-inlaid wares. The ancient people of China have known the gold and silver. According to the Book of Hills and Seas-Wuzang Mountains, there were mines of 98 mineral resources distributed throughout the country, 19 of which had gold and 20 of which had silver. The gold mines near Xi'an City included Mt. Yingshan, Mt. Taichang, Mt. Shuli(now in Qianyang County), Mt. Longshou, Mt. Yangxu(in Luonan County), Mt. Yanghua, Mt. Chi, Mt. Shen(now in Ansai County), and other places. The silver mines were mainly distributed in Mt. Dashi(now in Mei County), Mt. Shuli, etc. According to the book, the gold was rich in the north of Mt. Lantian. With rich gold and silver resources, the gold and silver wares emerged as early as Shang and Zhou Dynasties such as the gold products ("gold bullion and small gold leaf") from the site of Gaocheng County of Hebei Province and ruins of the Yin Dynasty in north China. A large batch of gold and silver wares were unearthed from the Xiongnu Graves of Spring and Autumn and Warring States periods of China (including Aluchaideng of Hanggin Banner of Inner Mongolia to north of Xi'an City, Xigoupan of Zhunge'er qi (place in Inner Mongolia), and Nalin Gaotu Village of Shaanxi Province, etc.), such as the eagle-shaped gold crown, gold crown belt, animal paillette and gold deer-shaped monster, of which the animal images are very common in the gold ornaments and have complicated craftsmanship, different shapes and vivid forms. Many gold and silver wares were excavated from Xi'an City, Baoji City, Xianyang City, etc., especially the gold and silver wares of Qin Dynasty, such as the dragon-head-shaped Panlong gold belt hook, gold animal ornaments, gold duck-billed belt hook, gold ornament for horses, gold animal figure, gold foam, etc. of Yongcheng site, the Capital of the Qin State. This shows the development of Qin culture. When all states had disputes and the powerful leaders changed from time to time, the Qin state in the western China made great efforts to build a strong state and fought with the eastern states for supremacy. Many gold wares were excavated from the detached palace, ancestral temple of a ruling house, and tombs surrounding Yongcheng, the capital of Qin state, including the harness, ornaments and weapons besides above wares. Of them, the golden handle of an iron sword have hollowed-out, deformed and interlaced dragon pattern and embedded with the turquoise. After that, the Qin State was strengthened and expanded to the east until the unification of Qin State. Its economy was flourishing and the handicraft industry was developed, especially the metal-inlaid craftsmanship and gilt craftsmanship. This marked the development of handicraft industry with complicate techniques and superb skills. The hollowed-out looking-back and crouching gold tiger and gold tiger tally collected in Xi'an Cultural Relic Protection and Archaeology Institute were excavated from Fengxiang County of Baoji City, and they have distinctive characteristics in molding and technique and with the same styles. The gold tiger tally is similar to those unearthed from Weijiaya Village of Qianhe Town and collected in the museum of Chencang District of Baoji City. In addition, the gold and silver wares excavated in Xi'an City include the gilt belt hook, gilt bronze belt hook with embedded shell, metal-inlaid belt hook with three cicada designs, silver-inlaid forged pieces, metal-inlaid cylindrical vehicle ornaments, etc., The silver-inlaid turtledove-shaped cap is in the shape of turtledove with the inlaid silver as the decorative pattern and carved the following at the base: "Made in the 23rd years in a peaceful and prosperous society" as the decoration of spear handle. This displays that the metal-inlaid and gilt wares were commonly used in Warring States periods. The social reform in the Spring & Autumn and Warring States periods of China brought great change of economy, culture and handicraft industry, and the new wares and new craftsmanship were developed as the traditional ritual vessels were on the decline. The gold and silver wares had novel shapes, gorgeous decoration and reflected the brand-new and lively outlook of the whole society at that time. The unification of the country by first Emperor Qin laid a foundation for the social development and the handicraft industry was also developed. Records of the Grand Historian History of Qin writes:"Qin Shi Huang was buried in Mount Li and his tomb was ornamented with golden images of birds." The large gold foams unearthed in the vault of tomb of Qin Shi Huang and the gold and silver accessories found in the No.2 bronze chariot and horses shows the great achievements in gold and silver wares making. In the Han Dynasty, the state was powerful, and there were numerous gold, silver, and gold and silver wares in Han Dynasty according to the historical record. For instance, the Book of Han Biography of Gong Yu writes:"The Guanghan of ancient Shu kingdom was rich in gold and silver wares and five million taels of gold was used respectively for each year" and so it is called the dynasty with abundant gold. It also records that the emperor of Western Han Dynasty awarded gold to his chancellors for more than one hundred times. The Records of the Grand Historian Ping Huai Shu records:"The Biaoqi(a title of generals in ancient times) General-in-chief went to fight with the tartars and chopped off eighteen or nineteen thousand of enemy's heads, so five hundred thousands taels of gold was awarded to him." Records of the Grand Historian-Prince Xiao of Liang writes:"When prince Xiao of Liang was alive, his property was in an immerse amount. After his death, there were over four hundred taels of gold in his mansion". The Debates on Salt and Iron writes:"The copper mines of Lingyang lie to" the Jingzhou and Yangzhou and "the mountains of Danyang and Zhangshan have copper mines". The Commentary on the Waterways Classics-Water writes: "There are gold dusts in Lancang River and the people of Yue State collect them to smelt the gold". The Records of the Grand Historian-Collected Biographies of the Commercial and Industrial Management writes:"there are gold and tin in the south of the Yangtze River", and "the gold exists in Yuzhang County". According to the Records of the Huayang Kingdom, "there are small rivers from the small mountains and the sources of rivers are gold and silver mines in Fu County. After washing and smelting, the gold and silver can be produced", and there are gold and silver mines and gold dusts in Jinshou County, Bonan County, etc. According to the Extensive Gleanings of the Taiping Era which describes the brother of empress of Emperor Guangwu, Guo Kuang, "he accumulates hundreds of millions of taels of gold, has four hundred servants and uses the gold to make wares. The sound of smelting and casting can be heard in the capital and surrounding areas". This shows the large scale of gold and silver workshops. Collected in Xi'an Cultural Relic Protection and Archaeology Institute, a 219 gold cakes weighing from 254.5g to 227.6g were excavated in bricks and tiles plant in Beishilipu East Village, TanjiaTownship, Weiyang District, Xi'an in November 1999. Most of them have stamps. Judging from the excavation and stacking condition, these gold cakes were hastily buries, which may be buried underground when peasant uprising or before that dynasty was to perish and when people were escaping. They were precious metallic currency at that time. In addition, gilt silver phoenix weight, gilt inlaid silver with crouching tiger shape and gilt eagle-shaped butt end of spear excavated in Han dynasty tombs are collected as well. Thus, it can be seen that the noble had so much gold. Craftsmanship of gold and silver wares was improved greatly in Han Dynasty. The previous embossment and vertical sculpture were not adopted any more; the simple, unsophisticated and extensive was changed; its craftsmanship was separated from traditional technique of bronze craftsmanship and gradually stepped on the way of independent development. In Han Dynasty, hammering and welding technique were widely used for molding. Molding and casting technique was less used. In general, the details of pattern were processed only after they were hammered into vertical sculpture and shallow embossment. In addition, wire inlay, welding and golden leaf were used. With small body and skillful manufacturing, gold cup was excavated in Lujiakou Village, northern suburb of Xi'an City in 1996. Its craftsmanship is to decorate clouding with staggered gold thread and inlay kallaite with wire welding, golden leaf and inlaying technique. For the stove, the pot is filled with rice, as if it was cooking(originally inlayed turquoise dropped). Meanwhile, "Rili" was carved at the bottom. In 1972, gilt eagle-shaped butt and of spear was excavated in Xi'an No.2 Brick Plant, gilt and inlayed by beads(most of the beads are intact). The Silk Road was blazed in Han Dynasty. Thus, economic communications between Han Dynasty and the west was enhanced and foreign culture was introduced into China, including gold and silver wares. The silver box excavated in South Yue Emperor's grave of Western Han Dynasty in Guangzhou was manufactured with adoption of hammering technique. Its water-drop-shaped petal ornamentation has three dimensional effects. Archaeologists and antiquities experts believe that it was the silver wares in Persia or Roman area introduced into China via the Silk Road. The aforesaid craftsmanship of gold stove is the technology from foreign countries. Afterwards, gold and silver wares with such technique are frequently discovered.

The craft of gold and silver wares is complicated and fine, with high skills. The craft can be specifically divided into mould-casting, hammering, gilding, welding, mixed gold and silver inlaying, gold plating, wire inlaying, and gold bead welding and decoration, etc.: The mould-casting is similar to the bronze craft, the gold shall be heated to 1063℃, milted into liquid gold and poured into the mould to harden into shape, while the melting temperature of silver is 960℃. The hammering makes use of the extensibility of gold and silver, hammer the gold and silver into flake, then put in the implements or mould to make the gold and silver cool and bond firmly. Gilding, or "fire gilding" and "mercury gilding" is to add gold nugget or broken gold in mercury proportionally at temperature of 400℃ to make the gold melt in mercury, and cool into the mushy solid, which is commonly known as "gold mud", then coat the "gold mud" on the surface of implements, roast tenderly with fire to make the mercury evaporate, and the gold will leave on the surface of implements. This technology is invented in the Warring States Periods, and China is the first country in the world to use this technology. Carving designs: it is to carve various kinds of patterns on the surface of gold and silver wares with burin. Since the skills can be mastered expertly, the patterns carved are vivid and smooth. Inlaying: it is to inlay the turquoise, crystal, pearl, gemstone, etc., on the surface of gold and silver wares to increase the magnificence and value of implements, and to make the implements more luxuriant and gorgeous. Mixed gold and silver inlaying has become mature in the Warring States Period. It is to design and make the hollow molding of mixed gold and silver on the mould of cast copper on silverware, inlay the mixed gold and silver in the hollow dermatoglyphic pattern on the surface of copper or silverware, polish it smooth to show various kinds of patterns, which will be more luxuriant. Wire inlaying and gold bead welding and decoration crafts is to hammer the gold and silver into thin slice, shear the very thin thumped gold and silver slice into thin strips, twist the strips into wire, (from the unearthed gold wire, there are shearing the slice into strips and drawing into wire) and weave into patterns. Gold bead welding and decoration craft is to heat the gold wire and agglomerate the gold wire into grains, or heat one end of the gold wire to meltdown and the bead will drop. Wire inlaying patterns and gold bead can be welded on the decoration of the implements, and some have embedded gemstone, etc.

In the period of Wei, Jin, Southern and Northern Dynasties, the society was instable and the economy was wrecked in a certain degree. In addition, people of different nations lived together and were assimilated, with foreign economy and culture exchanged actively. The introduction of Buddhism and other arts urged the development of culture and art in that stage. Gold and silver wares also developed comparatively, while the structure and pattern design showed obvious culture and art features of that period, i. e. the combination of traditional culture and foreign culture. The number of gold and silver wares manufactured and used in this period was reduced comparatively. Some scholars researched archaeological materials and proposed some reasons: the output of gold and silver at that time was reduced; the production of implements was limited; and Buddhist images was produced in a large amount because of the bloom of Buddhism. The fabrication of gold and silver wares which were popular among upper classes was improved remarkably. List of Implements for Emperor and Memorial of Miscellaneous Articles wrote by Cao Cao mention that for standing statue of Sakyamuni, 50 thousand kilograms of solid gold and 300 hundred kilograms of yellow gold were used, as well as pure gold censers and spittoons, pure silver censers and plates, etc. Pure gold and silver were required for manufacturing gold and silver wares. The Records of Qielan at Luoyang states that Wang Yuanchen in Hejian City in Northern Wei Dynasty, was fond of birds, used silver manger for feeding horses, gold locking collar tying horses, collected more than one hundred gold bottles and silver urns, as many gold and silver cutleries and wine sets, etc. There are many records about presenting, devoting, stealing and confiscating gold silver wares. Changan City was the Buddhism center during the period of Wei, Jin, and Southern and Northern Dynasties. Buddhism was flourishing and spread widely. Fine gold Buddha statues unearthed in Xi'an areas are copious, such as Gilt Bronze Sitting Buddha marked Kharosth unearthed in Stone Buddha Temple in Huangliang town in Changan, Gilt Bronze Standing Buddha in the fifth year of Tianhe unearthed in the northern suburbs of Xi'an, and four sheep-head gold pendants, which were cloth adornments of minority nations in the North, and the instances of minority nations moving to the central plain area. Several gold coins of Lower Empire(also called Byzantine Empire), which was equal to Northern Dynasty, collected in Xi'an Cultural Relics Protection Archaeological Institute, reflect the situations that western countries made trade relations with Changan via the Silk Road.

The Tang Dynasty is the golden age for the manufacture and use of gold and silver wares in a large number, with various types, and beautiful fabrication. Gold and silver craftsmanship in ancient China reached the peak at that period. Gold and silver wares unearthed in Xi'an are abundant. Xi'an Cultural Relics Protection Archaeological Institute have collected many gold and silver wares in the Tang Dynasty; the specific places include Jangguo Road, Shapo Vullage, Qujangchi, Sanzhao Village, Northwestern Polytechnical University, the site of Xingqing Palace, Zaoyuan Village of Xinzhu town, Xi'an railway station, Zhu Village in Changan District, Maqizhai Village of Daminggong town, Xi'an brickyard, Panjia Villgae, Bureau of Urban and Rural Construction, etc., Shaanxi Provincial Museum also stores numerous gold and silver wares unearthed in Xi'an, for example, more than 270 wares unearthed in Hejia Village in southern suburbs, Gold and silver wares were for the noble. Housing and Implements in The Tang Law Dredges Opinion recorded that food vessels of implements for people under the first rank, shall not be made from pure gold and genuine jade. Jottings of Tnaghuiyao recorded that in September of the second year of Shen Long (706 A.D.), in Yi Zhi rules, food vessels of implements for people under the first rank shall not use unrefined gold and uncarved jade, that for people under the sixth rank shall not use silver. The upper classes were fond of sumptuous banquets mostly, and invited more than one hundred chancellors frequently, with gold and silver wares, just as that described in Tang poetry: who can bring wine with gold cips, in exchange for beauties to show dances in epicurean repast. 100 Ci-poetry wrote by Wang Jian remarked that there are five thousand designs for one kind of gold plate, red shortcakes can make for peonies. The literature also recorded that governor Wang Bo of Huainan Province, offered more than 5,900 gold and silver wares to the Emperor as tribute for three times. Form this case, we can know the grand situation of using gold and silver wares at that time, while it reflected an aspect of social politics, economy and culture. Economy and culture in the Tang Dynasty was prosperous: the Silk Road was developed further; economy and culture communication between China and foreign countries were more frequent and much developed. People in the Tang Dynasty, influenced by the Western, advocated foreign implements, and regarded using foreign goods as a fashion, especially gold and silver wares. From Wei and Jin Dynasties to Sui Dynasty, gold and silver wares were used in the upper classes because of its luxury, most of which were foreign imported goods. The Tang Dynasty inherited the previous dynasty, and the manufacture of gold and silver wares increased except foreign implements. The imperial and noble family had traditional mysterious thought of using gold and silver wares: one will not die and live longer if using gold and silver wares as food vessels, just as that recorded in Jewelry Part of Taiping Imperial Encyclopedia, from literatures and archaeological materials, gold and silver wares are not only for upper-scale practicality objects, but also more frequently used for reward and present, external contacts, etc., The types of gold and silver wares are various, mainly include food vessels such as bowl, plate, dish, cup; drink vessels such as bottle, ear cup, pot, tea cup; tea sets and containers such as silver box (for tea storage), tea sieve, silver salt container, silver jar, silver bath, silver spoon, silver cup, and tea roller; medical instruments such as elixir furnace, pomegranate crock, gold or silver bath, handle crock, crosspiece; sanitary appliances such as incense bag, censer, kettle; ornaments such as bodkin, hairpin, comb, dangling ornament, necklace, bracelet, armlet; religion instruments such as statue, cinerary casket, musical instruments used in a Buddhist or Taoist mass, inner and outer coffin; sundry goods such as silver lock, hinge, wine chip, and drinking game. The emblazonry is colorful, manifold, and extremely full of culture contents. The specific patterns include animal pattern such as dragons and phoenixes, mythical bird, swan goose, wasp, butterfly, heavenly steed, heavenly deer, lion, bear, turtle, monkey, capricorn; interlocking flowers, medallion, designs of composite flowers, plucked branches and flowers, etc. as well as various figure pattern. In general, it shows the characteristics and breath of the times: perfectly round and plump, magnanimous and splendid, full vigor and confidence. The animal and flower patterns evolves on a basis of reality, especially the patterns of medallion, plucked branches and flowers and interlocking flowers are plump, elegant and vital. Figures patterns are drawn from real life, including Jiyue dance, banquet, hunting and maid of honor life, etc., which are very different from the ornaments in the previous dynasty, but contain happy event, auspices and goodliness, tend to common customs, and blaze with color, with powerful and upward appearance.

The gold and silver wares were mainly imported before Tang Dynasty which lasted about 300 years and were developed with the social progress in Tang Dynasty. Their development is divided into four periods according to the archaeological excavation data, ware form and decorative patterns: from early Tang Dynasty to Emperor Gaozong of Tang(618 A.D.~683 A.D.); from Empress Wu Zetian and Emperor Xuanzong of Tang(684 A.D.~755 A.D.); from Emperor Suzong of Tang to Emperor Xianzong of Tang(756 A.D.~820 A.D.); and from Emperor Muzong of Tang to Emperor Aidi of Tang(821 A.D.~907 A.D.). Some scholars divide it into three periods and others divide it into six periods. In a word, judging from the period divide of gold and silver wares, it can be seen that the early gold and silver wares are distinctively affected by the foreign countries. Meanwhile, the styles of gold and silver wares become localized in China and for most wares, the craft technique was hammering and the specific patterns were carved after the pattern profile was hammered. They are relatively thick and heavy. Many silver wares are gild completely. During this period with great progress, the craftsmen of Tang Dynasty learned the western techniques and mastered the craftsmanship to make them more suitable for application and appreciation of the Chinese. In the middle and late periods, the gold and silver wares become mature, popular and diverse: the forms of bowl, dish and box were varied, the goblet and cups were not common and tea set, chip pot, holder, refuse vessel appeared. The decorative patterns are rich and varied and have strong atmosphere of civil life. It can be seen from collections in Xi'an Cultural Relic Protection and Archaeology Institute: The sunflower-shaped silver bowl with eight-honeysuckle-pattern unearthed from the western suburbs of Xi'an City and the silver bowl with deer Motif unearthed from the Shapo Village have strong style of grain silver wares and are the wares of this first period; raised three-legged silver plate and broken flower pattern and medallion (three pieces in total) unearthed in Chi Village of Qujang District of Xi'an have distinctive Chinese technological characteristics in the second period; silver plate with double-carp and lotus petal, silver plate with oriole, silver plate with double-wild goose, silver plate with Mandarin Ducks and wild goose, silver plate with pomegranate unearthed from Northwestern Polytechnical University were the third period (such wares have the Chinese characteristics in terms of form and decorative pattern); the "Governing Seven Kingdoms" six-petal silver box, Chinese flowering crab apple shaped circular leg silver box with parrot pattern and silver box with tortoiseshell pattern unearthed in Xi'an Jiaotong University were the fourth period. The molding is diverse in this period and the application scope was expanded. Such wares were used not only the royal or noble family but all the local officials and rich common people. The raw materials of gold and silver and their smelting were recorded in the historical data with very specific description, such as Book of New Tang Dynasty-Geology, Tongdian, Tang Liu Dian, and Annals of Yuanhe County. The operating of mining was classified into two systems: governmental mining and private mining, which are complementary with each other. Book of Old Tang Dynasty-Official writes: "for the copper and iron mines in all China, the private persons can mine but the governments will impose taxes." The private persons were allowed to mine in Tang Dynasty and the civil people were encouraged to exploit the silver and gold to obtain benefits from taxes. For the convenience of storage or carrying, the silver and gold were usually smelted, casted or hammered into the ingots in a certain form. By taxation, purchase, etc., most gold and silver all round China were collected to the imperial family and offices of local government. They were not circulated in the ordinary market, but become the raw materials to produce wares for the imperial family and offices of local government, for example, the "Yaozhou tribute" gold ingot, silver ingot of "Naozhou(695 A.D.)", silver ingot of "the sixth year of Qianfu", tribute silver ingot of "Lingnandao", and bridge-shaped silver ingot. The central government workshop, local government workshop and private workshop were established to manufacture the gold and silver wares. The central government workshop was under the control of the directorate for palace building and department for palace construction authority of handicraft industry serving the royal family and central government, mainly including the gold and silver workshops under the foundry office, left service office and middle service office. After the flourishing of Tang Dynasty, the emperor often issue edicts to the local officials to "collect" gold and silver wares. The "Crafts Institute" was specially established in the period of emperor Xuanzong of Tang(847 A.D.~858 A.D.) to make gold and silver wares for royal family and many gold and silver wares unearthed in Famen Temple are carved definitely that they were made by the Crafts Institute. In addition, the historical data and unearthed gold silver wares show that the central and local officials of high rank offered gold and silver wares as the tributes and such deeds become a fashion at that time. The silver plate with double-carp, lotus petal and "Tribute of Li Mian" unearthed in Northwestern Polytechnical University in 1975 and collected in Xi'an Cultural Relic Protection and Archaeology Institute was carved as the tribute. Li Mian is the imperial prime minister in feudal China of emperor Suzong of Tang, emperor Daizong of Tang and emperor Dezong of Tang. The historical book writes: "He is honest, upright and simple as the example of imperial official". The inscription describes the silver plates offered to the emperor by him when he assumes the office of the governor of Hongzhou. This proves the fashion of tribute offering was strong at that time. The local government workshops emerged in early Tang Dynasty and flourished in middle Tang Dynasty. The inscription of gold and silver wares unearthed shows that the main manufacturing places of gold and silver wares such as Yuezhou of Jiangnan east area (now Shaoxing of Zhejiang Province), Hongzhou (now Xichang of Jiangxi province) and Xuanzhou (now Xuanzhou of Anhui Province) of west area, and Runzhou of Zhexidao (now Zhenjiang of Jiangxi Province) were the local government workshops in south of China. The gold and silver wares made in Zhexidao were unearthed in Yao County of Shaanxi Province, Famen Temple of Fufeng County, etc. The private workshops were developed in the middle stage, especially in the south of China. Since the production volume of gold and silver was large, the raw materials were sufficient, and the government promoted the "monetary contributions in lieu of corve service", "government employment" and other new policies in the handicraft industry, the private handicraft industry of gold and silver was developed. The goblet with "Mashe" unearthed in cellar of Hejia Village of southern suburbs of Xi'an City,

Quadrilateral silver bowl and pentagonal silver plate with "Mamaming" and "Zhukou" and carved designs unearthed from the Liulin Beiyin Village of Yao County of Shaanxi province were manufactured from private workshops. According to the historical data of private gold and silver workshops, the organized alliance between civil society and private workshops was established, i.e. the guild, whose head was the guild head. The gold and silver guild was recognized by the government and assisted the government to deal with affairs. The development of office of local government and private workshops manifests the achievements of gold and silver industry in Tang Dynasty.

The development of commodity economy and prosperity of towns in Song Dynasty promoted the flourish of gold and silver wares. At that time, not only the kinsman of the emperor, princes, dukes and ministers and rich businessmen could enjoy the gold and silver wares, but also the medium farming family and rich citizens could use them. They were unearthed from the grave, tower footing and cellar and the gold and silver wares become fashionable for a time. In Song Dynasty, the use and manufacture of gold and silver wares were greatly increased, especially for the clothing. With wide application of gold and silver wares and ornaments, according to the incomplete statistics, 23 edicts were issued from Emperor Taizong of Song to Emperor Duzong of Song to forbid the gold and silver wares and ornaments, but it was unable to stop despite repeated prohibition. With the continuous innovation based on their development in Song Dynasty, new look with distinctive characteristics of the times was formed in Tang Dynasty. As the characteristics of fullness in form and tremendous momentum disappeared, the gold and silver wares were elegant, beautiful, ingenious and novel. The workmanship and forms of the gold and silver wares of Liao Dynasty and Jin Dynasty were rich in local distinctive national features. The gold and silver wares of Yuan Dynasty were similar to those of Song Dynasty, but the number of articles of daily use and furnishings was increased. The decorative patterns in Song and Yuan Dynasties were derived from the social life with broader and more secular content, whether the plant patterns such as the flowers and fruits or the animal patterns such as birds and beasts including the figures and beautiful women; their figuring paintings were vivid, vigorous and vital with the auspicious expression of health, longevity and richness. At the end of Chinese feudal society in Ming and Qing dynasties, the gold and silver wares present the styles of different times: they were simple and unsophisticated in Qing Dynasty; they were neat and gorgeous, fine and delicate. For the gold and silver wares used by emperor, royal family, duke, marquis, and the upper class people, their molding and decorative patterns were fine and luxurious. Many of them are encrusted with diamonds and contrasted finely with each other, luxurious and gorgeous. However, it is common for the gold and silver wares and ornaments to be used among the people and their crafts are colorful and exquisite. We can see their workmanship and skills from the small golden hair pin, gold ring and gold bracelet collected in Xi'an Cultural Relic Protection and Archaeology Institute.

The development history of gold and silver wares is a part of Chinese cultural development history. We can learn about the artistic styles of all times, which reflect the aesthetic consciousness of that age and display the mental outlook at those times. Its evolution records the cultural and historical development. The gold and silver wares collected in Xi'an Cultural Relic Protection and Archaeology Institute are great cultural wealth blazing with color and present the great achievements made by the Chinese people in the human history

Nov. 2011

Wang Changqi

　我が國が約3000年前に商代はすでに黄金を使い始めたが、かつ河南、河北、北京、山西などの商代遺跡及び墓中にかつて小型金飾を出土したことがある。銀は戦国の時までに使い始めてからかつ迅速に流行っているみたいだが。春秋戦国時代に、西安はその所在の秦国に金銀製造の手工業にとって各諸侯国中で最もきわだっている、製品の数量に拘らずまだ造型、製造プロセスレベルも全部すでに高いほどに達したが、1976~1986の間に関中西部の鳳翔一帯でつまり秦文化の遺跡中にかつて前後で発掘による約100件以上の金銀器を出土された。ところが、西安地区は考古学発掘作業の現場でいくつかの戦国の銀質あるいは【錯金銀帯釣】を出土された以外、あまり戦国前のその他の金銀器を見られないが、そこは秦人活動の中心地区にいないと関係があるかも知れない。

　秦代の金銀製品は多く実用器であるが、主に車に用いる。秦俑で見つけられた2セットの銅車馬の部品には、ただし金銀飾り件も約100件以上がある、金節約、金当盧、銀節約、金銀勒などがある。秦俑坑の第5個の【探方】内にも金節約などを出土した。金銀器の鋳造温度が高く、プロセス技術も複雑である。金銀器の制作は銅とその他の金属器の難度よりもっと大きく、しかも当地と周辺地区では出土した金銀器の規則程度と統一の造型風格から見えると、その地方役所の手工業の仕事場或は仕事場はその時の客観的な条件の下で金銀を作るわけにはいけない、寺工で指導したもとの役所の仕事場から鋳造加工したはずだ。

　両漢時期において、国力は勢いが盛んであったため、朝延は大量の黄金を持っているが、多く財政準備金或は流通流域に用いる、しかし金質容器ではきわめて珍しく、或はこの時期の鎏金プロセスがきわめて盛んに流行したので、その後鎏金器で代わった。

　漢代の金器の制作技術にとっては、代表性的な成績を持つのは【集定繰糸】と【粒状真珠】点溶接のプロセスを使用したんだ。【集定繰糸】は、たたかれた薄い金銀片を条状に切り、糸に磨くとそれを曲がり、図案を摘んでいる、器物の表面に貼付け溶接するものだ。【粒状真珠】点溶接は、細くはトウモロコシのような小金粒と金糸を金器表面に溶接されたのは装飾となる。

　1966年に未央区廬口族村の東漢のお墓から出土した金竈は、長寿を求めて金丹を精錬された丹灶に取材したんだ、つまり『文選·別賦』:「守丹灶而不顧、炼金鼎而方堅」という言葉からのいわゆる器物の模型だ。このかまどはかまど門、かまど腔、かまど台面、釜と煙突から構成するが、その長さは3センチ、幅は1.7センチ、高さは1.2センチ、重さは5.2グラム。かまど面は1釜を前置く、釜内はトウモロコシをいっぱいに入れている、粒々が見える。

　周囲には金糸と連珠から「S」になった刑絞を飾っているものが、下側には長舌型灰盤がある。かまど台の回りには雲気紋を飾っている。かまど台の右上角側には細金糸で旋回している煙突を付けている。かまど門の正上方と釜の四角に桃形の赤、紫、緑の諸色の寶石が5粒嵌めるのに、残念ながらもう落ちた。かまどの底部には篆書で「日利」二字の吉語を彫った署名がある。金かまどの造型は小さくて精巧で、イメージは真に迫り、品質は丹念で、装飾は華麗で、プロセスは複雑で、また銘文もある、高度な科学研究と芸術鑑賞の価値を持つ。かまど表面の釜内のトウモロコシは【粒状真珠】点溶接の技術で作ったもの、かまど表面の刺青と煙突は【集定繰糸】プロセスで作ったものだ。

西漢は有名な金が多く持つ王朝で、文献に記載されている通りに西漢皇帝と国家は恩賞、プレゼント、結納、貯蔵、ビジネスに用いられた黄金はよく見られて新鮮ではなかった、かつ数量も驚き、それぞれ朝代は珍しいことだ。

　『史記·平准書』のように記載：「大将軍、驃騎大出胡、得首虜八九万級，賞賜五十万金」と述べられたが、同書の『梁孝王世家』のように記載：「梁孝王未死時，財以巨万計，不可勝数及死，藏府余黄金尚四十余万斤」と述べられた？

　ただ一回大臣に恩賞したものは王の財産とこのように多くの黄金がある、しかも西漢歴史に関する記載中もの、それぞれの用途の黄金の数量は約200万斤に達した。

　たとえ再使用ものを含んでも、その時社会上の黄金の貯蔵量も1つの巨額の数字だ。

　考古発掘から出土した多くの黄金によって文献の記載を実証された、今まで全国にはすでに発見されたものは約30件の馬蹄金と麒趾金は漢の長安(今西安)地区に半分出土された。

　さらに驚くことは、1999年11月2日に西安市未央区譚郷北十里舗東村には219枚の金餅をただ一回出土されたが、各重量は約250グラム、直径は5.67~6.6センチ、厚さは0.82~1.64センチ、この数字は従来全国で発見された漢代の金餅よりの総計以上。

　銀は漢代で応用範囲は広く、容器は飾り件もあるが、西安漢代における銀容器が十分に少ない発見した、鎏(金)銀銅器が出土されたのはわりに多い。1973年に西安市未央区未央宮公社(郷)李下壕村から1組4件の【鎏金銀卧虎刑鎮】を出土した、底径は6.1センチ、高さは3.1センチ、単独の重さは400グラム、4件の形状の大きさは同様、鎮は虎形である、虎体はまき横になっている姿を呈する、首をそむけて下顎を後股にを掛けている、大口や広鼻、雙眼が少しあけている、両耳を後へすぼめる、4爪指を合わせてアーチ形になる、太長くて丈夫な尾は内に曲がって腹側に掛ける、形態が自然、眠りそうだ。

　1本は細陰刻線は鼻から後へ頭頂より背中に沿って尻まで虎体の形態を描き出したが、口、鼻、眉、ひげとひじ毛が全部陰線で描写する、身の斑紋も陰線でアウトラインを描き出した、この4件の虎形鎮は全体鎏金銀を処理する、鎏金銀プロセスにとって漢代で応用はもう非常に広く、ずっと清朝までに用いている。錯金銀銅器は多く戦国時期に見えられた、漢代において珍しい。

　三国両晋南北朝の時期に、黄金銀の生産高は激減し、考古で出土した金銀器の数量も多くないが、金飾りでの仏像が大量に現れました。北朝ほとんど歴代の帝王はすべて仏教に信仰される、彫刻の石仏と鋳造の銅仏は金で華麗な装飾し、大量の黄金を使いました。

　『南斉書·蕭穎胄伝』のように記載：「長沙の寺僧業が富んで、肥え鋳造された黄金が竜を制作して数千両を使うが、土中に埋められました。」と述べられたが、『魏書·釋老』の記載：「興光元年（西暦454年）秋に、敕有司は5級大寺の境内で、太祖はすでに五帝をおりたが、釋迦立像を5つ鋳造し、各長さは1丈6尺、すべて赤金で25万斤に達した。」述べられたが、天安2年(西暦467年)に、「天宮寺で釋迦立像を造った。高さが43尺、赤金で10万斤、黄金で6百斤。」、史籍は金で仏教造像を飾った記録が増えている、西安北郊外の漢長安城の遺跡内で考古発掘により出土された北朝の貼金石造像と鎏金銅造像の数量は非常に大したものだ。

魏晋から隋唐の時期まで、手工業の仕事場は役所の隷属性に対して次第に弱めなり、職人の身分は長期服役を順番服役に変更された。手工業の仕事場の経営方式の転換と職人身分の変化が普遍的な過程の中で、金銀器の制作業界は比較的に特殊で、変化も遅く、その原因は金銀の原料が貴重で、制作プロセスは複雑で、製品は大部分が少数者から楽しんで、金銀の手工業の仕事場を開設するのは強大な経済実力を必要とするだけではなく、職人も長期にわたり必ず才能を育成したこそずば抜けている技巧を持つ。

　8世紀中葉前の唐代は、その金銀制作がほとんど中央政府と皇室から独占された。

　唐代の中後期に、土地の国家所有制の解体に従って、徭役の上で金納を労役にしたのは更に普便になった。役所における仕事場の職人の身分は相対に自由で、南北朝の時期で新興された都市での私営手工業を発展させれたが、最後にも金銀の手工業の領域に波及された。

　手工業と商業の連絡は緊密になったが、唐代の中後期でその経済の重点を南に移動された社会の多くの背景の下で、金銀原材料の産地、供給などがわりに多く南方の客観的な条件に依存したので、このようにずっと皇室と中央役所によるしきりに制御された局面を突破された。

　中央政府はこの変化に順応し、地方役所では個人からさえ金銀器を造ることを許可されたのに、更に租税、宣索と献上する方式によって製品を取り上げられた。すると、中央役所の仕事場と地方役所の仕事場、及び個人の仕事場と共存する繁栄ぶりが現れました。地方役所と個人の金銀手工業はいったん興ったら、皇室と中央は前ようにしっかり製品の流れる方向を制御することができない、ほとんど百花斉放な唐代の金銀器製造は、新しい状態が現れました。金銀器物の使用により一定の程度の普及が現れました、それから中国古代の金銀器の生産と使用の新しい一章をめくりました。

　唐代の金銀器の製造は前代の特徴に区別した、その他の器物の付属装飾とする地位を抜けた、単独な器物制作を主流になっているが、金銀器類の大型器物の数量は大くに増加しました。唐代の金銀器が大量に見つけられたが、はっきり唐代の金銀の手工業界が繁栄で発達を反映した、文献中に少なく金銀の手工業の仕事場の問題に関しないのは考古学データによって検討を行なうものとする。文献の史料と出土された実物からの分析の結果を結び付るによると、唐代の金銀の手工業製作の生産部門が中央役所、寺院と個人の仕事場、まだいくつか移動の個体職人があると見つけることができる。

　中央役所の金銀器の仕事場は京都長安に設置された、主に【少府監掌冶署】？【少府監中尚署】より直接に3か所の金銀仕事場院と【文思院】を管轄される。

　『唐六典』少府監掌冶署条のように記載：「冶署令、銅鉄器物を製煉？鋳造する事を司る」，直接に金銀器の制作に言及しないが、しがしながらは注：「隋太府が全部が冶署令を司った二人はまだ金銀銅鉄器の属することを司るが、かつ諸冶を管理する」と云う、隋代の【掌冶署】はすでに金銀器物の製造の職責を負ったことが、唐代はあいかわらずそのようだ。『新唐書か？百官志』は記載するのがいっそう明らかで、掌冶署は「制御範囲には金銀銅鉄を製煉するおよび瑠璃の玉作を塗り飾ることを含む」。

　【少府監中尚署】は直接に“金銀仕事場院”が管籍される(『新唐書』巻48。このように、唐初は非常に明確な金銀製作の機関が2つある、1つは手は掌冶署内の仕事場で、次は中尚署下の金銀の仕事場院だ、全部は中央役所により統轄されると判断される。唐代の金銀器の制作はまだ1つの重用な場所がある、つまり都城の長

安内の【文思院】だ。

『東観奏記』のように記載：「武宗はとても長生久視の術に好むので、大明宮で望仙台を築く、勢いは天漢を侵略するようだ。上(宣宗)は即位に始まって、趙帰真にとって道士を責められた、棒に殺された、望仙台も中止された。大中8年に、復命は密生、右補闕陳嘏がすでに抵抗されたがかつその事を議論すること、すぐ修造をやめられた、その院を【文思院】にする。」

『唐会要』雑記：「（大中）8年8日、詔による望仙台を【文思院】に変更さろと命令された、……武宗は仙人の事に好むので、大明宮で台を築い、号による望仙を言う……」と云う。唐文思院は望仙台を改築したの特殊な機関だ。【文思院】の職責に関して、唐代の文献の中で直接記録していない。

宋代の【文思院】から唐代の情況を推側できる。『宋史？職官志』の少府監条のように記載：「文思院は、金銀、サイ玉の精巧な物の製造についての司る。」唐代の【文思院】もこの職責があるべきでした。

上記のように、中央政府より【少府監掌冶署】と【少府監中尚署】に属する金銀の仕事場院、および直接に皇室に従属する文思院を管轄されたと分かりました。【掌冶署】と金銀の仕事場院は、唐初からすでに置いた、その後で続きました。文思院は晩唐に盛んになった。考古で発見された金銀器が多く全部【金銀の仕事場院】と【文思院】にから出た、文献のスベースを埋めました。

西安西郊外から出土した1件の「宣徽酒坊」の銀注壷(朱捷元などの『西安西郊外から出土した唐「宣徽酒坊」銀酒注』)、その腹部：「宣徽酒坊、咸通十三年六月廿日別敕造七升地字号酒注壹枚，重壹百両，匠臣楊存実等造？監造番头品官臣冯金泰？都知高品臣张景谦？使高品臣宋师贞？」を刻んでいる。

ただ官府の仕事場の中でこそ、官職付きの人がと製品の製作過程に参加する。監造番头、都知？使などの官名と「宣徽酒坊」からの刻銘から見ると、この器物は唐代の中央役所の仕事場にからのみ、つまり【金銀の仕事場院】あるいは【文思院】。

現在見つけた晩唐の金の銀製品中で、【文思院】の作品は多く明確に【文思院】の字様を刻んで、だから「宣徽酒坊」の銀注壷がたぶん【金銀の仕事場院】の作品だ。

「宣徽」は唐代の【宣徽院】ということだ、宦官から管理し、郊祀？宴飨？供帳などを担当する。この器物中の「地字号」はセット器物中の番号だ、宮廷の宴会のために使った器物だ。

宮廷宴会で使った器物は、自然に中央役所の【金銀の仕事場院】から製作を担当する、「宣徽酒坊」の銀注壷の上の文字は、【金銀の仕事場院】が完備な生産管理システムがあることを表明しました。

銘刻中の「監造番頭」は監造を担当するための工官だが、「都知」と「使」はもっと高層の管理者で、楊存実は具体的に器物を作る職人だ。器物の生産過程は厳格なフローがある、それぞれの責任に負ける、近代的な生産責任制に類似する。

唐代の金銀職人は専門の職業だ、【掌冶署】、【金銀の仕事場院】などは唐代の前期の中央政府からの管理の官営の仕事場だ、多くの専門の金銀職人を掌握する。金銀器の製作は各種技巧の中で最も複雑で、難度も最高の技術の職種だ、所要の学習の訓練時間も最も長いだ。

それによって唐代は中央より制御の下で予備人材を教授し、育成する制度を実行することを制定した、『新唐書？百官志』から記載は金銀製品の職人の「鈿鏤の工」を含める、4年を学びました後に厳格

に審査評価を通じて正式の職人になることができる。

　役所の職人が不足の時に、かつ職人の後代で優先的に選ばれて父業を受け継ぐこと。

　身は特技の職人を抱いたため、よく代々伝わってっヴィる、ずっと役所のためにサービスする、役所の仕事場は特殊な技術の伝授と高まることを保証しました。[均田制]下での唐代の前期には、役所の手工業の仕事場の職人は主に各地から招集して来たので、人数は多く、生産規模も大きく、生産原料は主に地方から貢ぎ物を捧げた依頼だ。

　各地は金銀製造に従事した名匠は、ほとんど強制性に中央役所に招集されるので、集中はいっしょに各種の精巧で美しい器物の製造を行って、客観的には職人の間に互いに学び合うこと、長所を取り入れ短所を補う機会を提供しました。

　役所の金銀器の制作、原材料は十分にあるので、ツール、生産条件など及びコストを計算ない、制限をも受けない、誠心誠意に創作を行うことができる、従って製品の数量と品質は迅速な発展がある。

　西安地区から見つけた唐代の金銀器の数量は非常に大したものだ、種類は豊かで、あるものは紀年墓から出て、あるものは紀年の銘文が刻んであって、時間の上に唐朝のそれぞれの段階を含む。最も重要な以下の数ヶ所を見つけた。

　①1969年西安市？雁塔区？何家村窯蔵中から、2瓮約1000件以上の各類の文物を出土した、ただし、金銀器が270件、合計が碗、皿、たらい、壷、缶、ボックス、熏炉、熏球、かんざし首飾りなどがある。

　金碗の高さが5.5センチ、口径が13.5センチ、開口鼓腹、丸足はラッパ形を呈し、内壁から外へハンマ仕上げて成型、外には2層の蓮花びらがある。金碗の内側には[墨書]で「9両半」の3字がある、その重さを明示した。

　金碗は多く皇帝のために使用する、出土したのはきわめてめったに見られない、史料の記載は多くない。既存資料から見ると、それは唐代の金銀器の中でわずか見えた最も華麗で立派な金碗だ。

　この秘蔵品の中であるものが明確な紀年を持つ、ただし時代最も遅いのは"開元19年(西暦731年)庸調"が刻んでいる字形の銀餅があるので、この穴蔵貯蔵が形成した時間はこの時まで遠くないべきだ。

　②1963年に西安市雁塔区沙坂村の穴蔵貯蔵から出土した銀製品15件は、香袋、碗、杯、壷、ボックスなどがある。これらの器物の形状、紋様の風格と何家村の穴蔵貯蔵から出土した大部分の器物の非常に接近だ。その中の1件の環柄の銀杯は、高さが6.3センチ、口径が7センチ、丸口の深腹、ラッパ形の低リング足、環状柄。この杯がただ口辺の下側に1回り凸の弦紋がある、残りの部分は全部光素は紋様がなく、全体の器形は明らかに薩珊ベルシャ酒具に影響を受けた。

　③1975年に西安市灞橋区開元6年(西暦718年)墓からは銀製器5件を出土した形状、紋様の風格も何家村と類似した。例えば折技紋様の3足の銀壷は、蓋、胴体の2部品からなる。蓋を傘帽形にする、上側にボタンがある。壷口は微開、首しばり、丸鼓腹、まわり底、下側に3ひづめ足付き。

　蓋の表面に草葉の紋様を飾る。壷体に枝折の草花、鷺鳥が飾り、足部にピーコック尾羽のような紋様が飾る。紋様の円形の銀箱は上下で隆起し、子雌口で掛け合う。箱の片側に飛鳥腹ばいになっている鹿、草花、樹木、山並みが飾り、別の片側に鷺鳥、枝折花と僧侶が杖をついて象を1頭引いている図が飾

る。オシドリ紋様付きのクラム状の銀箱は環軸で箱体の2半に接合する。箱表面のテーマの紋様は、片側に首を混ぜ織っているおおかりとカササギ鳥が飾り、さらに枝折の花紋を配合する。別の表面にはオシドリが向かい合う状態、カササギと枝折の草花を配合するこのいくつかの器物の紋様は比較的に非常に細くて繁密で、僧侶は枚をとって象を引いている図は珍しい内容。器物は全部たたいて折り畳んで成型し、紋様はチーゼルで刻んで、さらに鎏金処理を行なう。

④1971年に西安市灞橋区?開元21年(西暦733年)韋美美墓から銀器を4件出土した、その中のオシドリの紋様の円形銀箱は最も精巧で美しく、箱は上下の両側に隆起し、子雌口で掛けあう。箱は両側センターにオシドリが蓮を踏んでいる図が飾り、両側は枝折の草花が引立てる。箱表面の両側に雲のかたまりの紋様が飾る。クラム状の銀箱の2半は環軸で接合する、オープン自由。箱表面のテーマの紋様がオシドリのくわえてゆるため状態の紋様が飾り、周囲には枝折の草花が飾り、刺青の部分は鎏金で処理する。

⑤1975年に西安市碑林区?西北工業大学穴蔵から銀器を4件出土した、その中に「李勉」の円形銀盤がある、8世紀中葉の器物だ。この盤は比較的に浅く、丸口や弧腹、平底部が少しく突出し、盤芯はスイカズラ葉で円を構成し、正中央に2匹のコイがいる、周囲の2回りに枝折の花葉で間飾ってスイカズラ紋様を回り、隙間に魚卵文で添加する。

刺青部分が鎏金で処理する。盤の外側の底部に「朝議丈夫、節都督洪州諸軍事を持つ、洪州刺史を守る、かつ州御史中丞を兼ね担当し、統一的に江南西道観察処置都団練、守捉および莫徭など使を管理し、紫金魚袋を与える、臣李励奉進」と銘文を刻んでいる。

『新唐書?李勉伝』記載による、李勉は唐代宗広徳2年(西暦764年)9月から大历2年(西暦767年)4月まで洪州刺史を担当し、江南西道観察などを統一に管理する、銘文によってこの銀盤は(代行)洪州(今江西南昌)を守る刺史李勉が代宗皇帝に貢ぎ物を献上いただいたんだ。

⑥1957年に西安市碑林区?和平門外穴蔵から銀器を7件出土した、その中の2層の蓮びらの銀茶托に「大中14年」(西暦860年)の銘文が付け。この茶托が丸底は深托、寛平辺、丸足。辺上に2層の蓮びらを彫刻する。回り内側に「大中14年(西暦紀元860年)8月に渾金涂茶拓子一枚を作る、金銀が合計重さは捌錢叁字」を刻む。

同時に茶托を合計7件出土した、別の6件とこの件の形状が少し差別がある、単層の蓮びらだ、ただしひとつの丸足内側に「左策使宅茶庫金塗装工拓子壹拾枚、合計重さは玖拾柒両伍錢一」を刻む。

⑦1980年に陝西省藍田県湯峪鎮楊家溝の穴蔵から銀器を約30件出土した、最も重要なのは"田嗣莒"の雙鳳紋様の花びら形の銀箱ものだ、箱身と箱蓋は5曲の花びら形で、丸足すでに失いました。箱表面が隆起し、正中央には雙鳳でくわえている綬帯を飾り、周辺は枝紋様と飛鴻を巻き付ける。

箱身には綬帯、オシドリはと枝巻きの紋様を飾り、器体の刺青部分に鎏金で処理する。

箱外の底部には「内園供奉合咸通7年(西暦866年)11月15日に造り、使臣田嗣莒、重さは一十五両五錢一字」を彫刻する。

⑧1977年に西安市蓮湖区棗園村の穴蔵から銀器を約4件出土した、並蒂団の紋様涎盂、雙鳳くわえている綬の五曲盤、6びら碗と「乾符6年(西暦879年)」の銀鋌はそれぞれ1件を含む。並蒂団の模様涎盂は今

まではまだ同類の銀器の出土ない。その上部にラッパ口を4曲の花びら形にする、下部の壺体が丸く突起、同様4びらを分けて、低丸足ものだ。

　ラッパ形口辺には3層刺青を彫刻する：壺口の周囲には変形の寶相の蓮びらが8つある、びらずつワスレグサの1本がある。周りに辺円形の並蕃が4本ある、びらずつ三角形の枝折花とワスレグサのそれぞれが1本飾る、繁縟団花を形成する。

　最もの外では1回り変形の仰蓮びらだ。腹壁には4組の枝折花がある、毎組は2本の花巻だ、中心は咲いている花の周りにいっぱい花葉を生えている、同様に形成した繁縟な団花は、団花の間に花に三角形の枝折花がある。花を彫刻している部位に全部鎏金で処理した。

　上記いくらヶ所に重要な発見の以外、唐代の宮廷遺跡と大型の貴族のお墓中にもいくつかの十分に貴重な金銀器を出土しました。例えば1979年10月12日西安市碑林区？西安交通大学内の唐興慶宮の遺跡から出土した都管七国の人物銀箱などについて、1983年に西安市未央区大明宮郷馬旗寨村？唐大明宮遺跡から宮女が猟をしている紋様の8つびらの単柄の銀杯などを出土する、それもきわめて高い芸術の価値と歴史学の価値を持っているが、盛唐の金銀器中のヘッドの作品と称する。

　以上の器物は年代はよく知っているので、かつ時間の上に全体の唐代を越えました。これらの器物はもし時間の前後によって並べるならば、いくつかの器物の形状を反映することができる。紋様などの方面の早や晩が異なる、従って大略的に1つの唐代の金銀器の発展変遷の序列を描き、かつ多くの器物の時代に対するの早や晩の特徴にかんする認識を得た、この年代の序列がその他の金銀器を年代を確定する時に1つの信頼できる比較の標準がある。

　西安地区から出土した唐代の金銀器を見渡し、初唐的金銀器の数量はより少ないが、器物の中にわりに多くのはペルシア薩珊式の金銀器の形状がある。後期にこれらの器形はすでに見えない或はほとんど少ない、主にの中国の伝統な銅器、陶磁器、漆器の器形を続き吸収した。

　これに対応して、器物の刺青はささいなもの、繊細ものを繁縟で煌びやかで美しいものに変える、外来の紋様は次第に独立の地位を失ったが、中国の伝統の装飾の図案と一体になっている、金銀飾りを完璧になり、成熟になる。中唐の以後、南方の金銀品プロセスは盛んに流行する、内廷に対するないしは全中国の金銀器プロセスの発展に対して大きい影響を生んだが、五代、宋の金銀器プロセスの発展のためには基礎を定めた。

　宋代の後で、金銀器の制造業は継続的な開発がある、商品化の程度も当然高まるすべきだが、主要な金銀器の製造加工センターすでに東部や南方へ転換しました。この時期の西安では、地理の上でにぎやかな京都を遠く離れた、都市の模型を縮小したり、人口も大幅に減らしたり、手工業生産の繁栄もそんざいしない、金銀の製造業も遠く昔に及ばない、すぐれた佳作もめったに見えない。

王長啓

2010年11月

Contents

춘추전국시대

春秋戰國時代

춘추전국(春秋戰國)시대

　지금으로부터 3,500년 전인 상대(商代) 중국에서는 이미 금은기(金銀器)가 생겨났다. 상주(商周)시대의 금은기는 중원지역 및 관할 소수민족지역에 분포되었으며, 그 공예기술은 금(金), 은(銀) 두 금속의 성질뿐만 아니라 당시 사회문명 발전수준과도 연관되어 있다. 상주시대, 중국 청동(靑銅) 공예의 급격한 발전은 금은기의 발전에 탄탄한 기술적 기반을 마련해줌으로써 더 넓은 영역에서 다양한 형태의 금은기를 볼 수 있게 되었다. 이 시대의 금은기는 제작기법이 비교적 간단하고 크기가 작은 편이며 민무늬로 된 것이 많았는데 금박(金箔), 금엽(金葉), 금편(金片) 등 순금(純金)제품이 다수였으며 주로 기물장식에 사용되었다. 서주시대(기원전 11세기~771년)에는 평탈법(平脫法) 공예가 새롭게 생겨나기도 했다.

　춘추전국시대(기원전 770~221년), 주(周)왕실의 몰락, 제후국 세력의 확장과 더불어 위엄 있고 신비로운 왕실용품은 점차 참신하고 화려하며 가볍고 정교하며 편리하고 실용적인 일용그릇으로 대체되었다. 사회생산력의 발전과 더불어 금은 장식기법은 풍부하고 다채로우며 참신한 면모를 나타냈고 그 장식효과는 더욱 화려해지고 금은입사기(金銀入絲器)가 대량 만들어졌다. 당시는 주로 청동기의 형태를 모방하여 금은기 그릇을 제작하였으며, 새로 생겨난 금은입사기 제품을 비롯해 순금 장신구가 여전히 유행하였다. 당시 금은제품의 제작과 사용은 모두 관부(官府)가 독점하였으며 신분, 지위, 부귀, 계급 등의 상징이 되었다.

The Spring and Autumn Period & Warring States Period

　Chinese gold and silver wares can be dated back to Shang Dynasty over 3,500 years ago. In Shang and Zhou Dynasties, gold and silver wares were used in the central plain and those ethnic areas under effect. Generally speaking, the techniques of gold and silver wares in Shang and Zhou Dynasties were closely related to the civilization of that era as well as the metal property, in which the highly developed bronze technics laid a firm technological groundwork for the gold and silver wares, which enabled the latter to perform their aesthetical functions in a broader sense. In this period, the gold and silver wares are mostly gold foils, gold leaves and gold sheets, which are pure in texture, easy in fabrication technics, small in shape and exiguous in decoration, serving as the utensil ornamentations. In Western Zhou Dynasty(11th cen. BC~771BC), there even emerged the flat rubbing technology of gold and silver wares.

　Due to the decline of Zhou's central power and the expansion of the individual enfeoffment states, the previous stiffly majestic imperial ware were gradually replaced by the conveniently novel dainty daily-ware in the Spring and Autumn Period and Warring States Period(770BC~221BC). With the improvement of productivity, the technics of gold and silver ornament bloomed with various forms and magnificent ornamental effects, emerging gold-inlay or silver-inlay ware. The shape of gold and silver wares was mainly of bronze-ware imitation. Besides the newly emerged gold-inlay and silver-inlay ware, decorations in pure gold were still in the mainstream. The gold and silver wares at this period of time were governmentally monopolized both in manufacture and use, as a symbol of social status.

001

누공회수금와호(鏤空回首金臥虎)

금(金) | 전국(戰國), 진(秦) | 길이 5.2cm 너비 3.3cm 높이 3.3cm 무게 155g
1979년 보계시 풍상현 주원(寶鷄市 風翔縣 周原) 출토

Crouching Hollowed-out Golden Tiger with Backward Head

Gold | Warring States Period(457BC~221BC) | L 5.2cm W 3.3cm H 3.3cm Weight 155g
Excavated from Zhouyuan Ruins in Fengxiang County, Baoji in 1979

　기물(器物) 장식품으로 속이 빈 호랑이 모양이다. 구멍으로 된 큰 눈, 넓은 코와 입, 위로 말린 큰 귀를 가진 호랑이는 입을 지그시 다물고 긴 꼬리를 위로 올리고 엎드려 있다. 호랑이의 몸에는 진주무늬와 권운문(卷雲紋)이 새겨져 있다.

금호식 (金虎飾)

금(金) | 전국(戰國), 진(秦) | 길이 4.8cm 높이 2.3cm 무게 35.6g
1979년 보계시 풍상현 주원(寶鷄市 風翔縣 周原) 출토

Gold Tiger Amulet

Gold | Warring States Period(457BC~221BC) | L 4.8cm H 2.3cm Weight 35.6g
Excavated from Zhouyuan Ruins in Fengxiang County, Baoji in 1979

호랑이 모양의 장식품이다. 커다란 눈과 귀를 가진 호랑이는 머리를 쳐들고 이빨을 드러냈으며, 긴 꼬리를 휘감고 다리를 구부리고 엎드려 있다. 전체 문양은 오목새김으로 되어 있다. 호랑이의 배 안쪽 절반은 네모 모양으로 볼록하게 나오고 절반은 오목하게 들어갔는데, 볼록면과 오목면의 길이, 너비, 깊이는 거의 상호 대응된다. 이는 기물(器物)에 상감(象嵌)해 넣는 장식품의 일종이다.

이 장식품은 금(金)으로 만들어진 것으로는 보기 드문 작품이다. 비록 크기가 작지만 전반적인 제작기법이 정교하고 생동감이 넘치며 형상 또한 웅대하고 기이하여 예술적 · 역사적 가치가 높다.

유금은대구(鎏金銀帶鉤)

은(銀) | 전국(戰國), 진(秦) | 길이 21cm 너비 1.3~3.8cm 두께 0.9~1.6cm 무게 210g
1996년 서안시 미앙구 우가장(西安市 未央區 尤家莊) 출토

Gilt Silver Belt Hook
Silver | Warring States Period(457BC~221BC) | L 21cm W 1.3~3.8cm Thickness
0.9~1.6cm Weight 210g
Excavated from Youjiazhuang Village Weiyang District Xi'an in 1996

　　구(鉤)의 표면에는 금(金)을 입히고 옥(玉)을 상감하였으며 신령하고 상서(祥瑞)로운 짐승 및 기타 여러 가지 무늬를 새겼다. 구수(鉤首)는 넓은 입과 코, 동그란 눈, 볼록한 눈썹, 기다란 귀를 가진 유니콘 모양이다. 흉복(胸腹) 부위에는 신령한 짐승 하나가 입을 벌리고 유니콘의 목 부위를 물고 있으며 양측으로 날카로운 송곳니가 보인다. 정수리에는 직사각형의 구멍이 나 있는데 원래 상감물(象嵌物)이 있었던 것으로 추정된다. 정수리 양쪽에는 새털 모양의 장식이 있으며 위쪽을 향해 좀 더 올라가면 쇠뿔 모양의 뿔이 두 쌍이 있는데 뒤로 감긴 한 쌍은 작은 편이고 앞으로 감긴 한 쌍은 큰 편이며, 각각 빗줄무늬와 마디무늬를 새겼다. 뿔의 측면은 오목한 띠 모양으로 되었다. 두 뿔 사이에는 원형의 청옥(青玉)을 상감하고 뿔의 끄트머리에는 볼록 장식을 배치하였는데 이는 아래쪽의 옥을 고정하기 위함이다. 뿔 뒷부분의 가운데 면은 오목하고 모서리가 볼록하다. 양측에는 표면이 벗겨진, 원형에 가까운 흔적이 있는데 금입사(金入絲)가 벗겨진 것으로 추정된다. 위로 더 올라가면 사나운 날짐승이 날카로운 부리에, 둥근 눈을 하고 서 있다. 눈에 상감하였던 옥은 떨어지고 없으며 눈썹 위 한 쌍의 뿔은 가늘고 길며 맨 끝은 구의 몸과 연결되었다. 뿔 사이는 오목면으로 되었고 볼록한 모서리와 날개는 위를 향하며 두 다리를 곧게 세우고 날카로운 발톱을 드러냈다. 발 사이에는 반원 모양의 구멍이 있는데 이는 옥을 상감하였던 자리이다. 날짐승의 뿔 위쪽에는 한 쌍의 나선 모양의 쇠뿔 장식이 있고 맨 위쪽 가운데에는 원

형 옥이 박혀 있으며, 양측은 오목한 띠 모양으로 되어 있고 옥 중심은 못으로 고정되어 있다. 맨 끝에는 네모난 구멍이 있다. 구의 아랫면 중간 부분에는 원기둥 모양의 고정쇠가 있는데 그 위에는 전서체(篆書體)로 '心(심)' 자가 새겨져 있다. 이 구와 뒤에 나오는 도금감패동대구(鍍金嵌貝銅帶鉤)는 모두 표면에 짐승 얼굴, 날짐승 등을 돋을새김함으로써 전국(戰國)시대 북방 초원의 금은기(金銀器) 공예 풍격을 띠고 있다.

　　구(鉤)는 대구(帶鉤)의 약칭이다. 고대에는 가죽띠를 잠그거나 여러 가지 장식품을 달아 놓는 데 사용했다. 가늘고 길며 구부러진 구는 한쪽 끄트머리가 갈고리 모양이며 뒷면에는 원형 고정쇠를 배치하였다. 중국 북방 유목민족이 최초로 사용한 대구는 춘추(春秋)시대 중원으로 전해져 갑옷에 사용되다 점차 왕공(王公) 귀족들에게도 널리 사용되었다. 전국 및 진한(秦漢)시대에 대구가 널리 성행하였는데 물새, 비파, 장패(長牌), 짐승 얼굴, 숟가락, 주걱 등 모양이 다양하다. 그중 여우, 호랑이, 사슴, 용, 물고기 등 동물 모양을 가진 대구가 다수였다. 삼국(三國) 이후, 대구는 고리 모양의 대휼(帶鐍)로 대체되었으나 청대(青代) 전기까지 여전히 사용되었다.

　　도금(鍍金)공예는 전국시대에 나타났는데 중국 고대 금속 가공 전통공예 중의 하나로 화도금(火鍍金), 소금(燒金) 또는 홍도금(汞鍍金)이라고도 한다. 이는 이금(泥金)을 기물의 표면에 바른 후 무연탄으로 구워 수은은 증발시키고 황금은 기물의 표면에 남게 하는 수법이다. 이금은 황금덩이 혹은 황금조각을 부수어 400℃ 온도에서 황금과 수은을 1:7의 비율로 수은 속에 녹아들게 한 다음 시간이 지나 냉각되면 생성되는 흙 모양의 고체이다. 춘추전국시대 순금(純金) 제품은 보편적으로 사용되었지만 순은(純銀)이나 은(銀)을 위주로 한 제품은 보기 드물었다. 금은 자연계에서 유리(游離) 상태로 존재하여 쉽게 발견하고 이용할 수 있지만 은은 화합물(化合物) 상태로 존재하여 당시 과학기술로는 발견 및 추출이 어려웠기 때문이다. 이 금은대구의 출토는 춘추전국시대의 과학기술사를 연구하는 데 중요한 의의가 있다.

004

유금감패대구(鎏金嵌貝帶鉤)

동(銅) | 전국(戰國), 진(秦) | 길이 23.4cm 너비 1.1〜3.4cm 두께 1.5cm 무게 245g
1996년 서안시 미앙구 우가장(西安市 未央區 尤家莊) 출토

Gilt Hook with Shell-inlay

Copper | Warring States Period(457BC〜221BC) | L 23.4cm W 1.1〜3.4cm Thickness 1.5cm Weight 245g
Excavated from Youjiazhuang Village Weiyang District Xi'an in 1996

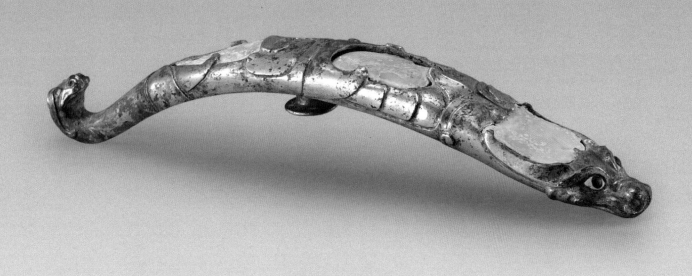

　표면에 금(金)을 입히고 부분적으로 조개를 상감(象嵌)한 굽은 봉 모양의 대구(帶鉤)이다. 몸통이 편평한데 뒷면은 오목한 모양이다. 짐승 머리 모양의 구수(鉤首)는 넓은 입, 약간 위로 말린 넓은 코가 있으며 그 양측에는 작은 구멍이 있고 눈에는 검은색 구슬을 상감하였다. 볼록한 눈썹은 가느다랗게 뒤로 늘어지고 눈썹 위의 가느다란 두 뿔(오목한 띠 모양)은 목까지 길게 뻗은 후 아래로 말렸다. 목은 가늘고 길며 목과 가슴은 한 가닥의 홈으로 나뉘었다. 흉부 윗부분은 우임단의(右袵短衣) 모양이고 가운데 부분에는 거꾸로 된 '心(심)' 자 모양의 조개를 상감하였다. 몸통 양측의 안쪽으로 굽은 발 모양 장식과 대구 아랫부분의 꼬리 마냥 위로 말린 '回(회)' 자 모양 장식은 각각 가운데의 조개 장식과 위쪽 타원형의 조개 장식을 고정하기 위해 배치한 것이다. 대구의 꼬리는 안쪽으로 말린, 입을 약간 벌린 짐승머리 모양으로 눈썹 위 가느다란 두 뿔은 길게 뻗었으며 들창코는 볼록하고 너부죽하다. 두 눈에는 검은색 구슬을 상감하고 콧마루에는 두 가닥의 볼록한 띠로 장식하였다. 두 각(角) 사이에는 앞부분이 볼록하고 뒷부분이 오목한 직사각형의 조개를 상감하였다. 두 개의 오목한 띠 모양 장식은 양측에서 안쪽을 향해 아래로 말려 그 아래의 조개 장식을 고정시켜 주고 뒤의 볼록 모양 장식은 타원형 조개 장식을 고정시켜 준다. 대구 뒷면의 오목한 부분에는 썩은 나무의 잔흔이 남아 있으며 가운데에는 원주(圓柱) 모양의 고정쇠가 있는데 '반전서체(反篆書體)'와 유사한 글씨체로 위에는 "左(좌)" 자, 아래에는 "無(무)" 자를 새겼다.

005

착은비파형대구(錯銀琵琶形帶鉤)

동(銅) | 전국(戰國) | 길이 5.1cm 너비 1.5cm 높이 2cm 무게 67g
1998년 서안시공안국(西安市公安局)으로부터 받음

Silver-gilded Lute-shaped Belt Hook

Copper | Warring States Period(457BC~221BC) | L 5.1cm W 1.5cm
H 2cm Weight 67g
Transferred by Xi'an Public Security Bureau in 1998

비파 모양의 구(鉤)는 짧고 작으며 튼실하다. 구의 머리는 짐승머리 모양으로 되었는데 눈, 뿔과 다리는 은입사문(銀入絲紋)으로 표현되었다. 뒷면 뒤쪽에 달린 고정쇠는 굵고 짧으며, 융기(隆起)된 표면에는 은입사와문(銀入絲渦紋)을 새겼다.

금은입사(金銀入絲) 공예를 일명 금은착(金銀錯)이라고도 한다. 금(金)과 은(銀)은 원래 아름다운 색상을 띠고 있어 이로 장식하면 무늬가 복잡하면서도 아름다울뿐더러 전체적으로 웅장하고 우아해 보인다. 또한, 금은은 유연성이 있어 이러한 장식 공예가 더욱 널리 이용될 수 있었다. 금은입사 공예는 춘추(春秋) 말기에 출현하여 전국(戰國)시대에 발전하였으며 서한(西漢)시대에 와서는 금속공예기법의 일종으로 보편화되었다. 춘추전국시대의 금은입사 공예는 먼저 동기(銅器)의 틀 위에 금은입사 무늬를 양각(陽刻)하고 청동기(靑銅器)가 만들어진 다음 금은사(金銀絲)를 무늬의 홈에 상감(象嵌)하고 연마(硏磨)하거나 두드려 박아 넣는 등의 방법을 사용하여 청동기의 표면을 평평하게 하는 기법을 말한다. 금은입사기물 가운데 금입사기(金入絲器)가 가장 먼저 생겨나고 전국 중기에 이르러 은입사동기(銀入絲銅器)와 금은동기(金銀銅器)가 생겨나기 시작하였다. 금은입사동기가 춘추전국시대에 널리 사용된 것은 이 시기 사회배경과 밀접한 관계가 있다. 당시 주(周)왕실 세력은 쇠퇴하였으나 각지 제후(諸侯)들의 세력은 날로 확대되었고 사회경제 발전과 더불어 귀족계층이 부단히 확대됨으로써 사치품에 대한 수요는 점점 늘어났다. 또한 당시 금은의 채굴량이 제한되어 있어 대량의 순금, 은으로 기물을 제작하는 것은 불가능하였다. 하지만 금은입사 공예를 사용하면 재료가 많이 절약되므로 대량으로 만들 수 있었기 때문에 금은입사동기는 춘추전국시대에 대량으로 제작되다가 서한시대에 이르러 차츰 감소되었다.

006

착은기하문곡봉식대구(錯銀幾何紋曲棒式帶鉤)

동(銅) | 전국(戰國) | 길이 11.8cm 너비 1.5cm 높이 2.2cm 무게 101g
1997년 서안시문물국(西安市文物局) 수집

Silver-Gilded Belt Hook With Geometry Patterns

Copper | Warring States Period(457BC~221BC) | L 11.8cm W 1.5cm H 2.2cm Weight 101g
Collected by Xi'an Culture Relic Bureau In 1997

원기둥 형태의 대구(帶鉤)는 짐승머리 모양의 구수(鉤首) 및 구부정한 몸통으로 구성되었으며 뒷면에는 타원형 고정쇠가 있다. 몸통에는 기하문(幾何紋)을 은입사(銀入絲)하였는데 어자문(魚子紋)으로 기하문 사이를 가득 채웠다.

007

착은기하문비파형대구(錯銀幾何紋琵琶形帶鉤)

동(銅) | 전국(戰國) | 길이 11.6cm 무게 103g
1997년 서안시문물국(西安市文物局) 수집

Silver-gilded Lute-shaped Belt Hook with Geometry Patterns

Copper | Warring States Period(457BC~221BC) | L 11.6cm Weight 103g
Collected by Xi'an Culture Relic Bureau In 1997

　호형(弧形) 비파 모양의 대구(帶鉤)이다. 구수(鉤首)의 일부분은 손상되었으며, 뒷면에는 타원형의 고정쇠가 있다. 구의 윗면에는 금은입사(金銀入絲) 무늬를 새겼다. 표면에 새긴 도안은 관현문(寬弦紋) 두 쌍에 의해 두 부분으로 나뉘는데 모두 변형기하문(變形幾何紋) 및 꽃으로 장식하고 그 사이를 어자문(魚子紋)으로 가득 채웠다.

008

착은선문이룡형대구(錯銀蟬紋螭龍形帶鉤)

동(銅) | 전국(戰國) | 길이 16.6cm 무게 132g
1997년 서안시문물국(西安市文物局) 수집

Silver-gilded Hornless-dragon-shaped Belt Hook with Cicada Patterns

Copper | Warring States Period(457BC~221BC) | L 16.6cm Weight 132g
Collected by Xi'an Culture Relic Bureau in 1997

　이무기[螭龍] 형상으로 만들어진 대구(帶鉤)이다. 걸이는 용머리 모양으로, 몸통은 호형(弧形) 원기둥 모양으로 되었다. 뒷면에는 둥근 빵 모양의 고정쇠가 있다. 표면에는 다섯 가닥의 관현문(寬弦紋)을 균일하게 배치하고 그 사이에는 서로 등진 변형된 매미무늬 한 쌍을 새겨 넣었으며 은(銀)을 상감(象嵌)하였다. 전국(戰國)·진한(秦漢) 시기, 도교(道教)의 신선사상(神仙思想)이 널리 유행하였는데, 도사들은 곤충인 매미가 껍데기를 벗고 변태과정을 거치므로 '상서(祥瑞)로운 동물'로 여겼으며 사람의 육체도 매미의 껍데기와 마찬가지로 육체가 죽어도 영혼은 부활할 수 있다고 생각하였다. 이 대구에 새겨진 은입사(銀入絲) 매미무늬가 곧 이런 신선사상의 반영이다.

착은수운문대구(錯銀獸雲紋帶鉤)

동(銅) | 전국(戰國), 진(秦) | 길이 11.3cm 무게 79g
함양시 요점향(咸陽市 窯店鄕) 출토

Silver-gilded Belt Hook with Animal Moire

Copper | Warring States Period(457BC~221BC) | L 11.3cm Weight 79g
Excavated from Yaodianxiang County in Xianyang

이무기[螭龍] 형상으로 만들어진 대구(帶鉤)이다. 걸이는 용머리 모양으로, 몸통은 호형(弧形) 원기둥 모양으로 되었다. 뒷면에는 원형의 고정쇠가 있는데 이는 가죽벨트의 양쪽을 연결해 주는 작용을 한다. 대구의 표면은 은입사(銀入絲)한 후 권운문(卷雲紋)을 새기고 권운문 사이에는 어자문(魚子紋)을 새김으로써 용 몸의 인갑(鱗甲)을 표현하였다.

'영원(郢爰)' 금판(金版)

금(金) | 전국(戰國), 초(楚) | 길이 2cm 너비 1.7cm 높이 0.43cm 무게 15.5g
1940년대 위남시 교사(渭南市 交斜) 출토

Ancient Ying's Gold Coin

Gold | Warring States Period(457BC~221BC) | L 2cm W 1.7cm H 0.43cm Weight 15.5g
Excavated from Jiaoxie Village in Weinan City in 1940's

장방형(長方形)에 가까운 복두형(覆斗形) 금판(金版)이다. 윗부분은 조금 오목하게 들어가고 세 변에는 테두리가 있으며 나머지 한 변에는 자른 흔적이 남아 있다. 테두리 안쪽에는 "郢爰(영원)"이란 글자를 음각하였다. 아랫부분은 울퉁불퉁하며, 주조 시 흔적이 남아 있다. '영원'은 전국(戰國)시대 초(楚)나라의 금화(金貨)로 지금까지 출토된 금화 중 가장 오래된 것이다. '영(郢)'은 초나라 도읍의 명칭이며, '영원' 같은 황금화폐는 주로 초나라에서 유행하였다. 화폐에 새겨진 인문(印文)은 초나라의 성읍(城邑)의 명칭과 연관되는데 그중 가장 많이 사용된 '영원'은 초나라 수도인 영에서 주조한 것이다. 이 황금화폐는 하사품으로 사용될 뿐 유통되지는 않았다.

춘추전국(春秋戰國)시대, 초나라는 중국의 유명한 황금산지였다. 『관자(管子)』 「경중갑편(輕重甲篇)」에는 "초나라에는 여한(汝漢)에서 나는 황금이 있다"고 기록되어 있다. 여기서 '여(汝)'는 여하(汝河)를 말하는데 고대(古代) 여하는 하남성(河南省) 서부의 복우산(伏牛山)에서 발원하여 하천의 중류에 와서 풍부한 사금광상(沙金礦床)을 이루었다. '한(漢)'은 한수(漢水)를 말하는데 섬서성(陝西省) 영강현(寧强縣)에서 발원하여 동쪽으로 섬서 남부의 한중(漢中), 안강(安康)을 지나 호북(湖北)을 가로질러 무한(武漢)에서 장강(長江)으로 흘러들었다. 선진(先秦) 시기, 여, 한은 초나라의 금(金) 산지(産地)로 이름을 날렸다.

금판(金版)은 금판(金鈑)・인자금(印子金)・원금(爰金)이라고도 불렸다. 흔히 전국시대 초나라에서 주조한 황금화폐를 가

리키는데 뒷면이 호형(弧形)인 사각형, 직사각형, 원형 등 여러 가지 모양이 있다. 대부분 지금의 장강 중하류 및 황하(黃河) 하류의 호북(湖北)・호남(湖南)・하남(河南)・안휘(安徽)・강소(江蘇)・산동(山東) 남부의 초나라 일대에서 출토되고 섬서 관중(關中) 지역에서도 일부 출토되었다. 온전한 금판 하나의 무게는 약 500g이고 금판에 찍은 인문의 종류만 해도 무려 60가지나 된다. 이미 발견된 인문에는 영원(郢爰)・진원(陳爰)・격원(鬲爰)・노금(盧金)・소정(少貞)・전애(專愛) 등이 있다. 그중 영원이 가장 많고 진원이 두 번째로 많으며 그 외의 것은 보기 드물다. '애(원)'이란 글자는 교환을 뜻하는데 후에 무게 단위로 사용되었다. 기타 문자는 당시의 지명에서 온 것도 있다. 盧金(노금), 少貞(소정)은 '爐金(노금)', '小鼎(소정)'이라고 해석되나 정련(精鍊)이라는 뜻이다. 금판은 크기가 일정하지 않은 작은 덩이로 잘라서 사용하였으며 그 무게는 작은 덩이의 실제 무게로 계산되었다. 사용되기 시작한 시기는 불명확하나 서한 초기까지 사용되었다. 서한(西漢) 시기 모조품이 비교적 많았는데 대부분 명기(冥器)로 사용되었다.

진한시대

秦漢時代

진한(秦漢)시대

지금까지 출토된 진대(秦代, 기원전 221~206년) 금은기(金銀器)는 그다지 많지 않다. 섬서성(陝西省) 임동현(臨潼縣) 진시황릉(秦始皇陵)에서 출토된 청동기(靑銅器) 및 금은기를 볼 때 진대 금은기는 주조, 용접, 세선세공(細線細工), 상감, 마찰 및 광택을 내거나 여러 가지 기계를 연결하거나 접착하는 등 종합적인 공예기법을 사용하였음을 알 수 있다. 양한시대(兩漢時代, 기원전 206~기원후 220년), 강대한 국력을 바탕으로 국가는 대량의 황금을 보유할 수 있었다. 또한 당시 신선사상이 유행하였는데 방사(方士)들은 금은은 수명을 연장시키고 장생불로하게 한다고 생각하였다. 이로써 금은기의 제작 및 금은기물(金銀器物)에 대한 상층귀족들의 수요를 직접적으로 자극함과 동시에 금은기의 사용에 신비로운 색채를 더했고 이후 금은기의 생산 및 사용에 커다란 영향을 끼쳤다. 한대(漢代) 금은기는 수량은 물론 품종, 제작기법 또한 선진(先秦)시대를 훨씬 능가했다. 당시 금은기 중 가장 흔히 볼 수 있는 것은 장신구이고 금은기물은 많지 않았을 뿐더러 형태 또한 간결하여 민무늬가 많다. 한대 금은기는 상감(象嵌), 도금(鍍金), 금은입사(金銀入絲), 광택을 내는 공예기법을 지속적으로 사용하는 동시에 금은으로 금박(金箔)이나 이금(泥金)을 만들어 칠기(漆器) 또는 견직물을 장식하는 데 사용하기도 했다. 무늬는 일반적으로 추엽(錘揲), 용접을 통해 만들었으며 당시 장인들은 철금주(綴金珠), 겹사양감(拾絲鑲嵌) 등의 기법도 터득하고 있었다. 이로써 금은기의 발전과 번영에 기반을 마련하였다. 실크로드의 개통으로 한왕조(漢王朝)와 중앙아시아, 서구 로마 제국 간에 비교적 밀접한 경제·문화 교류가 지속됨으로써 서구의 금은기가 중국에 전해지면서 서구의 작주(炸珠, 고대 금속가공공예의 일종으로 황금 용액을 따뜻한 물에 부어 금속알갱이를 만들거나 금가루를 불에 녹여 알갱이가 되었을 때 냉각시키는 형식이다)·세선세공·나사(捼絲) 등과 같은 제작기법도 함께 전해졌다.

Qin & Han Dynasty

Till now, gold and silver wares in Qin Dynasty(221BC~206BC) haven't been largely unearthed. From the unearthed bronze ware and gold and silver wares unearthed from funerary pits in Mausoleum of the First Qin Emperor, Lintong, Shaanxi, we could find that technics of foundry, inlaid cast, rasping, polishing, linking by multiple mechanism and stickiness were applied in Qin's gold and silver wares. Because of the flourishing national power, there was a large amount of gold in Han Dynasty(206BC~220AD). In addition to the then popular immortal thinking, in which the alchemist alleged that gold and silver had the function of prolonging life and preventing death, the manufacture of gold and silver wares expanded in the upper noble class. This veiled the gold and silver wares with a sense of mystery, profoundly affected the production and use of the later generations. In terms of quantity, types and fabrication, Han's gold and silver wares are far better than that of Pre-Qin Period.

In this period, gold and silver wares were still mainly in ornaments, with few plain-surfaced ware. Besides technics of casting, inlaying and plating, gold and silver were made into sheets or paste for the use of lacquers or silks in Han Dynasty. The patterns were hammered or jointed on the surface. Meanwhile, the technics of welding golden beads and wiry inlay were also mastered by the craftsmen, which established firm groundwork for the development of the gold and silver wares. The Silk Road bridged the economic and cultural exchange between Had Dynasty and Central Asia and Roman Empire, when Western gold and silver wares and techniques(quenching, wiry and piling etc.) came to China.

011

착은선문대구(錯銀蟬紋帶鉤)

동(銅) | 진(秦) | 길이 11.5cm 무게 101g
1983년 서안시(西安市) 문물상점(文物商店)으로부터 넘겨받음

Silver-inlay Belt Hook with Cicada Patterns

Copper | Qin Dynasty(221BC~206BC) | L 11.5cm Weight 101g
Transferred by Xi'an Culture Relic Shop in 1983

이무기 형상의 호형(弧形) 원기둥 형태의 대구(帶鉤)이다. 걸이는 용머리 모양이며 대구의 뒷면에는 원형 고정쇠가 있다. 표면에는 서로 마주한 두 조의 은입사(銀入絲) 매미무늬를 새기고 무늬 사이에는 은입사 어자문(魚子紋)을 새겨 넣었다.

착은대(錯銀鐓)

동(銅) | 진(秦) | 길이 13.2cm 너비 3.6cm 두께 2.6cm 무게 222g
1966년 서안시문물관리위원회(西安市文物管理委員會) 수집

Silver-inlay Rammer

Copper | Qin Dynasty(221BC~206BC) | L 13.2cm W 3.6cm Thickness 2.6cm Weight 222g
Collected by Xi'an Culture Relic Administration Committee in 1966

직사각형 통 모양의 대(鐓)는 너비가 일정치 않은 철현문(凸弦紋)에 의해 두 부분으로 나뉘는데 각각 서로 다른 자태를 뽐내는 봉황을 새겼다. 깃털이 흩날리는 봉황은 마치 하늘거리며 날고 있는 것 같아 그 형태가 아름답기 그지없다. 금속세공 공예로서의 금은입사(金銀入絲)는 춘추(春秋) 말기에 흥기하여 전국(戰國) 시기에 더욱 발전하였다. 당시 금입사기물(金入絲器物)이 비교적 많은 반면에 은입사기물(銀入絲器物)은 드물었다. 무늬가 정교하고 아름다운 이 은입사대는 당시 은입사기물의 대표작이다.

대는 장병기(長兵器)의 부품으로 자루 끄트머리에 부착한다. 고대 중국에서는 병사들이 병기를 놓을 때 일반적으로 자루가 아래로 향하게 틀 위에 꽂았으므로 금속대는 장대를 보호하는 역할을 하였다.

(1) (2)

013

착은환형차식(錯銀環形車飾)

동(銅) | 진(秦) | 지름 (1) 10.6cm (2) 9cm 무게 (1) 238g (2) 139g
1967년 서안시 미앙구 미앙궁향 대백양촌(西安市 未央區 未央宮鄉 大白楊村) 수집

Silver-inlay Annular Vehicle Decoration

Copper | Qin Dynasty(221BC~206BC) | D (1) 10.6cm (2) 9cm Weight (1) 238g (2) 139g
Collected in Dabaiyang Village in Weiyang in 1967

　두 개의 수레 장식이다. 수레 장식은 납작하면서도 동그란 고리 모양이
고 양면 도안이 일치한데 모두 기하권운문(幾何卷雲紋)을 새기고 두 줄무
늬 사이에는 기하유운문(幾何流雲紋)을 새겨 넣었으며 무늬마다 은입사
(銀入絲)를 상감(象嵌)하였다.

착은구형비모(錯銀鳩形秘冒)

동(銅) | 전국(戰國), 진(秦) | 길이 7.1cm 높이 8.5cm 기둥지름 3.1×2.4cm 무게 142g
1980년 서안시 연호구 홍묘파촌(西安市 蓮湖區 紅廟坡村) 출토

Silver-inlay Turtledove-shaped Cap of Dagger Handle

Copper | Warring States Period to Qin Dynasty(457BC∼206BC) | L 7.1cm H 8.5cm D 3.1×2.4cm Weight 142g
Excavated from Hongmiaopo Village Lianhu District, Xi'an in 1980

자루집은 비둘기 형태이다. 비둘기는 고개를 돌린 채 긴 꽁지를 한데 모으고 몸을 웅크리고 좌 (座) 위에 앉아 있다. 비둘기 몸에는 은입사(銀入絲) 무늬를 새김으로써 깃털을 생동하게 표현하였다. 전반적인 형태가 살아 있는 듯한 느낌을 준다. 좌는 원통형으로 자루를 고정시켜 주는 작용을 한다. 좌 안쪽에는 "廿三年服工□治古, 三十八(입삼년복공□치고, 삼십팔)" 11자 명문이 음각되어 있다.

자루집은 모자 형식의 장식으로 창이나 물미[鐏]의 위쪽에 위치하고 다른 쪽 끝에는 대(鐓, 밑바닥이 평평한 금속덮개)와 준(鐏, 원추형의 금속덮개)이 있다. 모두 장대를 보호하는 역할을 한다.

착은구형비모(錯銀鳩形秘冒)

015

착금은통형차식(錯金銀筒形車飾)

동(銅) | 진(秦) | 길이 9cm 입지름 5.8cm 무게 425g
1967년 서안시 미앙구 미앙궁향 대백양촌(西安市 未央區 未央宮鄉 大白楊村) 수집

Gold-and-silver-inlay Bucked-shaped Vehicle Decoration

Copper | Qin Dynasty(221BC∼206BC) | L 9cm Mouth D 5.8cm Weight 425g
Collected in Dabaiyang Village in Weiyang District, Xi'an in 1967

원통형의 수레 장식이다. 한쪽에는 볼록하게 두드러져 나온 원형 가장자리가 둘러져 있다. 표면의 무늬는 쌍쌍이 대칭되었고 네 마리의 변형 매미무늬가 사이사이 배치되어 있으며 매미무늬의 머리는 크고 몸은 작아 삼각형에 가깝다. 무늬는 모두 끌로 새겨졌고 무늬 안쪽에는 금은(金銀)을 상감(象嵌)해 넣었는데 매미 머리의 두 눈과 등의 두 날개를 표현한 것이 소박하면서도 장중한 느낌을 주고 선 흐름이 거침없다.

016

금공심주(金空心珠)

금(金) | 서한(西漢) | 지름 1.55cm 무게 9.1g
1966년 서안시문물관리위원회(西安市文物管理委員會) 수집

Hollow Golden Bead

Gold | West Han Dynasty(206BC∼25AD) | D 1.55cm Weight 9.1g
Collected by Xi'an Culture Relic Administration Committee in 1966

12개의 순금(純金) 고리를 용접하여 만든 공심주(空心珠)이다. 구형(球形)에 가까운 형태로 고리마다 하나의 면을 이룬다. 고리의 외곽에는 금구슬 다섯 더미를 배치하였는데 하나의 더미는 4개의 작은 금구슬로 구성되었다. 공심주의 속은 비었다. 이는 형태상 산동(山東) 치박(淄博)의 서한(西漢) 제왕묘(齊王墓), 광주(廣州) 선열로(先烈路) 용생강(龍生崗) 4013호 동한(東漢) 무덤에서 출토된 것과 매우 비슷한데 모두 한철금주(焊綴金珠) 공예기법으로 만들어진 것이다. 서아시아·남유럽 일대에서 기원한 한철금주 공예는 서한(西漢)시대에 중국에 전해진 것으로 금은(金銀) 조각을 가늘게 자르거나 토막 낸 다음, 가열하여 알알이 응고시킨 뒤 냉각시켜 용접하여 연결하는 기법이다. 이 공심주는 조형이 기묘하고 이국적인 색채가 짙다.

진한(秦漢)시대, 서아시아·남유럽·북아프리카를 포함한 지중해 지역은 서로마제국(기원전 27년 옥타비아누스에 의해 세워짐. 395년 서로마제국과 동로마제국으로 분리되었는데 476년 서로마제국이 멸망하고 1453년 동로마제국이 멸망함)의 통치하에 있었다. 선진(先秦)시대 중국과 서양의 무역교류에 관한 명확한 기록은 없다. 한무제(漢武帝) 시기에 와서 박망후(博望侯) 장건(張騫)이 동서무역을 잇는 실크로드를 개척하면서 무역이 흥성하였다. 중국의 비단, 자기 등 상품은 서역, 중앙아시아를 통해 로마제국으로 전해져 상류 지배계급의 사랑을 받았다. 이 공심주가 바로 중국과 로마제국 사이의 무역교류를 증명하는 좋은 예이다.

017

착금은구연운문방(錯金銀鉤連雲紋鈁)

동(銅) | 서한(西漢) | 높이 61.5cm 입둘레 16cm 최대배둘레 33.5cm 굽둘레 19.5cm 무게 34kg
1964년 서안시 연호구 남소항(西安市 蓮湖區 南小巷) 출토

Gold-and-silver-inlay Pot with Goulian Moire

Copper | West Han Dynasty(206BC∼25AD) | H 61.5cm Mouth L 16cm Belly L 33.5cm Bottom L 19.5cm Weight 34kg
Excavated from Nanxiaoxiang in Lianhu District, Xi'an in 1964

네모난 입, 짧은 목, 정육면체에 가까운 몸체, 네모 모양의 굽을 가진 술항아리이다. 어깨와 불룩한 배는 매끄럽게 이어졌는데 윗배에는 서로 대칭되는 포수함환(鋪首銜環)이 부착되어 있다. 배 아래쪽에는 "三月卄日□斤(3월20일□근)", "私官□□六□□□(사관□□육□□□)"과 "十八斗半斗(18두반두)" 등 19글자 명문(銘文)이 새겨져 있다. 술항아리의 실제 측량 용적은 35.4리터이다. 몸체 전면에 금은입사(金銀入絲) 구연운문(勾蓮雲紋)을 꽉 차게 배치하였는데 위치마다 무늬도 다르다. 입술에는 단순 구연운문을 한 바퀴 두르고 4척능(四脊棱) 양측에는 대각의 구연운문을, 목과 배에는 큰 마름모 모양의 구연운문을 새겼다. 무늬 가운데 중심선은 좌우 무늬가 서로 대칭되게 하였다. 굽의 사면에도 기하학적 구련운문을 대칭으로 새겨 넣었다. 술항아리의 무늬는 구상이 기발하고 조형이 섬세하며 배치가 균일해 예술성과 실용성을 모두 갖춘 정교한 그릇이다. 술항아리와 함께 동등(銅燈), 동훈로(銅熏爐), 동당(銅鐺) 등도 한대(漢代) 장안성(長安城) 남상림원(南上林苑) 유적지에서 출토되었다. 출토지점과 매장유적을 볼 때 술항아리는 서한(西漢)시대의 황실용품인 것으로 추정된다.

유금봉조종(鎏金鳳鳥鍾)

동(銅) | 서한(西漢) | 높이 78.4cm 입지름 22.8cm 배지름 42.6cm 굽지름 23.7cm 무게 20.13kg
2003년 서안시 미앙구 문경로 조원촌(西安市 未央區 文景路 棗園村) 출토

Gilt Phoenix Drinking Vessel

Copper | West Han Dynasty(206BC~25AD) | H 78.4cm Mouth D 22.8cm
Belly D 42.6cm Bottom D 23.7cm Weight 20.13kg
Excavated from Zaoyuan Village in Weiyang District, Xi'an in 2003

표면에 전체적으로 도금(鍍金)한 이 종(鍾)은 술항 아리의 일종으로 뚜껑과 몸통으로 구성되었는데 두 부분이 만나는 곳은 자모구(子母口)를 이룬다. 볼록한 뚜껑 중앙에는 봉황 모양의 꼭지가 있다. 구슬을 입에 문 봉황이 머리와 꽁지를 쳐들고 날개를 모으고 서 있는 형상인데 전체적인 선 흐름이 매끄러워 살아 움직이는 듯하다. 몸통은 약간 벌어진 입, 잘록한 목, 원형의 풍만한 배를 가지고 있다. 윗배 양측에는 포수 함환(鋪首銜環) 손잡이를 대칭되게 배치하고 굽, 입, 어깨, 배 등 부분에는 관현문(寬弦紋)을 양각하였다.

고대 중국인들은 금이나 은으로 만든 식기를 사용하면 수명이 연장되고 심지어 장생불로한다고 여겼다. 장생불로(長生不老) 사상은 최초로 주(周)나라 때의 『시경(詩經)』에서 반복적으로 나타난 '만수무강(萬壽無疆)'이란 어구에서 엿볼 수 있다. 진대(秦代)에 이르러 장생불로를 바라는 사람들의 소망이 더욱 강렬해졌으며 신선, 도인들의 입을 거치면서 이야기가 보다 부풀려졌고 또한 이런 이야기들은 흔히 황금과 이어졌다. 한무제(漢武帝) 때 방사(方士) 이소군(李少君)은 "단사(丹砂)로는 황금을 만들 수 있고 또한 황금으로 만든 그릇을 쓰면 장수하고 장수하면 바다 속의 봉래산(蓬萊山)의 신선을 만나 볼 수 있고, 만나서 제사를 올리면 장생불로하게 된다"라고 말했다. 당대(唐代) 금제, 은제 그릇이 유행하게 된 것은 "금과 은으로 만든 그릇을 쓰면 장생불로한다"는 전통적인 관념이 그대로 반영된 현상이라 하겠다. 동종(銅鍾) 표면에는 금을 입혔는데 이는 금은식기의 또 다른 표현형식에 속한다.

이 도금 동종은 한대(漢代) 장사파(長斜坡) 단실묘(單室墓)의 작은 방에서 함께 출토된 것으로 모양과 구조가 똑같은 도금 동종이 한 점 더 출토되었다. 무덤의 부장품으로 동정(銅鼎, 동으로 만든 솥), 동방(銅鈁, 동으로 만든 네모난 술그릇) 등 청동기(靑銅器) 17점, 견형도호(繭形陶壺, 고치형 도기 항아리) 5점과 옥조각 101점이 있다. 무덤의 모양과 구조 및 출토된 부장품으로 미루어 볼 때 이는 서한(西漢) 문경(文景) 시기 일등급 제후의 귀족 묘로서 도금 동종은 황실용품에 속하는 것으로 추정된다.

유금양등(鎏金羊燈)

동(銅) | 서한(西漢) | 길이 27.4cm 너비 11.1cm 높이 21.8cm 무게 2,970g
1982년 보계시 봉상현 성북(寶鷄市 鳳翔縣 城北) 출토

Gilt Goat-shaped Lamp

Copper | West Han Dynasty(206BC~25AD)
L 27.4cm W 11.1cm H 21.8cm Weight 2,970g
Excavated from Fengxiang County Baoji City in 1982

　금(金)을 입힌 양등(羊燈)은 조명기구의 일종이다. 등잔은 양(羊) 형상으로 양은 머리를 높이 쳐들고 앞을 주시하고 있으며 앞다리를 뒤로, 뒷다리를 앞으로 향한 자세로 웅크리고 앉아 있다. 두 뿔은 안쪽으로 말렸으며 몸체는 둥글고 꼬리는 짧다. 양의 배는 속이 텅 비어 있는데 이는 등유를 저장하는 곳이다. 양의 등과 몸은 서로 분리할 수 있게 만들고 머리 뒷부분에는 조립식 손잡이를 배치하고 둔부에는 올림 손잡이를 배치하였다. 두 손잡이를 이용하여 분리해 낸 등을 머리 위에 올려놓아 오목한 타원형 등잔대로 사용할 수가 있다. 또한 등잔대 한쪽 밖으로 좀 튀어나온 귀때에는 심지를 놓을 수 있도록 하였으며 불을 끌 때 등잔대 안의 남은 기름이 그 홈을 타고 양의 배 안으로 흘러 떨어지도록 만들어졌다. 등잔대를 도로 닫아 놓으면 원상태로 돌아가는데 그 형태가 자연스럽고 무게감이 있으며 고풍스럽다. '羊(양)'은 '祥(상)'과 발음이 비슷하여 한대(漢代)에는 양에 상서(祥瑞)로움의 뜻을 담았다. 이를테면 한대 청동기(青銅器) 표면에 흔히 보이는 "宜候王, 大吉羊(祥)[의후왕, 대길양(상), 후왕들의 제사에 대길한 양]" 등과 같은 명문(銘文)이 그것이다. 유금양등은 실용성과 예술성이 하나로 융합된 작품이다. 하북성(河北省) 만성중산왕(滿城中山王) 유승(劉勝) 무덤에서 이와 형태, 크기가 같은 유금양등이 출토된 적이 있는데 이는 한대 제후와 왕만 동등(銅燈)을 사용할 수 있었음을 말해 준다.

020

금병(金餠)

금(金) | 서한(西漢) | 지름 5.67~6.6cm 두께 0.82~1.64cm 무게 247g
1999년 서안시 미앙구 담가향 북십리포동촌(西安市 未央區 譚家鄕 北十里鋪東村) 출토

Gold Discuses

Gold | West Han Dynasty(206BC~25AD) | D 5.67~6.6cm Thickness 0.82~1.64cm
Weight 247g
Excavated from Shilipu Village Tanjia County Weiyang District, Xi'an in 1999

'감금[柿子金]'이라고도 불리는 금병(金餠)은 원판형에 표면이 약간 볼록하고 밑 부분은 안쪽으로 오목하게 들어갔다. 오목하게 들어간 곳에는 'V' 혹은 '干(천)' 자 모양의 절인(截印)이 남아 있으며 해서체(楷書體)로 "吉(길)", "陽城(양성)" 등과 같은 명문(銘文)이 새겨져 있다. 이 밖에 "令之(영지)"[인지(麟趾)의 속칭]라는 글자를 새긴 것도 있는데 이는 금병이 인지금(麟趾金)의 또 다른 형태였음을 말해 준다. 말굽금[馬蹄金]과 인지금은 제왕이 상을 내리거나 선물하는 데 쓰이거나 대량거래 시 고급화폐로 쓰였다. 보통 모형주조법(模型造法)을 사용하여 금병을 주조하는데 한 개 무게가 약 247g가량이고 가장 무거운 것은 254.4g, 가장 가벼운 것은 227.6g이다. 날인(捺印)을 새긴 것이 다수이고 문자, 부호를 함께 새긴 것도 있는데 이를테면 명사, 수사, 방위명사, 성씨, 복합어 및 V · U · S형 부호 등과 같은 것이다. 219점 되는 금병을 세 더미로 무질서하게 매장한 것으로 보아 성급히 매장했음을 알 수 있다.

서한(西漢) 초기, 진대(秦代) 말기 농민전쟁으로 말미암아 나라가 극도로 빈곤하였다. 문경의 치[文景之治] 이후, 나라가 날로 부강해짐에 따라 화폐체계에 관해서도 일련의 개혁을 단행하여 네모난 구멍이 있는 동그란 동전이 주로 유통되고 다음으로 하얀 녹비[鹿皮]가 화폐형식으로 유통되었으며 금병과 같은 화폐는 제후들의 공납품, 군주의 하사품 또는 대량화물 거래에 사용되었다. 서한 말기, 외척 왕망(王莽)은 정권을 탈취하고 국호를 '신(新)'이라고 하였다. 왕망의 통치하에 천하가 어지러워지자 서한 왕족 유(劉)씨 왕들이 군대를 일으켜 왕망의 신조(新朝)를 뒤엎었다. 이로부터 금병의 주조 연대는 서한 문경 시기(기원전 179~141년)까지 거슬러 올라갈 수 있으며 매장 연대는 왕망 신조(9~23년) 말기 전후로 추정할 수 있다.

021

유금은봉조진(鎏金銀鳳鳥鎮)

동(銅) | 서한(西漢) | 길이 6.4cm 너비 5.7cm 높이 4.7cm 무게 555～576g
1988년 서안시 미앙구 장가보(西安市 未央區 張家堡) 출토

Gilt Silver Phoenix Weight

Copper | West Han Dynasty(206BC～25AD) | L 6.4cm W 5.7cm H 4.7cm Weight 555～576g
Excavated from Zhangjiabu Village Weiyang District, Xi'an in 198

　형태와 크기가 똑같은 봉조진(鳳鳥鎮) 4점이다. 여의(如意) 모양의 관을 쓴 봉황은 입이 짧고 뾰족하며 목에는 고리 모양의 은색 목걸이를 걸었다. 눈을 약간 뜨고 엎드린 채 고개를 돌려 등 위 깃털을 다듬고 있는데 앞을 향한 양쪽 발은 구부렸고 두 날개는 살짝 세워졌으며 꽁지는 땅 위에 살포시 드리워졌다. 양쪽 깃과 꽁지에는 사이사이 금, 은을 입히고 남은 부분에는 금만 입혔다.

　진(鎮)은 용도가 다양하다. 한대(漢代)에 부장품(副葬品)으로 사용되었는데 죽은 사람 소맷부리에 놓는 것은 압수(壓袖. 소매를 누름)라고 하고 무덤 안의 장막 네 모서리에 놓는 것은 압장(壓帳. 장막을 누름)이라고 한다. 성당(盛唐) 이전에 사람들은 바닥에 자리를 깔고 앉을 때 무게가 나가는 진을 네 모서리에 놓아 돗자리를 평평하게 하였다. 일반 서민들이 사용하던 진은 비교적 단순한 모양이나 상층귀족들은 서민들과 달리 순동진(純銅鎮), 도금동진(鍍金銅鎮), 금은입사동진(金銀入絲銅鎮)과 같은 호화로운 진을 사용하였다. 여기서 소개한 도금동진은 당시 상류층의 호화로운 생활을 보여 준다. 성당 이후, 비교적 높은 책걸상과 같은 실내 용품들이 나타나면서 사람들의 생활습관이 변화됨에 따라 돗자리에 사용하던 진도 점차 모습을 감추었다.

유금착은와호형진(鎏金錯銀臥虎形鎭)

동(銅) | 서한(西漢) | 높이 3.1cm 밑지름 6.1cm 무게 400g
1973년 서안시 미앙구 미앙궁향 이하호촌(西安市 未央區 未央宮鄉 李下壕村) 출토

Gilt Silve-inlay Crouching-tiger-shaped Weight

Copper | West Han Dynasty(206BC~25AD) | H 3.1cm Bottom D 6.1cm Weight 400g
Excavated from Lixiahao Village Weiyang District, Xi'an in 1973

형태와 크기가 같은 호형진(虎形鎭)이다. 고개를 돌리고 사타구니에 아래턱을 받치고 넓은 입과 넓은 코에, 두 눈은 약간 뜨고 두 귀를 오므리고 있으며 네 발을 한데 모아 궁형(弓形)을 이루었다. 굵고 긴 꼬리는 안으로 휘감아 배에 놓았는데 형태가 자연스러우며 졸린 듯한 모습이다. 가는 선 한 가닥을 코에서부터 정수리를 지나 등을 따라 둔부까지 음각(陰刻)함으로써 호랑이의 형태를 도드라지게 하고 입, 코, 눈썹, 수염 및 팔꿈치의 털과 몸의 얼룩무늬는 모두 음선(陰線)으로 그 윤곽을 그렸다. 도금(鍍金) 공예와 은입사(銀入絲) 공예를 함께 사용하였으며 은입사 공예는 표면의 그림을 따라 얕은 홈을 내고 은실을 홈에 넣은 다음, 연단(鍊鍛)·압연(壓延)·마찰과 평평하게 하는 과정을 통해 만들어진다. 조화롭게 어우러진 호형진 표면의 금은(金銀) 색상에서는 화려함과 웅장함이 넘친다. 밑부분의 중심에는 동그란 구멍을 내고 그 속에 납을 넣어 무게를 증가시킬 수 있도록 하였다. 맹호(猛虎) 형상으로 만들어진 동진(銅鎭)은 마귀를 쫓아내고 액막이를 한다는 의미를 담고 있다.

023

호웅상투진(虎熊相鬪鎭)

동(銅) | 서한(西漢) | 높이 3.8cm 밑지름 7.4cm 무게 580g
1979년 서안시(西安市) 문물상점(文物商店)으로부터 넘겨받음

Weights of Fighting Tiger and Bear

Copper | West Han Dynasty(206BC~25AD) | H 3.8cm Bottom D 7.4cm Weight 580g
Transferred by Xi'an Culture Relic Shop in 1979

형태와 크기가 같은 호웅상투진(虎熊相鬪鎭) 2점이다. 도금(鍍金) 공예로 만든 진(鎭)은 호랑이와 곰이 서로 싸우는 형상으로 속이 꽉 차고 밑 부분이 평평하다. 맹호는 눈을 동그랗게 뜨고 귀를 쫑긋하게 세우고 커다란 입으로 곰의 배를 물었는데 앞발로 곰의 몸을 짓누르고 왼쪽 뒷다리로 바닥을 딛고 오른쪽 뒷다리로 곰의 한쪽 귀를 밟고 있다. 곰은 발버둥 치며 고통을 호소하고 있는데 한쪽 발로 호랑이의 오른쪽 귀를 거머쥐고 다른 한쪽 발로 간신히 지탱하고 있으며 죽기 살기로 오른쪽 뒷다리를 이용해 호랑이의 어깨를 내리누르고 있다. 호랑이의 사납고 용맹스러움과 곰의 우람하면서 굼뜬 모습이 선명한 대비를 이룬다. 호랑이의 수염, 눈썹과 곰의 털을 짧은 직선으로 표현하여 호랑이의 사납고 흉악함과 곰의 놀란 모습을 한층 더 부각시켜 손에 땀을 쥐는 격렬한 싸움을 생생하게 표현하였다.

61

유금함환포수(鎏金銜環鋪首)

동(銅) | 서한(西漢) | 길이 11cm 너비 12.5cm 무게 208~230g
1966년 서안시 연호구 홍묘파촌(西安市 蓮湖區 紅廟坡村) 출토

Gilt Chinese Door-knocker with Ring-handle

Copper | West Han Dynasty(206BC~25AD) | L 11cm W 12.5cm Weight 208~230g
Excavated from Hongmiaopo Village Lianhu District, Xi'an in 1966

　　금을 입힌, 짐승 얼굴 모양의 문고리이다. 눈썹은 가느다랗고 각지며 끄트머리가 올라가고, 두 눈은 약간 튀어나왔다. 코는 삼각형을 이루며 아래쪽 고리에는 동환(銅環)이 걸려 있다. 얼굴 양측에는 발톱이 드러나 있으며 소용돌이 모양처럼 표현된 얼굴 수염에서 노한 듯한 모습을 엿볼 수 있다.

　　전설에 의하면 용의 아홉 아들 가운데 하나인 포수는 조용한 것을 좋아하며 직책에 충실하였다고 한다. 하여 사람들은 문고리, 그릇 손잡이 등 장식품으로 사용하였다. 포수를 문고리 장식품으로 사용한 것은 전국(戰國)시대로부터 시작되어 오늘날까지 유행하고 있으며, 포수를 두드림으로써 사람들의 이목을 끄는 용도 외에도 신분을 나타내고 악귀를 쫓아내며 행운을 부르는 작용도 한다. 정교하게 만든 포수는 온화하고 점잖으며 귀한 티가 나는데 서한(西漢) 경사(京師) 장안(長安) 부근에서 출토된 것으로 보아 당시 황실용품의 일부였음을 알 수 있다.

인지금(麟趾金) · 마제금(馬蹄金)

금(金) | 서한(西漢) | (1) 길이 6.4cm 너비 5.2cm 높이 3.4cm 무게 257.65g (2) 높이 3.5cm 지름 5.6cm 무게 246.4g
1974년 서안시 안탑구 어화채향 북석교촌(西安市 雁塔區 魚化寨鄕 北石橋村) 출토

Kylin-toe-shaped Coin and U-shaped Coin

Gold | West Han Dynasty(206BC~25AD) | (1) L 6.4cm W 5.2cm H 3.4cm Weight 257.65g (2) H 3.5cm D 5.6cm Weight 246.4g
Excavated from Beishiqiao Village Yuhuazhai County Yanta District, Xi'an in 1974

(1)　　　　　　　　　　　　　　(2)

　　마제금(馬蹄金)과 인지금(麟趾金)은 모두 한대(漢代) 화폐의 일종이다. 마제금은 말발굽 모양에 속이 비었고 밑부분은 타원형이며 가운데가 오목하게 들어가고, 사면의 경사진 벽이 위로 올라가면서 점차 가운데로 모이는데 전벽(前壁)이 가장 높고 좌우벽(左右壁)이 점차 낮아지며 후벽(後壁)은 중심과 가까워지면서 점차 낮아지고 뒤편 오른쪽에는 구멍이 있다. 인지금은 기린의 발 모양과 비슷한데 정면은 원형에 가깝고 뒷면은 속이 비었으며, 주변 벽은 위쪽의 한 점에서 모인다. 입구가 좁고 밑바닥이 넓어 짐승의 둥근 발굽 같다. 한대 이전부터 황금화폐가 있었다. 태시(太始) 2년(기원전 95년), 한무제(漢武帝)는 '천마가 서쪽에서 오고 기린이 남쪽에서 오는' 꿈을 꾸고는 그것을 상서(祥瑞)로운 징조로 여겼는데 실제로 천마는 서역(西域,지금의 중국 신장 및 중앙아시아 지역) 대완국(大宛國)에서 나는 한혈마(汗血馬)를 가리켰고 기린은 당시 유행하던 도교(道敎) 신선설(神仙說)에서 상상해 낸 신령스러운 짐승이었다. 그리하여 무제는 화폐를 말굽, 기린 모양으로 바꾸어 제후왕들에게 상을 내리는 데 사용했다. 서한(西漢)시대에는 주로 동전이 유통되었으며 금폐(金幣)는 주로 제왕이 상, 선물, 하사품을 내릴 때 쓰였다.

　　금은(金銀)은 세계에서 가장 일찍 사람들의 주목을 받은 귀금속이다. 일찍 은상(殷商)시대부터 중국의 금은 공예가 성숙하였으며 춘추(春秋)시대에 이르러서는 황금화폐가 유통되기 시작하였고, 전국(戰國)시대에 이르러서는 중원(中原) 및 남방의 초(楚)나라에서 대량의 황금이 유통되어 대상인, 귀족들 사이에서는 대부분의 경우 황금으로 거래하였다. 진시황(秦始皇)이 중국을 통일한 뒤 황금은 상등(上等) 화폐로 사용되었으며, 진대(秦代)의 문물제도를 이어 한대에서도 여전히 황금이 상등 화폐로 사용되었다. 신망(新莽)시대, 국가가 보유한 황금은 70여만 근에 달했으며 위진(魏晉) 이후 황금은 점차 유통영역에서 모습을 감추었으나 여전히 가치척도, 저장수단의 기능을 갖고 있었으며 백은(白銀)이 널리 유통되었다. 당대(唐代)에 와서 국가에서 은본위제도(銀本位制度)를 확립함으로써 황금화폐는 저장의 용도로 쓰이고 거의 유통되지 않았다. 명대(明代) 중기에 이르러 상품경제의 급속한 발전과 더불어 백은이 보편적으로 유통되는 화폐가 되었다.

손잡이가 거북 모양인 금인귀뉴(金印龜鈕)이다. 네모난 받침대 위의 거북은 머리를 쳐들어 코끝이 하늘을 향하는데 눈을 동그랗게 뜨고 입을 벌렸다. 볼록한 등에는 육각형 무늬가 새겨졌고 육각형 안쪽 및 주위에는 연주문(聯珠紋)이 새겨졌으며 네 발에는 바둑점 무늬가 가득하다. 제작이 정교하고 조형이 사실적이면서도 과장스럽게 묘사함으로써 형상이 생동감이 있고 거북의 질감을 남김없이 표현하였다. 금인(金印) 면에는 선 흐름이 원숙하고 매끄러우며 힘 있는, 정교한 '王精(왕정)' 두 글자가 음각되어 있다.

도장[璽印]은 고대에 개인이나 관청 및 종교계에서 사용하던 상호 간 사회교류의 부신(符信)이자 증표이다. 주로 금·은·동·납·철·옥·호박(琥珀)·돌·나무·뼈·뿔·이빨·도자기·유리 등 재료로 만들어졌는데 그중 금은은 중국에서 가장 일찍 사용된 도장 재료였다. 한대(漢代) 관인(官印) 중 옥인(玉印)은 일반적으로 제왕, 왕비의 전용품이었는데 손잡이는 모두 이호(螭虎) 혹은 용 모양이었다. 왕·제후·태자·승상·태위 및 중앙에 귀복한 소수민족 수령은 거북이나 낙타 모양의 손잡이가 달린 금인, 이천석(二千石) 또는 중이천석(中二千石) 고관은 거북 손잡이가 달린 은인(銀印), 천석(千石)에서 이백석(二百石) 고관은 동인(銅印)을 사용하였다. 제후 이하 관리들이 사용하는 것을 인(印), 장군들이 사용하는 것을 장(章)이라 일컬었다. 이러한 도장 사용제도는 진한(秦漢)시대부터 수당(隋唐)시대까지 별다른 변화가 없었으며 송대(宋代) 이후에는 제왕(帝王)의 도장만 옥(玉)으로 만들고 백관(百官)의 도장은 모두 동(銅)으로 만들었다. 이는 당시 행정제도의 필요에 의한 것이며 관원 등급제도의 상징이기도 하다.

관인 이외에 사인(私印)도 있는데 사인은 재료나 손잡이 양식에 제한이 없었고 품계에 따른 규정도 없었다. 지난 수천 년간, 관청에서부터 민간에 이르기까지 도장은 독창적이면서도 다양하였다. 재질이 다양하고(동을 주로 하였음) 형태와 크기가 다양하였고 손잡이 양식도 풍부하였으며, 인면(印面)과 인문(印文) 역시 저마다 달랐다.

한대 이래의 도장 사용제도와 인문의 서체를 살펴볼 때 이 금인은 신망(新莽)시대 이름이 '정(精)'인 왕후가 몸에 지녔던 물품인 것으로 추측된다. 도장은 관청 및 개인 용무에 사용하는 증표일 뿐만 아니라 권력과 계급의 상징이었는데 금으로 만들어진 데서 이 금인 사용자의 신분을 미루어 짐작할 수 있다. 이 도장은 신망시대 유물 중 우수한 작품으로 손꼽힌다.

026

'왕정(王精)' 금인(金印)

금(金) | 신망(新莽) | 길이 1.1cm 너비 1.1cm 높이 0.5cm 손잡이길이 1cm 손잡이너비 0.7cm 무게 17.1g
1966년 서안시 비림구 사파 한묘(西安市 碑林區 沙坡 漢墓) 벽돌공장에서 출토

Golden Seal with Character Wang Jing

Gold | Xin Dynasty(9AD~23AD) | L 1.1cm W 1.1cm H 0.5cm handle L 1cm handle W 0.7cm Weight 17.1g
Excavated from Shapo Village Beilin District, Xi'an in 1966

금조(金竈)

금(金) | 동한(東漢) | 길이 3cm 너비 1.7cm 높이 1.2cm 무게 5.2g
1966년 서안시 미앙구 노가구촌(西安市 未央區 盧家口村) 출토

Golden Kitchen Range

Gold | East Han Dynasty(25AD~220AD) | L 3cm W 1.7cm H 1.2cm Weight 5.2g
Excavated from Lujiakou Village Weiyang District, Xi'an in 1966

부뚜막과 솥 모양으로 만든 금조(金竈)의 표면에는 금을 입히고 부분적으로 녹송석(綠松石)을 박아 넣었으나 지금은 떨어지고 없다. 금조는 타원형에 가까운 모양으로 아궁이문, 아궁이, 부뚜막, 솥, 굴뚝으로 이루어졌다. 부뚜막 앞에는 솥이 놓여 있는데 그 속에는 한철금주(焊綴金珠, 금구슬을 용접·연결함) 공예로 만든 좁쌀 모양의 금이 알알이 담겨져 있으며, 주위에는 세선세공(細線細工) 공예로 새긴 호형(弧形)무늬가 군데군데 배치되어 있고 띠무늬가 둘려져 있다. 오른쪽 모서리에는 가는 금실을 휘감은 굴뚝이 우뚝 서 있다. 솥 앞 양쪽에는 녹송석을 상감했던 흔적이 남아 있으며 정면 위쪽 가운데 있는 아치형 장식 위쪽에는 녹송석 하나를 상감하고 아래에는 땔나무를 넣는 아궁이가 있다. 아궁이 주위에는 금실과 구슬로 된 'S' 모양, 활 모양 무늬가 나 있고 나머지 세 면에도 똑같은 무늬가 있는데 서로 이어진 무늬는 한왕조(漢王朝) 때 성행하던 유운문(流雲紋)이다. 아궁이문 아래쪽에는 타원형의 재 담는 그릇이 놓여 있다. 부뚜막 모형 밑부분에는 전서체(篆書體)로 된 '日利(일리)'라는 길상어(吉祥語)가 새겨져 있다.

솥은 취사용 도구로 사람들이 일상생활 가운데서 음식을 익히는 주요 기구이다. 이러한 용도에 관한 기록은 서책에서도 찾아볼 수 있는데 『석명(釋名)』 「석궁실(錫宮室)」에는 "솥[竈]은 '만든다'는 '조(造)'와 동음으로 음식을 만든다는 뜻이다"라고 기록되어 있다. 가장 오래된 솥은 신석기시대 - 앙소문화(仰韶文化) 시기에 출현되었다. 명기(冥器)로 사용된 부장품(副葬品)인 솥은 진한(秦漢)시대에서 북조(北朝)시대의 무덤에서 주로 출토되었다. 특히 양한(兩漢)시대에 도자기나 동(銅)으로 만든 명기(明器) 솥을 부장하는 풍속이 성행하였는데 이 때문에 출토품 중 도자기 및 동을 재료로 한 솥이 많은 반면, 금솥은 희소하다. 서한(西漢)시대 솥은 민무늬에 불구멍이 하나뿐인 것이 많았으나 동한(東漢) 중기 이전에 불구멍이 3개, 4개로 늘어났고 표면에 각종 주방기구와 식품을 모사하거나 새겨 넣었다. 동한 중기 이전에는 주로 둥근 머리 솥이 유행하였으며 동한 말기에 와서는 네모 머리 솥이 유행하였다.

한왕조의 지배계급은 '효로써 천하를 다스린다'라고 주장하였고, 따라서 장례를 치를 때 '죽음을 삶과 같이 여길 것'을 주장하였기에 장례를 융숭하게 치르는 기풍이 성행하였다. 한왕조 때 흔히 도자기로 된 부뚜막 모형을 부장품으로 하였으며 금제 부뚜막은 극히 드물었기 때문에 금제 부뚜막의 소유자는 지체가 상당히 높았음을 알 수 있다. 전국진한(戰國秦漢) 시대에 도교(道教) 신선사상(神仙思想)이 성행하였는데 '금단(金丹)'을 복용하면 신선이 된다'는 관념이 바로 이런 사상의 반영이다. 당시 사람들이 알고 있는 금속 가운데 산과 알칼리에 잘 견디고 부식되지 않는 황금은 화학적 성질이 가장 안정적인 것으로 알려져 사람들은 황금을 복용하면 금의 특수한 성질이 몸에 전해져 장생불로(長生不老)하며 신선이 된다고 생각하였다. 『남사(南史)』「도홍경전(陶弘景傳)」에서 "도홍경은 신부(神符) 비결을 얻으면 신단(神丹)을 만들 수 있으리라 여겼다는 기록이 있다. 그러나 그에 맞는 약재가 없어 고민하던 중 황제가 황금, 주사(朱砂), 증청(曾青), 웅황(雄黃) 등을 하사하여 그것으로 서리같이 흰 비단(飛丹), 즉 신단을 만들었다. 이를 복용한 도홍경은 전에 비해 몸이 훨씬 가벼워졌다. 황제는 그 비단을 복용하고 효험이 있으니 도홍경을 더욱 존중했다"라고 기록하였는데 여기서의 금제 부뚜막은 장생하는 금단을 만드는 단조(丹竈) 모양을 본뜬 것이고 그 위 좁쌀 모양의 알갱이는 '금단'을 뜻한다. 금제 부뚜막은 조형이 정교하고 형상이 핍진(逼眞)하며, 솜씨가 섬세하고 장식이 화려하며, 기법이 복잡할 뿐만 아니라 명문(銘文)이 새겨져 있어 과학적 연구가치와 예술적 감상가치가 높다.

028

유금응형식(鎏金鷹形飾)

동(銅) | 동한(東漢) | 길이 27.4cm 너비 8.5cm 두께 3cm 무게 1,050g
1972년 서안시 연호구(西安市 蓮湖區) 서안제2기(西安第二機) 벽돌공장에서 출토

Gilt Eagle-shaped Goblet

Copper | East Han Dynasty(25AD~220AD) | L 27.4cm W 8.5cm Thickness 3cm Weight 1,050g
Excavated from the Second Brick Factory in Lianhu District, Xi'an in 1972

　형태, 크기, 무게가 같은 장식품 두 점이다. 매의 모양새를 본떠 만든 것으로 표면은 모두 도금(鍍金)했다. 기물(器物)은 대체적으로 직사각형인데 윗부분은 매의 머리 모양이다. 매 머리는 우뚝 서 있고 매 머리에 있는 눈과 볏에는 유리(琉璃)와 녹송석(綠松石)을 박아 넣었다. 뾰족한 갈고리 모양의 부리와 목은 화난 독수리가 목의 깃털을 세우고 있는 형상을 묘사했다. 배 부분도 똑같은 모양으로 와문(渦紋)을 새긴 녹송석을 박아 넣었는데 포획물을 향해 날아가려는 매를 연상케 한다. 나머지 네 곳 역시 같은 모양으로 되어 있어 네 마리의 매 머리 같으며 똑같이 녹송석을 박아 넣었다. 손잡이 쪽 구멍이 난 곳에는 관현문(寬弦紋)을 한 바퀴 둘렀다. 손잡이 아래쪽에는 타원형으로 된 구멍이 있고 측면에는 뚫려진 구멍이 있어 못으로 고정시킬 수 있게 하였다. 이 두 개의 황금으로 도금한 매 모양의 장식품은 그 전체의 모양이 매의 무리 같기도 하고 서로 잇닿은 갈고리 모양과도 같아 추상성과 상징성이 어우러져 위압감과 공포감을 느끼게 한다.

　사금(砂金) 제련(製鍊), 모형 제작, 주조(鑄造), 상감(象嵌)과 도금 기술을 동시에 사용하였다. 정교한 제작과 풍부한 구상, 치밀한 짜임새와 기이하며 장중한 모양으로 보아 황실 또는 고관대작들이 의식을 거행하거나 행차할 때 쓰던 의장기(儀仗器)의 일부인 것으로 추측된다.

위진남북조시대

魏晉南北朝時代

위진남북조(魏晉南北朝)시대

위진남북조(220~589년)시대는 사회가 동란(動亂) 속에 빠져서 왕조교체가 빈번하고 민족 간 충돌이 끊임없었고 아울러 여러 민족들이 서로 융합되었으며, 대외교류가 확대되었고, 불교와 불교예술의 전파로 당시 금은기(金銀器)는 뚜렷한 시대적 특징을 갖게 되었다. 당시 금은기는 수량이 양한(兩漢)시대에 비해 대폭 늘어났을 뿐만 아니라 제작기술이 보다 세련되었다. 이때 흔히 볼 수 있었던 금은기는 탁(鐲, 팔찌), 채(釵, 뒤꽂이), 잠(簪, 남녀 사용 구분 없는 일반적인 비녀), 환(環, 고리) 등과 같은 장신구였다. 진한(秦漢)시대와 달리 그릇의 종류와 수량이 대폭 증가되었는데 특히 순은(純銀) 기구(器具)가 대량으로 출현하였다. 이는 금과 은의 성질이 서로 다르기 때문이다. 금의 물리적 성질은 비교적 안정적이어서 자연계에서 유리(遊離) 상태로 존재하여 사람들이 쉽게 발견하고 이용할 수 있으나 은광(銀鑛)은 화합물 상태로 기타 광물질과 공존하기에 발견과 제련(製鍊)이 어려워 은의 사용은 금에 비해 수천 년가량 늦다. 고대 중국의 은그릇은 전국(戰國)시대 초(楚)나라에서 최초로 나타났는데 그 양이 매우 적었으며 위진남북조시대에 크게 늘었다. 당시 중국 전통 풍격을 띤 금은기는 청동기(靑銅器)의 영향에서 벗어나 한대(漢代)에 비해 정교하고 발달된 제작기법을 갖추었고 도금(鍍金), 누공(鏤空) 등 기법을 널리 사용하였다. 당시 금은기는 여전히 장식품을 위주로 하였는데, 은반(銀盤), 은대야[銀盆], 은이(銀匜), 은호(銀壺)와 금배(金杯) 등 금은 그릇도 있었지만 그 수량이 극히 적었다. 사회의 불안정 및 외래 불교의 신속한 전파와 더불어 불교 조상(造像)[특히 금동불상(金銅佛像)]이 크게 늘었으며 불교 조각예술의 보편적인 소재인 인동(忍冬), 연화(蓮花), 비천(飛天) 등 도안(圖案)들이 금은기에 나타나기 시작하였다. 대외교류가 빈번해짐에 따라 서아시아 · 페르시아 사산왕조(Sasan王朝, 226~642년)의 은제품은 무역상품 혹은 진상품으로서 중국에 전해졌는데 비록 수량은 제한적이지만 중국의 북조(北朝) 및 수당(隋唐)의 금은기 풍격에 커다란 영향을 미쳤다. 이 시기 대부분 금은기 장신구는 모두 선명한 민족색채를 띠었다. 그리고 많은 금은기의 형태, 무늬는 뚜렷한 서역 · 서아시아 · 남유럽의 풍격을 갖고 있었다.

Wei-Jin & North-South Dynasty Period

In Wei-Jin and North-South Period(220AD~589AD), the society was in chaos, which was caused by the repeatedly changed dynasties and constant conflicts between different peoples. While the introjection between different peoples, increased foreign trade and the spread of Buddhism enabled gold and silver wares in this period of time to be unique with the characteristic of the age. The number of gold and silver wares increased and the technics became more mature. In this period, decorations as bracelets, hairpins, rings etc., remained to be common. Compared with Qin-Han period, the type and number of daily ware increased, especially silver-ware, which were determined by the different qualities between gold and silver. The dissociative gold is stable in quality, which is easy to be found and used, while silver coexists with other minerals as compound, which is difficult to be found and abstracted. Thus, silver are used about a thousand years later than gold. The earliest silver-ware were found in Chu in Warring States Period in a small amount. This situation hadn't been changed until Wei-Jin and North-South Period. In this period, Chinese gold and silver wares almost got rid of the influence of bronze-ware, with far more delicate and developed technics and the wide use of gilt and hollowing. In terms of type, decorations were still the main works, with small amount of silver plate, silver basin, silver ladle, silver pot and golden cup. Due to the turbulence, exotic Buddhism was rapidly spread. Thus, Buddha statues, especially gilt statues greatly increased. Honeysuckle, lotus and flying Apsaras were the common subjects on the gold and silver wares. Because of the frequent foreign trade, silver works of West Asian Sassanian Dynasty were transferred or paid as tribute to China. The little amount of exotic works greatly influenced the domestic style in North Dynasty and Sui-Tang Period. Gold and silver wares in this period of time were of vivid exotic features, whose fabrication and patterns were the imitation of the style in West Region, West Asia and South Europe.

029

동류금좌불(銅鎏金坐佛)

동(銅) | 십육국(十六國) | 높이 13.2cm 무게 855g
1979년 서안시 장안구 황량향(西安市 長安區 黃良鄉) 석불사(石佛寺) 출토

Gilt Copper Sitting Buddha

Copper | Sixteen States Period(304AD~439AD) | H 13.2cm Weight 855g
Excavated from Shifo Temple in Huangliang Town Chang'an County Xi'an in 1979

　금을 입힌 불좌상(佛坐像)이다. 넓은 이마를 가진 둥글넓적한 얼굴에는 미소가 어려 있으며 묶은 바리때 모양의 육계(肉髻)를 하였다. 둥근 옷깃의 통견(通肩)식 가사를 입고 그 위에 가슴 앞을 지나는 대의(大衣)를 양어깨에 걸쳤다. 대좌(臺座) 위에 결가부좌(結跏趺座)의 모습으로 앉아, 양손을 겹쳤는데 왼손이 안쪽에 있으며 손바닥은 모두 몸 쪽을 향한 선정인(禪定印)을 짓고 있다. 대좌는 기하(幾何), 능형(菱形)무늬를 새긴 앞면이 네모나고 뒷면이 둥근 모양이다. 불상 머리 뒤에는 구멍 2개가 뚫려 있는데 이는 광배(光背)를 고정시키기 위한 것이다. 대좌 뒤쪽에는 "이 불상은 지맹(智猛)이 선사한 것으로 마열가(摩列迦)의 후예 불사타가혜열(弗斯陀迦慧悅)에게 삼가 드린 것이다"라는 뜻이 담긴 카로슈티(Kharosth) 문자가 한 줄 새겨져 있다. 불사타가혜열은 대월지(大月氏)의 명문 귀족인 마열가의 후예인 것으로 추정된다.

　선정인은 불교 수인(手印) 중 하나이다. 불교에는 여러 수인이 있는데 '인상(印相)' 혹은 '인계(印契)'라 일컬으며 각기 특정한 의미를 내포한다. 정인(定印)이라고도 불리는 선정인은 보통 두 손을 가지런히 배 앞에 놓아 양손을 펴서 왼손을 아래로 하여 겹치고, 두 엄지손가락의 끝을 서로 맞댄 손 모양을 말한다. 이 수인(手印)은 잡념을 버리고 마음을 모아 삼매경(三昧境)에 이름을 뜻한다. 결가부좌는 전가좌(全跏坐), 가좌(跏坐)라고도 하며 불상 중에서 가장 흔히 보이는 좌법의 하나이다. 불교에서는 이런 좌법을 가장 편안하고 쉽게 피로하지 않으며 마음을 바로잡을 수 있는 자세라 여겨 좌선할 때 늘 사용한다. 불상은 불교의 전파와 더불어 중국에 전해진 것으로, 불교문화의 중요한 구성요소이자 불교 신도들이 봉안하고 기도하는 대상이다. 청동불상은 인도에서 기원하였으며 궁이나 절에 봉안하였다. 중국 불상의 주조(鑄造)연대는 한명제(漢明帝) 유장(劉莊) 영평(永平) 10년(67년)으로 거슬러 올라간다. 당시 명제는 장인에게 명해 불상을 조각하여 청량대(淸凉臺) 및 현절릉(顯節陵)에 봉안하였다. 청동불상은 처음엔 금인(金人)으로 불리다가 이후 금동상(金銅像)으로 불렸다. 대체로 남북조(南北朝)부터 당대(唐代)까지가 전성기이며 일반적으로 도금(鍍金) 공예로 그 표면을 장식하였기에 도금 추엽상(鍾鍱像)이라 부르기도 했다.

030

유금일불이보살입상(鎏金一佛二菩薩立像)

동(銅) | 서위(西魏) | 높이 13.3cm 무게 251g
1970년대 서안시 연호구(西安市 蓮湖區) 당(唐) 예천사(醴泉寺) 유적지에서 출토

Gilt Statues of One Buddha and Two Bodhisattvas

Copper | Western Wei Period(535AD~556AD) | H 13.3cm Weight 251g
Excavated from Liquan Temple of Tang Dynasty in Lianhu District, Xi'an in 1970's

금을 입힌 불상은 높은 육계(肉髻), 둥글넓적한 얼굴에 넓은 이마, 턱은 네모에 가깝다. 두 눈을 지그시 뜨고 아래쪽을 바라보고 있으며 입꼬리가 올라가 미소를 띤 듯하다. 겉에는 목깃이 두 겹이고 늘어진 형태의 통견(通肩)식 가사, 안에 승지지(僧祇支)를 입고 아래에는 긴 치마를 입었다. 손은 손바닥이 밖을 향하고 오른손은 하늘을, 왼손은 땅을 향하는 시무외(施無畏)·여원인(與願印)을 취하고 있다. 이는 불보살(佛菩薩)이 중생이 원하는 바를 모두 만족시켜 줄 수 있음을 뜻하는 것으로 여원인은 일반적으로 시무외인과 통인(通印)을 맺으며, 맨발로 복련좌(覆蓮座) 위에 서 있는데 벌어진 대좌 아랫부분에는 둥근 받침대 하나가 있다. 좌우에는 각각 높은 화관을 쓴 협시보살(脇侍菩薩)이 있는데 어깨에는 비단으로 짠 천의(天衣)를 걸치고 아래에는 긴 치마를 입었다. 손을 합장하고 맨발로 연화좌(蓮花座) 위에 서 있다. 광배는 배[舟] 모양으로 그 둘레에는 활활 타오르는 불꽃무늬를 새겼다. 화염무늬의 정중앙에 앉은 자세의 화불(化佛)이 조각되어 있는데 머리에 원형 광배(光背)를 두르고 있다. 불상 뒷면에는 "佛弟子王得□供養佛一軀(불제자 왕득□이 부처를 봉안하였다)"라는 글이 새겨져 있다.

031

유금입불(鎏金立佛)

동(銅) | 북위(北魏) | 높이 9.6cm 무게 248g
1970년대 서안시 연호구(西安市 蓮湖區) 당(唐) 예천사(醴泉寺) 유적지에서 출토

Gilt Standing Buddha

Copper | Northern Wei Period(386AD~534AD) | H 9.6cm Weight 248g
Excavated from Liquan Temple of Tang Dynasty in Lianhu District, Xi'an in 1970's

　서 있는 자세의 금을 입힌 불상이다. 나선무늬로 된 높은 육계(肉髻), 동그스름하면서도 수려한 얼굴, 넓은 이마, 어깨까지 드리운 두 귀, 도드라진 눈두덩이를 가졌다. 두 눈을 살짝 뜨고 아래쪽을 바라보며 입꼬리는 위로 올라갔는데 유쾌하고 편안한 표정은 자연스럽고 친근해 보인다. 위에는 둥근 옷깃의 통견(通肩)식 가사를, 아래에는 긴 치마를 입고 맨발로 서 있다. 오른손은 시무외인[施無畏印, 불보살이 취하는 수인(手印) 중 하나로 손의 모습은 오른손을 꺾어 어깨높이까지 올리고 다섯 손가락을 가지런히 펴서 손바닥이 밖으로 향하게 한 형태이다. 이 수인은 부처가 중생에게 대자(大慈)의 덕을 베풀어 중생이 원하는 바를 달성하게 함을 나타내는데 중생에게 무외(無畏)를 베풀어 공포로부터 벗어나게 하고, 우환과 고난을 해소시키기에 시무외라 불렀다]을 지었다. 왼손은 엄지손가락을 손바닥 가운데로 굽히고 나머지 네 손가락을 아래로 곧게 펴 손바닥을 밖으로 하여 내린 여원인(與願印)을 하였다.

　불상은 어깨가 넓고 체구가 웅장하며 신체에 얇은 옷자락이 밀착되어 허벅지 굴곡이 뚜렷하게 드러난다. 촘촘한 옷무늬는 볼록한 줄무늬로 되어 있다. 이는 간다라 불상의 기본특징으로 입체감이 강한 사실(寫實)적인 옷주름에서 발전된 도안화된 옷 무늬이다.

032

유금천존입상(鎏金天尊立像)

동(銅) | 북위(北魏) | 높이 13.4cm 너비 4.5cm 무게 115g
1976년 서안시 연호구 대백양촌(西安市 蓮湖區 大白楊村) 수집

Gilt Standing Buddha Statue

Copper | Northern Wei Period(386AD~534AD) | H 13.4cm
W 4.5cm Weight 115g
Collected in Dabaiyang Village in Weiyang District, Xi'an in 1976

높은 관을 쓴 천존(天尊)은 둥그스름한 얼굴에 짧은 수염을 가졌다. 열린 V형에 넓은 소매로 된 긴 도포를 걸치고 안에는 둥근 옷깃의 긴 치마를 입고 허리에 띠를 둘렀다. 가슴 앞에 모은 양손으로 보물을 받쳐 들고 연화좌(蓮花座) 위에 서 있다. 연화좌와 그 아래 연꽃 줄기가 하나로 어우러진 것이 마치 줄기 위에 활짝 핀 연꽃이 천존을 받쳐 주는 듯하다. 어깨 뒤에는 복숭아 잎 모양의 광배(光背)가 있는데 바깥쪽의 불꽃무늬와 안쪽의 타원형 연꽃무늬로 나뉜다. 천존상은 모형(模型) 주조(鑄造) 및 세부 문양을 끌로 조각하는 방법을 통해 만들어졌다. 천존은 도교의 최고신이지만 이 천존상에서는 인물을 제외한 광배, 발밑의 연꽃, 연꽃 줄기 등 모두 불교를 본떠 만든 것이다. 이는 표현기법상 도교가 불교를 모방하였음을 말해 준다.

양진남북조(兩晉南北朝) 시기, 서역(西域) 천축(天竺, 지금의 인도)에서 유입된 불교가 점차 흥성해지고 중국 토착 신앙인 도교도 날로 강대해졌다. 교세를 다투는 가운데 두 종교는 화이지변(華夷之辯), 윤리강상(倫理綱常) 등 중국 전통관념 및 국력, 재력의 차이로 인해 치열한 충돌을 일으켰다. 그 과정에서 엄밀한 이론체계를 가진 불교와 달리 상대적으로 빈약한 이론체계를 가진 도교는 불리한 위치에 놓였다. 그러나 두 종교는 서로 충돌하면서도 다른 한편으로 철리(哲理)·의식(儀式)·방법·신보(神譜) 등 여러 면에서 서로 융합되었다. 북조(北朝) 시기, 두 종교 사이의 융합은 단순한 모방에 불과하였고 초당(初唐) 이후에 건축, 조각, 철학적 체계 등에서 진정한 의미의 융합이 시작되었다.

천화오년석가모니유금조상(天和五年釋迦牟尼鎏金造像)

동(銅) | 북주(北周) | 높이 10.2cm 무게 550g
1970년대 서안시 미앙구(西安市 未央區) 출토

Gilt Sykyamuni Statues Built in the 5th Year of Tian He

Copper | Northern Zhou Period(557AD~581AD) | H 10.2cm Weight 550g
Excavated from Weiyang District, Xi'an in 1970's

　나발(螺髮) 머리에 솟아 오른 육계(肉髻)를 한 석가모니 입상이다. 위에는 둥근 옷깃의 통견(通肩)식 가사, 아래에는 긴 치마를 입었는데 얼굴은 동그스름하면서도 수려하고 둥근 눈썹은 콧등까지 이어져 있다. 살짝 뜬 두 눈, 오뚝한 콧마루, 약간 올라간 콧방울과 입꼬리에서 표현된 유쾌하고 편안한 표정은 유난히 친근하고 자연스러워 보인다. 오른손은 다섯 손가락을 가지런히 펴서 손바닥을 밖으로 하여 어깨 높이까지 올린 시무외인(施無畏印), 왼손은 쭉 뻗어 손바닥이 밖으로 향하게 하고 손가락을 약간 굽혀 여원인(與願印)을 하였으며 맨발로 복련좌(覆蓮座) 위에 서 있다. 연화좌 앞쪽 가운데에는 수인(獸人)이 있는데 양팔로 바나나가 담긴 둥근 쟁반을 떠받친 채 웅크린 자세를 취한 모습이다. 수인 양측에는 각각 머리를 쳐든 호법사자가 배치되어 있다. 긴 갈기털이 나 있는 사자는 입을 크게 벌려 이빨을 드러냈는데 그 모습이 마치 포효하는 것만 같다. 뒷다리는 반쯤 구부리고 앞다리 중 한쪽은 쳐들고 다른 한쪽은 땅에 버티고 서 있으며 꼬리는 곧추 세웠다. 연화좌 아래에는 발이 네 개인 선(宣) 자 방형대좌(方形臺座)가 있다. 광배(光背)는 누공(鏤空)하여 만든 배 모양으로 가장자리에 활활 타오르는 불꽃무늬를 새기고 그 안쪽에 연주문(聯珠紋)과 화판문(花瓣紋)을 새겼다. 방형대좌 뒷면에는 "天和五年三月八日比丘馬法先爲七世父母法界衆生敬造釋迦牟尼像一軀供養(천화 5년 3월 8일, 비구 마법선이 칠세부모, 법계중생을 위해 석가모니상 1구를 만들어 봉안한다)"는 발원문(發願文) 여덟 줄이 새겨져 있다. 비구는 남거사(男居士)를 일컫고 마법선은 인명(人名)이다.

　석가모니의 속명(俗名)은 고타마 싯다르타로 기원전 6세기 후반 고대 인도 가비라위국 석가종족 정반왕(淨飯王)의 아들로 태어나 성인이 된 후 출가하여 수행하였다. 이후 성불하자 사람들은 '석가모니[석가족(釋家族)의 성자라는 뜻임]'라 존칭하였으며 열반(涅槃)한 뒤 불교의 최고신으로 받들었다. 석가모니상에는 좌상(坐像), 와상(臥像), 입상(立像) 등이 있다. 입상은 흔히 석가모니가 위에 승지지(僧祇支), 아래에 긴 치마를 입고 겉에 통견(通肩) 대의를 걸친 채 연화좌 위에 서 있는 형상이다. 오른손으로는 시무외인, 왼손으로는 여원인을 하고 있는데 유행설법(游行說法)하여 중생을 제도하려는 석가모니의 소망을 뜻한다. 천화(天和)는 북주(北周)의 무제(武帝) 우문옹(宇文邕)의 연호이며 천화 5년은 570년이다. 이 불상은 제작이 정교하고 아름다우며, 표면에 전체적으로 금을 입혀 금빛 찬란한데다 완벽하게 보존되어 진귀한 작품이라 할 수 있다.

034

양수금패식(羊首金牌飾)

금(金) | 북조(北朝) | 길이 4.64cm 너비 4.31cm 무게 2g
2002년 서안시 임동구 대왕진(西安市 臨潼區 代王鎭) 출토

Golden Tablet Decorated with Goat Head

Gold | Northern Dynasty Period(386AD~581AD) | H 4.64cm W 4.31cm Weight 2g
Excavated from Daiwang Town Lintong District, Xi'an in 2002

　　형태, 크기, 무게가 같은 장식용 금패(金牌) 4점이다. 금패는 윤곽이 복숭아 모양인데 가장자리에는 음현문(陰弦紋)을 한 바퀴 둘렀다. 그 안쪽에는 아래턱을
맞대고 같은 방향으로 머리를 돌린 양 머리 장식 2개가 배치되어 있다. 모두 오뚝한 코, 지그시 다문 입, 동그랗게 뜬 눈, 뒤로 오므린 귀를 가졌다. 정수리에서
뻗어 나온 거대한 뿔은 귀를 에돌아 'U' 자형을 이루었는데 짙은 북방 초원문화 특징을 띠었다. 문양은 금형 누름기법으로 만들어져 입체감이 뛰어나다. 금패
의 양측 및 아래위에 나 있는 작은 구멍 2개는 고정용으로 추정되는데 의복이나 기물(器物)의 장식에 사용되었음을 알 수 있다. 중국 역사상 양진남북조(兩晉南
北朝)시대(265~581년)는 '오호난화(五胡亂華)' 시기였다. 섬서(陝西) 관중(關中)을 포함한 진령(秦嶺) · 회하(淮河) 이북의 중국 북방지역은 당시의 흉노(匈奴),
선비(鮮卑), 갈(羯), 저(氐), 강(羌) 등 소수민족에 의해 번갈아 통치되었다. 수많은 소수민족들이 주변에서 중원(中原)으로 이주했는데 '섬서 관중의 백만 인구
중 타민족이 절반'이라는 기록이 있다. 3백여 년 동안 계속된 소수민족 통치는 관중지역에 민족특색이 강한 유적과 유물을 남겼다. 여기서 소개한 금패가 바로
그중의 하나이다.

동로마제국 테오도시우스 2세 반신상(半身像) 금화(金貨)

금(金) | 북조(北朝) | 지름 1.8cm 무게 3g
1980년 서안시(西安市) 금속재활용업체에서 수집

Golden Coin with the Bust of East Roman Empire's Theodosius II

Gold | Northern Dynasty Period(386AD~581AD) | D 1.8cm Weight 3g
Collected in Xi'an Metal Recycle Company in 1980

금화 2점이다. 이는 동로마제국(395~1453년, 비잔틴제국이라고도 함)의 황제 콘스탄티누스가 화폐개혁을 실시하면서 유통된 금화이다. 양면에는 도안과 명문이 새겨져 있다. 앞면은 동로마 황제 테오도시우스 2세(408~450년)의 반신상이다. 왼쪽으로 약간 돌린 머리에는 투구를 썼으며 볼에는 관의 구슬이 드리워져 있고 몸에는 'V'형 옷깃의 갑옷을 입고 전포(戰袍)를 둘렀다. 투구 및 갑옷의 윤곽은 연주문(聯珠紋)으로 나타냈다. 오른손에 든 표창(標槍)을 오른쪽 어깨에 메었는데 왼쪽 귀밑머리 사이로 창끝이 보인다. 외곽에는 "DNTHATTA", "SIVSPPAVI"라는 라틴 문자가 새겨져 있는데 이는 'D(ominus)N(oster)THATTA',

'SIVPSPP(ius)F(elix)AV'의 약자로 '우리의 주상(主上), 경애하는 행복의 지존(황제) 테오도시우스여'라는 뜻이다. 뒷면은 그리스 신화에 나오는 승리의 여신상이다. 이 여신은 등 뒤에 날개가 달렸다. 오른손에 십자가를 들었는데 십자가 한쪽에는 팔각성(八角星)이 있으며 왼손은 배 아래 쪽에 놓았다. 외곽에는 "VICTORIA", "AAVGGGA"를, 여신 발아래 부분에는 "CONOB"를 새겼다. 여기에서 "CONOB"는 'Constantinople Obsignata'의 약자로 '콘스탄티노플에서 주조하였다'는 뜻이다. 콘스탄티노플은 동로마 제국의 수도(오늘날 터키의 최대 도시인 이스탄불로 비잔틴이라고도 함)이다. 금화 양면에 고대 로마 황제와 신령이 함께 있는 것으로 보아 양자가 대등한 관계였음을 알 수 있다.

중국과 서양의 무역 교류는 일찍부터 있어 왔는데 한대(漢代) 실크로드의 개통 이후 점점 더 빈번해졌다. 삼국양진남북조(三國兩晉南北朝)시대, 북방의 전란으로 인해 사회경제의 막대한 손해가 있었지만 경제 교류는 여전히 지속되었다. 당대(唐代)는 중국 역사에서 가장 흥성하던 시기로 국력이 강성하고 경제가 발달하였다. 이로써 중앙아시아, 서아시아, 북아프리카를 통치하던 아랍제국의 상인들에 의해 대량의 중국 상품이 실크로드를 통하여 지중해 동부의 동로마제국에 전해졌는데 이 금화가 바로 동서양 상업 무역의 역사적 증거이다. 무덤 속 사자(死者) 입 안에서 동로마의 금화가 많이 발견되었는데 1988년 서안(西安) 함양(咸陽) 공항의 당대 하약(賀若)씨 무덤, 2003년 서안시(西安市) 미앙구(未央區) 정상촌(井上村) 북주(北周, 557~581년)의 강업묘(康業墓)에서 출토된 금화 등이 그 예이다. 금화의 용도는 죽은 자의 입 안에 넣어 부장품으로 쓰이는 것이다. 죽은 자의 입에 물건을 물리는 것은 고대 북방 민족의 보편적인 장례 풍속으로 춘추전국(春秋戰國) 이전에는 흔히 익힌 음식을 물렸다. 진한(秦漢) 시기에 이르러 초기 도교 신선사상이 점차 전파되면서 장생불로(長生不老)하고 죽은 뒤 불후의 존재가 되려는 원시적인 욕망도 부풀어 올랐다. 황금은 영원히 부식되지 않으며 옥석은 하늘의 영성을 갖고 있다 여겨 사람들은 금옥으로 된 것을 입거나 먹으면 그 특성이 사람의 몸에 전해진다고 생각했다. 옥함(玉琀), 금루옥의(金縷玉衣), 금화가 바로 사람들의 이러한 염원을 구현한 것이다.

동로마제국 레오 1세 반신상(半身像) 금화(金貨)

금(金) | 북조(北朝) | 지름 1.8cm 무게 2g
1966년 서안시 안탑구 동하가촌(西安市 雁塔區 東何家村) 출토

Golden Coin with the Bust of East Roman Empire's Leo I

Gold | Northern Dynasty Period(386AD~581AD) | D 1.8cm Weight 2g
Excavated from Donghejia Village in Yanta District, Xi'an in 1966

순금으로 만든 원형의 소리두스(Solidus) 금화이다. 앞면은 동로마제국 레오 1세(457~474년) 황제의 반신상이다. 레오 1세는 왼쪽을 향해 얼굴을 약간 돌리고 있는데 머리에 쓴 투구 정수리 부분에는 깃털 장식이 있고 뒷머리에는 관끈 두 가닥이 휘날리며 볼에는 관의 구슬이 드리워져 있다. 안에 갑옷을 입고 겉에 가슴 부분이 파인 전포를 둘렀다. 왼손에는 방패를 들었는데 왼쪽 어깨가 방패에 의해 가려졌다. 외곽에는 로마제국의 상용문자인 라틴문자로 된 명문(銘

文) "NIVSTINVSPP UG" 13글자가 새겨져 있는데 오른손 부분에서부터 시계방향으로 배열된 명문은 정수리의 깃털 장식 부분에서 두 마디로 나뉜다. 뒷면은 승리의 여신상이다. 정면으로 서 있는 여신은 몸을 약간 왼쪽으로 기울였는데 높은 관을 쓰고 긴 적삼을 걸쳤다. 왼손에는 십자가(십자가는 기독교의 상징이다. 기독교의 한 교파인 동방정교회(東方正敎會)는 이 시기 이미 동로마제국의 국교가 되어 있었다)를 들고 오른손에는 권력을 상징하는 대나무 마디 모양의 지팡이를 잡고 있다. 십자가 아래에는 육각성(六角星)이 있고 등에는 한 쌍의 날개가 달려 있다. 외곽에는 라틴문자 "VICTORIA", "AAUGGG"가 새겨져 있다. "VICTORIA"는 승리의 여신을 뜻하며 "AUG"는 'Augustus'의 약자로 음역하면 아우구스투스, 의역하면 '존엄한 자'라는 뜻이다. 이는 기원전 27년 로마제국 원로원에서 초대 황제 옥타비아누스에게 부여한 존칭인데 그 후의 황제들도 이 존칭을 사용하였다. AUGGG는 G를 3번 반복한 것으로 'Augustus'의 다수를 뜻한다. 마지막 자모는 그리스 문자로 알파벳에서 4번째에 배열되는데 여기에서는 서수(序數) 제'4'로 사용되어 콘스탄티노플 제4 주폐국(鑄幣局)에서 주조하였음을 뜻한다. 콘스탄티노플에는 주폐국이 도합 10곳이 있었다. 전체 구절은 '존엄한 자들의 승리의 여신, 제4(국)'이라 옮길 수 있다. 여신 발아래에는 'Constantinople Obsignata'의 약자인 "CONOB"가 새겨져 있는데 "콘스탄티노플에서 주조하였다"는 뜻이다. 금화 주조연대는 중국 북위(北魏) 문성제(文成帝)로부터 효문제(孝文帝) 시기 초기와 맞물린다.

소리두스는 동로마제국의 화폐명이다. 로마에서는 기원전 1세기부터 무게가 황금의 40분의 1파운드(대략 7.7~8.4g)에 달하는 '아우레우스(Aureus) 금화'를 사용하였다. 4세기, 콘스탄티누스 황제의 화폐개혁을 통하여 무게가 황금의 72분의 1파운드(대략 4.4~4.54g)에 달하는 비교적 가벼운 금화가 주조되었는데 이를 소리두스(Solidus)라고 명하고 일명 노미스마(Nomisma)라고 하였다. 이는 동로마제국의 화폐체계가 독립적인 발전단계에 들어섰음을 말해 준다. 이러한 금화는 각 시기마다 무게가 약간 달랐을 뿐, 1453년 동로마제국이 멸망할 때까지 줄곧 사용되었다.

수당시대

隋唐時代

수당(隋唐) 시대

　　300여 년간의 수당시대 금은기(金銀器)는 비약적인 발전을 이루었다. 수대(隋代, 581~618년)는 그 통치기간이 매우 짧아 금은기 역시 자기만의 독특한 풍격을 만들어 내지 못하고 대부분 이전의 풍격을 이어 왔다. 당대(唐代, 618~907년)는 고대 중국 사회발전의 전성기로 경제가 번영, 발전하였으며 대외교류가 전에 없이 활발하였다. 이 시기 금은기는 고대 중국 금은 공예의 정점에 달해 수량 및 종류가 많고 조형이 특이하며 무늬가 다채로울뿐더러 제작 또한 정교하고 아름답다. 당대의 금은기는 크게 식기, 일용그릇, 장식기구, 종교기구, 금은화폐 등으로 나뉘는데 유형마다 양식이 다양하다. 이 시기 장식무늬는 강렬한 시대적 특징을 갖고 있는데 동물무늬와 식물무늬가 주를 이룬다. 동물무늬는 모양이 다양하고 굳건하며 힘 있어 보이고 식물무늬는 다채롭고 화려하다. 이 시기에는 수렵, 화장, 악무(樂舞) 등 사회생활을 반영하는 소재들이 대량 출현하였으며 도금불상도 위진남북조(魏晉南北朝)시대에 이어 계속 성행하였다. 공예 또한 복잡하고 정교하였는데 추격(錘擊, 원석에 타격을 가하는 방법), 주조(鑄造), 용접, 절삭(切削), 유결(鉚結, 땜질하여 응결), 참각(鏨刻), 투각(鏤空), 상감(象嵌) 등 기법을 널리 사용하였다. 당대 금은그릇은 생활적인 면을 많이 담았으며 실용성을 위주로 실용성과 심미성을 상호 결합하였다. 조형과 구조를 살펴보면 합리적인 기능성과 선진적인 과학성이 구현되어 있으며, 장식 면에서는 금은의 속성을 보존하면서도 풍부하고 다양한 문양 및 기법으로 금은의 아름다움을 나타내었다. 당대 금은기는 다음과 같은 여러 발전단계를 거쳤다. 초당(初唐, 618~683년): 수량과 종류가 적으며 형태 및 무늬는 서역, 서아시아 일대의 풍격이 짙다. 성당(盛唐, 684~755년): 종류가 다양해지고 제작기법이 단순하며 양식이나 무늬의 외래문화 요소가 줄어들거나 없어졌다. 형태는 주로 중국의 전통적인 동기(銅器), 도자기, 칠기(漆器)의 형태를 답습하고 발전시켰다. 무늬는 가늘고 세세하던 것에서 복잡하고 현란하게 바뀌었는데 외래의 무늬가 점차 독립적인 지위를 잃고 중국 전통 장식도안과 하나로 융합되면서 금은기의 장식이 더욱더 완미하고 성숙해지게 되었다. 중당(中唐, 756~820년): 음식기구가 대부분이었으나 그 양이 적었다. 이 시기의 가장 뚜렷한 특징은 방생기물(仿生器物, 식물이나 동물 형상을 본떠 만든 것)의 출현이다. 만당(晚唐, 821~907년): 종류가 다양하고 수량 또한 많았다. 무늬는 종교 색채가 짙고 유가(儒家) 경전(經典) 속의 인물 이야기를 도안으로 한 것도 나타났다. 초당 시기에는 중앙정부와 황실에서 금은기의 제조업을 독점하였다. 당대 중기 이후 사회경제의 지속적인 발전과 더불어 수공업과 상업의 번영에 따라 당시 경제 중심은 동쪽에서 남쪽으로 옮겨가게 되었고 이와 함께 남방의 금은광이 대량으로 채굴되면서 이러한 독점이 사라지고 지방정부, 개인수공업자의 금은기 제조업이 점차 발전했다.

Sui & Tang Dynasty

　　The three-hundred-year-reign of Sui-Tang period witnesses the unprecedented development of gold and silver wares. During the short period of Sui Dynasty(581AD~618AD), gold and silver wares inherited the previous styles without much innovation. In the peak period of Chinese ancient society, Tang Dynasty(618AD~907AD) was prosperous in both economy and diplomacy. In this period, gold and silver wares were rich in number, type and pattern, with delicate sculpting, reflecting the top level of Chinese ancient technics on gold and silver making. Gold and silver wares could be categorized into table ware, daily ware, decorative ware, religion ware and coins in Tang Dynasty, with each type various in fabrication. The patterns strongly indicated the characteristics of that age, with various vigorous animal patterns and swinging magnificent plant patterns. Besides, there were also patterns of hunting, dressing and dancing, which reflected the social life. In Tang Dynasty, gilt Buddha statue continued its popularity since Wei-Jin and the Northern and Southern Dynasties. Technics of hammering, casting, jointing, cutting, polishing, riveting, chiseling, hollowing and enchasing etc. were widely applied, which were complicated but delicate. The artistic design of gold and silver wares was life-based, practical while aesthetical. Functionality and scientificity could be found in its sculpting and structure. By various decorative patterns, the beauty of gold and silver is both preserved and expanded. There are four phases of the development of gold and silver wares. In the early Tang period(618AD~683AD), the number and type of gold and silver wares were limited, with the shapes and patterns of obvious West Regional and Western Asian style. In the grand Tang(684AD~755AD), the types of gold and silver wares increased and the technics simplified. Both shape and pattern were no longer influenced by the foreign elements, but inherited Chinese traditional style. In terms of shape, it assimilated the shape of traditional Chinese copper ware, pottery and lacquer. By adding Chinese traditional vignettes, the patterns were changed from trivial to luxuriant, enabling the decorative patterns to be perfect and mature. In mid-Tang period(756AD~820AD), the main type of gold and silver wares was table-ware. Among the small amount of works, bionic works were the highlight. In late Tang period(821AD~907AD), the gold and silver wares were rich in type and number. The patterns were characterized with religion, with the patterns of classic Confucian stories. In terms of manufacture, gold and silver wares were monopolized by the central government and imperial family in early Tang period. After the mid-Tang period, with the development of social economy, the boom of handicraft and commercial industries, the southeastward of ancient economic center and the large-scale exploitation of southern bullion mines, the former monopoly was broke by the local feudal officials and private handicraftsmen.

유금누공관세음보살입상(鎏金鏤空觀世音菩薩立像)

동(銅) | 수(隋) | 전체높이 13.4cm 무게 101g
1970년대 서안시 연호구(西安市 蓮湖區) 당(唐) 예천사(醴泉寺) 유적지에서 출토

Gilt Standing Hollowed-out Avalokitesvara Statue

Copper | Sui Dynasty(581AD~618AD) | H 13.4cm Weight 101g
Excavated from Liquan Temple of Tang Dynasty in Lianhu District, Xi'an in 1970's

관세음보살 입상이다. 머리에는 화관을 썼는데 관대(冠帶)가 양팔을 따라
손목까지 드리워졌으며, 목에는 방울 달린 목걸이를 하였다. 어깨에는 대좌 위
까지 흘러내린 천의(天衣)를 둘렀다. 상반신을 드러내고, 배꼽 아래로는 몸에
밀착되는 얇고 긴 치마를 입었다. 내린 오른손에는 정병(淨瓶)을, 어깨 높이로
올린 왼손에는 불진(佛塵)을 들고 높은 수미좌(須彌座)에 맨발로 서 있는데 대
좌 아래에는 방형대좌(方形臺座)가 있다. 어깨의 윗부분에는 잎 모양의 광배
(光背)가 있으며 꼭대기에는 연꽃 위에 앉은 화불(化佛)이 조각되어 있다.

관음·관자재(觀自在)·아바로키테슈바라 등 여러 가지 이름으로 불리는
대자대비(大慈大悲)의 관세음보살은 33가지 화신(化身)을 가지며 12가지 재
난을 구제할 수 있다. 귀하거나 천하거나 현명하거나 미련함을 따지지 않고 중
생을 구제할 것을 주장하기에 '고난에 처한 사람을 구제하는 대자대비의 관세
음보살'이라고 존칭하였다. 보살의 설법지는 지금의 절강성(浙江省) 보타산
(普陀山)이라 전해지고 있다. 그의 탄생일은 하력(夏曆) 2월 19일, 성도일(成道
日)은 하력 6월 19일, 열반일(涅槃日)은 9월 19일이다. 초기 불경을 보면 관세
음은 대세지보살(大勢至菩薩)의 형으로서 발원(發願), 수행(修行)하여 중생을
구제하였으며 형제가 함께 아미타불(阿彌陀佛)을 모시는데 셋을 합하여 '서방
삼성(西方三聖)'이라 불렀다는 기록이 있다. 불교신자들은 그의 도행과 공덕
이 부처님의 경지에 이르렀다고 생각하여, 그의 이름을 부르면 고난에서 벗어
날 수 있다고 믿었기에 관세음이라고 불렀다. 초당(初唐) 시기, 태종(太宗) 이
세민(李世民)과 이름자가 같다 하여 '관세음'을 '관음'이라 고쳤다. 초기의 관
음은 남자 형상이었는데 그 후 남녀 구분이 모호해졌으며 원대(元代) 이후 차
츰 젊고 아름다운 여자 형상으로 변화되었다. 일반적으로 관음은 흰옷을 입고
하얀색 연화좌(蓮花座) 위에 서거나 앉아 있으며, 중생을 구제하기 위하여 손
에 정병을 들고 감로를 뿌리는 모습을 하고 있다.

038

동흠조유금아미타불상(董欽造鎏金阿彌陀佛像)

동(銅) | 수(隋) | 전체높이 41cm 대좌길이 24.6cm 너비 24cm 무게 13.27kg
1974년 서안시 안탑구 팔리촌(西安市 雁塔區 八里村) 출토

Gilt Amitabha Statue Made by Dong Qin

Copper | Sui Dynasty(581AD~618AD) | H 41cm
Pedestal L 24.6cm W 24cm Weight 13.27kg
Excavated from Bali Village Yanta District, Xi'an
in 1974

불상은 방형대좌(方形臺座) 위에 부처 1구, 보살 2구, 역사(力士) 2구, 향훈(香薰)과 앉아 있는 사자 두 마리로 이루어졌다. 아미타불은 대좌 뒤쪽 중간 부분의 허리가 잘록한 연화좌(蓮花座) 위에 결가부좌(結跏趺坐)를 하고 앉아 있다. 상반신은 앞으로 약간 기울였는데 오른손을 위로 들어 손바닥을 펴서 밖으로 향한 모습의 시무외인(施無畏印)을 취하고 왼손을 아래로 내려 손바닥을 밖으로 향한 모습의 여원인(與願印)을 취하였다. 나발(螺髮) 머리에 얼굴은 반듯한데 눈썹과 눈, 콧수염은 붓으로 점묘하였으며 입술에는 빨갛게 바른 흔적이 어렴풋하게 보인다. 안에는 승지지(僧祇支)를 입고 겉에는 편단우견(偏袒右肩)으로 가사를 걸쳤는데 옷이 몸에 밀착되어 굴곡이 돋보이며 옷주름이 간결하고 세련되게 표현되었다. 머리 뒤에는 복숭아 모양의 광배(光背)가 있는데 안쪽을 연꽃무늬, 외곽을 활활 타오르는 불꽃무늬로 장식하였다. 맨발로 연화좌 위에 서 있는 두 협시보살(脇侍菩薩)은 관대(冠帶)가 무릎까지 드리워진 높은 보관(寶冠)을 썼다. 몸체가 길며 허리는 가냘프다. 상반신을 드러내고 아래에는 발목까지 오는 긴 치마를 입었는데 어깨에 두른 천의(天衣)는 복부, 팔꿈치를 거쳐 자연스럽게 아래로 드리워졌다. 목에는 방울 달린 목걸이 및 영락(瓔珞), 팔과 손목에 팔찌를 착용했다. 머리 뒤에는 연잎 모양의 광배가 있다. 우협시보살은 위로 들어 올린 오른손에 연꽃 봉오리를 들고 있으며, 왼손 손바닥이 아래로 향하게 하고 손가락을 곧게 펴서 가슴 앞에 놓았다. 좌협시보살은 자연스레 내린 오른손에 연꽃 봉오리를 받쳐 들고 가슴 위로 올린 왼손 엄지손가락과 식지(食指)로 보주(寶珠) 하나를 집었다. 두 보살 앞에는 금강역사(金剛力士)가 맨발로 서 있다. 모두 상반신을 드러냈는데 근육이 울퉁불퉁하고 복부가 불룩하게 나왔다. 들창코에 큰 입을 가졌으며 두 눈을 부릅뜨고 노려보고 있는 모습이다. 머리에 쓴 보관의 관대는 몸 양측으로 흘러내리며 어깨에 걸친 천의는 땅에 닿았다. 목에는 목걸이 및 영락 장식, 머리 뒤에는 연잎무늬가 새겨진 원형 광배가 있다. 우측 역사는 오른손으로 검을 쥔 듯하며, 손바닥이 아래를 향한 채 조금 들어 올린 왼손으로 검날을 누르는 듯하다. 좌측 역사는 오른손을 가슴 앞에 놓고 왼손을 반쯤 주먹 쥔 채 약간 들어 올린 것이 마치 금강저(金剛杵)를 잡고 있는 것 같다. 대좌의 한복판에는 덩굴가지와 연꽃으로 둘러싸인 향훈이 놓여 있고 그 아래에는 나체 난쟁이가 하나가 힘껏 향훈을 받쳐 들고 있는데 그 조형이 생동하기 그지없다. 대좌 앞에는 기골이 장대한 두 마리의 사자가 웅크리고 앉아 앞발을 비스듬히 디디고 있다. 불상, 연화좌(蓮花座), 방형대좌 등은 따로 주조(鑄造)하여 그 사이에 끼울 수 있는 구멍을 내 서로 연결하거나 분해할 수 있게 하였다. 대좌의 오른쪽과 뒷면에는 "開皇四年七月十五日, 寧遠將軍 武強縣承 董欽敬造彌陀像一區, 上爲皇帝陛下 父母兄弟姐妹妻子具聞正法. 贊曰 : 四相迭起 一生俄度 唯乘大車 能□平路, 其一. 真相□□ 成形應身 忽生蓮座 來救□輪, 其二. 上思因果 下念群生 求離火宅 先知化城 , 其三. 樹斯勝善 惑諸含識 共越閻浮 鏡食香食, 其四 (개황 4년 7월 15일, 영원장군 이며 무강현승인 동흠이 미타상 1구를 정성들여 만들어 위로는 황제폐하를 위하고 아래로는 부모, 형제, 자매, 처자가 모두 올바른 불법을 경청하게 함이다. 이를 찬양하여 이른다. 첫째, 사상이 거듭 일어나고 한생이 잠깐 사이에 흘러가나니 오직 큰 수레를 타야만 평탄한 길에 오를 수 있도다. 둘째, 진상이 □□. 형태가 이루어지면 그 몸도 따르게 되는 법이니 홀연히 연좌가 생겨나서 찾아와서 □륜을 구해 주는구나. 셋째, 위로는 인과를 생각하고 아래로는 군생들을 염려하면서 불타는 집안에서 구출해 내어 성으로 변했음을 먼저 알게 하는구나. 넷째, 이 승선을 세워 여러 가지 함식을 알게 하고 염부를 함께 넘어서서 경식향식을 하게 하는구나)"라는 명문(銘文) 118글자가 새겨져 있다. 이 불상은 제작이 정교하고 아름다우며 표면에 전체적으로 금을 입힌데다 완벽하게 보존되었기에 웅장하면서도 화려하다.

개황은 수문제(隋文帝)의 연호로 개황 4년은 584년이다. 북조(北朝) 말기 불교 세력의 팽창으로 인해 국가 재정수입의 막대한 손실을 가져왔다. 이에 주무제(周武帝) 우문옹(宇文邕)은 건덕(建德, 572~578년) 연간 억불정책을 실시하였다. 북주(北周)를 멸망시키고 수왕조(隋王朝)를 건립한 양견(楊堅)은, 불교 신도들의 옹호를 받기 위하여 불교를 대대적으로 제창하였다. 따라서 민간에서는 불상을 주조하는 열풍이 불었다. 이 불상은 당시 사회 모습을 그대로 보여 줄뿐더러 명문 및 연호가 온전히 남아 있어 고고학적 시기와 불교 도상학(圖像學)의 연구에 있어서 매우 중요한 의의를 지닌다.

039

유금동입불(鎏金銅立佛)

동(銅) | 수(隋) | 전체높이 12.6cm 무게 325g
1970년대 서안시 신성구(西安市 新城區) 출토

Gilt Copper Standing Buddha Statue

Copper | Sui Dynasty(581AD~618AD) | H 12.6cm Weight 325g
Excavated from Xincheng District, Xi'an in 1970's

    높은 육계(肉髻)에 넓은 이마, 초승달 같은 눈썹, 긴 눈매, 튀어나온 네모난 턱을 가진 불상이다. 둥그스름한 얼굴에는 미소가 어려 있으며, 양쪽 귓불은 어깨까지 늘어져 있다. 위에는 둥근 옷깃의 통견(通肩)식 가사, 아래에는 긴 치마를 입었다. 오른손은 다섯 손가락을 오른쪽으로 향하게 하고 손바닥을 밖으로 하여 어깨 높이까지 올린 시무외인(施無畏印), 왼손은 손바닥을 밖으로 하고 엄지손가락을 안쪽으로 약간 굽히고 나머지 네 손가락을 펴서 내린 여원인(與願印)을 짓고 있다. 크고 높은 방형대좌(方形臺座)가 원형대좌(圓形臺座)와 맨발로 서 있는 불상을 받쳐 주고 있다. 인체조형의 비례로부터 볼 때 이 불상은 머리가 큰 편이고 얼굴이 네모나며 몸체가 웅장하고 다리가 짧다. 이러한 풍격은 북주(北周) 때에 생겨난 것으로 주로 수대(隋代) 불상의 특징이다.

040

유금누공관세음보살입상(鎏金鏤空觀世音菩薩立像)

동(銅) | 수(隋) | 전체높이 14.8cm 무게 108g
1970년대 서안시 연호구(西安市 蓮湖區) 당(唐) 예천사(醴泉寺) 유적지에서 출토

Gilt Standing Hollowed-out Avalokitesvara Statue

Copper | Sui Dynasty(581AD~618AD) | H 14.8cm Weight 108g
Excavated from Liquan Temple of Tang Dynasty in Lianhu District, Xi'an in 1970's

    보살은 머리에 높은 화관을 썼는데 그 관대(冠帶)가 양팔을 따라 아래로 흘러내렸으며, 어깨에 걸친 천의(天衣)는 팔을 휘감고 대좌(臺座) 위에 드리워졌다. 상반신은 맨몸에 목걸이를 착용하고 하반신은 몸에 밀착되는 얇고 긴 치마를 입었다. 아래로 내린 오른손에는 정병(淨甁)을, 위로 올린 오른손에도 뭔가를 들고 맨발로 복련좌(覆蓮座) 위에 서 있는데 연화좌(蓮花座) 아래에는 방형대좌(方形臺座)가 있다. 어깨 위에는 불꽃무늬가 새겨진 배 모양의 광배(光背), 꼭대기에는 앙련좌(仰蓮座) 위에 앉아 있는 화불(化佛)이 조각되어 있다.

소은부(小銀釜)

은(銀) | 당(唐) | 높이 3.65cm 입지름 3.76cm 배지름 6.19cm 밑지름 2.78cm 무게 85g
2002년 서안시 장안구 축촌향 양촌(西安市 長安區 祝村鄕 羊村) 출토

Little Silver Kettle

Silver | Tang Dynasty(618AD~907AD) | H 3.65cm Mouth D 3.76cm Belly D 6.19cm
Base D 2.78cm Weight 85g
Excavated from Yangcun Village Zhucun County Chang'an District, Xi'an in 2002

은솥[銀釜]은 입술이 안쪽으로 오목하게 들어간 입구와 평평한 밑바닥을 가지고 있다. 배부는 좁다란 볼록한 턱에 의해 상하 두 부분으로 나뉘는데 호형(弧形)에 가까운 윗배의, 입술과 가까운 쪽에는 세 줄로 된 음현문(陰弦紋)이 한 바퀴 둘러졌으며 아랫배는 사선으로 내려오면서 점차 좁아진다. 그릇 형태가 불균형하며 전체적으로 살짝 동황색을 띤다.

솥[釜]은 음식물을 조리하는 도구로서 일명 '부(䰞), 확(鑊)'이라고도 하며 둥근 입구, 호형의 배, 얇은 벽, 둥근 바닥을 가진 형태가 많다. 신석기시대 초기에 생겨난 것으로 이에 관한 기록은 사서에서도 찾아볼 수 있다. 『예함문가(禮含文嘉)』에는 "수인씨(燧人氏)가 나무를 마찰하여 불씨를 얻는 방법을 전파함으로써 익힌 음식을 먹을 수 있어 배탈이 나지 않으니 짐승과 구별되었다"고 기록되어 있고, 『고사고(古史考)』에는 "황제가 솥, 시루[甑]를 만들었다"고 기록되어 있다. 부는 격(鬲, 솥의 일종)으로부터 진화되어 온 것인데 격의 발이 점점 짧아지다가 나중에 없어지는 과정을 거쳐 부가 된 것이다. 전국(戰國)시대 둥근 밑굽, 둥근 배에 오므라든 입구, 테두리가 밖으로 꺾인 솥이 나타났으며 한대(漢代)에 이르러 솥, 시루, 대야 등 각자 모양을 취해 한데 묶어 주문 제작하였다. 이때의 솥

은 배 중간 부분에서 뒤엎은 사발 모양의 윗부분과 입술이 평평한 대야 모양의 아랫부분으로 나뉘는데 아래위는 못[鉚釘]으로 고정된다. 가장 일찍 도자기 솥이 출현하였던 상주(商周)시대에는 도자기솥과 구리솥이 병존하였다. 『맹자(孟子)』「등문공(騰文公)」에는 "허 씨가 도자기솥으로 밥을 짓고 철제농기구로 밭을 가는가?"라고 하였는데 이는 전국시대 평민들도 솥과 시루를 사용했음을 말해 준다. 양한(兩漢)시대에는 구리 솥을 보편적으로 사용하였고 수당(隋唐)시대 이후 솥은 점차 정형화되었으며 그 후 냄비[鍋]로 대체되었다. 역대의 솥은 모양과 제작법이 조금씩 다르긴 하나 기능은 거의 같다. 춘추전국(春秋戰國)시대에는 솥을 용기 계량단위로 사용하기도 하였는데 솥 하나가 6말[斗] 4되[升] 또는 2, 3곡(斛)으로 차이가 있었다.

중당(中唐) 이전, 특히 초당(初唐) 시기에 금은기(金銀器)의 제작은 중앙정부와 황실에서 독점하였고 장인(匠人)들은 신분이 대대로 세습되었다. 수대(隋代) 말년의 전란으로 인해 뛰어난 장인의 수가 줄어들고 공예수준과 제련기술이 퇴보하면서 비교적 조악(粗惡)한 그릇들이 만들어졌다. 또한 금은기는, 당대 이전에는 흔히 장식, 감상 및 소장품으로 사용되었을 뿐 실용적 가치가 적었으나 당왕조(唐王朝) 때부터는 실용성을 갖추기 시작하였다. 이 은솥은 형태가 작으므로 실용가치가 없이 오직 부장품(副葬品)에 속한다.

소면은완(素面銀碗)

은(銀) | 당(唐) | 높이 9.6cm 입지름 13.35cm 굽지름 6.24cm 무게 465g
2002년 서안시 장안구 축촌향 양촌(西安市 長安區 祝村鄕 羊村) 출토

Silver Bowl with Plain Surface

Silver | Tang Dynasty(618AD~907AD) | H 9.6cm Mouth D 13.35cm Base D 6.24cm Weight 465g
Excavated from Yangcun Village Zhucun County Chang'an District, Xi'an in 2002

　약간 벌어진 입구, 호형(弧形)의 깊은 배, 나팔 모양의 낮은 굽을 가진 민무늬 완(碗)이다. 굽의 가장자리는 넓으면서도 두껍다. 전체적으로 은회색을 띠면서 동황색이 감돈다.

　완(碗)은 음식그릇으로서 음식을 담거나 차나 술을 마시는 데 쓰인다. 입구가 벌어지고 배는 호형이며 밑굽은 둥그렇거나 전병(煎餠) 모양인 형태가 많다. 그 재질은 도자기 따위이고 금이나 은은 많지 않은데 주로 지배계급의 상층부에서 사용하였다. 완은 신석기시대에 출현했으며 상주(商周)시대에 나타난 청동완(靑銅碗)은 현대의 사발과 유사하다. 양진(兩晉) 때에 나타나서 점차 보편화된 청자완(靑瓷碗)에는 불교의 영향으로 인해 연잎무늬가 많이 보인다. 당대(唐代) 초기와 성당(盛唐) 시기에는 백자완(白瓷碗)의 수량이 대폭 증가하였고 금은완(金銀碗)은 궁궐에서나 고관대작들이 많이 사용하였으며, 그 무늬는 주로 화초 · 봉황 · 원앙새 · 물고기 · 비둘기 같은 것이었다. 당대 후기에 와서 완의 종류가 점차 다양해짐에 따라 연잎 모양, 해당화 모양, 해바라기 잎 모양의 입구를

가진 완 등이 나타났다. 명청대(明淸代)에 와서 그 종류가 더욱 많아졌고 용 · 봉황 · 소나무 · 대나무 · 매화 · 화초 같은 상서(祥瑞)로운 뜻이 담긴 도안이나 무늬가 주를 이루었다.

　이 은완(銀碗)은 수대(隋代) 말기와 당대 초기의 완과 달리, 배가 비교적 깊으며 굽은 조금 넓고 두껍다. 당대 초기 금은 제품은 독립적인 계통을 이루지 못하였기에 주로 다른 기물의 모양을 본떴다. 당대 초기의 술잔[盅] 모양의 완은 입구가 곧고 배가 깊으며 굽은 옥벽 모양이다. 당대 중기와 당대 후기에 유행하였던 별구완(撇口碗)은 입구가 벌어지고 입술부위가 약간 구부러져 있으며 복부가 비스듬한 형태로 옥벽 모양의 굽은 벽이 점점 더 얇아지고 가운데 공간이 점차 커졌다. 당대 후기에서 오대(五代, 907~960년)에 이르러 연잎 · 해당화 · 해바라기 잎 모양의 입구, 골을 판 흔적이 있는 몸체, 고리 모양의 굽을 가진 형태로 변화하였다.

043

심복소면은완(深腹素面銀碗)

은(銀) | 당(唐) | 높이 10cm 입지름 13.7cm 밑지름 7cm 무게 538g
1971년 서안시 연호구 홍묘파촌(西安市 蓮湖區 紅廟坡村) 출토

Silver Bowl with Deep Abdomen and Plain Surface

Silver | Tang Dynasty(618AD~907AD) | H 10cm Mouth D 13.7cm
Base D 7cm Weight 538g
Excavated from Hongmiaopo Village in Lianhu District, Xi'an in 1971

표면이 전체적으로 은회색을 띠는 민무늬 완(碗)이다. 입구가 벌어지고 배는 깊으며 벽은 호형(弧形)인데 아랫배가 서서히 내려오면서 좁아진다. 밑굽은 둥글며 굽은 밖으로 벌어졌다. 완의 발전과정을 볼 때 이 완은 당대(唐代) 초기의 것임을 알 수 있으며 황실 정원에서 출토되고 부피 또한 크다는 점에서 황실용품인 것으로 추정된다.

044

소면소은완(素面小銀碗)

은(銀) | 당(唐) | 높이 2.6cm 입지름 10.1cm 무게 96g
1979년 서안시 파교구 홍경진 전왕촌(西安市 灞橋區 洪慶鎮 田王村) 출토

Small Silver Bowl with Plain Surface

Silver | Tang Dynasty(618AD~907AD) | H 2.6cm Mouth D 10.1cm Weight 96g
Excavated from Tianwang Village Hongqing Town Baqiao District, Xi'an in 1979

민무늬 완(碗)은 입구가 벌어지고 벽은 호형(弧形)이며 굽은 둥그렇다. 입구의 가장자리 부분에는 귀때가 달려 있다.

팔곡전지문은완 (八曲纏枝紋銀碗)

은(銀) | 당(唐) | 높이 3.79cm | 입지름 11.58cm | 무게 194g
1972년 서안시 안탑구 곡강향 곡강지촌(西安市 雁塔區 曲江鄕 曲江池村) 출토

Eight-petaled Silver Bowl with Enwinding Branches

Silver | Tang Dynasty(618AD∼907AD) | H 3.79cm Mouth D 11.58cm Weight 194g
Excavated from Qujiangchi Village Qujiang County Yanta District, Xi'an in 1972

여덟 꽃잎 모양을 본떠 만든 완(碗)이다. 운두가 조금 낮고 벽은 약간 굽었으며 아랫배는 서서히 좁아져 내려오다 밑쪽에서 나팔형 굽을 이루었다. 외벽의 꽃잎 사이에 파낸 골은 내벽에서 볼록선 여덟 줄이 생겨나게 하여 몸체가 꽃잎 모양이 되게 하였다. 볼록선을 따라 화초 여덟 그루를 배치하였다. 그루마다 대칭되는 화엽(花葉)이 있는데 화엽의 끝부분에는 동그란 꽃잎 1개, 뾰족한 꽃잎 2개가 있으며 화초 아랫부분에서 서로 연결되어 팔각형을 이루었다. 안바닥에는 겹으로 된 연주문(聯珠紋), 그 사이에는 '八(팔)'자 모양으로 된 인동(忍冬)무늬가 새겨져 있다. 외벽의 무늬도 똑같은데 꽃잎마다 대칭되는 전지문(纏枝紋)을 새겼다. 굽

가장자리는 비교적 큰 연주무늬로 장식하였다. 완은 추엽(錘揲) 기법으로 만들어졌으며 무늬는 끌로 새기고 안팎 무늬에는 모두 금을 입혔다.

인동무늬의 소재인 인동은 '금은화(金銀花)'라고도 불리는데 '겨울철에도 시들지 않는다'는 뜻에서 이러한 이름을 가지게 되었다.

인동무늬는 서방에서 중국에 전파된 중요한 무늬 중 하나로 위(魏)·진(晉)·남북조(南北朝) 시기에 널리 유행하였다. 당대(唐代)의 인동무늬는 3~5개의 반쪽꽃잎으로 이루어졌는데 장식용으로 쓰일 때는 두 잎을 대칭되게 하거나 가지 또는 넝쿨과 결합하여 무늬 양식을 만들었다. 연주문(聯珠紋)은 작고 둥근 고리와 구슬을 배열하여 만든 것으로 흔히 그릇의 입구, 밑굽 또는 모가 난 곳에서 보인다. 금은기(金銀器)의 주요 무늬 중 하나인 연주문은 당대 전반에 걸쳐 줄곧 존재하였는데 8세기 중엽 전에는 큰 연주문, 8세기 중엽 이후에는 작은 연주문이 유행하였다.

이 은완은 섬서성(陝西省) 서안시(西安市) 하가촌(何家村)의 당대 금은기 가마터에서 출토된 토우(土偶)가 든, 손잡이가 달린 금술잔의 인동무늬와 똑같다. 중앙아시아·소그디아나(Sogdiana, 중앙아시아의 샤라프샨 하천과 카슈카 다리아 유역 지방의 옛 이름)의 은기(銀器) 풍격을 띤 것으로 보아 8세기 중엽 이전의 소그디아나 은제품에 속함을 알 수 있다.

원앙홍안절지관화문은완(鴛鴦鴻雁折枝串花紋銀碗)

은(銀) | 당(唐) | 높이 9cm 입지름 21.7cm 밑지름 4.7cm 무게 399g
1975년 서안시 비림구(西安市 碑林區) 서북공업대학(西北工業大學) 출토

Silver Bowl with Patterns of a Mandarin Duck and a
Swan Goose in the Branches of Flowers

Silver | Tang Dynasty(618AD~907AD) | H 9cm Mouth D 21.7cm Base D 4.7cm
Weight 399g
Excavated from Northwestern Polytechnical University in Beilin District, Xi'an in 1975

입구가 크고 운두가 낮아 쟁반 모양과 흡사한 은제 완(碗)이다. 안바닥에
는 원앙새 한 마리와 기러기 한 마리가 모란 속에서 노니는 모습을 그렸는데,
머리를 쳐든 수컷 원앙새가 가슴을 내밀고 날개를 활짝 펼친 것이 마치 날아
오르려는 것 같기도 하고 이미 떠나 버린 암컷 원앙새를 찾는 것 같기도 하다.
기러기는 긴 목을 빼어 울창한 가지를 에돌아 고개를 돌리고 꽃잎을 지그시
문 채 날개를 치며 날아오를 것만 같다. 주위에 펼쳐진 송이송이 모란들은 원

앙새, 기러기와 하나가 되어 단화(團花)무늬를 이루었다. 내외 벽에는 각기 여섯 떨기의 두 겹으로 된 절지화(折枝花)가 참각(鏨刻)되어 있는데 앞부분만 보이
고 나머지는 꽃잎에 가려졌다. 입구 부분에는 금박을 입혀 꽃무늬를 조각하는 공예기법을 사용하여 변형 꽃잎 무늬를 새겼다. 전체적으로 은백색을 띠며, 금빛
이 반짝이는 완은 화려하고 정교하며 세련된 것을 추구하는 당대(唐代) 사람들의 풍격을 그대로 보여 주었다. 밑굽에는 "趙一(조일)" 두 글자가 묵서(墨書)되어
있다. 당대로부터 전해 내려온 기물(器物)의 표면에는 흔히 소유자의 이름이나 시간이 표기되어 있어 성이 조씨인 사람이 표기한 것으로 추측된다.

　춘추(春秋) 말기에 시작되어 전국(戰國) 이후에 성행한 참각(鏨刻) 공예는, 성형된 기물의 표면을 두드려 각종 무늬를 만드는 공예를 일컫는다. 추엽(鍾揲) 기
법으로 금은기(金銀器)를 장식하면서부터 참각은 세부(細部)를 가공하는 중요한 수단으로서 자리매김하게 되었다. 절지문(折枝紋)은 '지자화(枝子花)', '생색
화(生色花)'라고도 불린다. 이는 화초의 가지 또는 일부분을 취하여 무늬를 만드는 것으로 흔히 꽃이나 꽃봉오리, 잎으로 구성되는데 그 형태가 사실적이긴 하
나 수많은 절지(折枝) 사이에는 아무런 연관성이 없다. 꽃들을 송이송이 표현하는 절지관화문(折枝串花紋)은 주로 8세기 전반기부터 9세기 후반기에 유행하였
다. 잎을 배열하여 만든 엽판문(葉瓣紋)은 8세기 중엽에 나타났으나 그다지 유행하지 않았으며, 9세기 때 금은기 장식무늬에서 흔히 볼 수 있었다. 두 겹으로 된
절지관화문은 8세기 중엽 유행하였다. 이로부터 이 완은 중당 시기의 은제품이었음을 알 수 있다.

화판형유금원앙문은완(花瓣形鎏金鴛鴦紋銀碗)

은(銀) | 당(唐) | 높이 5.5cm 입지름 21.6cm 무게 359g
1979년 서안(西安) 기차역 광장 출토

Petal-shaped Gilt Silver Bowl with Mandarin Duck

Silver | Tang Dynasty(618AD~907AD) | H 5.5cm Mouth D 21.6cm Weight 359g
Excavated from Xi'an Railway Station Square in 1979

은회색을 띠는 완(碗)이다. 벌어진 입구는 4개의 꽃잎 모양이고 배는 호형(弧形)이다. 외측면의 오목 선은 몸체를 네 부분으로 나누고 있다. 입구의 안쪽은 중첩된 꽃잎무늬, 내벽은 민무늬로 장식되었다. 안바닥 복판에는 암수 원앙이 짝을 이뤄 한가롭게 노닐고 있는 모습을 그렸다. 그중 하나는 고개를 숙이 고, 다른 하나는 뒤를 돌아보고 있다. 그 주위에는 금빛 나는 절지화(折枝花)를 새겨 넣고 가장자리에는 꽃잎무늬를 둘렀다. 외벽에는 활짝 편 화초 한 떨기를 새겼는데 꽃잎들이 겹겹이 중첩되어 큰 단화(團 花) 네 송이를 이루었다. 단화 2조 사이에는 금빛 나는 작은 꽃을 상하로 배열하였다. 밑굽에는 워낙 굽 이 있었으나 일부가 손상되고, 해서체(楷書體)로 된 명문(銘文) "臣康進(신강진)" 3글자가 새겨져 있는 것이 보인다. '康(강)'은 당대(唐代)의 한 지방 관원의 이름이다. 이 은완은 바로 그가 조정에 바쳤던 공 납품이다.

꽃잎무늬는 8세기 중엽에 생겨나 9세기 때 각종 기물(器物)에서 널리 유행하였으며, 단화(團花)무늬 는 8세기 중엽 이후에 유행하였다. 이 밖에, 기존의 문헌 및 고고학적 발굴 자료를 살펴보면 당대에는 지 방관리들이 조정에 금은기물(金銀器物)을 공납하는 풍조가 성행하였는데 초기부터 성당(盛唐) 시기까 지는 금은정류(金銀鋌類), 중·후기에는 그릇류가 주를 이루었음을 알 수 있다. 따라서 이 완은 8세기 중 엽 이후의 금은제품으로 추정된다.

048

홍안단화문은완(鴻雁團花紋銀碗)

은(銀) | 당(唐) 높이 5.54cm 입지름 22cm 밑지름 10.9cm 무게 310g
1975년 서안시 비림구(西安市 碑林區) 서북공업대학(西北工業大學) 출토

Silver Bowl with Pattern of Swan Goose and Cluster Flowers

Silver | Tang Dynasty(618AD~907AD) | H 5.54cm Mouth D 22cm Base D 10.9cm
Weight 310g
Excavated from Northwestern Polytechnical University in Beilin District, Xi'an in 1975

입구가 벌어지고 배는 호형(弧形)이며 밑굽이 평평한 둥근 은완(銀碗)이다. 입구와 배는 오목선에 의해 4개 부분으로 똑같게 나뉘는데 안쪽 입구에는 운곡문(雲曲紋)이 둘러져 있다. 내벽의 4부분에는 각각 한 떨기 타원형의 단화(團花)를 새겼는데 잎들이 크고도 무성하다. 안바닥 가장자리에는 바람에 흩날리는 듯한 연잎을 두르고 그 중앙에는 기러기 두 마리가 날개를 펼치고 목을 길게 뻗어 서로 마주 보고 있는 것을 그렸다. 무늬가 다양한 안쪽과 달리, 겉면에는 무늬가 없다. 밑굽 언저리에는

용접한 흔적이 있는데 굽이 떨어져 나간 것으로 보인다. 무늬는 모두 끌로 조각하였으며 표면에는 금을 입혔다.

단화문(團花紋)은 통속적으로 일컫는 단어로 꽃은 대체로 원형이며 어느 특정한 식물의 꽃에 속하지 않고 일반적으로 윤곽이 원형인 장식무늬를 가리킨다. 금은기(金銀器)에 사용되는 이러한 무늬들은 모두 정면이나 굽어보는 각도에서 활짝 핀 꽃을 바라본, 꽃잎이 중심으로부터 여러 층으로 펼쳐진 모양이다. 보상화(寶相花)와 달리, 이는 사실적인 꽃으로 주로 8세기 중엽에 유행하였다. 입구에 새겨진 운곡문은 각기 타원형 안에 위치하는데 이러한 문양은 8세기 중엽 이후 유행된 것이다.

기원전 6세기, 지중해 지역 주변 국가 및 고대 페르시아 · 아케메네스 왕조(기원전 558~330년)에서 여러 개 꽃잎 모양의 은완이 유행하기 시작하여 중앙아시아 및 서아시아에서 줄곧 그 전통이 이어져 내려왔다. 5~6세기에 만들어진 소그디아나(Sogdiana, 중앙아시아의 샤라프샨 하천과 카슈카 다리아 유역 지방의 옛 이름)의 은완이 바로 꽃잎 모양의 요철이 있는 그릇 벽을 특징으로 한다. 7세기 초 소그디아나의 여러 개 꽃잎 모양으로 만든 은완은 중국에 유입된 즉시 유행하였다. 초기에는 입구까지 골을 파지 않았으나 7세기 후반 점차 중국화되면서 꽃잎이 점차 커지고 개수가 점점 줄어들었다. 8세기 이후, 꽃잎과 그릇이 한층 더 융합되면서 입구까지 골을 파게 되었다. 이 은완의 표면에 새긴 단화 · 연잎 · 기러기 등 문양들은 모두 중국 전통문양이고 완의 형태 또한 소그디아나의 것과 완전히 구별되는데 이미 중국화(中國化)가 완성된 것이다. 문양의 유행된 시기로부터 그 제작연대가 중당(中唐) 초기였음을 알 수 있다.

석류화문은완(石榴花紋銀碗)

은(銀) | 당(唐) | 높이 4cm 입지름 19cm 무게 370g
1966년 서안시 비림구(西安市 碑林區) 서북공업대학(西北工業大學) 출토

Silver Bowl with Guava Patterns

Silver | Tang Dynasty(618AD~907AD) | H 4cm Mouth D 19cm Weight 370g
Excavated from Northwestern Polytechnical University in Beilin District, Xi'an in 1966

벌어진 입구, 호형(弧形)의 배, 둥근 밑굽을 가진 은완(銀碗)이다. 두드려서 그릇 형태를 만들고 표면에 새긴 문양에는 금을 입혔다. 안쪽 문양은 3부분으로 나뉘는데 안바닥에는 넓은 잎과 활짝 핀 꽃 세 송이가 원형을 이룬 무늬가 새겨지는데 석류 4개를 중심으로 아름다운 도안을 펼쳐냈다. 내벽에는 석류와 화초로 이루어진 절지단화(折枝團花) 5조가 균등한 간격으로 배치되어 있고 입구에는 잎무늬가 둘러져 있다. 가지와 잎이 무성하고 전체 문양의 배치가 알맞으며 선 흐름을 표현함이 거침없다. 겉면에는 무늬가 없다. 넓은 잎으로 장식한 문양은 성당(盛唐)에서 만당(晚唐) 시기에 주로 유행하였다. 이로부터 미루어 보아 이 은완은 대체로 당대(唐代) 중·후기의 것이었음을 알 수 있다.

호접문은완(蝴蝶紋銀碗)

은(銀) | 당(唐) | 높이 4.8cm 입지름 14.5cm 밑지름 4.58cm
무게 103.8g
1966년 서안시 비림구(西安市 碑林區) 서북공업대학(西北工業大學) 출토

Silver Bowl with Butterfly Patterns

Silver | Tang Dynasty(618AD~907AD) | H 4.8cm Mouth D 14.5cm
Base D 4.58cm Weight 103.8g
Excavated form Northwestern Polytechnical University in Beilin District, Xi'an in 1966

입구가 안쪽으로 오므라들고 배는 가파른 직선으로 내려오며 밑굽이 작고 평평한 완(銀碗)이다. 무늬를 안쪽에만 새기고 겉면에는 새기지 않았다. 안쪽 입구에는 관현문(寬弦紋) 한 줄을 두르고 배에는 나비 네 마리를 음각하고 그 사이사이를 꽃으로 장식하였다. 밑굽에는 날개를 나풀거리는 나비 한 마리를, 밑굽과 가까운 곳에는 관현문 두 줄을 두르고 그 사이에 불규칙적인 해당화무늬를 새겼다. 모든 문양에는 금을 입혔다. 이는 당대(唐代) 말기의 완 중 수준 높은 작품이다.

홍안절지화문은반(鴻雁折枝花紋銀盤)

은(銀) | 당(唐) | 높이 3cm 지름 24cm 무게 470g
1975년 서안시 비림구(西安市 碑林區) 서북공업대학(西北工業大學) 출토

Silver Plate with Patterns of a Swan Goose and Branches of Flowers

Silver | Tang Dynasty(618AD~907AD) | H 3cm D 24cm Weight 470g
Excavated from Northwestern Polytechnical University in Beilin District, Xi'an in 1975

벌어진 입구, 호형(弧形)의 배[腹], 둥근 밑굽을 가진 은쟁반이다. 민무늬인 겉면과 달리, 안쪽에는 여러 가지 문양들을 새겼다. 입구에는 구름무늬 한 줄을 두르고 배에는 절지(折枝)·모란·화초로 조합된 여섯 떨기의 꽃을 균일하게 배치하였다. 안바닥 중앙에는 넓은 잎의 절지·모란 무늬를 새겼는데 무성한 가지와 잎, 송이송이 활짝 피어난 모란 속에는 날개를 펼치고 꽁지를 높이 치켜든 채 비상하는 기러기 한 마리가 있다. 반짝이는 두 눈을 가진 기러기의 목, 등, 가슴의 깃털은 마치 바람에 하느작거리는 것만 같다. 밑굽 중심에는 "十一兩二分(11냥 2분)" 5글자가 새겨져 있다. 이 쟁반은 금박을 입히고, 무늬를 새겨 넣으며 추엽(錘揲) 등 기법으로 만들어졌으며, 문양은 모두 끌로 조각하였다.

추엽(錘揲)은 일명 '타작(打作)'이라 불리기도 하는데 금은기(金銀器) 제작기법의 일종이다. 이는 금은의 전성(展性, 얇게 펴지는 성질)과 연성(延性, 가늘고 길게 늘어나는 성질)이 큰 특징을 이용하여 천연 또는 제련된 금은정류(金銀鋌類)의 재료를 단조(鍛造)하여 가공·제작할 수 있도록 만드는 공예기법이다. 원래 서아시아 금은기 제작기법의 일종이었는데 남북조(南北朝) 말기 중국에 유입되어 당왕조(唐王朝) 때 성행하였다.

쟁반 위의 금으로 단장한 화초 및 기러기는 유난히 아름다우며 합리적으로 배치한 문양은 절묘하고 짜임새가 잘 이루어졌다.

'이면봉진(李勉奉進)' 쌍어문만초화은반(雙魚紋蔓草花銀盤)

은(銀) | 당(唐) | 높이 1.2cm 입지름 17cm 무게 198g
1975년 서안시 비림구(西安市 碑林區) 서북공업대학(西北工業大學) 출토

A Tribute of Silver Plate with Double-fish Pattern and Plants by Li Mian

Silver | Tang Dynasty(618AD~907AD) | H 1.2cm Mouth D 17cm Weight 198g
Excavated from Northwestern Polytechnical University in Beilin District, Xi'an in 1975

벌어진 입구에 입술은 넓으며 얕은 배는 호형(弧形)이고 밑굽이 평평한 은쟁반이다. 안쪽에는 둥글게 원을 이룬 인동(忍冬) 잎 안에 절지화(折枝花) 잎속에서 노니는 한 쌍의 물고기로 장식하였다. 원의 외곽도 절지화 잎으로 장식하고 띄엄띄엄 진주무늬를 새겨 넣었다. 이는 추엽(錘揲) 기법을 사용한 것으로 먼저 각 문양을 그린 다음에 끌로 세부적으로 조각하고 나중에 금을 입힌 것이다. 밑굽에는 "조의대부(朝議大夫)·사지절(使持節)·도독홍주제군사(都督洪州諸軍事)·수홍주자사(守洪州刺史) 겸 어사중승(御史中丞)·충강남서도(充江南西道) 관찰처 치도단련(觀察處 置都團練), 수착(守捉), 막요(莫徭) 등을 역임하고, 자색포에 금어대(金魚袋)를 하사받은 신 이면(李勉)이 받들어 올림"이라는 내용의 명문이 새겨져 있다. 홍주(洪州)는 지금의 강서성(江西省) 남창시(南昌市)이고 『신당서(新唐書)』에 의하면 당 대종(代宗) 광덕(廣德) 2년(764년) 9월~대력(大歷) 2년(767년) 4월, 이면(李勉)은 홍주자사(洪州刺史), 강남(江南) 서도관찰(西道觀察) 등 관직을 맡았으며 숙종(肅宗), 대종(代宗), 덕종(德宗) 3대 왕조를 걸친 중당(中唐) 시기의 저명한 3대 왕조 원로로서 "청렴하고 소박하여 종신의 본이다"라고 칭송을 받았다. 당시 이면은 지방관리를 지내면서 조정에 공납을 올렸는데 이는 중당 시기 관리들이 부패하였음을 말해 준다. 당대(唐代) 지방관리가 황제에게 재물을 공납하는 부패한 풍조는 고종(高宗) 시기에 시작되어 무후(武後) 시기, 현종(玄宗) 시기에 이르러 날로 성행하였다. 당대 중·후기 번진할거(藩鎭割據)로 인해 조정에 공납되는 조세가 점점 줄어들었다. 지방관리들이 승진의 기회를 노리면서 부패풍조가 더욱 심해졌다.

물고기무늬는 당대 금은기(金銀器)에서 흔히 볼 수 있는 문양이다. 고대 중국은 어수(魚水)로 군신관계를 비유하였는데, 이는 물고기와 물처럼 임금과 신하의 관계가 매우 친밀함을 뜻하며 신하가 군주를 향한 충성심으로 표현하기도 한다.

당대 중기 이후, 북방의 빈번한 전란으로 사회경제에 막대한 손실을 가져왔다. 반면 남방 상황은 상대적으로 안정되어 지속적인 경제발전을 가져왔으며 수공업 및 상업이 고도로 발전하였고 양주[揚州, 지금의 (江蘇省) 양주시(揚州市)], 익주[益州, 지금의 사천성(四川省) 성도시(成都市)]와 같은 새로운 경제의 중심지가 형성되어 고대 중국 경제 중심지가 동에서 남으로 이동하였다. 게다가, 남방 금은광이 대량 개발되면서 초당(初唐) 시기 금은기 제작업이 중앙정부 및 황실에 의해 독점되었던 상황이 타파되자 조정에서는 지방관부에 이어 민간에서도 금은기를 제작할 수 있도록 허가하였다. 이로써 중앙정부, 지방관부, 민간 수공업 공장이 공동으로 금은기를 제작하게 되었으며 특히 동남지역에서 이 같은 경향이 두드러졌다. 이 은쟁반은 당대 홍주 지방관부 수공업 공장에서 제작한 제품 중의 하나이다.

화판형착금화조문은반(花瓣形錯金花鳥紋銀盤)

은(銀) | 당(唐) | 높이 3.2cm 입지름 22.2cm 무게 525g
1977년 서안시 파교구 신축향 조원촌(西安市 瀟橋區 新築鄉 棗園村) 출토

Petal-shaped Gold-inlay Silver Plate with Patterns of Flowers and Birds

Silver | Tang Dynasty(618AD~907AD) | H 3.2cm Mouth D 22.2cm Weight 525g
Excavated from Zaoyuan Village Xinzhu County in Baqiao District, Xi'an in 1977

원형의 은반(銀盤)이다. 밖으로 꺾인 테두리, 각진 입구, 호형(弧形)의 곧은 배, 평평한 바닥을 지녔다. 배는 안쪽의 볼록선으로 오엽화형(五葉花形)을 이루었다. 겉면에는 무늬가 없다. 안쪽 무늬는 3부분으로 나뉘는데 구연(口沿)과 배의 볼록선 부분에는 잎무늬를 새기고 오엽화형으로 나뉜 안쪽에는 날개를 펼치며 날아가는 두 마리 새의 모습을 담았다. 한 마리는 고개를 돌리고 있고 다른 한 마리는 뒤를 쫓고 있다. 새들 사이를 매화로 아름답게 꾸몄다. 안바닥 가장자리에는 화초 다섯 송이를 배치하고 그 사이에 단화(團花)를 새겨 넣었다. 단화 중심에는 꽃 세 송이가 있는데 송이마다 세 꽃잎으로 구성되었다. 바닥과 배가 만나는 볼록선 아래에는 꽃 다섯 송이가 있으며 꽃에 의해 다섯 부분으로 나뉜 테두리에는 각기 큰 단화를 새겨 넣었다. 안바닥 중앙에는 수대(綬帶, 비단끈)를 입에 문 봉황 두 마리가 날개를 펼치고 긴 꽁지를 하느작거리며 선회하고 있다. 문양은 끌로 조각하고 표면에는 금을 입혔다.

봉황은 중국 고대 전설 속의 신조(神鳥)로서 상서(祥瑞)로움을 뜻한다. 당대(唐代) 금은기(金銀器)를 살펴보면, 초기에는 단독으로 서 있는 봉황, 중·후기에는 짝을 이루는 봉황이 많았음을 알 수 있다. 수대문(綬帶紋)은 꽃처럼 맨 끈 모양의 무늬를 말한다. '수(綬)'와 '수(壽)'는 발음이 비슷한데 두 마리의 새가 비단끈을 물고 있는 것은 행복·원만·장수·길상(吉祥)을 뜻한다. 당대 금은기에 사용된 수대문은 주로 9세기 후반기에 유행하였다.

고대 중국의 쟁반은 둥근 모양이 주를 이루었다. 당대 무측천 이후, 중앙아시아·소그디아나(Sogdiana, 중앙아시아의 사라프산 하천과 카슈카 다리아 유역 지방의 옛 이름) 문화의 영향을 받는 한편 중국 전통 풍격을 띤 꽃 모양의 은쟁반이 점차 유행하였는데 일명 해바라기 모양의 은쟁반이라 하였다. 성당(盛唐) 시기 해바라기 모양의 은쟁반 중심에는 짙은 소그디아나의 예술풍격을 띤 단독적인 동물무늬를 볼 수 있었다. 성당 이후에 와서는 그 풍격이 점차 중국화되면서 은쟁반의 입구가 더욱 넓어지고 밖으로 벌어졌으며, 동물과 화초로 쟁반 중심을 장식함으로써 입구가 좁은 소그디아나의 은쟁반과 완연히 구별되었다.

무금무학해당형은반(撫琴舞鶴海棠形銀盤)

은(銀) | 당(唐) | 입지름 21cm 밑지름 15cm 무게 241.5g
1968년 1월 1일 서안시도시건설국(西安市都市建設局)으로부터 넘겨받음

Crabapple-shaped Silver Plate with the Pattern of Figures and a Dancing Crane

Silver | Tang Dynasty(618AD~907AD) | Mouth D 21cm Base D 15cm Weight 241.5g
Transferred by Xi'an Bureau for Municipal Design in 1968

해당화 모양의 은쟁반은 입술이 넓으며 굽은 이미 떨어지고 없다. 안바닥 왼쪽에는 머리를 묶어 올린 일사(逸士)가 교령(交領)의 두루마기를 걸치고 앉아 거문고를 연주하고 있으며, 그 거문고 소리를 엿듣고 있는 동자가 지팡이를 들고 뒤에 서서 공손히 기다리고 있는 장면을 묘사하였다. 일사 맞은편에는 거문고 소리에 맞춰 춤추는 학 한 마리가 있다. 사방에 돌산을 배치하고 훤초(萱草)로 빈 공간을 채웠고 가장자리에는 능형(菱形) 기하(幾何)무늬 및 여의(如意) 구름무

늬를 각각 한 줄씩 둘렀다. 입술 부분에는 석류, 선도(仙桃)와 절지화(折枝花)를 사이사이 새겨 넣었다. 추엽(鎚揲) 및 끌로 조각하는 기법을 겸해 사용함으로써 이와 같은 무늬를 연출할 수 있었다.

일사, 동자, 거문고와 주변의 학, 석류, 선도, 절지화가 어우러져 아름다운 은일고사도(隱逸高士圖)가 그려졌다. 거문고, 바둑, 서예, 그림은 문인 사대부가 신심을 닦고 교양을 쌓는 수단이며, 선도는 중국 전통 문양에서 무병장수의 상징이고 휘영청 밝은 달 아래 솔바람이 불고 하얀 구름 아래 학이 노니는 모습은 도가(道家)에서 추구하는 자유로운 생활의 반영이다.

초당(初唐)과 성당(盛唐) 시기에는 분방하고 호방한 사회적 분위기의 영향을 받아 사람들은 너그럽고 진취적이며 자신감이 넘치는 태도를 갖게 되었으며 몸과 마음을 다해 충실한 삶을 살았다. 안사의 난(安史之亂, 755~763년) 및 이후의 사회동란으로 말미암아 중국 전통 사회의 정치체계가 동요되고 사람들의 이상과 생활정취가 무너졌다. 그 후, 당(唐)문화에서 송(宋)문화로 전환되면서 중국 전통문화는 점차 성당 시기의 개방적인 분위기에서 폐쇄형으로 변화되고 문인 사대부들은 적극적으로 사회와 융합하던 태도에서 소극적인 태도로 바뀌어 사회를 등지게 되었다. 사람들의 심미 정취도 번잡함을 피해 조용한 곳을 찾아 마음을 가라앉히고 도를 닦아 세속에 물들지 않은 고상한 정신세계를 추구하는 쪽으로 변하게 되었다.

화판형철화은반(花瓣形凸花銀盤)

은(銀) | 당(唐) | 높이 1cm 입지름 15.5cm 무게 (1) 207g (2) 182g
1972년 서안시 안탑구 곡강향 강지촌(西安市 雁塔區 曲江鄉 江池村) 출토

Petal-shaped Protruding Silver Plate

Silver | Tang Dynasty(618AD~907AD) | H 1cm Mouth D 15.5cm Weight (1) 207g (2) 182g
Excavated from Qujiangchi Village Qujiang County Yanta District, Xi'an in 1972

은회색을 띠는 둥글납작한 모양의 은쟁반 2점이다.
입술이 넓고 테두리는 밖으로 꺾이고 운두가 낮고 밑
굽이 평평하다. 안바닥에는 금을 입힌, 화초 한 그루를
새겼다. 매화 네 송이 가운데 가지 끝머리의 큼직한 꽃
잎 5개를 가진 매화는 활짝 핀 모습인데 안바닥 한복판
에 놓여 있다. 나머지 꽃봉오리 세 송이는 금방이라도
피어날 것만 같다. 모형주조법(模型鑄造法)으로 만든
쟁반 내측에는 화초무늬가 있고, 금을 입힌 그 표면이
약간 볼록하고 매끌매끌하다. 문양들은 먼저 금을 입
힌 다음 끌로 조각하여 만들었다. 뒷면은 민무늬이고
오목하게 들어갔다. 그 어떠한 가공 흔적이 없는 것으
로 보아 다른 물품에 상감(象嵌)했던 것이었음을 알 수
있다.

(1)

(2)

056

철화은반(凸花銀盤)

은(銀) | 당(唐) | 입지름 15.5cm 무게 241.3g
1972년 서안시 안탑구 곡강향 서곡강지촌(西安市 雁塔區 曲江鄉 西曲江池村) 출토

Silver Plate with Protruding Flowers

Silver | Tang Dynasty(618AD~907AD) | Mouth D 15.5cm Weight 241.3g
Excavated from Qujiangchi Village Qujiang County Yanta District, Xi'an in 1972

밖으로 젖혀진 테두리, 호형(弧形)의 배, 낮은 운두를 가진 둥글납작한 모양의 은쟁반이다. 안바닥에는 보상화(寶相花)를 새겼는데 꽃잎은 매우 크며 꽃봉오리 2개는 막 터질 듯이 부풀어 있다. 추엽(鎚揲) 기법으로 만든 문양 위에 금을 입혔다. 겉면에는 무늬가 없다. 이 쟁반은 앞서 소개한 두 은쟁반과 똑같은 지점인, 당대(唐代) 곡강(曲江) 유적지인 서안(西安) 남교(南郊) 곡강지촌(曲江池村)에서 출토되었다. 당대의 장안성(長安城) 동남쪽에 위치한 곡강(曲江)은 진한(秦漢)시대 황실의 내원이었다. 당왕조(唐王朝) 때 이곳은 이름난 명소로 과거에 급제한 자를 위해 연회를 베푸는 장소로 사용되기도 하였는데 3점의 은쟁반은 아마도 연회를 베풀 당시 부주의로 강에 떨어뜨렸던 것으로 추측된다.

057

고족은소반(高足銀小盤)

은(銀) | 당(唐) | 높이 2.73cm 지름 4.6cm 굽지름 2.29cm 무게 27g
2002년 서안시 장안구 축촌향 양촌(西安市 長安區 祝村鄉 羊村) 출토

Small Silver Plate with a High Pedestal

Silver | Tang Dynasty(618AD~907AD) | H 2.73cm D 4.6cm Base D 2.29cm Weight 27g
Excavated from Yangcun Village Zhucun County Chang'an District, Xi'an in 2002

벌어진 입구, 경사진 얕은 배, 평평한 밑굽에 나팔형의 높은 굽다리를 갖춘 소반(小盤)이다. 표면에는 원래 금을 입혔으나 대부분 벗겨졌다.

반(盤)은 물이나 음식을 담는 데 쓰이는 그릇으로 도자기·금은·동 등 재료로 만들어진다. 상(商)나라 초기에 나타난 반은 배가 둥글고 굽은 있으나 고리가 없는 형태가 보편적이다. 흔히 그릇 안쪽에 귀어문(龜魚紋)을 새기고 일부는 입구 부분에 '서 있는 새' 모양의 장식품을 부착하기도 한다. 서주(西周)~춘추(春秋)시대에는 고리, 귀때 및 굽이나 발 3개를 갖춘 형태가 많

았다. 전국(戰國)시대에는 직사각형으로 된 것이 있었는가 하면 입술이 넓고 밑굽이 둥글며 고리가 없는 것도 있었다. 남북조(南北朝)시대에 와서는 청자쟁반이 성행하였는데 불교의 영향을 받아 연꽃무늬 청자쟁반이 주를 이루었다. 그 후, 주로 청자쟁반을 사용함과 동시에 다른 재료로 된 것도 함께 사용하였다. 수(隋)~당대(唐代) 중기에는 대외 정치, 경제, 문화교류가 전에 없이 활발해지면서 강렬한 이국적 풍격을 띤 쟁반들이 제작되었다. '안사의 난(安史之亂)' 이후, 대외 문화교류가 여전히 빈번하였지만 중국 전통문화는 외적인 발전으로부터 내적인 발전으로 변화하면서 쟁반을 포함한 모든 그릇에서 외래문화 요소가 점차 줄어들고 중국 전통문화의 영향력이 점차 커졌다. 오대(五代) 이후에는 쟁반의 모양 및 장식이 완전히 중국화되었으며 송원(宋元)과 명청(明淸) 시기를 거쳐 쟁반의 종류 및 장식이 더욱 다양해지고 장식용 쟁반 및 그와 짝을 이루는 받침대도 나타났다.

이 쟁반은 조형이 수대(隋代)의 고족자반(高足瓷盤, 높은 굽다리를 가진 사기쟁반)과 매우 흡사한데 도자기 모양을 본떠 만든 것이다. 이는 초당(初唐) 시기의 금은그릇이 아직 독립적인 발전단계에 이르지 못하였음을 말해 준다.

058

사산식팔곡은장배 (薩珊式八曲銀長杯)

은(銀) | 당(唐) | 높이 2.65cm 지름 5.25~8.96cm 무게 44g
2002년 서안시 장안구 축촌향 양촌(西安市 長安區 祝村鄉 羊村) 출토

Eight-petaled Long Silver Cup with Sassanian Style

Silver | Tang Dynasty(618AD~907AD) | H 2.65cm D 5.25~8.96cm Weight 44g
Excavated from Yangcun Village Zhucun County Chang'an District, Xi'an in 2002

팔엽화형(八葉花形)의 타원형 민무늬 은장배(銀長杯)이다. 운두가 높은 편이고 꽃잎들은 서로 대칭되며 가로 방향으로 층차 구분이 나 있다. 밑굽까지 미치지 않은 외벽의 곡선은 안쪽으로 오목하게 들어갔으며 굽은 떨어지고 없다.

이 장배는 볼록선이 뚜렷하고 타원형의 굽이 있는 등 페르시아 사산왕조(Sasan王朝, 226~642년)의 풍격이 짙다. 해당화 모양의 은배(銀杯)는 다곡장배(多曲長杯)라 불리기도 하는데 3~8세기 중엽 이란 고원에서 유행하였던 은잔의 일종으로 그 형태는 길쭉한 타원형이고 기벽은 꽃잎 형상이다. 이 시기의 이란 고원은 페르시아 사산왕조의 통치하에 있었기 때문에 이와 같은 은잔을 일명 사산식다곡장배(薩山式多曲長杯)라고도 한다. 4세기 말에 장배의 제작기술이 중국에 유입되면서 8개 또는 12개 꽃잎 모양의 볼록선이 선명한 장배가 나타났다. 7세기 후반기에는 다곡장배가 점차 중국화되어 화판(花瓣)이 그리 뚜렷하지 않고 요철이 심하지 않았다. 8세기 중엽 이후에 와서는 꽃잎 모양의 기벽(器壁)이 매끈해지고 볼록선은 종적으로 분포되고 꽃잎 개수가 4개로 줄어들었는데 원래의 기하학적인 꽃잎무늬를 점차 사실적인 식물형태로 표현함으로써 완전히 중국화된 예술적 효과를 나타냈다.

059

단환타원형은배 (單環橢圓形銀杯)

은(銀) | 당(唐) | 높이 4.48cm 입지름 15.2×10.1cm 밑지름 10.1×6.2cm 무게 172g
2002년 서안시 장안구 축촌향 양촌(西安市 長安區 祝村鄉 羊村) 출토

Oval Silver Cup with Single Ring

Silver | Tang Dynasty(618AD~907AD) | H 4.48cm Mouth D 15.2×10.1cm Base D 10.1×6.2cm Weight 172g
Excavated from Yangcun Village Zhucun County Chang'an District, Xi'an in 2002

은회색을 띠는 민무늬 은배(銀杯)이다. 길쭉한 타원형의 몸체에 벌어진 입구, 호형(弧形)의 배, 평평한 밑굽을 갖추었다. 입구와 밑굽도 모두 타원형이다. 몸체의 지름이 긴 쪽 목에는 고리 모양의 손잡이가 달려 있다.

은발(銀鉢)

은(銀) | 당(唐) | 높이 7cm 입지름 15.6cm 무게 269g
1964년 서안시문물관리위원회(西安市文物管理委員會) 수집

Silver Bowl

Silver | Tang Dynasty(618AD~907AD) | H 7cm Mouth D 15.6cm Weight 269g
Collected by Xi'an Culture Relic Administration Committee in 1964

　벌어진 입구, 호형(弧形)의 깊은 배, 둥근 밑굽을 갖춘 은회색을 띠는 민무늬 발(鉢)이다. 발은 음식을 담는 데 쓰이는 완(碗)의 일종으로 신석기시대에 처음 나타났다. 초기에는 도자기만 사용하였으나 문명 시대에 접어들면서 동(銅)이나 철(鐵)도 사용하였다. 동한(東漢) 초기, 불교가 중국에 유입되면서 법기(法器)도 함께 전해졌다. 형태상 중국에서 만든 이러한 완과 불교도들이 사용하는 발(鉢)이 유사하므로 범어(梵語)의 '발다라(鉢多羅)'라는 명칭을 그대로 옮겨 부르기도 하고 '발'이라 약칭하였다. 범어 '발'은 '응기(應器)', '응량기(應量器)'를 뜻하므로 '바리때[鉢器]'라고도 한다. 도자기나 철로 된 것이 많았으며 옥, 마노(瑪瑙), 금은(金銀)으로 된 것도 있었으나 진귀하고 수가 적었다.

매화식은배(梅花飾銀杯)

은(銀) | 당(唐) | 전체높이 5.94cm 입지름 4.97cm 밑지름 2.8cm 무게 64g
서안시 장안구 축촌향 양촌(西安市 長安區 祝村鄉 羊村) 출토

Silver Cup With Plum-blossom Patterns

Silver | Tang Dynasty(618AD~907AD) | H 5.94cm Mouth D 4.97cm Base D 2.8cm Weight 64g
Excavated from Yangcun Village Zhucun County Chang'an District, Xi'an

　표면이 전체적으로 은회색을 띠는 은배(銀杯)이다. 입구가 밖으로 벌어지고, 둥근 몸체는 어깨에서 급히 좁아졌다가 서서히 넓어진다. 위에는 가운데가 융기된 뚜껑, 밑굽에는 나팔형의 굽이 달려 있다. 뚜껑 중심에는 6개 꽃잎의 형상으로 된 매화 장식이 부착되어 있는데 그 중앙에는 우산 모양의 꼭지가 있다. 넓은 가장자리의 아래쪽에는 거꾸로 된 나발 모양의 턱을 둠으로써 아래 그릇과 만나게 하였다.

062

속요은배(束腰銀杯)

은(銀) | 당(唐) | 높이 2.4cm 입지름 5.36cm 밑지름 2.89cm 무게 41g
2002년 서안시 장안구 축촌향 양촌(西安市 長安區 祝村鄉 羊村) 출토

Silver Cup with Thin Middle

Silver | Tang Dynasty(618AD~907AD) | H 2.4cm Mouth D 5.36cm Base D 2.89cm Weight 41g
Excavated from Yangcun Village Zhucun County Chang'an District, Xi'an in 2002

　벌어진 입구로부터 아래로 내려오면서 서서히 좁아지는 민무늬 은배(銀杯)이다. 아랫배에는 가로로 꺾인 부분이 있다. 둥근 밑굽에는 나팔형의 굽이 달려
있었으나 지금은 떨어지고 없다.

　이 은배는 조형상 성당(盛唐) 시기의 배(杯)와 판이하나 수대(隋代) 말기~당대(唐代) 초기의 도자기완(陶瓷器碗), 고족배(高足杯), 고족반(高足盤)과 비슷
한 풍격을 지닌다. 이러한 조형 풍격은 당시의 식습관과 밀접한 관련이 있다. 당대 초기의 사람들은 바닥에 자리를 깔고 앉는 것에 익숙해 비교적 낮은 탁자를
사용하였다. 따라서 배(杯), 완(碗)을 제작할 때 이러한 생활방식 및 환경에 따라 제작할 수밖에 없었다. 배는 손에 들고 사용하므로 각진 형태가 사람들의 시각
효과를 만족시킬뿐더러 안정감, 풍만감, 상승감을 준다. 현종(玄宗) 천보(天寶, 742~756년) 연간 이후, 실내 진열품에 비교적 높은 탁자와 의자가 생겨남으로써
음식기에 일련의 변화가 생겼다. 배, 완 등 그릇의 배부[腹部]가 부드러운 곡선 모양으로 변화되어 시각적인 편안함을 주었다.

063

고족소은배(高足小銀杯)

은(銀) | 당(唐) | 높이 2.25cm 입지름 5.18cm 무게 23g
2002년 서안시 장안구 축촌향 양촌(西安市 長安區 祝村鄉 羊村) 출토

Small silver Cup with High Pedestal

Silver | Tang Dynasty(618AD~907AD) | H 2.25cm Mouth D 5.18cm Weight 23g
Excavated from Yangcun Village Zhucun County Chang'an District, Xi'an in 2002

　전체가 약간 동황색을 띠는 민무늬 은배(銀杯)이다. 입구는 밖으로
벌어지고 윗배에서 좁아지다가 아랫배로 내려오면서 다시 넓어진다.
평평한 밑굽 아래에는 나팔형의 낮은 굽이 있다. 전국(戰國) 시기에 처
음 나타난 고족배(高足杯)는 입구가 세워지거나 벌어지고 기벽(器壁)
이 곧으며 원통형의 깊은 배, 둥근 밑굽, 나팔형의 높은 굽을 지닌 형태
가 많았다. 이 은배는 조형적으로 전통적인 중국 고족배와 달리, 6세기
동로마제국 및 유럽 흑해 북쪽 연안의 것과 유사해 동로마제국의 것을
본떠 만든 공예품으로 추정된다.

064

사녀수렵문팔판단병은배(仕女狩獵紋八瓣單柄銀杯)

은(銀) | 당(唐) | 높이 4.2cm 지름 9cm 무게 183g
1983년 서안시 미앙구 대명궁향 마기채(西安市 未央區 大明宮鄕 馬旗寨) 출토

Eight-petaled and Single-handled Silver Cup with
Maiden Hunting Patterns

Silver | Tang Dynasty(618AD~907AD) | H 4.2cm D 9cm | Weight 183g
Excavated from Maqizhai Village Daminggong County Weiyang District, Xi'an in 1983

연주(聯珠) 모양의 밖으로 꺾인 테두리, 호형(弧形)의 배[腹]를 지닌 팔엽화형(八葉花形) 은배(銀杯)이다. 밑부분의 연꽃은 오목선에 의해 나뉜 윗부분의 꽃잎들을 받쳐 준다. 밑굽에는 워낙 굽이 달려 있었으나 떨어지고 없다. 꽃잎 모양의 삼각형 손잡이는 그 외곽을 연주 모양으로 장식하고 여의(如意) 구름 모양의 손가락 받침대를 입구와 수평이 되게 부착하였다. 받침대 중심에는 꽃사슴무늬를 새기고 손잡이 아래쪽에는 배와 용접되어 있는 갈고리 모양의 장식이 있다. 안바닥에는 해수서수유어도(海水瑞獸游魚圖), 외벽에는 사이사이 남자수렵도(男子狩獵圖)와 사녀희악도(仕女戱樂圖)를 새겨 넣었다. 외벽의 오목선 부분은 버들잎 무늬로 장식하였다. 이 은배는 추엽(鎚揲) 기법으로 만들어졌는데 꽃무늬는 평참(平鏨, 끌로 반듯하게 새김)하고 바탕에는 어자문(魚

子紋)을 새겼으며 무늬마다 금을 입혔다. 문양이 정교하고 아름다우며 공예기술 또한 뛰어나 성당(盛唐) 시기 금은기(金銀器) 중 수작으로 손꼽힌다.

사슴은 고대에 선한 동물로 여겨졌다. 사슴무늬가 당대(唐代) 금은기 중 주로 식기에 장식된 것은 당시 제도와 연관되는 것으로 추측된다. 과거제는 수왕조(隋王朝) 때 실시되어 당왕조(唐王朝) 때에 와서는 선비들이 과거급제하면 향음주례(鄕飮酒禮)를 베풀었다. 따라서 『시경(詩經)』의 「녹명(鹿鳴)」을 녹명연(鹿鳴宴)이라고 부르기도 하였다. 그러므로 이 배에 새겨진 사슴무늬 역시 도공의 아름다운 소망을 표현한 것이다.

손잡이가 달린 꽃잎 모양의 은기(銀器)는 중앙아시아 · 소그디아나(Sogdiana, 중앙아시아의 샤라프샨 하천과 카슈카 다리아 유역 지방의 옛 이름) 예술품 가운데 하나로 동서양 무역 교류가 빈번해지면서 초당(初唐) 시기 중국에 유입되었다. 7~8세기 전반기의 은배는 8개 꽃잎 또는 항아리 모양의 몸체에 받침대가 있는 손잡이를 갖추었다. 8세기 중엽 이후에 몸체는 원통형이나 밑굽이 둥근 사발 모양으로 변화되고 형태가 가늘고 길던 데서 굵고 짧아져 입구의 지름이 운두보다 커졌다. 이는 당대 문화가 소그디아나 기물(器物)의 조형에 깊은 영향을 미쳤음을 말해 준다.

065

유금용문타은배(鎏金龍紋橢銀杯)

은(銀) | 당(唐) | 길이 12.7cm 너비 7.1cm 높이 4cm 무게 114g
1966년 서안(西安) 벽돌공장에서 출토

Oval-shaped Gilt Silver Cup with Dragon Pattern

Silver | Tang Dynasty(618AD~907AD) | L 12.7cm W 7.1cm H 4cm Weight 114g
Excavated from Xi'an Brickyard in 1966

타원형 몸체에 벌어진 입구, 볼록한 배를 지닌 은배(銀杯)이다. 입구는 불규칙적인 팔엽화형(八葉花形)으로 장식되었다. 내벽은 가로로 된 곡선 모양의 볼록선에 의해 5개 부분으로 나뉘었다. 위쪽의 대칭되는 부분에는 선산(仙山)이 띄엄띄엄 분포된 넘실거리는 파도무늬를 새기고, 가운데 대칭되는 부분에는 어자문(魚子紋)을 바탕에 시문(試紋)하고 선산, 연꽃, 덩굴무늬를 새겼으며, 안바닥에는 파도가 출렁이는 바다 속에서 용의 머리에 물고기 몸체를 한 마갈(摩羯) 두 마리가 서로 마주하고 연꽃을 노니는 도안을 새겨 넣었다. 외벽 역시 5개 부분으로 나뉜다. 위쪽에는 산중을 달리는 꽃사슴 한 마리와 사자 한 마리를, 가운데 부분에는 연꽃 주위를 사이에 둔 학 두 마리가 각각 수대(綬帶, 비단끈)를 물고 날개를 펼치며 하늘로 날아오르는 도안을 새겼다. 타원형 밑굽으로 대칭을 이루는 아랫부분 양측에는 화초 속에서 너울너울 춤추는 여인의 모습을 담았다. 여인은 교령(交領)에 좁은 소매로 된 옷을 입었는데 어깨에 걸친 긴 띠가 바람에 나부낀다. 굽은 일부가 떨어져 나가고 없다. 떨어진 부분은 타원형을 이루며 남은 부분에는 전지활엽화문(纏枝闊葉花紋)이 새겨져 있다. 이 은배는 모형주조법(模型鑄造法)으로 형태를 만든 다음 끌로 새기거나 추엽(鎚揲) 기법으로 가공, 제작하여 무늬를 새겨 넣었다. 비록 형태상 짙은 페르시아 사산왕조(Sasan王朝, 226~642년)의 예술풍격을 띠나 무늬에 나타난 회화풍격은 중국 전통문화의 범주에 속한다.

'綬(수)'와 '壽(수)'는 발음이 같아 '학 두 마리가 함께 수대를 무는 것'은 '행복하게 오래 살다'라는 의미를 담고 있다.

066

해당형마갈은배(海棠形摩羯銀杯)

은(銀) | 당(唐) | 높이 3.2cm 입지름 13.6cm 밑지름 7cm 무게 87.8g
1968년 서안시도시건설국(西安市都市建設局)으로부터 넘겨받음

Crabapple-shaped Silver Cup with
Cetacean Pattern

Silver | Tang Dynasty(618AD~907AD) | H 3.2cm Mouth D 13.6cm
Base D 7cm Weight 87.8g
Transferred by Xi'an Bureau for Municipal Design in 1968

살짝 벌어진 입구, 호형(弧形)의 배[腹], 둥근 밑굽을 갖춘 은배(銀杯)이다. 권족(圈足)은 떨어지고 없다. 입구와 배는 타원형을 이룬다. 가장 길고 짧은 지름
에 의해 나뉘는 입구의 네 부분에는 각각 연잎 반쪽을 새겼다. 연잎의 가장자리가 바닥에 펼쳐진 연잎과 배부에서 맞닿는데 연잎무늬는 율동감이 넘치며 촘촘
한 잎맥들의 선 흐름은 거침없이 표현되었다. 안바닥 중앙에는 마카라(Makara) 두 마리가 볼록한 화염 모양의 진주를 에워싸고 희롱하는 모습을 새겼다. 형태
및 문양은 추엽(錘揲) 기법으로 만들고 꽃무늬는 끌로 평평하게 새겼다. 금을 입힌 안쪽과 달리 겉면은 민무늬이다.

연잎무늬는 세세한 잎맥까지 사실적으로 표현하였다. 연꽃이 달린 것도 있는데 주로 9세기 말에 유행하였다. 마카라는 고대 인도 불교에서 전하는 동물로
긴 코, 예리한 이빨, 물고기의 몸에 꼬리가 달렸는데 일명 마가라(摩伽羅, 摩迦羅)라고도 하며 중국어로 고래(鯨魚), 자라(巨鼈)로 번역된다. 『현응음의(玄應音
義)』에는 "마갈어(摩羯魚)라 불리기도 하는 마가라어(摩伽羅魚)를 정확히 마가라어(摩迦羅魚)라 하며 바다 속의 왕인 고래를 일컫는다"라고 기록되어 있다. 물
속의 정령이자 생명의 근본이라 여겨진 마카라는 고대 인도의 전통문양인데 고대 인도의 조각 작품이나 사원 건축 탑문을 그린 회화 작품에서 그 모습을 찾아
볼 수 있다. 불교의 유입과 더불어 중국의 석굴(石窟), 금은기(金銀器)에서도 마갈무늬를 볼 수 있었으며 물고기 형상과 비슷한 무늬는 만당(晚唐) 시기에 주로
사용되었다. 호형의 배, 둥근 밑굽을 갖춘 은장배(銀長杯)는 페르시아 사산(Sasan) 은장배가 중국으로 들어와 변형된 형태로 배가 더욱 깊고 나팔형의 권족이
달렸다. 표면에는 일반적으로 연잎무늬를 새긴다. 이 은배는 중국, 인도, 사산 문화가 모두 담겨 있는데 정치 · 경제 · 문화 교류의 산물이다.

103

해당형황리화조은배 (海棠形黃鸝花鳥銀杯)

은(銀) | 당(唐) | 높이 3cm 입지름 13cm 밑지름 10.2cm 무게 122g
1968년 서안시도시건설국(西安市都市建設局)으로부터 넘겨받음

Crabapple-shaped Silver Cup with Chinese
Oriole and Flowers

Silver | Tang Dynasty(618AD~907AD) | H 3cm Mouth D 13cm Base D
10.2cm Weight 122g
Transferred by Xi'an Bureau for Municipal Design in 1968

해당화 모양의 몸체와 굽에 밖으로 약간 벌어진 입구를 갖춘 은
배(銀杯)이다. 호형(弧形)의 벽은 아래로 내려오면서 서서히 좁아
진다. 은배는 추엽(錘揲) 기법으로 성형하고 무늬를 반듯하게 한
뒤에 금을 입혔다. 표면 전체에 어자문(魚子紋)을 시문(試紋)하였
다. 안바닥 중앙에는 여의운문(如意云紋) 다섯 개가 장식되어 있
고 그 사이를 기러기 두 마리가 날고 있다. 둘레는 타원형의 연판
문(蓮瓣文)으로 장식하였다. 기러기 한 마리는 목을 빼들고 앞을
바라보며 다른 한 마리는 고개를 돌려 뒤를 바라본다. 내벽 가운데
에는 여의운문 한 줄, 안쪽 입구에는 파식해당문(破式海棠紋, 해당
화의 일부분을 취한 무늬)을 둘렀다. 외벽에는 절지화(折枝花)무늬를
촘촘하게 새기고, 볼록선에 의해 나뉜 부분마다 다양한 모습의 꾀
꼬리를 생동감 있게 표현하였다. 앞을 바라보며 나는 듯한 모습을
한 지름이 짧은 쪽의 꾀꼬리는 땅으로 내려앉으려는 것 같고 날개
를 모으고 고개를 돌린, 긴지름 쪽의 꾀꼬리는 꽃 속을 거니는 듯
하다. 꾀꼬리의 아래위에는 연판문을, 굽에는 파도무늬를 둘렀다.
문양이 복잡하고 세밀하여 아름답다.

068

해당형봉조문은배(海棠形鳳鳥紋銀杯)

은(銀) | 당(唐) | 높이 4.9cm 입 긴지름 14.8cm 입 짧은지름 8cm 밑굽 긴지름 7.9cm 밑굽 짧은지름 5cm 무게 168g
1975년 서안시 미앙구(西安市 未央區) 출토

Crabapple-shaped Silver Cup with Phoenix Patterns

Silver | Tang Dynasty(618AD~907AD) | H 4.9cm Mouth D 8~14.8cm Base D 5~7.9cm Weight 168g
Excavated from Weiyang District, Xi'an in 1975

   밖으로 살짝 젖혀진 테두리, 깊은 호형(弧形)의 배[腹], 평평한 밑굽, 높은 굽을 지닌 은배(銀杯)이다. 전반적인 형태는 해당화 모양인데 추엽(錘揲) 기법으로 만들어졌으며 무늬는 끌로 조각하고 표면에는 금을 입혔다. 민무늬인 겉면과 달리 안쪽에는 여러 가지 무늬를 새겼다. 안쪽 입구에는 꽃잎무늬 한 줄을 두르고 내벽의 볼록선에 의해 나뉘는 네 부분에는 각각 단화 한 떨기를 장식하였다. 안쪽 바닥에는 화판문(花瓣文)을 한 바퀴 두르고 그 안쪽에는 꼬리를 물고 나는 봉황 두 마리를 새겼다. 남은 부분은 덩굴무늬로 장식하였다.

'가아(哥兒)' 해당형소면은배(海棠形素面銀杯)

은(銀) | 당(唐) | 높이 3.8cm 입지름 13×8.5cm 무게 114g
1966년 서안시 신성구(西安市 新城區) 서안통신 케이블공장에서 출토

Plain-surfaced and Crabapple-shaped Silver Cup with 'Ge Er' Inscription

Silver | Tang Dynasty(618AD~907AD) | H 3.8cm Mouth D 13×8.5cm Weight 114g
Excavated from Xi'an Cable Works in Xincheng District, Xi'an in 1966

벌어진 입구, 둥근 밑굽을 갖춘 해당화 모양의 민무늬 은배(銀 杯)이다. 외벽은 볼록선에 의해 꽃잎 4개로 나뉜다. 해서체(楷書 體)로 된 "哥兒(가아)" 두 글자가 새겨져 있는 밑굽에는 해당화 모양의 굽이 있었으나 떨어지고 없다.

(1)

(2)

소면은시(素面銀匙)

은(銀) | 당(唐) | 길이 (1) 12.3cm (2) 16.67cm 무게 (1) 11g (2) 25g
2002년 서안시 장안구 축촌향 양촌(西安市 長安區 祝村鄉 羊村) 출토

Plain-surfaced Silver Spoon

Silver | Tang Dynasty(618AD~907AD) | L (1) 12.3cm (2) 16.67cm Weight (1) 11g (2) 25g
Excavated from Yangcun Village Zhucun County Chang'an District, Xi'an in 2002

은숟가락 두 점이다. 하나는 우묵한 시면(匙面)에 길고 납작하며 구부정한 자루가 달려 있다. 자루의 한쪽은 조금 넓으며 다른 한쪽은 조금 좁다. 다른 하나 도 역시 자루가 길고 구부정한데 끄트머리 쪽을 향하는 부분은 사능형(四棱形)에서 끝부분에 이르러 삼각기둥을 이루며 넓고 평평한 다른 한쪽은 우묵한 타원 형의 시면과 연결되었다.

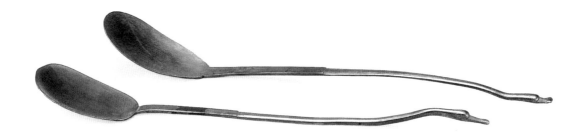

071

아수장병은시 (鵝首長柄銀匙)

은(銀) | 당(唐) | 길이 25.6cm 무게 82g
1979년 서안시 파교구 홍경진 전왕촌(西安市 灞橋區 洪慶鎭 田王村) 출토

Long-handled Silver Spoon with Goose Head

Silver | Tang Dynasty(618AD~907AD) | L 25.6cm Weight 82g
Excavated from Tianwang Village Hongqing Town Baqiao District, Xi'an in 1979

은숟가락의 시면(匙面)은 우묵한 타원형이며 자루의 한쪽 끝에는 거위 머리 모양을 하고 있다. 시면과 가까운 자루 부분은 납작하며 파도모양으로 구부러지며 거위 머리 부분까지 이르는데 거위 부리는 납작하며 코가 높고 눈이 작으며 동그랗다.

072

압수은시 (鴨首銀匙)

은(銀) | 당(唐) | 길이 26.5cm 무게 48.3g
1964년 서안시문물관리위원회(西安市文物管理委員會) 수집

Silver Spoon with Duck Head

Silver | Tang Dynasty(618AD~907AD) | L 26.5cm Weight 48.3g
Collected by Xi'an Culture Relic Administration Committee in 1964

우묵한 타원형 시면(匙面)에 길고 구부정한 자루가 달려 있는 은숟가락이다. 시면과 가까운 자루 부분은 아래위가 모두 평평하고 끄트머리를 향한 곳은 윗부분이 조금 휘었고 아랫부분은 평평하다. 자루 끝은 오리 머리 모양인데 기다란 부리, 높은 코, 작고 동그란 눈을 가졌다. 숟가락 표면은 은회색을 띠며 문양은 모두 음각하였다.

장병소면은시(長柄素面銀匙)

은(銀) | 당(唐) | 길이 32cm 무게 29g
1974년 서안시문물관리위원회(西安市文物管理委員會) 수집

Planin-surfaced Silver Spoon with a Long Handle

Silver | Tang Dynasty(618AD~907AD) | L 32cm Weight 29g
Collected by Xi'an Culture Relic Administration Committee in 1974

민무늬 숟가락은 은회색을 띤다. 시면(匙面)은 우묵한 타원형이며 자루는 길고 납작하며 약간 굽은 형태이다. 시면과 이어진 부분은 넓은 편이고 중간 부분은 삼각형에 가까우며 끄트머리 쪽의 허리 부분이 약간 튀어나왔다. 자루 끄트머리의 뒷부분에 해서체(楷書體)로 "吉才(길재)"란 두 글자를 음각(陰刻)하였다.

(1)

(2)

소면은쾌(素面銀筷)

은(銀) | 당(唐) | 길이 (1) 29.2cm (2) 19cm 무게 (1) 26.2g (2) 19.4g
1974년 서안시문물관리위원회(西安市文物管理委員會) 수집

Plain-surfaced Silver Chopsticks

Silve | Tang Dynasty(618AD~907AD) | L (1) 29.2cm (2) 19cm Weight (1) 26.2g (2) 19.4g
Collected by Xi'an Culture Relic Administration Committee in 1974

은회색을 띠는 기둥 모양의 민무늬 젓가락이다. 전체는 가늘고 길며 오리 부리 모양의 한쪽은 굵은 편이고 다른 한쪽은 가는 편이다.

젓가락은 일찍이 '저(箸)' 또는 '근(筋)'이라고 하였으며 명대(明代)에 와서는 '쾌(筷)'라고 부르기 시작했다. 식사도구로 음식을 집어 먹는 데 쓰인다. 성당(盛唐) 시기의 지배계급들은 고귀한 신분을 나타내기 위해 화려하고 사치스러운 식사도구를 사용하였는데 이 때문에 실용적인 금은식기가 날로 성행하였다. 『개원천보유사(開元天寶遺事)』에는 현종(玄宗) 때 "송경(宋璟)이 재상으로 있을 때 조야(朝野)에서는 모두 미를 추구하였는데 봄 연회에서 황제는 자기가 쓰던 금젓가락을 내시한테 명하여 송경에게 하사하였다"는 기록이 있다. 초당(初唐) 시기의 금은젓가락은 길이가 짧은 편이었으나 성당 시기부터 점차 길어져 30센티미터에 달하는 것도 있었다.

075

환저소은분(圜底小銀盆)

은(銀) | 당(唐) | 높이 1.85cm 입지름 6.1cm 무게 33g
2002년 서안시 장안구 축촌향 양촌(西安市 長安區 祝村鄉 羊村) 출토

Small Silver Basin with Round Bottom

Silver | Tang Dynasty(618AD~907AD) | H 1.85cm Mouth D 6.1cm
Weight 33g
Excavated from Yangcun Village Zhucun County Chang'an District,
Xi'an in 2002

열은 동황색을 띠는 민무늬 은분(銀盆)이다. 입구가 곧고 배[腹]는 호형(弧形)으로 되었으며 밑굽이 둥글고 운두가 낮다.

분(盆)은 물을 담는 그릇이다. 고대 사람들이 제사를 지낼 때 피를 담는 그릇으로 쓰였으나 후에는 세척 그릇으로 많이 사용되었다. 도자기나 청동기로 만든 것이 주를 이룬 반면에 금은제(金銀製)는 수가 적었다. 상주(商周)시대에 처음 나타나 한대(漢代) 이후에는 철제품이 널리 유행하였다.

076

평저소은분(平底小銀盆)

은(銀) | 당(唐) | 높이 2.92cm 입지름 6.66cm 밑지름 2.95cm 무게 58g
2002년 서안시 장안구 축촌향 양촌(西安市 長安區 祝村鄉 羊村) 출토

Small Silver Basin with Flat Bottom

Silver | Tang Dynasty(618AD~907AD) | H 2.92cm Mouth D 6.66cm
Base D 2.95cm Weight 58g
Excavated from Yangcun Village Zhucun County Chang'an District,
Xi'an in 2002

동황빛이 살짝 감도는 민무늬 은분(銀盆)이다. 벌어진 입구는 각지며 배[腹]는 약간 호형(弧形)이고 밑굽은 평평하다.

화조접문은분(花鳥蝶紋銀盆)

은(銀) | 당(唐) | 높이 7.1cm 입지름 27.5cm 밑지름 17.6cm 무게 440.5g
1972년 서안시문물관리위원회(西安市文物管理委員會) 수집

Silver Basin with Patterns of Flower, Bird and Butterfly

Silver | Tang Dynasty(618AD~907AD) | H 7.1cm Mouth D 27.5cm Base D 17.6cm Weight 440.5g
Collected by Xi'an Culture Relic Administration Committee in 1972

벌어진 입구는 조금 각지고 배[腹]는 곧고 비스듬하며 밑굽이 평평한 은분(銀盆)이다. 오엽화형(五葉花形) 입구에는 나풀거리는 잎 무늬, 입구와 배가 인접한 곳에는 관현문(寬弦紋)을 둘렀다. 내벽은 볼록선에 의해 5개 부분으로 나뉜다. 부분마다에는 활짝 피어난 화초 위에서 쉬고 있는 새 한 마리의 모습을 담았으며 볼록선 위쪽에는 나비무늬, 아래쪽에는 새싹을 새겼다. 안바닥에는 연지화(連枝花) 속에서 노니는 봉황 두 마리를 새기고 내벽과 안바닥이 만나는 곳에는 두 줄의 현문 사이 아래위로 띄엄띄엄 배열된 연꽃을 새겼다. 외벽 역시 5개 부분으로 나뉘며 각 부분을 연잎으로 장식하였다. 표면에 새긴 무늬에는 모두 금을 입혔다.

대류은이(帶流銀匜)

은(銀) | 당(唐) | 높이 3.5cm 입지름 13.5cm 밑지름 8cm 무게 151g
1979년 서안시(西安市) 문물상점(文物商店)으로부터 넘겨받음

Stream Silver Ladle

Silver | Tang Dynasty(618AD~907AD) | H 3.5cm Mouth D 13.5cm Base D 8cm Weight 151g
Transferred by Xi'an Culture Relic Shop in 1979

입구가 곧고 둥글며 배[腹]는 호형(弧形)이고 밑굽이 평평하다. 이(匜)는 전체적으로 은회색을 띠는데 곳곳에 동록(銅綠)이 나 있다. 입구에는 해당화 모양의 반(鋬, 손잡이)이 있으며, 가운데 아랫부분에는 배와 연결된 오리 주둥이 모양의 귀때가 있다. 안바닥에는 즐치(櫛齒)무늬로 된 정사각형이 선각(線刻)으로 표현되어 있는데 4변에 각각 한 송이의 연꽃이 바깥으로 뻗어 있고 연꽃 사이마다 구름무늬가 새겨져 있다. 정사각형 중심의 연꽃 네 송이에 둘러싸인 음양태극도(陰陽太極圖)에서 불교와 도교의 결합을 알 수 있다.

이(匜)는 세면도구로 주로 상주(商周)시대에 유행하고 한대(漢代) 이후부터는 유행하지 않았다. 그 형태가 장배(長杯)와 비슷한데 한쪽에 귀때가 있고 다른 한쪽에는 손잡이가 달려 있거나 굽을 갖춘 것도 있다. 흔히 동(銅), 도자기(陶瓷器), 금(金), 은(銀) 등 다양한 재료로 만들어진다.

태극도(太極圖)는 도교를 상징하는 도안으로 태극(太極)은 음(陰)과 양(陽)이 조화되어 우주만물을 이루었음을 의미한다. 송대(宋代) 주돈이(周敦頤)는 『태극도설(太極圖說)』에서 다음과 같이 해석하였다. "무극(無極)이자 태극이다. 태극이 움직이면 양이 생기고 움직임이 극에 달하면 도리어 고요해지며 고요하면 음이 생기고 고요함이 극에 달하면 다시 움직이게 된다. 양이 음으로 변하여 합하면 수화목금토(水火木金土)가 생성되며 이 오기(五氣)가 차례로 분포되고 사시(四時)가 운행되니…… 음기와 양기가 합하여 만물을 생성하고, 만물이 끊임없이 번성하니 변화가 무궁하다." '연꽃은 진흙에서 나오지만 더러움에 물들지 않는다'는 그림은 불교의 대표적인 도안 중 하나이다. 도교는 중국의 민간신앙으로 동한(東漢) 초기에 나타났으며, 고대 인도에서 기원한 불교는 동한 초기 육로와 해로를 통하여 중국에 유입되었는데 도교와 불교가 만나면서 분쟁이 끊이지 않았다. 중당(中唐) 이후 유교, 불교, 도교가 점차 융화되었다.

079

육능형착금연지화문치구은관(六棱形錯金連枝花紋侈口銀罐)

은(銀) | 당(唐) | 높이 12.2cm 입지름 10.2cm 무게 217.5g
1980년 서안시(西安市) 기차역 광장에서 출토

Six-edged Gold-inlay Silver Jar with Wide Edge and Patterns of Branches of Flowers

Silver | Tang Dynasty(618AD~907AD) | H 12.2cm Mouth D 10.2cm Weight 217.5g
Excavated from Xi'an Railway Station Square in 1980

　　입구가 벌어지고 목이 잘록하며 배[腹]가 약간 볼록한, 은회색을 띠는 은관(銀罐, 단지)이다. 밑굽에는 굽이 있었으나 떨어지고 없다. 입구와 목 아랫부분에는 각각 관현문(寬弦紋)이 둘러져 있는데 그 사이에 있는 세로선 여섯 줄은 목을 똑같은 6개 부분으로 나누고 각 부분마다 꽃을 한 송이씩 새겨 넣었다. 배 역시 아래위로 줄무늬가 둘러져 있고 6개 부분으로 나뉘며 각 부분에는 전지화(纏枝花) 두 송이가 장식되어 있다. 밑굽과 가까운 부분에도 전지화 무늬가 둘러져 있다. 무늬는 끌로 조각하고 그 위에 금을 입혔다.

080

'대당(大唐)' 관은합(款銀盒)

은(銀) | 당(唐) | 높이 9.1cm 지름 17.7cm 무게 1,260g
2002년 서안시 장안구 축촌향 양촌(西安市 長安區 祝村鄉 羊村) 출토

Silver Case with 'Da Tang' Inscription

Silver | Tang Dynasty(618AD~907AD) | H 9.1cm D 17.7cm
Weight 1,260g
Excavated from Yangcun Village Zhuncun County Chang'an
District, Xi'an in 2002

　　납작한 원통형 몸체의 합(盒)으로 몸통과 뚜껑이 만나
는 곳은 자모구(子母口)를 이룬다. 뚜껑은 윗면에 철현문
(凸弦紋) 두 줄이 둘러져 있고 가장자리가 비스듬하게 기
울어졌으며 벽은 곧다. 몸통의 입구와 벽은 곧으며, 두 부
분이 이어지는 곳에는 얕은 턱을 만들어 뚜껑이 닫히도록
하였다. 벽 아래의 가장자리는 안쪽으로 굽었다. 평평한
바닥 중심에는 해서체(楷書體)로 "大唐(대당)" 두 글자가
음각되어 있다.

113

081

소면은분(素面銀盆)

은(銀) | 당(唐) | 높이 5.87cm 입지름 25.48cm 무게 601g
2002년 서안시 장안구 축촌향 양촌(西安市 長安區 祝村鄕 羊村) 출토

Plain-surfaced Silver Basin

Silver | Tang Dynasty(618AD~907AD) | H 5.87cm D 25.48cm
Weight 601g
Excavated from Yangcun Village Zhucun County Chang'an District,
Xi'an in 2002

동그란 모양의 민무늬 은분(銀盆)으로 살짝 오므라든 입
구, 호형(弧形)의 얕은 배[腹], 평평한 바닥을 가졌다. 밑굽
에는 천으로 쌌던 흔적이 조금 남아 있다.

082

대개은합(帶蓋銀盒)

은(銀) | 당(唐) | 전체높이 7.23cm 입지름 5.86cm 배지름 9.11cm 밑지름 3.58cm 무게 166g
2002년 서안시 장안구 축촌향 양촌(西安市 長安區 祝村鄕 羊村) 출토

Silver Case with a Cover

Silver | Tang Dynasty(618AD~907AD) | H 7.23cm Mouth D 5.86cm Belly D 9.11cm
Base D 3.58cm Weight 166g
Excavated from Yangcun Village Zhucun County Chang'an District, Xi'an in 2002

둥글납작한 모양의 합(盒)으로 몸통과 뚜껑이 만나는 곳은 자모
구(子母口)를 이룬다. 뚜껑은 약간 융기(隆起)되었으며, 가운데 구멍
난 곳에는 원래 꼭지가 달려 있었으나 지금은 유실되고 없다. 가장자
리에는 현문(弦紋) 한 줄이 음각(陰刻)되어 있다. 몸통의 입구는 안쪽
으로 오므라들었고 역시 현문 두 줄이 음각되어 있다. 배는 볼록하며
바닥이 작고 평평하다.

083

환저소은합(圜底小銀盒)

은(銀) | 당(唐) | 높이 2.5cm 입지름 7.84cm 무게 69g
2002년 서안시 장안구 축촌향 양촌(西安市 長安區 祝村鄕 羊村) 출토

Small Silver Case with Round Bottom

Silver | Tang Dynasty(618AD~907AD) | H 2.5cm Mouth D 7.84cm Weight 69g
Excavated from Yangcun Village Zhucun County Chang'an District, Xi'an in
2002

뚜껑이 유실되어 몸통만 남은 은합(銀盒)으로 벌어진 입구, 호형
(弧形)의 얕은 배[腹], 둥근 밑굽을 가졌다. 입구의 안팎에는 현문(弦
紋) 한 줄, 안바닥 가장자리에는 복선(復線) 현문 두 줄이 음각되어 있
다. 찻잔 받침 모양인 밑바닥 중심은 둥글납작하고 가운데가 볼록한
것이 마치 운두가 낮은 쟁반 같다. 전체적으로 동황색을 띠는데 부분
적으로 동록(銅綠)이 있는 것으로 미루어 보아 동은합금(銅銀合金)
제품에 속함을 알 수 있다.

084

소면연지은합(素面臙脂銀盒)

은(銀) | 당(唐) | 높이 2.25cm 입지름 4.57cm 무게 28.5g
1981년 서안시(西安市) 제1건축공정회사에서 출토

Plain-surfaced Silver Rouge Case

Silver | Tang Dynasty(618AD~907AD) | H 2.25cm Mouth D 4.57cm Weight 28.5g
Excavated from Xi'an No.1 Construction Engineering Co. in 1981

은회색을 띠는 민무늬 합(盒)이다. 둥근 모양이고 몸통과 뚜껑이 만
나는 곳은 자모구(子母口)를 이룬다. 뚜껑은 융기되고 몸통은 직립이며
바닥은 평평하다.

소면은분합(素面銀粉盒)

은(銀) | 당(唐) | 높이 3.06cm 입지름 6.3cm 무게 76.5g
1977년 서안시 연호구 반가촌(西安市 蓮湖區 潘家村) 당나라 무덤에서 출토

Plain-surfaced Silver Puff Case

Silver | Tang Dynasty(618AD~907AD) | H 3.06cm Mouth D 6.3cm Weight 76.5g
Excavated from Tang Tomb Panjiacun Village in Lianhu District, Xi'an in 1977

은회색을 띠는 둥근 모양의 민무늬 합(盒)이다. 융기(隆起)된 뚜껑 가장자리를 부드러운 곡선으로 처리하여 몸통과 자모구(子母口)를 이루도록 하였다. 몸통의 벽은 곧고 밑바닥은 둥글다. 합 안에는 명주실로 만든 분첩(粉貼) 1개와 변질된 분이 담겨 있다.

화판형연지금합(花瓣形臙脂金盒)

금(金) | 당(唐) | 높이 1.2cm 지름 4.8cm 무게 32g
1966년 서안시 비림구(西安市 碑林區) 서북공업대학(西北工業大學) 출토

Silver Rouge Case in the Shape of Petals

Gold | Tang Dynasty(618AD~907AD) | H 1.2cm D 4.8cm Weight 32g
Excavated from Northwestern Polytechnical University in Beilin District, Xi'an in 1966

팔엽화형(八葉花形)의 합(盒)으로 뚜껑과 몸통은 형태가 똑같으며 맞닿는 부분은 자모구(子母口)를 이룬다. 뚜껑과 바닥이 모두 융기되었다. 뚜껑 문양은 이중구조로 장식되었는데 인동(忍冬)과 복숭아 모양의 꽃잎 8개가 방사형으로 펼쳐지는데 꽃잎의 뾰족한 부분이 밖을 향하고 바깥쪽 복숭아 모양의 꽃은 뾰족한 부분이 중심을 향한다. 그 안에는 여의전지화문(如意纏枝花紋)을 새기고 뚜껑과 몸통의 가장자리 화판(花瓣)마다 작은 꽃 세 송이를 새겼다. 몸통 역시 뚜껑과 같은 무늬로 장식하였다. 이 연지합(臙脂盒)은 조형과 문양의 배치가 일본 백학(白鶴)미술관에서 소장하고 있는 복숭아 모양의 팔곡은합(八曲銀盒)과 비슷한데, 모두 동일한 시기의 것으로 추측된다. 능화형(菱花形)과 규화형(葵花形)의 기물은 주로 7세기 후반, 8세기 초 및 8세기 중엽 이후 유행하였다.

쌍조원형은분합(雙鳥圓形銀粉盒)

은(銀) | 당(唐) | 높이 1.3cm 지름 3.1cm 무게 5.2g
1965년 서안시 안탑구 곡강향 삼조촌(西安市 雁塔區 曲江鄕 三兆村) 출토

Round Silver Puff Case with Pairs of Birds

Silver | Tang Dynasty(618AD∼907AD) | H 1.3cm D 3.1cm Weight 5.2g
Excavated from Sanzhao Village Qujiang County in Yanta District, Xi'an in 1965

둥글납작한 모양의 분합(粉盒)으로 뚜껑과 몸통
이 만나는 곳은 자모구(子母口)를 이룬다. 전체를
어자문(魚子紋)으로 장식하고 그 위에 화조(花鳥)
무늬를 새겨 넣었다. 뚜껑에는 두 마리의 새를 나란
히 배열하였는데 꽃을 물고 날아가는 새들 주변에
꽃과 가지가 둘러져 있다. 몸통 바닥에도 두 마리
새가 있는데 꽃을 물고 날개를 치며 날아오르는 모
습으로, 곳곳마다 봄빛이 완연하여 난새[鸞鳥]가 노
래하고 제비가 춤추는 광경이다.

합(盒)은 당대 금은그릇 가운데서 수량이 가장
많으며 종류가 다양하다. 시기에 따라 합의 형태도
다른데 8세기 중엽 이전에는 굽이 없는 둥근 모양
의 은합, 초당(初唐) 시기에는 민무늬 합이 주를 이
루었으며 성당(盛唐) 시기에 이르러서야 비로소 동
식물 무늬로 장식한 합이 유행하였다.

088

쌍후희희원형소은합(雙猴嬉戲圓形小銀盒)

은(銀) | 당(唐) | 높이 0.9cm 지름 4.2cm 무게 19g
1958년 서안시도시건설국(西安市都市建設局)으로부터 넘겨받음

Small Round Silver Case with a Pair of Playing Monkeys

Silver | Tang Dynasty(618AD~907AD) | H 0.9cm D 4.2cm Weight 19g
Transferred by Xi'an Bureau for Municipal Design in 1958

둥근 모양의 은합(銀盒)이다. 융기된 몸통 및 뚜껑
은 낮은 아치형을 이루며, 두 부분이 만나는 곳은 자모
구(子母口)를 이룬다. 전체적으로 어자문(魚子紋)을
새겼는데 뚜껑과 몸통의 문양은 다소 다르다. 뚜껑과
바닥 모두 활엽수 그늘 아래에서 노닐고 있는 원숭이
두 마리를 새기고 꽃잎 무늬로 빈 공간을 채워 아름다
움을 더했다. 측면에는 구름무늬를 띄엄띄엄 배치하
였다. 뚜껑에 조각된 원숭이들은 서로 마주 앉아 있으
며, 몸통에 조각된 원숭이 중 한 마리는 나뭇가지에 매
달려 있고 다른 한 마리는 나무에 오를 준비를 하고 있
다. 이는 전통적인 의미가 담긴 도안이다.

118

화판형류금은합(花瓣形鎏金銀盒)

은(銀) | 당(唐) | 높이 4.6cm 입지름 10.1cm 무게 102.5g
1980년 서안시(西安市) 기차역 광장에서 출토

Gold-decorated Silver Case in the Shape of Petals

Silver | Tang Dynasty(618AD~907AD) | H 4.6cm Mouth D 10.1cm Weight 102.5g
Excavated from Xi'an Railway Station Square in 1980

은회색을 띠는 꽃잎 모양의 은합(銀盒)이다. 곧은 입구와 윗배는 외벽의
오목선에 의해 똑같은 4개 부분으로 나뉘어져 연호(連弧) 모양이 되었다.
원래 권족(圈足)이 있었으나 부분적으로 손상되었다. 입구의 한쪽에는 고
리, 다른 한쪽에는 파손된 경첩이 달려 있다. 경첩은 뚜껑을 여닫는 데 쓰인
다. 안면과 바닥에는 무늬가 없다. 외벽의 윗부분에는 단화(團花) 네 떨기
를 두르고 사이사이 풀잎무늬를 새겨 넣었다. 아랫배에는 끄트머리가 뾰
족한 꽃잎과 원호형(圓弧形) 꽃잎이 어우러져 있다. 잎맥까지 선명하게 나
타난 꽃잎들은 모두 추엽(錘揲) 기법으로 만들어진 것이다. 꽃잎 아래에는
연주문(聯珠紋) 한 줄이 둘러져 있다. 합의 조형, 단화의 형태, 연주문의 장
식으로부터 미루어 보아 8세기 중엽 이후에 만들어졌음을 알 수 있다.

도관칠국인물은합(都管七國人物銀盒)

은(銀) | 당(唐) | (1) 대합 높이 5cm 지름 7.5cm 굽지름 6cm 배깊이 3cm 무게 121g
(2) 중합 높이 3.4cm 지름 6.4×4.9cm 굽지름 5×3.5cm 무게 38.2g
(3) 소합 높이 2.3cm 지름 4.7×3.7cm 무게 30g
1979년 서안시 비림구(西安市 碑林區) 서안교통대학(西安交通大學)에서 출토

Silver Cases Engraved with Figures from Seven Countries

Silver | Tang Dynasty (618AD~907AD)
(1) H 5cm D 7.5cm Base D 6cm Belly Depth 3cm Weight 121g
(2) H 3.4cm D 6.4×4.9cm Base D 5×3.5cm Weight 38.2g
(3) H 2.3cm D 4.7×3.7cm Weight 30g
Excavated from Jiaotong University in Beilin District, Xi'an in 1979

(1)

(2)

(3)

육판나팔형(六瓣喇叭形) 큰 합, 굽이 달린 앵무문해당형(鸚鵡紋海棠形) 중합, 귀배문(龜背紋)이 새겨진 작은 합으로 이루어진 삼단식 은합이다. 외층의 큰 합은 뚜껑 면이 불룩하고 몸통과 뚜껑이 만나는 곳은 자모구(子母口)를 이루며 평평한 밑바닥에는 나팔형의 높은 굽이 달려 있다. 뚜껑의 가운데 부분에 새겨진 육각형 도안의 변에 각각 계란형 도안을 둘렀다. 육각형 안에는 코끼리를 탄 사람이 있고 그 앞에는 머리에 물건을 인 채 배알하는 사람이 있으며 뒤에는 우산을 든 사람이 있다. 코끼리 몸에는 안천(鞍韉, 안장과 말다래)이 갖춰져 있다. 한 사람은 오른쪽에 서 있고 수행하는 다른 한 사람은 왼쪽에 서 있으며 또 다른 한 사람은 앉아 있다. 배알하는 사람 앞에는 "都管七個國(도관칠개국)", 가운데는 "昆侖王國(곤륜왕국)", 아래에는 "將來(장래)"라는 제방(題榜)이 있다. 곤륜왕국의 오른쪽으로부터 시계방향으로 파라문국(婆羅門國), 토번국(土蕃國), 소륵국(疏勒國), 고려국, 백척□국(白拓□國), 오만국(烏蠻國) 순서로 여러 나라 및 지역의 풍토와 인정을 드러내는 도안들이 배열되어 있다. 파라문국 도안에는 왼쪽에 선장(禪仗)을 짚고 가사를 입은 승려가 서 있고 오른쪽에는 의견을 묻는 듯한 사람 둘이 있다. 가운데에는 작은 입구에서 불꽃 모양의 방사물(放射物)이 나오는 네모난 병(甁)이 놓여 있다. 왼쪽에는 나라 이름, 오른쪽에는 '□賜(구사)' 두 글자가 새겨져 있다. 토번국 도안은 사람 둘이 재빠르게 달아나는 튼튼한 소 한 마리를 쫓고 있는 모습이다. 왼쪽 윗부분에는 제방이 새겨져 있다. 소륵국 도안에는 오른쪽에 칼을 든 두 사람, 왼쪽에 공손하게 서 있는 사람과 활을 들고 있는 다른 한 사람이 표현되어 있다. 정중앙에는 제방이 새겨져 있다. 고려국 도안은 왼쪽에 가부좌(跏趺坐)를 하고 있는 존자(尊者)의 좌우에 네 사람이 서 있는 모습이다. 모두 깃이 꽂힌 관(冠)을 쓰고 소매가 넓은 두루마기를 걸치고 위리(葦履)를 신었다. 정중앙에는 "高麗(고려)"라는 제방이 있다. 백척□국 도안에는 왼쪽에 포단(蒲團) 위에 앉아 있는 노인과 오른쪽에 노인에게 드릴 헌물을 들고 있는 한 소년이 있다. 정중앙에 제방이 있다. 오만국 도안에는 왼쪽에 발걸음을 내딛고 있는 두 존자, 오른쪽에 손님을 맞이하는 모습의 사람 셋이 있다. 모두 낭각(囊角) 머리를 하고 소매가 넓은 긴 치마를 입었다. 오른쪽에는 제방이 새겨져 있다. 뚜껑 및 몸통의 외측 면에 전지(纏枝)무늬를 바탕에 시문(試紋)하고

십이지신(十二支神) 도안과 함께 "子時半夜, 醜時雞鳴, 寅時平□, 卯時日出, 辰時食時, 巳時禺中, 午時正中, 未時日卷, 申時脯時, 酉時日入, 戌時黃昏, 亥時人定(자시는 한밤중, 축시는 닭이 우는 때, 인시는 아침, 묘시는 일출, 진시는 아침밥 먹는 시간, 사시는 점심 무렵, 오시는 정오, 미시는 해가 서쪽 방향으로 기우는 때, 신시는 두 번째로 밥 먹는 시간, 유시는 해가 지는 때, 술시는 황혼, 해시는 밤이 깊어 조용한 때)"라는 제방이 새겨져 있다. 중합은 뚜껑이 융기되고 몸통과 뚜껑이 만나는 곳은 자모구(子母口)를 이루며 입구는 해당화 모양이고 바닥은 평평하며 굽은 나팔형이다. 뚜껑에는 전지권초문(纏枝卷草紋)을 바탕에 시문하고 입에 꽃가지를 문 채 꼬리를 물고 나는 앵무새 두 마리를 새겨 넣었다. 뚜껑 가장자리에는 앙련(仰蓮)의 연판을, 합의 입구 위쪽에는 파식해당형(破式海棠形) 도안을 새겼다. 작은 합은 거북 등 모양으로 표면이 융기되고 바닥이 평평하다. 뚜껑 면에 거북 등 무늬가 새겨져 있고 나머지 부분에는 무늬가 없다. 안에는 수정구슬 2개와 갈색의 올리브 모양의 마노(瑪瑙)구슬 1개가 들어 있다. 이 삼단식 은합은 조형이 아름답고 기법이 섬세하며 무늬 또한 화조(花鳥)에서 인물에 이르기까지 모두 저마다의 독특한 풍채를 지님으로써 당대 은기 중의 수작에 속할뿐더러 당대 대외 문화 교류가 활발했음을 보여 준다.

인물을 장식 소재로 한 것은 당대(唐代) 금은기(金銀器)의 두드러진 특징이다. 8세기 중엽 이전에는 수렵, 악기(樂伎), 사녀(仕女), 8세기 중엽 이후에는 인물고사(人物故事), 유락(游樂) 등의 내용이 주를 이루었다. 이 은합은 9세기 남조국(南詔國, 748~937년, 지금의 중국 운남 지역)에서 만들었는데 1980년대 섬서성(陝西省) 부풍현(扶風縣) 법문사박물관(法門寺博物館)에서 소장한 9세기 후반기의 당대(唐代) 쌍사문화판형(雙獅紋花瓣形) 은합, 섬서성 남전현문물국(藍田縣文物局)에서 소장한 '전사거(田嗣莒)' 쌍봉문화판형(雙鳳紋花瓣形) 은합과 형태가 비슷한데 당선종(唐宣宗) 대중(大中)에서 당의종(唐懿宗) 함통(咸通) 연간(847~873년)의 은합에 속한다. 날로 쇠락하는 당왕조와 달리 남조국은 국력이 점점 더 강대해져 당왕조를 부단히 침략하였다. 여러 차례 패배한 당왕조로부터 대량의 토지를 빼앗은 남조국은 교만해져 당왕조를 업신여겼다. 앞서 소개한 7국은 당왕조의 번국에 속하는데, 남조국 은합을 보면 번국을 쟁탈하려는 남조국의 욕망을 엿볼 수 있다.

쌍봉함수대문오곡은합(雙鳳銜綬帶紋五曲銀盒)

은(銀) | 당(唐) | 높이 8cm 지름 15,33cm 무게 502g
1980년 서안시 남전현 탕욕진 양가구촌(西安市 藍田縣 湯浴鎭 楊家溝村) 출토

Five-carved Silver Case in the Pattern of Double Phonenixes Biting Ribbon

Silver | Tang Dynasty(618AD~907AD) | H 8cm D 15,33cm Weight 502g
Excavated from Yangjiagou Village Tangyu County Lantian District, Xi'an in 1980

납작한 오곡원형(五曲圓形) 은합(銀盒)으로 뚜껑과 몸통이 만나는 곳은 자모구(子母口)를 이룬다. 뚜껑 및 바닥은 모두 융기되었으며 뚜껑 윗면은 변형된 철현문(凸弦紋)에 의해 안팎으로 나뉘었다. 안쪽에는 네 가닥으로 매듭지어진 비단끈을 문 봉황 한 쌍과 덩굴무늬가 동그랗게 장식되어 있으며, 오엽화형(五葉花

形)의 바깥쪽에는 만초(蔓草), 인동(忍冬) 무늬를 바탕에 시문(試紋)하고 날아가는 기러기 한 쌍을 새겼다. 뚜껑 및 몸통 측면에는 수대(綬帶), 원앙새, 만초로 이루어진 무늬를 아래위로 배치하였다. 합 전체의 무늬 사이는 어자문(魚子紋)으로 장식되어 있다. 주제무늬는 거푸집에 찍어내고 어자문은 끌로 조각하고 표면에는 모두 금을 입혔다. 바닥에는 "內園供奉合(盒), 鹹通七年十一月十五日造 , 使臣田嗣菖 , 重一十五兩五錢一字(내원공봉합, 함통 7년 11월 15일 제작, 사신 전사거, 무게 15냥 5돈, 일자 모양)"이란 글귀가 네 줄로 나뉘어 새겨져 있다.

당대(唐代) 시기, 관직이 있는 사람만이 관청 수공업 공장의 제품 생산에 참여할 수 있었다. '내원(內園)', '사신(使臣)' 등 관료기구와 관직명으로 미루어보아 이 은합은 당대 중앙관청이나 황실의 수공업 공장인 금은작방원(金銀作坊院) 또는 문사원(文思院)에서 만든 것임을 알 수 있다. 금은기(金銀器)에 명문(銘文)을 새겨 넣는 풍속은 8세기 중엽 이후부터 시작되었다. 성당(盛唐) 시기 이전 중앙정부에서 금은기의 제작을 독점하였지만 중·만당(中·晚唐) 시기에 와서는 지방관청 및 개인 수공업 공장이 발전하면서 독점이 사라지고 따라서 제작 기구를 밝히기 위해 이러한 풍속이 생겨났던 것이다.

이 은합과 함께 은정(銀鋌) 3점, 원앙수대문은반(鴛鴦綬帶紋銀盤) 1점, 앵무단화문은반(鸚鵡團花紋銀盤) 1점, 오판소면은완(五瓣素面銀碗) 1점, 절지단화은해완개(折枝團花銀海碗盖) 1점, 팔판사출수대문은완(八瓣四出綬帶紋銀碗) 1점, 앵무포도문운두합(鸚鵡葡萄紋雲頭盒) 2점, 은숟가락 1점, 은젓가락 3점 등이 출토되었다. 그밖에 은장식품, 마구(馬具) 장식품 등도 출토되었다. 이러한 은기(銀器)는 절지단화(折枝團花) 무늬가 주를 이루며, 비단끈 무늬가 다음으로 많다. 이는 장생(長生)하기를 소망하는 지배계급들의 강렬한 염원을 반영한다. 당대 후기는 전쟁이 빈번한 시대였다. 은기와 마구 같은 것이 함께 매장된 데에서 은기 소유자가 철수하면서 급히 매장했던 것으로 추측된다.

092

단화문금은타호(團花紋金銀唾壺)

은(銀) | 당(唐) | 높이 9.8cm 입지름 14.6cm 무게 392g
1977년 서안시 파교구 신축향 조원촌(西安市 灞橋區 新筑鄉 棗園村) 출토

Gilt Silver Spittoon in Floral Pattern

Silver | Tang Dynasty(618AD~907AD) | H 9.8cm Mouth D 14.6cm Weight 392g
Excavated from Zaoyuan Village Xinzhu County in Baqiao District, Xi'an in 1977

이 타호(唾壺)는 입구가 반구(盤口)이며, 잘록한 목에 복부는 둥글고 바닥이 평평하며 굽은 낮다. 입구, 몸체 및 굽은 모두 4개 꽃잎 모양이다. 반구에는 세 겹의 문양이 새겨져 있다. 입구에는 8개 꽃잎의 연꽃이 둘러져 있고, 가운데 부분에는 동글납작한 아마릴리스 네 송이와 삼각형의 절지화(折枝花) 및 원추리 하나가 장식되어 있는데 얼기설기 얽힌 꽃줄기와 활짝 피어난 꽃들은 복잡다단한 단화(團花)를 이루었다. 바깥쪽에는 앙련(仰蓮)의 연판(蓮

瓣) 한 줄을 둘렀다. 복부의 외벽에는 절지화로 이루어진 단화 네 떨기와 그 사이에 끼여 있는 삼각형의 절지화가 새겨져 있다. 떨기마다 활짝 핀 꽃 주위에 꽃잎들로 가득한 모습이다. 무늬에는 모두 금을 입혔다.

　타호는 입을 가시거나 가래를 뱉는 데 쓰이는 그릇으로 일찍 진한(秦漢) 시기부터 널리 사용되었다. 옛 사람들은 흔히 안궤(案几)나 침대 위에 놓아두었다. 제왕과 귀족들은 금은이나 옥석, 평민들은 도자기로 된 것을 사용하였다. 반구, 가느다란 목, 볼록한 배, 평평한 밑굽이나 낮은 굽을 가진 형태가 많았다.

　타호는 당왕조(唐王朝) 때 보편적으로 사용하던 생활그릇으로서 도자기로 만든 것이 대부분이며, 금은으로 만든 것이 극히 적었다. 서안시문물보호고고학연구소에서 소장한 건부(乾符) 6년(879년)의 은정(銀鋌)과 함께 조원촌(棗園村) 공사장에서 출토된, 이 타호는 추엽(錘揲) 기법으로 만들어져 제작이 균일하여 매끄러운 느낌을 준다. 조형적으로 절강성(浙江省) 임안현(臨安縣) 만당(晚唐) '수추씨(水秋氏)' 무덤에서 출토된 '소면은타호(素面銀唾壺)'와 거의 일치한데 9세기 후기 당대(唐代) 금은기(金銀器) 중의 수작이다.

123

보상화은다탁(寶相花銀茶托)

은(銀) | 당(唐) | 입지름 7.27cm 무게 38.1g
1977년 서안시문물관리위원회(西安市文物管理委員會) 수집

Silver Saucer in Pattern of Composite Flowers

Silver | Tang Dynasty(618AD~907AD) | Mouth D 7.27cm Weight 38.1g
Collected by Xi'an Culture Relic Administration Committee in 1977

둥글납작한 모양에 호형(弧形)의 배[腹], 평평한 바닥, 나팔형의 굽을 갖
춘 찻잔받침이다. 은으로 만든 것으로 내벽에는 보상화(寶相花) 네 송이가
배치되어 있고 안바닥은 볼록하게 튀어나와 쟁반과 흡사하다. 겉면에는 무
늬가 없다. 판금(鈑金)으로 찻잔받침의 형태를, 추엽(錘擽) 기법으로 보상화
무늬를 만들고 표면에는 금을 입혔다. 보상화무늬는 당대(唐代) 특유의 무
늬로 원래 불교적인 장식무늬였다. 이는 연꽃에서 변화되어 온 무늬로 꽃,
꽃봉오리, 꽃받침, 잎사귀 등을 사방 혹은 여러 방향으로 대칭되게 뻗어나가
도록 배치해 층층이 중첩시키는 문양이다.

찻잔받침은 '다선(茶船)', '다탁자(茶托子)'라고도 불리며 쟁반 모양에 작
은 굽이 달린 형태이다. 가운데 오목하게 들어간 부분은 찻잔을 놓는 곳으
로 찻잔이 기울거나 찻물이 넘치는 것을 막아준다. 이는 찻잔과 세트를 이
루는 다구(茶具)의 하나이다. 찻잔받침은 진왕조(晉王朝) 때 생겨났는데 당
대에 와서 차를 마시는 풍습이 일반화되면서 유행하였다.

세경은병(細頸銀瓶)

은(銀) | 당(唐) | 높이 10.57cm 입지름 2.3cm 배지름 4.74cm 밑지름 3.23cm 무게 68g
2002년 서안시 장안구 축촌향 양촌(西安市 長安區 祝村鄉 羊村) 출토

Silver Bottle with a Narrow Neck

Silver | Tang Dynasty(618AD~907AD) | H 10.57cm Mouth D 2.3cm Belly D 4.74cm Base D 3.23cm
Weight 68g
Excavated from Yangcun Village Zhucun County Chang'an District, Xi'an in 2002

벌어진 입구, 길고 가느다란 목, 깊고 볼록한 배, 나팔형의 낮은 굽을 가진 은병(銀
瓶)이다. 표면은 전체적으로 은회색을 띤다. 목 아래에는 배부와 연결된 나팔 모양의
용접물이 있는데 서로 이어지는 곳은 턱을 이루었다.

병(瓶)은 '병(缾)'이라고도 불린다. 신석기시대에 생겨난 것으로, 고대 사람들은 물
을 긷거나 액체를 담아 저장하는 용기로 사용하였다. 지금까지 출토된 자기(瓷器), 불
교 석각(石刻)에 대한 고고학 연구에 따르면 목이 긴 은병은 주로 북조(北朝)부터 성당
(盛唐) 시기 중국 북방지역에서 유행하였음을 알 수 있다.

은괄설(銀刮舌)

은(銀) | 당(唐) | 길이 23.2cm 무게 12g
1965년 서안시 안탑구 곡강향 삼조촌(西安市 雁塔區 曲江鄉 三兆村) 출토

Silver Tongue Scraper

Silver | Tang Dynasty(618AD~907AD) | L 23.2cm Weight 12g
Excavated from Sanzhao Village Qujiang County in Yanta District, Xi'an in 1965

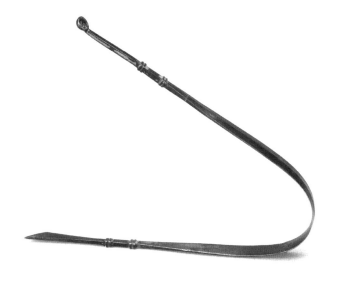

　은회색을 띠는 활 모양의 혀긁개로 한쪽에는 귀이개, 다른 한쪽에
는 사선의 작은 칼이 있다. 가운데가 조금 넓고 양쪽은 가늘며 네모난
편이다. 귀이개 및 칼자루와 가까운 부분은 철현문(凸弦紋) 두 줄로
장식되어 있다. 막대 모양의 자루는 한 면이 평평하고 다른 한 면은
융기되었다.

　서한(西漢) 말기에 나타난 혀긁개는 설태(舌苔)를 제거하는 도구
이다. 재질은 주로 죽목(竹木)이고 일부 금은동(金銀銅)도 있는데 극
히 적었다. 북송(北宋) 말기 칫솔이 생겨난 이후 점차 사라졌다.

은등대(銀燈臺)

은(銀) | 당(唐) | 높이 9.19cm 위 등잔받침 지름 5.07cm 아래 등잔받침 지름
6.53cm 굽지름 4.47cm 무게 120g
2002년 서안시 장안구 축촌향 양촌(西安市 長安區 祝村鄉 羊村) 출토

Silver Lampstand

Silver | Tang Dynasty(618AD~907AD) | H 9.19cm Upper D 5.07cm
Lower D 6.53cm Base D 4.47cm Weight 120g
Excavated from Yangcun Village Zhucun County Chang'an District, Xi'an in
2002

　등잔받침 2개와 기둥으로 이루어진 등잔받침이다. 위의 받침보
다 아래 것이 더 크다. 모두 테두리가 밖으로 약간 말리고 운두가 낮
으며 바닥이 평평하고 벽은 곧다. 중심부에는 동그란 구멍이 나 있
어 등잔받침을 대좌(臺座)에 고정시켜 주었다. 중심부와 가장자리
사이에는 가는 현문(弦紋)을 음각(陰刻)으로 둘렀다. 기둥은 속이
빈 요령(搖鈴) 모양이고 중간 부분이 가느다란 것이 대나무 마디 모
양과 흡사하며 마디가 연결된 부분마다 현문 한 줄을 음각으로 둘렀
다. 위쪽 관(管) 모양의 아랫부분 및 아래쪽 엎어 놓은 요령 모양의
가운데 부분에는 모두 작은 턱이 있어 등잔받침을 받쳐 준다. 구연부
(口沿部)는 밖으로 벌어져 권족(圈足)을 이룬다. 표면에는 동황색 빛
이 감도는데 부분적으로 동록(銅綠)이 슬어 있다.

유금쌍봉단화루공은향구(鎏金雙蜂團花鏤空銀香毬)

은(銀) | 당(唐) | 높이 6cm 너비 5.4cm 무게 61.5g
1965년 서안시 안탑구 곡강향 삼조촌(西安市 雁塔區 曲江鄕 三兆村) 출토

Gilt Hollowed-out Silver Censer Ball with Double
Bees and Floral Pattern

Silver | Tang Dynasty(618AD~907AD) | H 6cm W 5.4cm Weight 61.5g
Excavated from Sanzhao Village Qujiang County in Yanta District, Xi'an in 1965

향구(香毬)는 '금잡(金鍾)', '금은훈구(金銀薰球)'라고도 불린다.
당왕조(唐王朝) 때 향을 피우는 데 사용하던 기구이다. 공 모
양의 향구는 판금(鈑金) 공예로 만들어졌으며 표면을 전체적으
로 투각(透刻)하고 무늬에는 금을 입혔다. 아래위 반구(半球)로
구성되었는데 윗부분은 뚜껑이고 아랫부분은 몸통이다. 서로 맞
닿는 부분의 한쪽에는 쌍봉 모양의 경첩, 다른 한쪽에는 갈고리
가 있어 뚜껑을 여닫을 수 있게 하였다.

뚜껑 상단의 환뉴(環鈕)에는 연꽃 봉오리 모양의 고리를 걸
고 그 위에 은사슬을 연결하였다. 뚜껑 표면에는 단화(團花) 여
섯 송이를 새겼는데 상단의 단화 속에 새긴 꿀벌 네 마리와 몸통
밑부분에 새긴 절지단화(折枝團花)를 제외하고 나머지 단화 속
에는 모두 벌 한 쌍을 새겨 넣었다. 뚜껑과 몸통의 투각된 부분의
무늬는 모두 활엽무늬로 서로 대칭된다. 뚜껑과 몸통이 맞닿은
부분에는 덩굴무늬를 둘렀다. 향구 속에는 평형환(平衡環) 2개
가 있다. 향우(香盂)는 짧은 축으로 내환에 못으로 고정되어 있
으며 외환과 향구, 내외환 사이 역시 못[鉚釘]으로 연결되어 있
다. 원구(圓球)가 회전함에 따라 내외환도 회전할 수 있도록 하
였다. 향우 중심이 항상 아랫부분에 있어 평형상태를 유지해 향
이 탄 재가루나 불똥이 밖으로 흘러나오지 않게 된다. 따라서 옷
소매나 이불 속에서 회전시켜도 불이 꺼지지 않아 사람들은 '이
불 속의 향로'라고 불러왔다. 당대(唐代) 여성들이 즐겨 사용했
던 향구는 한편으로는 향을 태워 옷에 향내가 나도록 하였고 다
른 한편으로는 허리에 달고 다니는 장신구로도 삼았다. 이 밖에
이런 향구는 불교 행사에서 사용되기도 하였는데 이는 벽사(辟
邪)나 재난을 막기 위한 것으로 추측된다. 고고학 자료를 살펴보
면 향구는 당대에 지속적으로 유행하였음을 알 수 있다.

이 향구는 제작이 치밀하고 공예 또한 정교하여 당대 시기 장
인들의 뛰어난 금속 공예기술 및 기계제작 기술을 그대로 보여
준다.

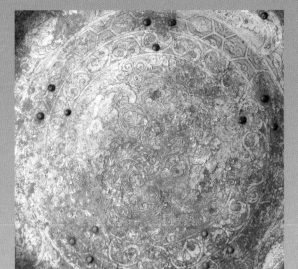

098

유금익수문대오족동로대(鎏金翼獸紋帶五足銅爐臺)

동(銅) | 당(唐) | 높이 11.5cm 입지름 37.3cm | 무게 6,150g
1958년 서안(西安) 기차역 광장에서 출토

Gilt Five-footed Bronze Coil Base with Winged Beast
Pattern

Silver | Tang Dynasty(618AD∼907AD) | H 11.5cm Mouth D 37.3cm Weight 6,150g
Excavated from Xi'an Railway Station Square in 1958

노대(爐臺)는 불교의 법기(法器) 가운데 하나인 향로의 일부이다. 입구가 벌어지고 바닥이 평평하다. 표면에는 복잡한 무늬를 5단으로 배치하고 전체적으로 금을 입혔다. 중심에는 튀어나온 눈, 큰 코, 넓은 귀, 긴 수염을 가진 날짐승 두 마리를 새겼는데 그 모양이 괴이하여 사자 같기도 하고 호랑이 같기도 하다. 두 날짐승은 흘러가는 구름을 입에 문 채 꼬리를 치켜세우고 날개를 펄럭인다. 문양을 표현함에 있어서 과장된 수법을 사용하였는데, 중심 부분에

는 날개 및 꼬리를 모두 꽃잎으로 장식한 날짐승들로 가득 채웠다. 두 번째 층에는 파곡문관지련(波曲紋串枝蓮), 세 번째 층에는 거북등무늬와 꽃잎무늬, 네 번째 층에는 큰 관지련(串枝蓮)을 한 바퀴 두르고 그 사이에 원앙 네 마리를 새겨 넣었다. 가지 위에 서 있거나 날개를 펄럭이며 노닐거나 고개를 돌린 채 당장이라도 날아갈 듯한 자세를 하고 있는 등 각양각색의 원앙들을 율동감 있게 표현하였다. 다섯 번째 층은 노대의 구연부(口沿部)로 잎무늬 한 줄이 둘러져 있다. 전체적으로 어자문(魚子紋)을 시문(試紋)하였다. 노대의 밑부분에는 유운(流雲) 모양의 굽다리 5개가 균일하게 배치되었는데 구름송이는 위로 말렸으며 굽다리의 끄트머리는 밖으로 벌어졌다. 굽다리에는 연잎 모양의 포수함환(鋪首銜環) 5개가 있으며 그 위에는 비단끈 무늬가 새겨진 술이 걸려 있다. 쟁반, 굽다리와 포수를 못으로 고정함으로써 안정감을 더해 주었다. 무늬와 표면의 금빛은 서로 어우러져 화려한 느낌을 준다.

이 노대는 섬서성(陝西省) 부풍현(扶風縣) 법문사(法門寺) 진신보탑지궁(眞身寶塔地宮)에서 도금와구연화문오족훈로(鍍金臥龜蓮花紋五足熏爐)와 함께 출토된 노대와 조형이 비슷하다. 이로 미루어 마찬가지로 향로의 받침대로 쓰였을 것으로 추측된다. 이 노대는 제작기법, 조형, 문양 등 여러 면에서 모두 정교함이 묻어나 당시 도금공예의 최고 수준을 보여 준 작품이다. 이 밖에 노대의 출토지는 서안시 기차역 광장으로 당대(唐代) 황제가 거처하던 태극궁(太極宮) 성동궁(城東宮) 유적지에 속한다. 이로써 당대 황실에서 예불(禮佛) 시 사용했던 황실용품이었음을 알 수 있다.

099

팔각형수렵문은경각(八角形狩獵紋銀鏡殼)

은(銀) | 당(唐) | 지름 20.7cm 무게 109g
1981년 서안시(西安市) 제1건축공정회사에서 출토

Octagonal Silver Mirror Shell with Hunting Patterns

Silver | Tang Dynasty(618AD~907AD) | D 20.7cm Weight 109g
Excavated from Xi'an No. 1 Construction Engineering Co. in 1981

　동경(銅鏡)의 장식품인 은경각(銀鏡殼)은 팔엽화형(八葉花形)이다. 은회색을 띠는 표면은 수렵무늬로 장식되었으며 중심에는 단화(團花) 모양의 둥근 꼭지
가 달려 있다. 무늬는 안과 밖으로 나뉜다. 안쪽에는 수렵무늬 두 조가 있는데 한 조는 달리는 말에서 몸을 돌려 활을 당기는 앞사람과 말 타고 뒤따르면서 활을
당기는 뒷사람이 함께 염소를 겨누고 있는 모습이다. 다른 한 조 역시 똑같은 구도인데 다만 염소 대신 멧돼지로 바뀌었을 뿐이다. 그 사이에는 산토끼와 꽃사
슴이 달리고 있고 주변을 관지화(串枝花)로 장식하였다. 외층무늬는 여덟 꽃잎의 가장자리에 새겨져 있는데 꽃을 마주하고 지저귀는 제비 두 마리와 산을 감도
는 흰 구름 및 무성한 화초무늬를 사이사이 배치하였다. 테두리에는 권운문(卷雲紋)을 둘렀다. 전체적으로 어자문(魚子紋)을 시문(試紋)하였으며 무늬는 모두
추엽(錘揲) 기법으로 만들었다.
　금은각경(金銀殼鏡)은 당대 동경의 주요 장식품으로 추엽(錘揲) 기법을 이용하여 거울 뒷면에 붙인 은판(銀板)이나 금판(金板)에 각종 문양을 새긴 것이다.
이 은경각의 도안들은 복잡하지만 질서 있게 배치되어 성당(盛唐) 시기 은장식품의 수작으로 손꼽힌다.

팔엽능화(八葉菱花) 모양이다. 거울 뒷면에는 금각(金殼)을 붙이고 그 위에 추엽(錘擪) 기법으로 부조식(浮雕式) 문양을 새겨 넣었다. 가운데 융기된 꼭지에는 추미식(追尾式) 쌍수(雙獸)를 새겼다. 철릉(凸稜)을 기준으로 두 부분으로 나눈다. 안쪽에는 덩굴무늬에 둥그렇게 둘러싸인 신수(神獸) 여덟 마리가 새겨져 있다. 신수는 걷거나 엎드리거나 기어가거나 뛰어오르거나 가지를 오르락내리락하면서 재롱부리는 모습이다. 바깥의 8개 능판(菱瓣)에는 철릉을 거쳐 안쪽 활짝 피어난 꽃마냥 뻗어 나온 덩굴무늬가 새겨져 있다. 그 사이사이에는 서로 얽힌 꽃가지도 있다. 판마다 꽃잎 4개를 가진 꽃봉오리가 능판의 꼭짓점을 마주하고 있고 양측에는 포도 열매가 드리워져 있으며 그 아래쪽에는 새 두 마리가 있는데 한 마리는 가지를 물고 있고 다른 하나는 씨를 쪼아 먹고 있다. 동경(銅鏡) 테두리 안쪽 틀에는 절지화(折枝花)로 장식하였다. 당대 동경 위에 새긴 포도무늬는 동서 문화교류의 산물로서 고대 그리스 사람들이 주신(酒神)인 디오니소스를 숭배하면서 생겨난 것이다. 디오니소스는 포도 재배와 주조업(酒造業)의 수호신이다. 로마신화에서 그를 바쿠스라고도 칭하는데 고대 그리스·로마 평민들의 사랑을 받는 신 가운데 하나이다. 고대 그리스·로마의 조각, 회화에서 디오니소스는 늘 포도의 나뭇가지 및 열매와 함께 표현되었다. 4세기 이후, 동로마제국은 고대 서방의 예술전통을 계승하였다. 동서양의 무역교류와 더불어 포도무늬는 초당(初唐) 시기에 중국에까지 전해졌는데 중국 전통 서수(瑞獸) 무늬와 함께 동경에 장식되었다. 당고종(唐高宗) 이치(李治) 시기에 나타난 포도문 동경은 무측천(武則天) 시기에 유행하였다가 당현종(唐玄宗) 후기에 이르러 점차 사라졌다.

이 금각경(金殼鏡)은 몸체가 두껍고 무거울뿐더러, 금판(金版)의 질이 부드럽고 표면이 매끈하며 가공 또한 섬세한데 참새 날개의 미세한 부분까지 생동감 있게 표현하였다. 안쪽에서 바깥으로 뻗어 나온 포도무늬 넝쿨 장식으로 미루어보아 이 거울은 성당(盛唐) 후기에 만들어졌음을 알 수 있다.

100

금배서수화지경(金背瑞獸花枝鏡)

금(金) | 당(唐) | 지름 19.68cm 무게 1,750g
2002년 서안시 파교구 마가구촌(西安市 灞橋區 馬家溝村) 출토

Gold-plated Mirror with Auspicious Animals and Flower Branches

Gold | Tang Dynasty(618AD~907AD) | D 19.68cm Weight 1,750g
Excavated from Majiagou Village Baqiao District, Xi'an in 2002

팔릉형은쇄(八稜形銀鎖)

은(銀) | 당(唐) | 길이 11.8cm 무게 46g
1966년 서안시문물관리위원회(西安市文物管理委員會) 수집

Octagonal Silver Lock

Silver | Tang Dynasty(618AD~907AD) | L 11.8cm Weight 46g
Collected by Xi'an Culture Relic Administration Committee in 1966

은회색을 띠는 자물쇠이다. 칼자루 모양의 갈고리는 속이 빈 팔릉형(八稜形)의 몸체를 통과하였다. 몸체에는 줄무늬 두 줄이 음각(陰刻)되어 있는 관대문(寬帶紋) 4개가 새겨져 있다. 갈고리에는 못[鉚釘] 3개가 배치되어 있으며 각각 꽃 장식이 달려 있다. 가운데 활짝 핀 꽃 정중앙은 삼엽화형(三葉花形)으로 투각되었으며 길이가 가장 길다. 뒤에 위치한 양쪽의 꽃들은 모두 꼭지 달린 감 모양이다.

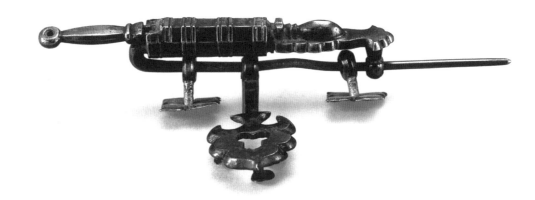

봉화문금잠(鳳花紋金簪)

금(金) | 당(唐) | 길이 14cm 무게 15g
1963년 서안시 비림구 사파(西安市 碑林區 沙坡) 벽돌공장에서 출토

Gold Hairpin with Phoenix and Flower Filigrees

Gold | Tang Dynasty(618AD~907AD) | L 14cm Weight 15g
Excavated from Shapo village Beilin District, Xi'an in 1963

순금(純金)으로 만든 잠(簪)이다. 머리에는 타원형 금편(金片)이 부착되어 있다. 잎무늬와 봉황 한 마리로 금편을 장식하였다. 봉황은 꽁지를 쳐들고 날개를 하늘거리며 모란꽃 위를 날아가는 형상이다. 잠의 몸체는 편평하고 길쭉하며 끝머리가 원추 모양이다.

신석기시대에 생겨난 잠은 머리를 얹거나 쪽을 진 후에 그 모양을 고정시키기 위해 사용하는 수식(首飾) 용구의 하나로 계(笄) 또는 비녀라고도 한다.

당대(唐代) 금은잠(金銀簪)은 이전에 비해 조형이 매우 복잡하였다. 꽃이나 용, 봉황 모양으로 된 것이 있는가 하면 수목, 산천, 인물 형상으로 된 것도 있었다. 금은뿐만 아니라 대모(玳瑁), 유리(琉璃)와 같은 진귀한 재료도 사용하였다. 이 금잠을 장식한 봉황과 모란 도안은 중국에서 부귀와 번영을 뜻한다. 봉황과 모란이 함께 금잠 위에 표현된 것에서 성당(盛唐) 시기 사람들의 부귀와 평안을 추구하는 염원을 엿볼 수 있다.

순형국화문류금은잠(盾形菊花紋鎏金銀簪)

은(銀) | 당(唐) | (1) 길이 13.1cm (2) 길이 16.5cm 각 무게 20.6g
1965년 서안시 비림구 사파촌(西安市 碑林區 沙坡村) 출토

Gilt Silver Hairpins with Chrysanthemum Pattern in the Shape of Shield

Silver | Tang Dynasty(618AD~907AD) | L (1) 13.1cm (2) 16.5cm Weight 20.6g for each
Excavated from Shapo Village Beilin District, Xi'an in 1965

잠(簪) 2점이다. 위쪽의 잠은 몸체가 편평하고 길다. 표면에는 금을 입혔는데 부분적으로 벗겨졌다. 머리는 방패 모양이다. 가장자리의 음각된 선문(線紋) 안쪽에는 가지와 잎이 흩어진 국화 한 송이가 음각되어 있으며 바탕에는 어자문(魚子紋)이 새겨져 있다. 아래쪽의 잠은 위의 잠과 형태가 똑같다. 머리 부분은 녹이 슬어 문양을 알아보기 어렵다.

(1)

(2)

순형모단화문금은잠(盾形牡丹花紋金銀簪)

은(銀) | 당(唐) | 길이 14.9cm 너비 3.4cm 무게 17g
1964년 서안시문물관리위원회(西安市文物管理委員會) 수집

Gilt Silver Hairpins with Peony Pattern in the Shape of Shield

Silver | Tang Dynasty(618AD~907AD) | L 14.9cm W 3.4cm Weight 17g
Collected by Xi'an Culture Relic Administration in 1964

조형과 무늬가 똑같은 편평한 잠(簪) 2점이다. 은으로 만든 다음에 표면에 금을 입혔다. 방패 모양의 머리에는 꽃봉오리가 달린 모란 한 송이가 새겨져 있다. 모란을 에워싼 가지와 잎은 촘촘하면서도 어수선하지 않다. 두 잠은 조형이 독특하고 배치가 합리적이다. 문양은 끌로 새기고 갈아서 빛을 낸 다음에 금을 입히는 기법을 사용하였다.

화초문은잠(花草紋銀簪)

은(銀) | 당(唐) | 길이 (1) 13cm (2) 8.7cm 각 무게 17g
1991년 서안시 파교구(西安市 灞橋區) 당나라 무덤에서 출토

Silver Hairpins with Flowers and Grass

Silver | Tang Dynasty(618AD〜907AD) | L (1) 13cm (2) 8.7cm Weight 17g for each
Excavated from Tang Tomb Baqiao District, Xi'an in 1991

편평한 잠(簪) 2점이다. 표면에는 금을 입혔는데 전체적으로 은회색을 띤다. (1) 버들잎 모양의 머리와 나선 모양의 몸체로 되어 있다. 가장자리가 연호형(連弧形)을 이루는 버들잎 안쪽에는 서로 잇닿은 잎무늬 3개가 배치되어 있으며 촘촘한 잎맥은 중심에서 가장자리로 뻗어 나왔다. (2) 꽃봉오리가 달린 연꽃 세 송이가 빼곡히 새겨진 머리와 나선 모양의 몸체로 되어 있다.

(1)　　　　　　　　　　　　　(2)

봉조문은채(鳳鳥紋銀釵)

은(銀) | 당(唐) | 길이 22cm 너비 9cm 무게 17.5g
1965년 서안시 연호구(西安市 蓮湖區) 출토

Silver Hairpin with Phoenix Pattern

Silver | Tang Dynasty(618AD〜907AD) | L 22cm W 9cm Weight 17.5g
Excavated from Lianhu District, Xi'an in 1965

몸체가 편평한 은채(銀釵)이다. 머리는 은행나무 잎 모양이다. 바탕은 진주무늬로 장식되었으며 가운데에는 둥둥 떠 있는 구름 사이로 봉황 한 마리가 날아가는 모습이 담겨 있다. 봉황은 관이 높다랗고 눈이 길쭉하며 머리의 깃털은 뒤로 흩날린다. 양쪽 날개는 가지런히 펼쳐졌으며 꽃잎 모양의 긴 꽁지는 바람에 하늘거린다. 은행나무 잎 가장자리는 투각(透刻)되었다. 표면에는 전체적으로 금을 입혔다.

107

은정수금채(銀錠首金釵)

금(金) | 당(唐) | 높이 29.8cm 무게 23.3g
1981년 서안시(西安市) 제1건축공정회사에서 출토

Gold Hairpin with a Silver Ingot

Gold | Tang Dynasty(618AD~907AD) | H 29.8cm Weight 23.3g
Excavated from Xi'an No.1 Construction Engineering Co. in 1981

순금(純金)으로 만든 채(釵)이다. 두 가닥으로 되었는데 몸체가 가늘고 길며 단면이 원형이다. 머리 부분은 배가 볼록한 사다리꼴 모양의 은정(銀錠) 2개를 연결한 듯하다. 연결된 부분은 봉긋하게 올라왔으며 양쪽에는 민무늬 채 한 가닥씩 이어져 있다.

108

소면금채(素面金釵)

금(金) | 당(唐) | 높이 19.2cm 무게 12.5g
1981년 서안시(西安市) 제1건축공정회사에서 출토

Plain Gold Hairpin

Gold | Tang Dynasty(618AD~907AD) | H 19.2cm Weight 12.5g
Excavated from Xi'an No. 1 Construction Engineering Co. in 1981

순금(純金)으로 만들어진 민무늬 채(釵)이다. 두 가닥으로 되었는데 머리는 '人(인)' 자 모양이고 몸체는 가늘고 길며 단면이 원형이다.

109

소면금채(素面金釵)

금(金) | 당(唐) | 높이 24.3cm 무게 23.5g
1987년 서안시 파교구(西安市 灞橋區) 제4군의대학 제2부속병원에서 출토

Plain Gold Hairpin

Gold | Tang Dynasty(618AD~907AD) | H 24.3cm Weight 23.5g
Excavated from The Fourth Military Medical University in Baqiao District, Xi'an in 1987

순금(純金)으로 만든 민무늬 채(釵)이다. 두 가닥으로 되었는데 몸체가 가늘고 길다. 단면은 원형이고 두 가닥이 연결된 부분은 '人(인)' 자 모양을 이루었다.

110

호수금채(弧首金釵)

금(金) | 당(唐) | 길이 11.3cm 너비 1.3cm 무게 19.99g
1979년 서안시 파교구 홍경진 전왕촌(西安市 灞橋區 洪慶鎭 田王村) 출토

Gold Hairpin with an Arced Head

Gold | Tang Dynasty(618AD~907AD) | L 11.3cm W 1.3cm Weight 19.99g
Excavated from Tianwang Village Hongqing Town In Baqiao District, Xi'an in 1979

머리꽂이로 쓰이는 민무늬 금채(金釵)이다. 머리는 호형(弧形)이고 몸
체는 끝이 뾰족하며 단면이 타원형인 기다란 막대 모양이다.

111

쌍엽문은채(雙葉紋銀釵)

은(銀) | 당(唐) | 길이 25.8cm 무게 20g
1986년 서안시 미앙구 삼교진(西安市 未央區 三橋鎭) 섬서(陝西) 제10면 방적공장 출토

Silver Hairpin with Double Leaves Pattern

Silver | Tang Dynasty(618AD~907AD) | L 25.8cm Weight 20g
Excavated from Shaanxi No. 10 Cotton Spinning Mill in Sanqiao Town
Weiyang District, Xi'an in 1986

은채(銀釵)는 두 가닥으로 나뉜다. 두 가닥 모두 단면이 원형으로 가늘고 긴 막대 모양이다. 두 가닥이 연결되는 부분은 중첩된 풀잎으로 장식되었다. 머리에
는 꽃잎 2개가 뻗어 있다. 풀잎과 꽃잎의 맥은 모두 끌로 조각하고 은채의 표면에는 전체적으로 금을 입혔다.

화조문은채(花鳥紋銀釵)

은(銀) | 당(唐) | 길이 17.1~34.1cm 무게 19.05g
1991년 서안시 파교구(西安市 灞橋區) 출토

Silver Hairpins with Flowers And Birds pattern

Silver | Tang Dynasty(618AD~907AD)
L 17.1~34.1cm Weight 19.05g
Excavated from Baqiao District, Xi'an in 1991

은채(銀釵) 8점이다. (1) 민무늬 은채로 머리가 은행나무 잎 모양이다. (2) 가운데로부터 양끝을 향해 두 가닥으로 뻗은 포크 모양이다. 머리에는 잎무늬가 새겨져 있고 사이사이에 반원 모양의 장식이 있다. 반원이 교차되는 곳의 안쪽에는 편평한 유정문(乳釘紋)이 배치되어 있다. (3) 길고 가늘며 편평한 모양이다. 머리에는 질경이 이삭 위를 나는 공작새 두 마리가 새겨져 있다. (4) 두 가닥으로 되어 있다. 머리는 활짝 핀 해바라기 꽃잎 모양이고 그 위쪽에는 바람에 나풀거리는 듯한 은사(銀絲) 두 가닥이 뻗어 있다. (5) 은채의 머리는 길쭉한 부등변 삼각형이다. 그 표면을 투각하였는데 권운문(卷雲紋)으로 안쪽을 장식하고 꽃잎마다에는 나는 새끼 제비 한 마리를 배치하였다. (6) 은채의 자루 끝머리에는 파초무늬가 새겨져 있으며 그 사이로 덩굴무늬를 새긴 풍성한 꽃이 피어 있다. 가지와 잎 사이는 모두 투각하였다. (7) 은채의 머리는 꽃잎 2개가 서로 얽히다가 편평한 모양의 가지와 잎으로 갈라진 형태이다. 끝머리에서 2~3개 꽃잎으로 갈라졌는데 가장자리에는 선문(線紋) 한 줄이 음각으로 둘러져 있다. 그 안쪽 양측에는 활짝 핀 연꽃이 각각 2개씩 배치되어 있다. (8) 은채는 몸체가 편평하다. 쌍엽(雙葉) 모양의 머리에는 긴 봉황 꽁지 한 쌍이 장식되어 있다. 겹겹이 새긴 유운(流雲)무늬 위에 표현된 종달새는 눈이 동그랗고 주둥이가 뾰족한데 날개를 펼치고 꽁지를 내려뜨린 채 자유로이 하늘을 나는 모습이다.

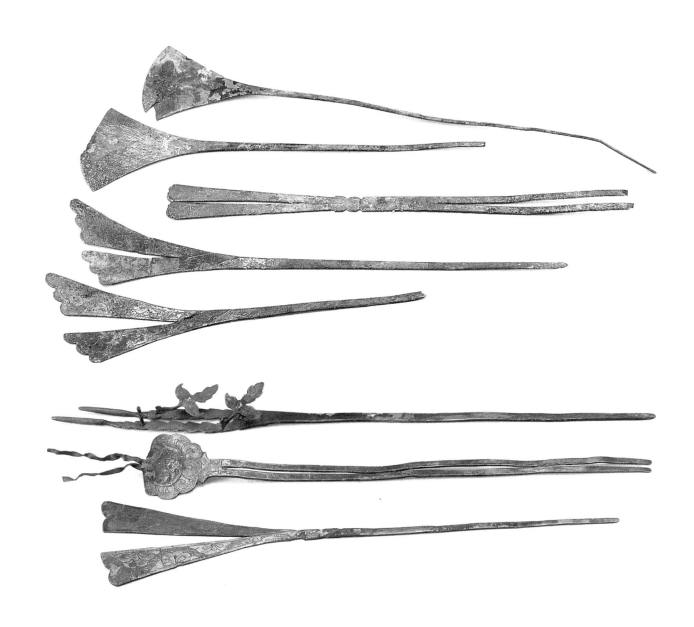

113

은채(銀釵)

은(銀) | 당(唐) | 길이 24.6~28.6cm 무게 64.8g
1993년 서안시 장안구 마왕진(西安市 長安區 馬王鎭) 출토

Silver Hairpins

Silver | Tang Dynasty(618AD~907AD) | L 24.6~28.6cm Weight 64.8g
Excavated from Mawang Town Chang'an District, Xi'an in 1993

부분적으로 회색 녹이 슬어 있는, 은백색을 띠는 은채(銀釵)이다. (1) 민무늬 은채로 머리가 '品(품)' 자 형이고 몸은 두 가닥으로 나뉘는데 가닥의 단면(斷面)은 원형이다. (2) 편평한 모양이다. 두 가닥은 깃털 모양의 무늬로 장식되었으며 가운데 부분에서 두 번 엉키다가 다시 갈라져 은채의 머리를 이루었다. 머리의 끄트머리는 삼각형으로 되었다.

(1)

(2)

114

마갈문은두채(摩羯紋銀頭釵)

은(銀) | 당(唐) | 잔편 길이 8.5cm 너비 4.6cm 무게 13.4g
1981년 서안시 미앙구 삼교진(西安市 未央區 三橋鎭) 출토

Silver Hairpin in Capricorn Pattern

Silver | Tang Dynasty(618AD~907AD) | L 8.5cm W 4.6cm Weight 13.4g
Excavated from Sanqiao Town Weiyang District, Xi'an in 1981

몸체가 파손되고 머리만 남아 있다. 표면에는 전체적으로 금을 입혔다. 머리는 꽃잎 모양인데 가운데에 연꽃 두 송이가 배치되어 있으며 그 위에는 둥근 공을 문 채 꼬리를 들고 튀어 오르는 마카라가 부착되어 있다. 인도의 전통 문양 중 하나인 마갈문(摩羯紋)은 길함을 뜻하는 문양으로 수당(隋唐)시대 불교의 성행과 더불어 중국에서 널리 성행하였다.

석류화문화채(石榴花紋花釵)

은(銀) | 당(唐) | 길이 17.5cm 무게 79.8g
1967년 서안시 신성구(西安市 新城區) 서안통신 케이블공장에서 출토

Flower Silver in Pomegranate Blossom Pattern

Sliver | Tang Dynasty(618AD~907AD) | L 17.5cm Weight 79.8g
Excavated from Xi'an Cable Works in Xincheng District, Xi'an in 1967

금을 입힌 은채(銀釵)로 부분적으로 손상되고 머리 부분만 남아 있다. 머리와 몸체를 이어주는 부분은 꽃잎 사이에 석류가 맺혀 있는 형상이다. 석류에서 꽃잎 2개가 뻗어 나와 은채의 머리가 되었다. 꽃잎은 투각(透刻)된 관지화(串枝花) 모양이고 잎줄기는 긴 편이다. 꽃잎 위에서는 종달새 한 마리가 노닐고 있다.

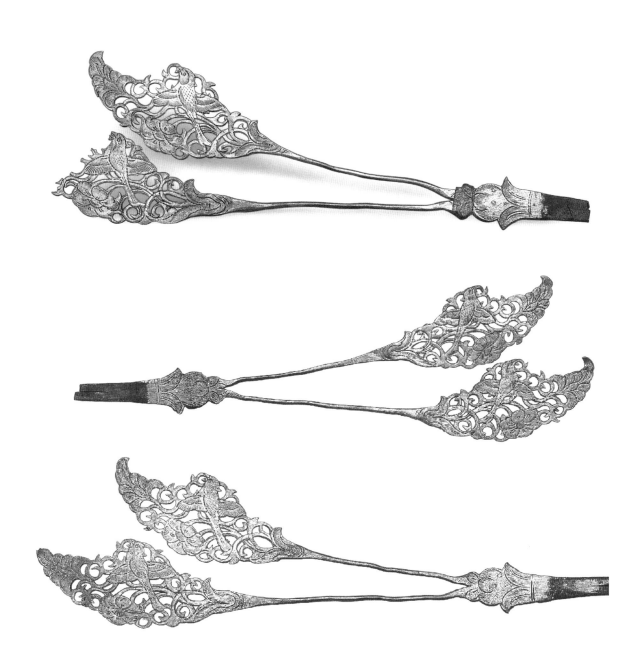

금주구(金珠扣)

금(金) | 당(唐) | 높이 0.7cm 지름 1.12cm 무게 3.4g
1971년 서안시 파교구 홍기향 곽가탄촌(西安市 灞橋區 紅旗鄉 郭家灘村) 출토

Gold Pearl Buttons

Gold | Tang Dynasty(618AD~907AD) | H 0.7cm D 1.12cm Weight 3.4g
Excavated from Guojiatan Village Honggi Town Baqiao District, Xi'an in 1971

속이 빈 원형 단추 2점이다. 외곽의 금편(金片)은 추엽(錘揲) 기
법으로 만들어졌는데 가운데가 약간 융기되었다. 그 속에 수정구
슬 하나가 상감되어 있다. 구슬 표면에는 타원형의 홈 3개가 나 있
다. 평평한 단추의 밑부분에는 가는 금사(金絲)가 뻗어 나온 작은
구멍 2개가 있다. 이는 단추를 고정시켜 주는 작용을 한다.

금화소(金花梳)

금(金) | 당(唐) | 길이 6.73cm 너비 1.7cm 무게 5.9g
1965년 서안시 안탑구 곡강향 삼조촌(西安市 雁塔區 曲江鄉 三兆村) 출토

Gold Flower Comb

Gold | Tang Dynasty(618AD~907AD) | L 6.73cm W 1.7cm Weight 5.9g
Excavated from Sanzhao Village Qujiang County in Yanta District, Xi'an in 1965

속이 빈 반달형 빗이다. 원래 나무 빗살이 달려 있었으나 파손되고 없다. 양면의 문양은 똑같은데 모두 세선세공(細線細工) 기법을 사용하였고 가운데에 매
화 한 송이, 양쪽에 원앙 한 쌍을 배치하였다. 꽃잎과 물방울무늬로 나머지 부분을 가득 채우고 작은 연주문(聯珠紋)으로 둘레를 장식하였다. 매화, 원앙, 물방울
등 부분에는 녹송석(綠松石)을 상감했으나 떨어지고 없다.

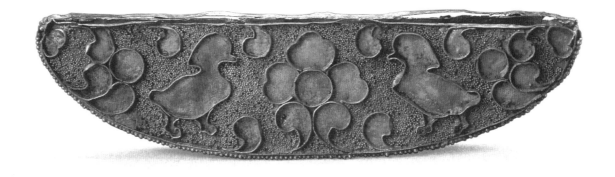

118

누공금화소(鏤空金花梳)

금(金) | 당(唐) | 길이 6.9cm 너비 5.5cm 무게 4.5g
1989년 서안시 연호구(西安市 蓮湖區) 출토

Hollow-out Gold Flower Comb

Gold | Tang Dynasty(619AD∼907AD) | L 6.9cm W 5.5cm Weight 4.5g
Excavated from Lianhu District, Xi'an in 1989

나무로 속을 만든 금빗이다. 톱니모양의 빗살은 거의 다 부러지고 일부만 남았다. 양면의 무늬는 동일한데 모두 가는 금사(金絲)를 추엽(錘擪)하여 만든 꽃과 가지, 잎이 부착되어 있다. 가운데에 매화 두 송이를 나란히 배치하고 그 양쪽을 가지와 잎으로 장식하였다. 문양들은 투각(透刻)하였다. 가지와 잎 위에 상감했던 장식물은 대부분 떨어지고 녹송석(綠松石) 한 알만 남았다. 송석 표면은 가는 선을 음각(陰刻)함으로써 잎맥을 나타냈다. 나무로 된 몸체 표면에는 작은 구멍이 있는데 금실로 양면의 꽃을 고정하였던 것으로 추측된다.

빗은 처음에 머리를 장식하는 데 이용하다가 차츰 머리를 정리하는 도구로 변화되었다.

당대(唐代) 여성들은 장식용으로 머리에 여러 개의 빗을 꽂았다. 따라서 당시(唐詩)에도 "구름같은 머릿단에 서각빗이 가로 꽂혔네"란 시구가 있다. 당왕조(唐王朝) 때는 금·은·무소뿔·옥·상아 등 재료로 반달모양의 빗을 장식하였다. 처음에는 간단히 쪽 앞부분에만 문양이 단순한 빗 하나를 꽂았는데 후에는 양쪽 귀밑머리 윗부분이나 쪽 뒷부분에도 꽂았다. 당대 말기에 와서는 빗 두 개를 한 세트로 하여 아래위로 마주 보게 꽂았고 또는 3개 세트를 쪽 앞부분과 양측에 꽂기도 했다. 손잡이의 장식은 날로 화려해져 금엽(金葉)을 입히고 그 위에 문양을 새긴 것도 있는가 하면, 금사(金絲)나 금알갱이로 각종 무늬와 도안을 만든 것도 있다. 성당(盛唐) 시기에는 비교적 작은 크기로 만들다가 중당(中唐) 시기에 이르러 점차 커졌으며 만당(晩唐) 시기에 크기가 더욱 커졌는데 머리의 두 배 높이인 것도 있었다.

119

유엽형은비천(柳葉形銀臂釧)

은(銀) | 당(唐) 지름 7.2cm 무게 89.8g
1964년 서안시문물관리위원회(西安市文物管理委員會) 수집

Silver Armlet in the Pattern of Willow Leaf

Silver | Tang Dynasty(618AD~907AD) | D 7.2cm Weight 89.8g
Collected by Xi'an Culture Relic Administration Committee in 1964

　가운데가 넓고 양쪽이 좁은, 열린 고리 모양의 편평한 비천(臂釧)이다. 표면은 은회색을 띤다. 겉면 가운데 볼록선은 비천 양끝과 연결되었다. 양쪽에는 은사(銀絲)가 여러 가닥 감겨져 있는데 끄트머리에서 작은 고리모양으로 매듭을 지었다. 끄트머리의 바깥쪽은 소용돌이 모양이고 편평한 안쪽은 민무늬로 되었다. 전체는 굽은 버들잎 모양이다.

　비천은 여성들이 팔에 착용하는 장신구로 서한(西漢)시대에 서역을 통해 중국에 전해졌다. 초기에는 단지 고리 모양으로만 만들어졌으나 양진(兩晉)시대에 와서 크기를 조절할 수 있는 것과 적게는 세 번 많게는 열 번 이상 감아 사용할 수 있는 것 등이 나타났다. 수당(隋唐) 초기에는 일반적으로 팔뚝에 착용하였으며, 성당(盛唐) 이후에는 위치가 점차 내려가다가 나중에는 손목 장신구가 되었다. 당대(唐代) 이후에는 양끝이 맞붙지 않은, 가운데가 넓고 양끝이 좁은 형태가 보편적이었다. 주로 옥이나 보석을 상감하거나 거푸집을 이용해 무늬를 찍어내는 등 기법을 사용하였다. 밧줄, 땋은 머리, 둥근 고리, 죽절(竹節) 및 구슬을 꿴 모양뿐만 아니라 양끝을 용머리 모양으로 장식한 것도 있었다.

120

유금동비천문은비천(鎏金銅飛天紋銀臂釧)

은(銀) | 당(唐) 지름 6.9cm 무게 27g 22g
1986년 서안시 미앙구 삼교진(西安市 未央區 三橋鎭) 출토

Gilt Silver Armlets in Flying Apsaras Pattern

Silver | Tang Dynasty(618AD~907AD) | D 6.9cm Weight 27g 22g
Excavated from Sanqiao Town Weiyang District, Xi'an in 1986

　버들잎 모양의 은제 비천(臂釧) 2점이다. 표면에는 전체적으로 금을 입혔다. 둘 다 비천을 두 부분으로 나누는 볼록선이 가운데에 배치되어 있으며 추엽(錘揲) 기법으로 만든 비천[飛天, 여자 선인(仙人)] 무늬가 새겨져 있다. 비천은 앞으로 뻗은 양손에 무언가를 들고 하늘을 나는 모습이다. 일명 '천인(天人)'이라고도 불리는 비천은 지위가 높은 천신(天神)으로 불교 도안에서 늘 하늘을 나는 다양한 자태의 모습으로 아름답게 묘사된다. 비천 장식은 당대(唐代) 이전의 사람과 신선 사이 장벽이 사라졌음을 말해주며 아름다운 생활을 영위하려는 사람들의 염원을 보여 준다.

'금광보전(金筐寶鈿)' 금화식(金花飾)

금(金) | 당(唐) | 길이 (1) 14.7cm (2) 6.9cm 너비 (1) 4.8cm (2) 6.2cm
무게 (1) 17g (2) 12g
1991년 서안시 파교구 파교진 여가보촌(西安市 灞橋區 灞橋鎮 呂家堡村) 출토

Gold Hair Ornaments in the Pattern of 'Jin Kuang Bao Dian'

Gold | Tang Dynasty(618AD~907AD) | L (1) 14.7cm (2) 6.9cm W (1) 4.8cm (2) 6.2cm
Weight (1) 17g (2) 12g
Excavated from Lvjiabu Village Baqiao Town Baqiao District, Xi'an in 1991

나비 및 봉황 모양의 꾸미개 2점이다. 나비 모양의 꾸미개는 좌우 대칭되는 가로로 된 'S'형 권연문(卷蓮紋)으로 이루어졌는데 날개를 펼치고 날고 있는 나비 같다. 연꽃의 가지와 잎들은 모두 편평한 금사(金絲)를 엮어 만든 것이다. 가지가 맞닿는 부분에는 금박을 용접하고 남은 부분은 투각(透刻)하였다. 가지와 잎 위에는 작은 크기의 금주문(金珠紋)을 새기고, 꽃잎과 이파리 부분에는 가늘고 얇은 금사를 엮어 가운데가 빈 테를 만들고 그 안쪽에 보석을 상감하였다. 봉

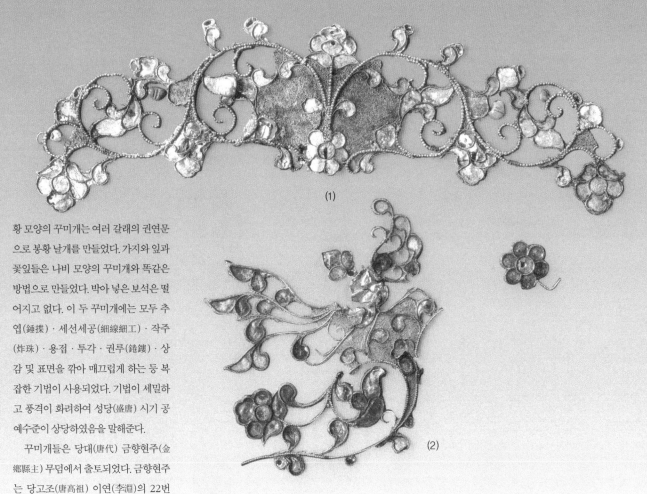

(1)

(2)

황 모양의 꾸미개는 여러 갈래의 권연문으로 봉황 날개를 만들었다. 가지와 잎과 꽃잎들은 나비 모양의 꾸미개와 똑같은 방법으로 만들었다. 박아 넣은 보석은 떨어지고 없다. 이 두 꾸미개에는 모두 추엽(錘揲)·세선세공(細線細工)·작주(炸珠)·용접·투각·권루(錔鏤)·상감 및 표면을 깎아 매끄럽게 하는 등 복잡한 기법이 사용되었다. 기법이 세밀하고 풍격이 화려하여 성당(盛唐) 시기 공예수준이 상당하였음을 말해준다.

꾸미개들은 당대(唐代) 금향현주(金鄕縣主) 무덤에서 출토되었다. 금향현주는 당고조(唐高祖) 이연(李淵)의 22번째 아들 등왕(滕王) 이원영(李元嬰)의 셋째 딸로 당고종(唐高宗) 영휘(永徽) 2년(651년)에 태어나 당현종(唐玄宗) 개원(開元) 10년(722년)에 졸하였는데, 향년 71살이다. 성당 시기의 인물인 금향현주 지위가 존귀한 이당(李唐) 종실이므로 다량의 진귀한 물품이 함께 부장되었다. 이 두 꾸미개는 금향현주가 머리

장신구로 사용한 것으로 추측된다.

고대 중국 부녀들은 치장하는 데 신경을 많이 썼다. 일찍 머리에 꽃을 꽂는 풍습이 있었다. 금은장신구는 지속적으로 매우 성행하였다. 성당 시기에는 부녀자들 사이에 높은 쪽머리가 유행하자 머리에 꽃을 꽂아 장식하는 풍습이 널리 퍼졌다. 상층 부녀들은 금제 꽃을 애용하였는데, 이를 금전(金鈿)이라 한다. 금전 위에 보석을 상감한 것은 보전(寶鈿)이라 한다. 고대 부녀들의 머리 장식은 장식용뿐만 아니라 신분, 지위의 상징물이기도 하였다. 『수서(隋書)』「예의육(禮儀六)」에서는 황후의 예복은 네 등급이 있다. 머리장식용 꽃은 12개이다. 삼비(三妃)는 9개, 공부인(公夫人), 현주(縣主), 이품(二品)의 명부(命婦)는 8개 꽃을 다는 등 개수는 지위에 따라 달라졌다. 당왕조는 수왕조를 그대로 답습하였다. 금향현주라 하면 이품의 명부로 장식용 꽃이 8개였을 것으로 추측된다.

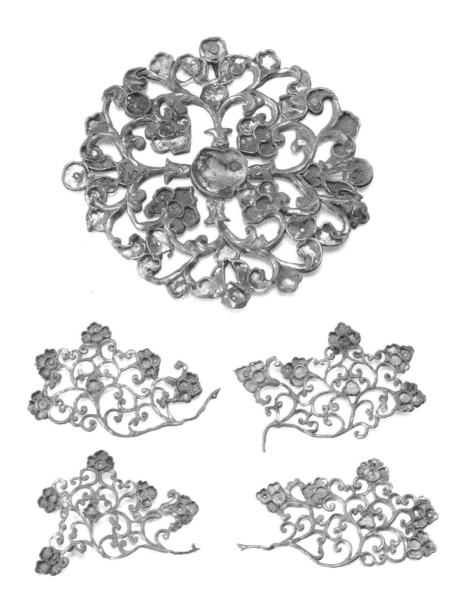

122

금만초화식(金蔓草花飾)

금(金) | 당(唐) | 길이 5~7.2cm 무게 102g
1971년 서안시 파교구 홍기향 곽가탄촌(西安市 灞橋區 紅旗鄉 郭家灘村) 출토

Gold Hair Ornament with Trailers

Gold | Tang Dynasty(618AD~907AD) | L 5~7.2cm Weight 102g
Excavated from Guojiatan Village Hongqi Town Baqiao District, Xi'an in 1971

　　덩굴무늬 꾸미개는 크게 잎 모양과 단화(團花) 모양으로 나뉘는데 가지와 잎이나 꽃으로 장식된 변형적인 관지연화(串枝蓮花)로 표현된다. 원래 둥근 모양이나 복숭아 모양의 보석이 박혀 있었으나 지금은 떨어지고 둥근 구멍만 남아 있다. 덩굴무늬 꾸미개에는 모두 6가지 형태가 있다. (1) 타원형이고 직경이 5.5~7cm이다. 중심에는 잎무늬가 사방으로 펼쳐지며 원형을 이루고 그 둘레에는 꽃 네 송이가 배치되어 있으며 꽃술 안팎에는 꽃잎이 둘러져 있다. 중심과 주위 꽃 사이 및 잎에는 보석이 박혀 있었으나 지금은 떨어지고 없다. 꽃 사이에는 고정용 구멍 8개가 나 있다. (2) 절지화(折枝花) 모양으로 길이가 8cm이고 너비가 4.5cm이다. 줄기에는 꽃과 가지와 잎이 연결되어 있으며 꽃가지 왼쪽에는 꽃 다섯 송이가 활짝 피어 있다. 네 꽃잎에는 보석이 상감되어 있었으나 지금은 떨어지고 없다. (3) 절지화 모양으로 줄기에는 꽃과 가지와 잎이 연결되어 있으며 꽃가지 오른쪽에는 꽃 다섯 송이가 피어 있다. 사엽화판(四葉花瓣)에 보석이 박혀 있었으나 지금은 떨어지고 없다. (4) 소엽절지화(小葉折枝花) 모양으로 길이가 3cm이다. 줄기에는 작은 잎이 가득 달려 있는데 잎마다 보석이 박혀 있었으나 지금은 떨어지고 없다. 잎에는 작은 구멍들이 나 있다. (5) 대엽절지화(大葉折枝花) 모양으로 길이가 3.5cm이다. 가지에는 큰 잎이 가득한데 잎마다 보석이 박혀 있었으나 지금은 떨어지고 없다. 잎에는 작은 구멍이 있다. (6) 매화 모양으로 길이가 6cm이다. 가지에는 매화가 피어 있으며 그 둘레는 연주문(蓮珠紋)으로 장식되어 있다.

금보리수(金菩提樹)

금(金) | 당(唐) | (1) 높이 13.5cm 상부 너비 7cm 하부 너비 0.5cm 밑동 너비 1.9cm 무게 11.6g
(2) 높이 11.6cm 상부 너비 7.5cm 하부 너비 0.3cm 밑동 너비 2cm 무게 8.6g
1971년 서안시 파교구 홍기향 곽가탄촌(西安市 灞橋區 紅旗鄕 郭家灘村) 출토

Gold Lindens

Gold | Tang Dynasty(618AD~907AD) | (1) H 13.5cm Upper W 7cm Lower W 0.5cm Base W 1.9cm Weight 11.6g
(2) H 11.6cm Upper W 7.5cm Lower W 0.3cm Base W 2cm Weight 8.6g
Excavated from Guojiatan Village Hongqi Town Baqiao District, Xi'an in 1971

보리수[菩提樹] 2점이다. 줄기, 나뭇가지, 꽃, 나뭇잎으로 이루어졌다. 크고 작은 나뭇가지에는 꽃과 나뭇잎이 가득하다. 밑동에서부터 마디가 있는 줄기 위로 넝쿨이 길게 휘감겨 있다. 나무줄기의 아랫부분마다 뿌리가 드러나 있으며, 꽃들에는 녹송석(綠松石)을 상감했던 것으로 보인다. 금수록화(金樹綠花), 경지유등(勁枝柔藤)은 화려하고 무게감이 있어 유난히 이목을 끈다. 나무줄기, 밑동 및 일부 잎사귀에 나 있는 작은 구멍들은 못으로 고정하기 위해 배치한 것이다. 이로써 보리수가 어떤 기물의 장식품으로 사용되었음을 알 수 있다. 두 보리수는 짜임새가 있으며 성기고 빽빽함이 알맞다.

보리수는 남아시아 일대의 수종으로 상록 교목에 속한다. 나뭇잎은 난원형(卵圓形)이고 줄기는 황백색을 띠며 꽃받침은 구형에 가까우며 그 속에는 꽃이 감춰져 있다. 타원형의 열매는 익으면 검은 자색을 띤다. 그 씨는 염주(念珠)로 쓰이는데 승려가 염불할 때 보리수를 직접 염주용으로 사용하기도 하였다. 전하는 바에 따르면 싯다르타는 보리수 아래에서 명상하던 중 깨달음을 얻어 성불하였다고 한다. 따라서 불교에서는 불교를 상징하는 보리수를 각수(覺樹), 도수(道樹)라고 부르기도 한다. 보리수의 제작 분포를 볼 때 불교는 당대(唐代)에 이미 중국사회에 융합되어 사람들의 문화생활에 영향을 미치고 있음을 알 수 있다. 추엽(錘揲) 기법으로 만들고 녹송석 장식까지 더하여 그 조형이 아름답고 율동감이 넘쳐 당대 장인들의 뛰어난 공예솜씨를 보여 주는 진귀한 작품이다.

(1)　　　　　　　　　　　　　　(2)

124

유금주룡(鎏金走龍)

동(銅) | 당(唐) | 길이 18cm 높이 10.8cm 무게 260g
1979년 서안시(西安市) 문물상점(文物商店)으로부터 넘겨받음

Gilt Walking Dragon

Copper | Tang Dynasty(618AD~907AD)
L 18cm H 10.8cm Weight 260g
Transferred by Xi'an Culture Relic Shop in 1979

용은 뾰족한 입 사이로 날카로운 이빨을 드러내고 긴 혓바닥을 말아 올렸으며 외뿔에 귀를 쫑긋 세웠다. 정수리의 곱슬곱슬한 머리는 뒤로 향했고 등은 톱날 같은 형상이다. 거니는 모양새를 하고 있는데 왼쪽 두 다리가 뒤로 향하고 오른쪽 두 다리가 앞을 향하고 있으며 끄트머리가 올라간 긴 꼬리를 질질 끌고 있다. 용의 다리는 기다랗고 발에는 발톱 3개가 달려 있다. 표면은 전체적으로 도금하고 몸체는 비늘무늬로 장식하였다. 발달한 근육, 힘찬 모습, 당당한 기세로부터 자신감과 활기찬 생명력을 엿볼 수 있다.

용은 상상 속의 동물이다. 용무늬는 중국 전통 장식문양 가운데 응용범위가 가장 넓고 생명력이 넘치며 민족적 특색을 띤 소재 중 하나이다. 당대(唐代) 시기의 황실에서는 용을 전용 도안으로 사용하지 않았기 때문에 이 유금주룡(鎏金走龍)은 용을 조각한 장인이 현실 속 동물을 기초로 하고 뛰어난 기교 및 정확한 형태로 조각하였다. 살아 있는 듯한 유금주룡은 성당(盛唐) 시기의 예술적 미를 표현하고 있다.

금난봉(金鸞鳳)

금(金) | 당(唐) | 높이 6.6cm 너비 6.7cm 무게 17g
1971년 서안시 파교구 홍기향 곽가탄촌(西安市 灞橋區 紅旗鄉 郭家灘村) 출토

Gold Luan & Feng(Legendary Birds in Chinese Folklore of the Phoenix Type)

Gold | Tang Dynasty(618AD∼907AD) | H 6.6cm W 6.7cm Weight 17g
Excavated from Guojiatan Village Hongqi Town Baqiao District, Xi'an in 1971

조형 및 장식기법이 똑같은 금난봉(金鸞鳳) 2점이다. 봉황은 앞쪽을 물끄러미 바라보는데 가슴을 쭉 펴고 두 발을 디디고 서 있으며 날개를 펼치고 당장이라도 날아갈 듯한 형상을 하고 있다. 정수리에는 높은 화관을 썼고 머리의 긴 깃털은 뒤로 흘날린다. 입이 짧고 목이 굽었으며 꼬리부분이 위로 말렸는데 깃털마다 가지와 잎 모양으로 층층이 위로 향하고 맨 끝은 한 무더기 꽃봉오리와 꽃잎으로 장식되었다. 가슴, 복부, 날개 깃털 등 부위에는 녹송석(綠松石)을 상감했으나 떨어지고 없다. 봉황의 날개, 꼬리, 발 등의 동작은 조화로우면서도 동태적인데 하늘 높이 솟구치려 할 때의 순간적인 동작을 매우 형상적으로 묘사하였다. 봉황의 화관, 날개 및 꼬리의 끄트머리와 양발에는 못으로 고정하기 위한 작은 구멍이 나 있다. 이 두 금난봉은 다음에 나오는 금룡(金龍), 금압(金鴨) 등과 함께 출토되었는데 모두 기물의 장식인 것으로 추측된다. 금난봉은 조형상 옹골지고 매끄러워 보이는데 이는 당대(唐代) 봉황 장식의 독

특한 특징이다. 당대 시기, '조류 가운데의 수장'으로 여겨진 봉황은 신령의 상징으로 숭고함과 존귀함을 뜻해 황후나 후궁을 의미하였다. 봉황은 중국 고대 방위를 상징하는 4령(四靈) 가운데 하나로서 남방을 상징하며 사철 중 여름을 상징하기도 한다.

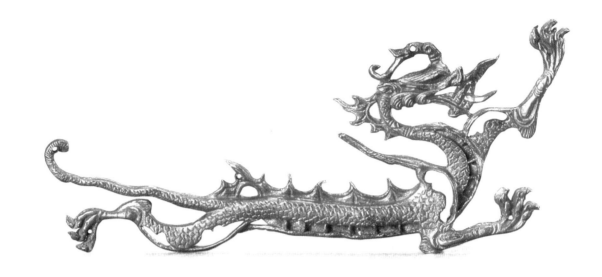

126

금룡(金龍)

금(金) | 당(唐) | 높이 4cm 길이 9.4cm 무게 11.2g
1971년 서안시 파교구 홍기향 곽가탄촌(西安市 灞橋區 紅旗鄉 郭家灘村) 출토

Gold Dragon

Gold | Tang Dynasty(618AD~907AD) | H 4cm L 9.4cm Weight 11.2g
Excavated from Guojiatan Village Hongqi Town Baqiao District, Xi'an in 1971

　　용은 하늘을 향해 질주하는 모습이다. 용의 머리는 긴 편인데 머리 위 외뿔은 뒤로 말렸으며 눈과 입이 크다. 눈과 귀 아래 부분에 세 가닥의 짧은 수염이 나 있다. 용은 앞다리를 앞으로 쭉 뻗고 뒷다리를 굽히고 뛰어오르는 모양을 하고 있는데 몸체가 비교적 곧으며 목, 등 부위는 뾰족하고 곧게 편 긴 꼬리의 끄트머리는 위로 말렸다. 용의 발은 3개의 발가락으로 되었으며 발톱은 예리하다. 용의 비늘을 묘사함이 촘촘하면서도 선명한데 전체적인 형태가 힘 있어 보인다. 몸체 아랫부분의 투각(透刻)한 곳에는 워낙 녹송석(綠松石)을 상감했었다. 용의 뿔, 발가락 및 꼬리 부분에 못으로 고정하기 위해 난 작은 구멍이 있는 것으로 보아 이 금룡은 기물(器物)의 장식품이었음을 알 수 있다. 용은 중국 고대 시기 방위를 상징하는 4령(四靈) 가운데 하나로 동방을 상징하며 사철 중 봄을 상징하기도 한다.

127

엽형금탁연주변양록송석식물
(葉形金托連珠邊鑲綠松石飾物)

금(金) | 당(唐) | (1) 길이 5.07cm 너비 3.05cm (2) 길이 5.09cm 너비 3.29cm
각 무게 18.5g
1986년 서안시 미앙구 삼교진(西安市 未央區 三橋鎭) 섬서(陝西) 제10면 방적 공장 출토

Leaf-shaped Gold-Quinto Ornament in the Pattern of Lianzhu Edge with Inlaid Kallaites

Gold | Tang Dynasty(618AD~907AD) | (1) L 5.07cm W 3.05cm
(2) L 5.09cm W 3.29cm Weight 18.5g for each
Excavated from Shaanxi No.10 Cotton Spinning Mill in Sanqiao Town Weiyang District, Xi'an in 1986

　　금테에 둘러싸인 불규칙적인 잎 모양의 장식 조각 2점이다. 가장자리에는 연주문(聯珠紋)을 두르고 그 안쪽에 녹송석(綠松石)을 상감하였다. 녹송석 위에는 연잎을 겹겹이 새겼는데 잎이 활짝 펼쳐지고 연꽃이 만발하였으며 그 사이로 한 쌍의 원앙새가 노닐고 있다.

128

금압(金鴨)

금(金) | 당(唐) | 높이 2.3cm 너비 3.3cm 무게 10.2g
1971년 서안시 파교구 홍기향 곽가탄촌(西安市 灞橋區 紅旗
鄉 郭家灘村) 출토

Gold Ducks

Gold | Tang Dynasty(618AD~907AD) | H 2.3cm W
3.3cm Weight 10.2g
Excavated from Guojiatan Village Hongqi Town Baqiao
District, Xi'an in 1971

　　오리 모양 장식품 2점으로, 조형 및 장식기법
이 똑같다. 앞쪽을 바라보는 오리는 주둥이가 길
쭉하고 목이 굽었으며 날개를 펼치고 두 발을 디
디고 서 있는데 날아갈 듯한 형상을 하고 있다. 뒤
로 드리운 꼬리는 여의운두형(如意雲頭形)을 이
룬다. 가슴, 복부와 날개 깃털 등 부위에는 원래
녹송석(綠松石)을 상감했으나 지금은 떨어지고
없다. 한쪽 날개 윗부분과 꼬리 끄트머리에는 각
각 작은 구멍이 있으며 구멍 안에 못[鉚釘]이 있
는데 이는 고정해 주는 작용을 한다. 이 금압(金
鴨)은 기물(器物)의 장식품에 속한다.

147

129

도형금식건(桃形金飾件)

금(金) | 당(唐) | (1) 길이 4.78cm 너비 3.37cm 무게 5g
(2) 길이 4.4cm 너비 3.58cm 무게 7g
1988년 서안시 연호구(西安市 蓮湖區) 서안계기공장에서 출토

Peach-shaped Gold Ornament

Gold | Tang Dynasty(618AD~907AD) | (1) L 4.78cm W 3.37cm Weight 5g
(2) L 4.4cm W 3.58cm Weight 7g
Excavated from Xi'an Instrument Plant in Lianhu District, Xi'an in 1988

복숭아 모양과 흡사한 장식 조각이다. 진주무늬를 바탕에 시문(試紋)
하였다. 가장자리에 자그마한 연주문(聯珠紋)을 새겨 넣고 연주문을 따
라 두 가닥의 금판(金版)을 둘렀다. 금판 안쪽은 연주문 모양의 동그란
합(盒)과 같은 장식이 가득 배열되었고 복숭아 모양의 중심은 꽃잎에 둘
러싸인 육판(六瓣) 매화꽃이다. 매화꽃과 잎무늬 안에 원래 보석을 상감
해 넣었는데 지금은 떨어지고 없다. 뒷면은 직사각형이다.

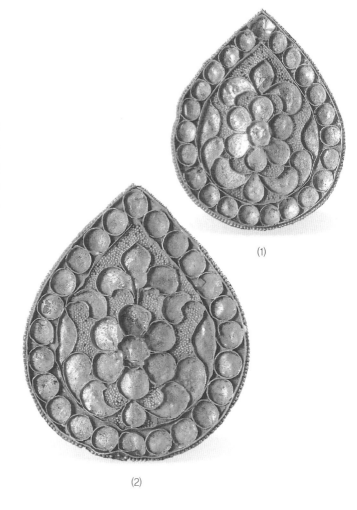

(1)

(2)

130

계심형금화식편(鷄心形金花飾片)

금(金) | 당(唐) | 길이 4.39cm 너비 3.72cm 무게 5g
1988년 서안시 연호구(西安市 蓮湖區) 서안계기공장에서 출토

Gold Flower Ornament in Heart-shaped Form

Gold | Tang Dynasty(618AD~907AD) | L 4.39cm W 3.72cm Weight 5g
Excavated from Xi'an Instrument Plant in Lianhu District, Xi'an in 1988

닭 심장 모양의 장식 조각이다. 가장자리에는 연주문(聯珠紋)을 두르고 가운데
는 추엽(鍾揲) 기법으로 매화무늬를 새겼는데 그 아래위에 꽃잎무늬 장식을 하였
으며, 나머지 부분에는 모두 진주무늬를 시문(試紋)하였다. 매화무늬 및 연주무늬
안에는 보석을 상감했으나 지금은 떨어지고 없다.

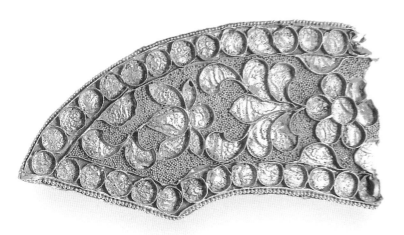

131

선형금화식편(扇形金花飾片)

금(金) | 당(唐) | 남은 조각 길이 8.3cm 너비 3.5cm 무게 18g
1988년 서안시 연호구(西安市 蓮湖區) 서안계기공장에서 출토

Fan-shaped Gold Flower Spike

Gold | Tang Dynasty(618AD~907AD) | L 8.3cm W 3.5cm Weight 18g
Excavated from Xi'an Instrument Plant in Lianhu District, Xi'an in 1988

이 장식조각은 펼쳐진 쥘부채 모양이고 부분적으로 파손되어 절반만 남은 상태이다. 장식 가운데는 꽃잎모양이며 가장자리에 연주문(聯珠紋)을 두르고 나머지 부분에 진주무늬를 새겼다. 꽃잎과 연주문 안에 보석을 상감했는데 떨어지고 없다. 뒷면 바탕에 인동문(忍冬紋), 진주무늬를 선각(線刻)하였다.

132

금합혈(金合頁)

금(金) | 당(唐) | 길이 5.3cm 너비 2.1cm 무게 21g 19g
1971년 서안시 파교구 홍기향 곽가탄촌(西安市 灞橋區 紅旗鄉 郭家灘村) 출토

Gold Hinge

Gold | Tang Dynasty(618AD~907AD) | L 5.3cm W 2.1cm Weight 21g 19g
Excavated from Guojiatan Village Hongqi County in Baqiao District, Xi'an in 1971

경첩은 궤(櫃)의 부속으로 두 날개가 축을 중심으로 맞물려 돌아갈 수 있게 만들었다.

경첩은 옷궤의 부분품으로써 축과 두 날개로 구성되었다. 금판형(金板形) 모양의 날개 위에는 복숭아무늬 1개, 구름무늬 2개, 작은 구멍 5개를 투각(透刻)하였는데 이는 경첩을 달기 위해 뚫은 못 구멍이다. 못[鉚釘]으로 축과 날개가 연결되어 축을 중심으로 맞물려 돌아갈 수 있다. 여기서 사용된 접합기법은 당대(唐代) 금은기(金銀器) 공예의 중대한 발명으로 접합하려는 부품과 기물(器物)에 작은 구멍을 뚫은 후에 못으로 고정시키는 방법을 말하는데 흔히 작은 기물에 많이 이용되었다. 이는 당시 간단한 기계공구가 있었음을 말해 준다.

133

은합혈(銀合頁)

은(銀) | 당(唐) | 길이 4.9cm 너비 1.79cm 무게 16.5g
1977년 서안시문물관리위원회(西安市文物管理委員會) 수집

Silver Hinge

Silver | Tang Dynasty(618AD~907AD) | L 4.9cm W 1.79cm Weight 16.5g
Collected by Xi'an Culture Relic Administration Committee in 1977

은으로 만든 경첩은 궤(櫃)의 부속이다. 경첩은 가운데의 축과 양쪽의 원호형(圓弧形) 날개 한 쌍으로 구성되었다. 뒷면에는 경첩을 달기 위한, 모자모양의 은못[銀釘] 3개가 배치되어 있다. 두 날개는 축을 중심으로 맞물려 돌아갈 수 있게 만들었다.

134

유금동용수은연쇄(鎏金銅龍首銀鏈鎖)

은(銀) | 당(唐) | 길이 102cm 지름 1.9cm 용머리 긴지름 3cm 무게 647g
1980년 함양시 요점(咸陽市 窯店) 출토

Gilt Silver Chain Lock with a Bronze Dragon Head

Silver | Tang Dynasty(618AD~907AD) | L 102cm D 1.9cm D of the Dragon head 3cm Weight 647g
Excavated from Yaodian Village Xianyang City in 1980

은사(銀絲)를 엮어서 만든 사슬 양끝에는 용머리 모양 자물쇠가 있다. 동으로 만든 용머리 표면에는 금을 입혔다. 외뿔이 나 있는 용머리는 큰 눈, 길쭉한 입, 날카로운 송곳니, 큰 귀, 긴 수염, 위로 굽은 코를 가진 형상이고 입에는 둥근 자물쇠 고리가 있다. 용머리와 사슬은 못[鉚釘]으로 연결되었다. 이 사슬은 함양시(咸陽市) 삼원현(三原縣)에서 출토된 북조(北朝)의 보살상 목걸이와 조형이 매우 비슷할 뿐만 아니라 비율 또한 거의 일치해 승려나 거사들이 예불호법(禮佛護法)을 위해 목에 걸었던 은목걸이인 것으로 추측된다.

불교에서는 고난을 즐거움으로 여길 것을 주장하는데 주로 불교도들이 현재에 만족하고 고난을 기꺼이 받아들일 것을 요구한다. 이 자물쇠는 제작이 정교하고 재료가 진귀한데 이는 당대(唐代) 사회 경제 및 불교 사원의 발전정도를 보여 준다.

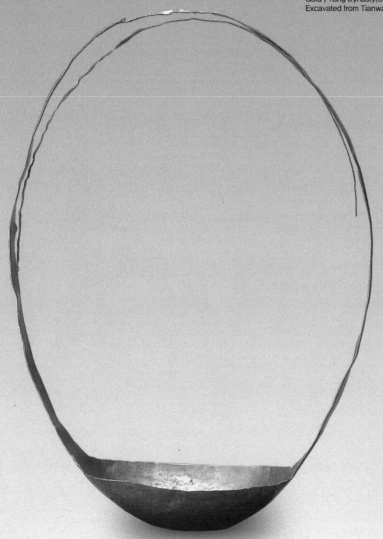

135

금합탁(金頜托)

금(金) | 당(唐) | 세로 66cm 가로 5.4cm 높이 9cm 무게 72g
1979년 서안시 파교구 홍경진 전왕촌(西安市 灞橋區 洪慶鎭 田王村) 출토

Gold Jaw Holder

Gold | Tang Dynasty(618AD~907AD) | L 66cm W 5.4cm H 9cm Weight 72g
Excavated from Tianwang Village Hongqing Town in Baqiao District, Xi'an in 1979

얇은 금속 조각을 추엽(錘揲)하여 만든 타원형의 민무늬 합탁(頜托)이다. 사람의 아래턱을 받쳐 주는 탁(托)도 타원형으로 되었는데 가운데가 오목한 구면(球面)이다. 양측에는 탁을 고정하기 위한, 길고 납작한 호형(弧形)의 자루가 달려 있다.

합탁은 장례용품으로 죽은 자의 몸이나 관(棺)에 넣어 함께 매장하는 물품을 말한다. 옛사람들은 흔히 금으로 만든 장례용품을 사용하였다. 옛사람들은 시체를 금으로 감싼 후 매장하면 시체가 부식되지 않는다고 믿었기 때문이다. 금은 화학적 성질이 안정적이어서 기타 금속과 화학반응을 일으키지 않아 영원히 변질되지 않는 특성이 있으므로 금으로 시체를 감싸면 시체가 부식되는 것을 방지할 것으로 믿었다. 금은은 귀금속에 속하므로 일정한 신분, 지위가 있는 사람만이 음식기나 장례용품으로 사용할 수 있었다. 따라서 금은기(金銀器)는 무덤 주인의 신분과 지위를 나타내주기도 하였다.

이 금합탁과 1999년 녕하(寧夏) 고원현(固原縣) 당고종(唐高宗) 의봉(儀鳳) 3년(675년), 사도덕(史道德) 무덤에서 출토된 금복면(金覆面) 속 금합탁과 조형이 똑같다. 사도덕의 선조는 당대(唐代) 시기, 중앙아시아 일대의 소무구성(昭武九姓, 소그디아나인) 가운데 사국인(史國人)으로 남북조(南北朝)시대에 중국으로 이주하면서 중앙아시아 소무구성의 장례풍속을 함께 가져왔다. 출토 시 사도덕의 입에 물었던 금화와 함께 출토된 원형 동물무늬 장신구와 연관시켜 보면, 상술한 금복면(金覆面)에서 표현된 장례풍속은 소그디아나인의 종교인 조로아스터교[기원전 6세기, 페르시아인인 조로아스터(Zoroaster)에 의해 창시된 종교로 페르시아 및 중앙아시아 여러 나라에서 널리 믿었다. 고대 페르시아제국 국왕 다리우스 1세가 조로아스터교를 국교로 정하여 광명과 행복을 상징하는 주신 아후라 마즈다(Ahura Mazda)를 숭배하였다. 또한 광명의 상징인 불을 숭배하여 주요 종교의식에 성화를 사용한다. 때문에 배화교(拜火教)라고도 불린다. 선과 악, 명과 암 간의 투쟁을 주장한다. 조로아스터교는 로마제국시대의 기독교 형성에 영향을 미쳤을 뿐만 아니라 위(魏)·진(晉)·남북조(南北朝)시대에 중앙아시아의 소그디아나인을 통해 중국에 전파되어 현교(祆教)나 배화교라 불렸다]와 관계가 있음을 짐작할 수 있다. 이로 볼 때 이 금합탁은 북조에서 당대 시기까지 중국 서북지역으로 이주한 소그디아나인들이 자기 민족의 장례풍속을 그대로 가져왔음을 알 수 있다.

151

조상(造像)은 투각(透刻)한 해바라기 모양의 높은 하대(下臺), 해당화 모양의 중대(中臺)와 중대에서 뻗어 나온 연꽃 줄기, 불상 1구와 보살상 2구로 구성되었다. 아미타삼존(阿彌陀三尊)이라고 불리는 서방삼성(西方三聖)은 중생을 극락세계로 인도하는 아미타불과 좌협시(左脇侍) 관세음보살(觀世音菩薩), 우협시(右脇侍) 대세지보살(大勢至菩薩)을 가리킨다. 아미타불은 높은 육계(肉髻), 둥글넓적한 얼굴, 큰 귀, 둥근 눈썹에 가는 눈을 가졌다. 목에는 이도(二道)가 새겨져 있다. 위에는 가사를 둘렀는데 그 안에 그물무늬로 장식한 승지지(僧祇支)가 훤히 보인다. 아래에는 치마식 긴 바지를 입었다. 오른손은 다섯 손가락을 가지런히 펴고 손바닥을 밖으로 하여 어깨 높이까지 올린 시무외인(施無畏印)을 취하였다. 왼손은 드리웠는데 손가락을 아래로 곧게 펴고 손바닥이 안쪽을 향하게 무릎 위에 놓아 항마인[降魔印, 또는 촉지인(觸地印)이라고 한다. 손을 무릎 위에 놓아 손가락을 아래로 향하게 하는 손 모양으로 잡귀를 굴복시킴을 뜻함]을 하였다. 두 발바닥이 위로 향하게 복부 앞쪽으로 놓아 결가부좌(結跏趺坐)를 하고 원형 대좌(臺座) 위에 앉아 있는데 대좌 둘레가 옷자락으로 가려졌다. 좌협시 관세음보살은 둥그스름한 얼굴, 반달 모양의 눈썹, 선한 눈, 오뚝한 코를 가졌다. 큰 귓불이 어깨에 닿을 듯하며 머리에 쓴 화려한 화불관(化佛冠)의 관대(冠帶)가 어깨까지 흘러내렸다. 목에는 이도(二道)가 새겨져 있으며, 방울이 달린 영락(瓔珞)을 착용하였다. 그중 두 가닥은 목에 둘러져 있고 다른 한 가닥은 오른쪽 어깨로부터 길게 아래로 드리워졌다. 상반신을 드러내고 하반신에는 긴 치마를 입었다. 어깨에 두른 천의(天衣) 자락 역시 아래로 흘러내렸으며, 손목에는 팔찌를 착용하였다. 위로 올린 오른손에는 버드나무 가지, 내린 왼손에는 정병(淨甁)을 들고 천을 두른 원형 대좌 위에 결가부좌를 하고 앉아 있다. 우협시 대세지보살은 좌협시 관세음보살과 거의 같은 형상이며, 다만 머리에는 보관을 쓰고, 목에 건 영락(瓔珞)이 왼쪽 어깨로부터 드리워져 있을 뿐이다. 보관(寶冠)의 관대가 어깨까지 드리워졌으며, 영락의 두 가닥은 목에 둘러져 있고 다른 한 가닥은 왼쪽 어깨로부터 길게 드리워져 있다. 손목에는 팔찌를 착용하였다. 올린 왼손에는 병(甁)과 흡사한 물건을 들고, 내린 오른손에는 연꽃 가지를 쥐었다. 세 불상의 머리 뒤에는 투각한 광배(光背)가 있다. 둘레는 활활 타오르는 불꽃무늬, 안쪽은 연꽃 가지·연잎·능형(菱形)·격자(格子)무늬, 가장자리를 불꽃무늬로 장식하였다. 꽃잎 모양의 높다란 하대와 중대에서 뻗어 나온 연꽃 줄기 3개가 위의 불상을 받쳐 준다.

아미타불은 불교의 사방사불(四方四佛) 가운데 하나이다. 불교에서 말하는 사방사불은 동방 향적세계의 아촉불[阿閦], 남방 환희세계의 보생불(寶生佛), 서방 안락세계의 무량수불, 북방 연화장엄세계의 미묘성불(微妙聲佛)을 말한다. 아미타불은 서방 안락세계의 주인이 되는 부처로, 전하는 바에 의하면 그 명호를 부르면 극락왕생할 수 있게 된다고 한다. 정토종(淨土宗)의 본존불인 아미타불은 명호가 매우 많은데 무량수불(無量壽佛)·접인불(接引佛)·지혜광불(智慧光佛)·환희광불(歡喜光佛) 등이 있다. 대세지(大勢至)는 보살 이름으로 불교에서는 그가 가는 곳마다 세계가 진동할 정도로 위세가 대단한데 불, 피, 전쟁 등 재난을 없앨 수 있을 정도라고 한다. 일반적으로 여자의 모습을 하고 있다. 머리에는 육계(肉髻)가 솟아 있으며, 그 위에는 광명을 저장하는 보병(寶甁)이 있다. 오른손에는 항상 청련(靑蓮)을 들고 있으며 왼손으로는 시무외인(施無畏印)을 짓고 있다. 전하는 바에 의하면, 대세지는 지옥에서 고통 받는 자가 고경(苦境)에서 벗어나도록 힘을 주는 지혜의 화신이라고 한다. 따라서 자비의 화신인 관세음과 함께 민간에서 공양 받고 있다.

136

유금서방삼성동조상(鎏金西方三聖銅造像)

동(銅) | 당(唐) | 전체높이 24cm 무게 1,350g
1977년 서안시 연호구 토문(西安市 蓮湖區 土門) 출토

Gilt Bronze Western Tri-Saints Statue

Copper | Tang Dynasty(618AD∼907AD) | H 24cm Weight 1,350g
Excavated from Tumen in Lianhu District, Xi'an in 1977

137

유금보살입상(鎏金菩薩立像)

동(銅) | 당(唐) | 전체높이 32cm 무게 2,050g
1978년 서안시 미앙구 삼교진(西安市 未央區 三橋鎭) 출토

Gilt Standing Buddha Statue

Copper | Tang Dynasty(618AD~907AD) | H 32cm Weight 2,050g
Excavated from Sanqiao Town in Weiyang District, Xi'an in 1978

보살은 서 있는 형상이다. 머리에는 아름다운 높은 화
관을 썼는데 그 위는 봉오리가 달린 연꽃 세 송이, 앞쪽은
화불(化佛)로 장식하였다. 얼굴은 둥근 편이고 양측으로
보증(寶繒) 장식이 늘어져 있으며, 입가에는 엷은 미소가
서려 있다. 삼도(三道)가 새겨진 목에는 영락(瓔珞) 및 목
걸이를 착용하였다. 영락은 발까지 길게 늘어졌으며, 복부
에서 X자로 교차된 곳에는 동그란 꽃 장식이 있다. 긴 치
마를 입고 맨발로 원형 대좌(臺座) 위에 서 있으며, 밑부분
의 앙련(仰蓮)과 복련(覆蓮)이 새겨진 대좌가 원형 대좌
및 보살을 받쳐 주고 있다. 보살 뒷면에는 광배(光背)를 고
정하기 위한 꼭지가 있으며, 치마끈 가운데 부분에는 고리
모양의 매듭이 달려 있다. 원형의 광배는 안쪽과 바깥쪽으
로 나뉘는데 바깥쪽에는 가지와 잎, 안쪽에는 이중(二重)
연판(蓮瓣)을 부조로 새겼다. 광배 위쪽에는 삼엽화형(三
葉花形)의 꽃장식이 있는데 그 중심은 동그랗게 튀어나오
고 테두리를 연판으로 한 바퀴 둘렀다. 꽃 장식 위 네모난
구름 모양의 매듭진 비단끈마다 각각 불탑을 조각하였다.
보살상 표면에는 전체적으로 금을 입혔다.

154

138

유금천왕입상(鎏金天王立像)

동(銅) | 당(唐) | 전체높이 8.5cm 무게 130g
1970년대 서안시 연호구(西安市 蓮湖區) 당(唐) 예천사(醴泉寺) 유적지에서 출토

Gilt Standing Devaraja Statue

Copper | Tang Dynasty(618AD∼907AD) | H 8.5cm Weight 130g
Excavated from Liquan Temple of Tang Dynasty in Lianhu District, Xi'an in 1970's

　천왕(天王)은 불교의 호법천신(護法天神) 가운데 하나이다. 화가 난 얼굴에 정수리 위로 높게 솟은 불꽃모양의 머리를 하고 있다. 드러낸 상반신에는 발달한 근육이 돋보인다. 허리에는 띠를 매고 어깨에는 천의(天衣)를 걸쳤으며, 아래에는 긴 치마를 입었다. 다섯 손가락 모두 왼쪽으로 뻗은 왼손은 손바닥이 아래를 향하게 내리고, 높이 쳐든 오른손에는 금강저(金剛杵)를 잡고 앙련(仰蓮)과 복련(覆蓮)을 새긴 연화좌(蓮花座) 위에 맨발로 서 있다. 어깨 위로는 원형 광배(光背)가 조각되어 있다. 호법천신은 불교에서 불법 및 중생을 수호하는 신을 말한다. 이 밖에, 금강저는 불교에서 사용하는 법기(法器) 중 가장 단단한 무기로 전해지고 있는데 만물을 물리치는 신비한 힘이 있다고 한다.

139

유금입불(鎏金立佛)

동(銅) | 당(唐) | 전체높이 16.1cm 너비 5.6cm 무게 344g
서안시 동교(西安市 東郊) 출토

Gilt Standing Buddha

Copper | Tang Dynasty(618AD∼907AD) | H 16.1cm W 5.6cm Weight 344g
Excavated from East Suburbs in Xi'an

　불상은 서 있는 형상으로 소발(素髮)에 높은 육계(肉髻), 둥그스름한 얼굴, 가느다란 눈썹, 수려한 눈, 오뚝한 코, 커다란 귀를 가졌다. 위에는 편단우견(偏袒右肩)으로 가사를 걸치고 아래에는 얇으면서도 밀착되는 긴 치마를 입었다. 오른손을 가슴 높이에서 굽혀 손바닥이 밖을 향하게 다섯 손가락을 곧게 편 시무외인(施無畏印)을 짓고 있으며, 왼손을 내려 보주(寶珠)를 받쳐 들고, 맨발로 앙련(仰蓮)과 복련(覆蓮)이 새겨진 대좌(臺座) 위에 서 있다. 연화좌(蓮花座) 아래에는 4단으로 된 팔각의 높은 받침이 있어 안정감을 더해 준다.

140

유금좌불(鎏金坐佛)

동(銅) | 당(唐) | 높이 15.8cm 무게 642g
1995년 서안시 안탑구(西安市 雁塔區) 출토

Gilt Sitting Buddha Statue

Copper | Tang Dynasty(618AD~907AD)
H 15.8cm Weight 642g
Excavated from Yanta District, Xi'an in 1995

불상은 육계(肉髻)가 높고 얼굴이 둥근 편이며 눈썹이 가늘고 길며 두 귀는 어깨까지 늘어져 있다. 두 눈을 지그시 감고 두툼한 입을 살짝 다물었으며 목에는 삼도(三道)가 새겨져 있다. 위에는 두 겹의 목깃이 있는 통견(通肩)식 가사를 입고 그 안에 승지지(僧祇支)를 받쳐 입었다. 어깨에 두른 대의(大衣)는 오른쪽 어깨로부터 복부 앞까지 흘러 내렸다가 왼쪽 어깨 뒤로 걸쳐졌다. 아래에는 긴 치마를 입었는데 허리에 두른 치마끈은 복부 앞부분에서 매듭을 졌다. 오른손은 손바닥이 밖을 향하게 가슴 높이로 들어 올렸는데 다섯 손가락이 파손되어 어떤 손모양을 취하였는지 단정 짓기 어렵다. 왼쪽 다리 위에 올려놓은 왼손은 다섯 손가락을 펴고 손바닥이 위를 향한 설법인[說法印, 불교의 수인(手印) 중 하나로 부처가 법을 설함을 뜻함. 보통 엄지와 중지 또는 검지를 서로 맞대고 나머지 손가락을 자연스레 편 모양]을 취하였다. 두 다리를 내려 맨발로 활짝 피어난 연꽃 두 송이를 밟고 대좌(臺座, 대좌가 파손되었음) 위에 걸터앉아 있다. 대좌는 치맛자락에 가려져 잘 보이지 않는다.

156

141

유금보살입상(鎏金菩薩立像)

동(銅) | 당(唐) | 전체높이 16.9cm 너비 5.8cm 무게 283g
1975년 서안시 동교 장가파촌(西安市 東郊 張家坡村) 출토

Gilt Standing Bodhisattva Statue

Copper | Tang Dynasty(618AD～907AD) | H 16.9cm W 5.8cm Weight 283g
Excavated from Zhangjiapo Village in East Suburbs in Xi'an in 1975

보살은 서 있는 형상이다. 머리에 높은 보관(寶冠)을 썼는데 관대(冠帶)가 어깨를 거쳐 대좌(臺座) 위로 흘러 내렸다. 상반신을 드러내고 하반신에는 얇으면서도 몸에 밀착되는 긴 치마를 입었는데 치마끈이 복부 앞쪽에서 매듭을 졌다. 어깨에 걸친 기다란 천의(天衣)는 양팔을 따라 수미좌(須彌座) 양측으로 드리워졌다. 풍만한 얼굴, 초승달 같은 눈썹, 각진 턱을 가진 보살은 방울 달린 목걸이와 팔찌를 착용하였다. 아래로 내린 왼손에는 정병(淨瓶), 위로 추켜든 오른손에는 불진(佛塵)을 들었다. 몸을 옆으로 기울이고 맨발로 앙련(仰蓮)과 복련(覆蓮)이 새겨진 수미좌 위에 서 있다. 수미좌 아래에는 4단으로 된 팔각의 높은 받침이 있다. 보살의 뒷면에는 광배(光背)를 고정시키기 위한 네모난 꼭지가 있다.

142

유금삼보살병좌조상(鎏金三菩薩竝坐造像)

동(銅) | 당(唐) | 전체높이 16.5cm 무게 62g
1970년대 서안시 연호구(西安市 蓮湖區) 당(唐) 예천사(醴泉寺) 유적지에서 출토

Gilt Tri-Bodhisattva Sitting Statue

Copper | Tang Dynasty(618AD～907AD) | H 16.5cm Weight 62g
Excavated from Liquan Temple of Tang Dynasty in Lianhu District, Xi'an in 1970's

세 보살 모두 머리에는 보관(寶冠)을 쓰고, 목에는 목걸이, 팔뚝과 손목에는 팔찌를 착용하였다. 상반신에는 옷을 걸치지 않고, 하반신에는 긴 치마를 입었다. 위로 들어 올린 오른손에는 무언가를 들고 있으며, 왼손은 왼쪽 무릎 위에 얹어 놓았다. 오른쪽 다리를 자연스레 내리고 왼쪽 다리를 연화좌(蓮花座) 위에 올려놓아 반가부좌(半跏趺坐)를 취하였다. 저마다 원형 대좌(臺座) 위에 앉아 있는데 대좌 아래에는 방형대좌(方形臺座)가 놓여 있다. 어깨 위에는 똑같이 불꽃무늬가 음각되어 있는 화판형(花瓣形)의 광배(光背)가 있다. 오른쪽 두 보살의 광배 꼭대기에는 좌불(坐佛)이 부착되어 있으나 왼쪽 보살의 광배는 부분적으로 손상되었다.

유금관세음보살좌상(鎏金觀世音菩薩坐像)

동(銅) | 당(唐) | 전체높이 10.5cm 대좌높이 4.5cm 무게 155g
1970년대 서안시 연호구(西安市 蓮湖區) 당(唐) 예천사(醴泉寺) 유적지에서 출토

Gilt Sitting Kwan-yin Bodhisattva Statue

Copper | Tang Dynasty(618AD~907AD) | H 10.5cm Pedestal H 4.5cm Weight 155g
Excavated from Liquan Temple of Tang Dynasty in Lianhu District, Xi'an in 1970's

　　보살은 머리에 화불관(化佛冠)을 썼는데, 관대(冠帶)가 양팔을 따라 팔뚝 바깥쪽으로 드리워졌다. 상반신은 거의 반나체 상태로 영락(瓔珞)만을 걸치고 아래는 얇으면서도 몸에 밀착되는 긴 치마를 입었다. 목에는 목걸이, 팔뚝과 손목에는 팔찌를 착용하였다. 오른손은 다섯 손가락을 오른쪽 위로 향하게 하고 손바닥을 밖으로 하여 어깨 높이까지 올린 손 모양이고, 왼손은 왼쪽 다리 위에 얹었다. 오른쪽 다리를 내려 작은 연꽃 위에 발을 올려놓고 왼쪽 다리를 자연스레 오른쪽 다리 위에 얹은 자세로 앙련(仰蓮)과 복련(覆蓮)을 새긴 연화좌(蓮花座) 위에 반가부좌(半跏趺坐)를 하고 앉아 있다. 연화좌 아래는 팔각을 이루며 그 아래로 방형대좌(方形臺座)가 놓여 있다. 타원형의 얼굴, 수려한 오관, 볼록한 가슴에서는 여성미와 평안한 기색이 흐른다. 머리를 약간 낮춰 굽어보는 자세를 취하고 있어 그 모습이 친근하면서도 기품이 있다.

유금누공보살좌상(鎏金鏤空菩薩坐像)

동(銅) | 당(唐) | 높이 13.3cm 무게 121g
1970년대 서안시 연호구(西安市 蓮湖區) 당(唐) 예천사(醴泉寺) 유적지에서 출토

Gilt Sitting Hollowed-out Bodhisattva Statue

Copper | Tang Dynasty(618AD~907AD) | H 13.3cm Weight 121g
Excavated from Liquan Temple of Tang Dynasty in Lianhu District, Xi'an in 1970's

　　앉은 형상의 보살로 표면에는 전체적으로 금을 입혔다. 머리에 쓴 높은 화관(花冠)의 관대(冠帶)가 어깨까지 드리워졌으며 어깨에 두른 긴 천의(天衣)가 대좌(臺座) 아래까지 흘러내렸다. 목에는 가는 선으로 음각한 목걸이가 장식되어 있다. 아래에는 얇으면서도 몸에 밀착되는 긴 치마를 입었다. 오른손은 오른쪽 무릎 위에 얹어 놓고 치켜든 왼손에는 보물을 받쳐 들었다. 왼쪽 다리를 복부 앞에 놓고 오른쪽 다리를 자연스레 내려 맨발로 연화좌(蓮花座)를 밟은 자세로 반가부좌(半跏趺坐)를 하고 높은 수미좌(須彌座) 위에 앉아 있다. 천이 걸쳐져 있는 수미좌 아래에는 방형대좌(方形臺座)가 있다. 보살 뒷면에는 불꽃무늬로 장식된, 투각한 복숭아 모양의 광배(光背)가 있는데 꼭대기와 양측에는 피어난 연꽃 속에서 가부좌(跏趺坐)를 하고 있는 화불(化佛)이 조각되어 있다.

145

유금좌불(鎏金坐佛)

동(銅) | 당(唐) | 전체높이 8.3cm 무게 122g
1970년대 서안시 연호구(西安市 蓮湖區) 당(唐) 예천사(醴泉寺) 유적지에서 출토

Gilt Standing Buddha Statue

Copper | Tang Dynasty(618AD~907AD) | H 8.3cm Weight 122g
Excavated from Liquan Temple of Tang Dynasty in Lianhu District, Xi'an in 1970's

불상은 파도모양의 높은 육계(肉髻), 둥그스름한 얼굴, 가느다란 눈썹, 큰 귀, 높
다란 콧마루를 가졌는데 두 눈을 지그시 뜨고 아래쪽을 주시하고 있으며 엄숙한 표
정을 짓고 있다. 편단우견(偏袒右肩)으로 가사를 입고 결가부좌(結跏趺座)를 하고
복련(覆蓮)이 새겨진 수미좌(須彌座) 위에 앉아 있다. 복련의 아래위에는 2단으로
된 팔각의 하대(下臺)가 배치되어 있고, 상대(上臺)는 드리워진 천에 의해 가려졌
다. 오른손을 굽혀서 어깨 높이까지 올리고 다섯 손가락을 세우고 손바닥을 밖으로
향하게 해 시무외인(施無畏印)을 지었으며 왼손은 손바닥이 안으로 향하게 하고 다
섯 손가락을 곧게 펴서 왼쪽 무릎 위에 놓아 항마인(降魔印)을 지었다. 불상 뒷면에
는 타원형의 꼭지가 있는데 그 위에 동그란 구멍이 있어 광배(光背)를 고정시킬 수
있다. 이 불상은 제작이 정교하며 기법 또한 완숙한데 특히 소요대좌(束腰臺座) 위
의 천 주름 표현이 생동감이 넘친다.

146

유금좌불(鎏金坐佛)

동(銅) | 당(唐) | 전체높이 6.6cm 무게 79g
1970년대 서안시 연호구(西安市 蓮湖區) 당(唐) 예천사(醴泉寺) 유적지에서 출토

Gilt Sitting Buddha Statue

Copper | Tang Dynasty(618AD~907AD) | H 6.6cm Weight 79g
Excavated from Liquan Temple of Tang Dynasty in Lianhu District, Xi'an in 1970's

불상은 소발(素髮)에 높은 육계(肉髻), 둥그스름한 얼굴에 넓은 이마, 가느다란
눈썹, 큰 귀를 가졌으며 두 눈을 지그시 뜨고 아래를 주시하고 있다. 목은 짧은 편이
다. 편단우견(偏袒右肩)으로 얇으면서도 몸에 밀착되는 가사를 입고 복련(覆蓮)이
새겨진 수미좌(須彌座) 위에 결가부좌(結跏趺座)를 하고 앉아 있다. 대좌(臺座)에
서 드리워진 천은 거꾸로 된 '山(산)' 자 모양과 흡사하며 복련 아래에는 2단의 팔각
받침이 있다. 어깨 높이까지 올린 오른손은 파손되었다. 왼쪽 무릎 위에 얹은 왼손
은 다섯 손가락을 곧게 펴고 손바닥이 안으로 향하게 하여 항마인(降魔印)을 짓고
있다. 불상 뒷면에는 광배(光背)를 고정시키기 위한 원형의 꼭지가 달려 있다. 불상
은 비례가 균형적이고 제작이 정교하며 옷주름에 율동감이 있다. 뿐만 아니라 표현
이 사실적이고 통속적이며 형상 및 표정 또한 현실생활 속의 권위 있는 사람을 방
불케 한다. 이는 당대(唐代) 불상의 특징에 속한다.

147

유금좌불(鎏金坐佛)

동(銅) | 당(唐) | 전체높이 11.3cm 너비 4.8cm 무게 204g
서안시 동교(西安市 東郊) 출토

Gilt Sitting Buddha Statue

Copper | Tang Dynasty(618AD∼907AD) H 11.3cm W 4.8cm Weight 204g
Excavated from East Suburbs in Xi'an

　　두 눈을 지그시 뜨고 있는 앉은 형상의 불상이다. 머리에는 나선형의 높은 육계(肉髻)가 솟아 있으며 얼굴은 윤이 난다. 가느다란 눈썹과 오똑한 콧마루는 서로 연결되었으며 입꼬리는 살짝 올라갔다. 미소가 서려 있는 얼굴에서는 장중함이 흐른다. 상반신에는 승지지(僧祇支)를 받쳐 입고 두 겹의 깃으로 된 통견(通肩)식 가사를 걸쳤으며 아래에는 긴 바지를 입었다. 결가부좌(結跏趺座)를 하고 앙련(仰蓮)과 복련(覆蓮)이 새겨진 수미좌(須彌座) 위에 앉아 있는데, 대좌(臺座)에서 흘러내린 천은 거꾸로 된 '山(산)' 자 모양을 이루며 대좌의 받침은 타원형으로 되었다. 오른손을 꺾어 어깨높이까지 올리고 다섯 손가락을 가지런히 펴서 손바닥이 밖으로 향하게 하여 시무외인(施無畏印)을 짓고 왼손은 손바닥이 안으로 향하게 하고 다섯 손가락을 펴서 왼쪽 무릎 위에 얹었다. 보살 뒷면에 달린 사각형의 평평한 꼭지에는 동그란 구멍이 있는데 이는 광배(光背)를 고정시키기 위한 것으로 보인다. 이 불상은 제작이 정교하고 섬세하며, 조형이 세련되고 사실적이다. 불상에서는 겸손하며 온화한 태도 및 소박하며 세속적인 정취가 짙게 풍기는데 당시의 현실생활을 그대로 반영해 주고 있다.

148

유금좌불(鎏金坐佛)

동(銅) | 당(唐) | 전체높이 8.4cm 너비 5.4cm 무게 219g
서안시 남교(西安市 南郊) 출토

Gilt Sitting Buddha Statue

Copper | Tang Dynasty(618AD~907AD) | H 8.4cm W 5.4cm Weight 219g
Excavated from South Suburbs in Xi'an

  불상은 고개를 약간 숙인 채 결가부좌(結跏趺坐)를 하고 앉아 있다. 정수리
에는 파도 모양의 높은 육계(肉髻)가 솟아 있는데 육계 앞쪽 정중앙에는 작은
돌기가 있다. 용모가 수려한데 계란형 얼굴에 어깨까지 늘어진 귀, 네모난 이
마, 살짝 올라간 입꼬리를 가졌다. 두 눈을 지그시 뜨고 아래를 주시하고 있으
며 얼굴에 미소를 띠고 있다. 목 부위에는 삼도(三道)가 새겨져 있다. 위에는
두 겹의 깃으로 된 통견(通肩)식 가사(袈裟)를 입고 아래에는 긴 치마를 입었
다. 오른손은 다섯 손가락을 가지런히 펴서 손바닥이 밖으로 향하게 하여 어
깨 높이까지 올린 시무외인(施無畏印)을 짓고, 왼손은 손바닥이 아래를 향하
게 하여 왼쪽 무릎 위에 얹었다. 불상은 풍만한 얼굴과 의미심장한 표정이 세
밀하게 부각됨으로써 넘치는 생동감과 활력이 표현되었다.

149

유금나한입상(鎏金羅漢立像)

동(銅) | 당(唐) | 전체높이 11.3cm 너비 4.2cm 무게 210g
서안시 남교(西安市 南郊) 출토

Gilt Standing Buddhist Arhat Statue

Copper | Tang Dynasty(618AD~907AD) | H 11.3cm W 4.2cm Weight 210g
Excavated from South Suburbs in Xi'an

  민머리에 넓적한 이마, 짙은 눈썹, 큰 귀를 가진 나한(羅漢)은 얼굴
에 미소를 머금고 있는데 전체적인 표정에서 온화하며 친근한 성격
이 돋보인다. 안에는 옷깃이 높은 장삼(長衫)을 받쳐 입고 밖에는 가
사(袈裟)를 걸쳤다. 두 손을 포개어 가슴 앞에 놓은 자세로 낮은 굽다
리 3개가 달려 있는 원형 대좌(臺座) 위에 서 있다. 나한상의 표면에
는 원래 금을 입혔으나 대부분 벗겨지고 없다.

150

관음보살입상(觀音菩薩立像)

동(銅) | 당(唐) | 전체높이 8cm 너비 2.1cm 무게 30g
1974년 서안시 북교(西安市 北郊) 출토

Standing Kwan-yin Bodhisattva Statue

Copper | Tang Dynasty(618AD~907AD) | H 8cm W 2.1cm Weight 30g
Excavated from North Suburbs in Xi'an in 1974

　　보살은 서 있는 형상이다. 머리에 보관(寶冠)을 썼는데 관대(冠帶)가 대좌(臺座) 위에 드리워져 있다. 둥그스름한 얼굴, 초승달 같은 눈썹, 가느다란 눈을 가졌으며 얼굴에는 미소가 서려 있다. 어깨 위에는 배 모양의 투각(透刻)한 광배(光背)가 있으며 광배의 꼭대기에 좌불(坐佛)이 부착되어 있다. 상반신을 노출하고 아래에는 망사처럼 얇은 긴 치마를 입었다. 몸을 오른쪽으로 뒤틀고 맨발로 원형 대좌 위에 서 있는데 그 자태가 매우 자연스럽다. 아래로 내린 왼손에는 정병(淨甁)을 들고 위로 들어 올린 오른손에는 불진(佛塵)을 들고 있다. 아래의 방형대좌(方形臺座)가 원좌 및 보살을 받쳐 주고 있다. 보살은 가슴이 볼록한 것이 여성성이 두드러져 보인다. 전체적으로 윤곽이 드러나고 얇고 부드러운 치마는 윤이 나면서도 부드러운 피부결과 아름다운 여성의 육체미를 그대로 보여 준다.

151

유금공양인(鎏金供養人)

동(銅) | 당(唐) | 전체높이 8.2cm 무게 56g
1970년대 서안시 연호구(西安市 蓮湖區) 당(唐) 예천사(醴泉寺) 유적지에서 출토

Gilt Buddhist Provider

Copper | Tang Dynasty(618AD~907AD) | H 8.2cm Weight 56g
Excavated from Liquan Temple of Tang Dynasty in Lianhu District, Xi'an in 1970's

　　포가계(抛家髻)를 한 공양인은 얼굴이 동그랗다. 위에는 소매가 넓은 두 겹의 깃으로 된 통견(通肩) 옷, 아래에는 긴 치마를 입었으며 허리에는 띠를 둘렀다. 앙련좌(仰蓮座) 위에 품위 있게 서 있는 공양인은 양팔을 모두 앞으로 뻗었는데 오른손에는 물건을 들었으며 왼손 손바닥은 위를 향하고 손가락을 조금 구부렸다. 앙련좌 아래는 가지와 잎으로 장식하였다.

152

유금좌불(鎏金坐佛)

동(銅) | 당(唐) | 전체높이 16.9cm 무게 427g
1970년대 서안시 연호구(西安市 蓮湖區) 당(唐) 예천사(醴泉寺) 유적지에서 출토

Gilt Sitting Buddha Statue

Copper | Tang Dynasty(618AD~907AD) | H 16.9cm Weight 427g
Excavated from Liquan Temple of Tang Dynasty in Lianhu District, Xi'an in 1970's

　수려한 용모의 불상은 머리에 높은 육계(肉髻)를 하고 풍만한 얼굴, 가느다란 눈썹과 눈을 가졌으며 명상하듯이 두 눈을 살포시 감고 있다. 오른손은 굽혀서 어깨 높이까지 올리고 다섯 손가락을 세우고 손바닥을 밖으로 향해 시무외인(施無畏印)을 짓고 왼손은 손바닥이 안으로 향하게 하고 다섯 손가락을 곧게 펴서 왼쪽 무릎 위에 놓아 항마인(降魔印)을 지었다. 위에는 소매가 넓은 두 겹의 깃으로 된 통견(通肩)식 가사를 입고 그 안에 승지지(僧祇支)를 받쳐 입었다. 목에는 삼도(三道)가 새겨져 있고 승지지 옷깃 부분에는 파도무늬, 복부에는 능형(菱形) 및 그물무늬가 새겨져 있다. 앙련(仰蓮)과 복련(覆蓮)을 새긴 수미좌(須彌座) 위에 결가부좌(結跏趺坐)를 하고 앉아 있는데 상대(上臺)는 가사(袈裟)와 드리워진 천으로 가려졌다. 수미좌 아래에는 2단의 오엽(五葉) 원형 대좌, 밑부분에는 타원형의 받침이 있으며 받침 아래에는 동그란 구멍이 있는 사각형의 평평한 꼭지가 양측으로 배치되어 있는데 이는 불상을 고정하기 위함이다. 불상 뒷면 역시 꼭지가 있었으나 지금은 손상되었다. 형체상 옹골지고 의젓함이 넘치는 불상은 살아 숨 쉬는 듯하고 넓은 마음과 속세를 초탈한 내재적 정신을 보여 주며 거침없이 표현된 옷 주름은 조각 기법상 전례 없는 완숙미에 이르렀음을 말해 주는데 이는 성당(盛唐) 시기의 대표적인 작품으로 손꼽힌다.

153

유금관세음보살입상(鎏金觀世音菩薩立像)

동(銅) | 당(唐) | 전체높이 10.9cm 너비 3.8cm 무게 120g
서안시 동교(西安市 東郊) 출토

Gilt Standing Kwan-yin Bodhisattva Statue

Copper | Tang Dynasty(618AD~907AD) | H 10.9cm W 3.8cm Weight 120g
Excavated from East Suburbs in Xi'an

　표면에 전체적으로 금을 입힌 보살 입상(立像)이다. 얼굴은 풍만하고 둥그스름하며 머리에는 보병(寶瓶)으로 장식한 화려한 보관(寶冠)을 썼는데 관의 보증(寶繒)이 양팔을 따라 아래로 흘러내렸다. 상반신을 드러내고 목에는 목걸이를 착용하고 어깨에는 천의(天衣)를 둘렀다. 자연스레 내린 왼손에는 정병(淨瓶)을 들고 어깨 높이까지 올린 오른손에는 불진(佛塵)을 들었다. 몸에 장식한 영락(瓔珞)은 왼쪽 어깨에서 다리로 흘러내리다 호형(弧形)을 그리면서 왼쪽 다리로 드리워졌다. 아래에는 몸에 밀착되는 얇은 긴 치마를 입고 맨발로 앙련(仰蓮)과 복련(覆蓮)을 새긴 수미좌(須彌座) 위에 앉아 있다. 불상은 용모가 수려하고 신체적 비례가 적절하며 온화한 기색을 띠고 있다. 몸체는 살짝 굽혀 'S'자 모양을 이루었는데 건강한 몸매와 고혹적인 자태는 예술조형상의 아름다운 선과 리듬의 운치를 충분하게 보여줌으로써 사람을 매혹시키는 아름다움이 있다.

154

유금누공관세음보살좌상(鎏金鏤空觀世音菩薩坐像)

동(銅) | 당(唐) | 전체높이 9.3cm 무게 44g
1970년대 서안시 연호구(西安市 蓮湖區) 당(唐) 예천사(醴泉寺) 유적지에서 출토

Gilt Sitting Hollow Kwan-yin Bodhisattva Statue

Copper | Tang Dynasty(618AD~907AD) | H 9.3cm Weight 44g
Excavated from Liquan Temple of Tang Dynasty in Lianhu District, Xi'an in 1970's

　보살은 머리에 보관(寶冠)을 쓰고 상반신을 드러냈으며 아래에는 몸에 밀착되는 얇으면서도 긴 치마를 입었다. 목에는 목걸이를 착용하고 어깨에는 팔을 휘감으며 대좌(臺座) 양편으로 흘러내리는 천의(天衣)를 둘렀다. 자연스럽게 내려뜨린 오른손은 손바닥이 아래를 향하게 오른쪽 무릎 위에 얹고 위로 굽힌 왼손에는 불진(佛塵)을 들었다. 왼쪽 다리를 복부 앞으로 굽히고 오른쪽 다리를 세워 맨발로 원형 대좌를 밟은 자세로 앙련(仰蓮)과 복련(覆蓮)이 새겨진 수미좌(須彌座) 위에 반가부좌(半跏趺坐)를 하고 앉아 있다. 어깨 위에는 꼭대기를 화불(化佛)로 장식한 배 모양의 광배(光背)가 있으며 천을 두른 대좌 아래에는 방형대좌(方形臺座)가 놓여 있다.

155

유금관세음보살입상(鎏金觀世音菩薩立像)

동(銅) | 당(唐) | 전체높이 14.3cm 무게 245g
1974년 서안시 미앙구(西安市 未央區) 출토

Gilt Standing Kwan-yin Bodhisattva Statue

Copper | Tang Dynasty(618AD~907AD) | H 14.3cm Weight 245g
Excavated from Weiyang District, Xi'an in 1974

　둥글넓적한 얼굴, 넓은 이마, 활처럼 휜 눈썹, 가늘고 긴 눈, 각진 턱을 가진 관세음보살상(觀世音菩薩像)으로 얼굴에는 미소가 어려 있다. 머리에는 정중앙을 앙련(仰蓮) 위에 서 있는 화불로 장식한, 높은 화관을 썼는데 그 관대(冠帶)가 양어깨로 흘러내렸다. 오른쪽 어깨로부터 영락(瓔珞)이 늘어져 내려와 무릎 아래까지 닿아 있다. 어깨에 천의(天衣)를 두른 상반신은 반쯤 드러내고 아래에는 몸에 밀착되는 긴 치마를 입었으며 허리에는 치마끈을 둘렀다. 구슬로 만든 목걸이를 착용하고 목에는 삼도(三道)가 새겨져 있고 가슴 역시 목걸이로 장식되어 있으며 팔목에는 팔찌가 있다. 손상되어 판단하기 어려운 왼팔과 달리, 오른팔은 들어 올린 것으로 보이는데 양손 모두 떨어져 나가 정확한 수인(手印)은 알 수 없다. 보살은 맨발로 앙련(仰蓮)과 복련(覆蓮)이 새겨진 대좌(臺座) 위에 서 있다. 대좌 아래에는 높다란 팔각 받침이 있고 머리 뒷면에는 광배(光背)를 고정시키기 위한 꼭지가 있다.

156

유금관세음보살입상(鎏金觀世音菩薩立像)

동(銅) | 당(唐) | 전체높이 12.6cm 무게 127g
1970년대 서안시 연호구(西安市 蓮湖區) 당(唐) 예천사(醴泉寺) 유적지에서 출토

Gilt Standing Kwan-yin Statue

Copper | Tang Dynasty(618AD~907AD) | H 12.6cm Weight 127g
Excavated from Liquan Temple of Tang Dynasty in Lianhu District, Xi'an in 1970's

　보살은 정수리에 화불(化佛)이 표현되어 있는 화관을 썼는데 그 관대(冠帶)가 양어깨를 따라 팔까지 흘러내렸다. 상반신을 반쯤 드러내고 아래에는 몸에 밀착되는 얇으면서도 긴 치마를 입었다. 목에는 목걸이 장식을 하고 어깨에는 천의(天衣)를 둘렀다. 오른쪽 어깨로부터 영락(瓔珞)이 늘어져 내려와 왼쪽 발목까지 닿아 있다. 들어 올린 오른손에는 불진(佛塵), 내려뜨린 왼손에는 정병(淨瓶)을 들었다. 몸을 옆으로 비스듬히 기울이고 맨발로 앙련(仰蓮)과 복련(覆蓮)이 새겨진 수미좌(須彌座) 위에 서 있으며 대좌(臺座) 아래 양측에는 불상을 고정하기 위한 꼭지가 배치되어 있다.

유금사리은곽(鎏金舍利銀槨)

은(銀) | 당(唐) | 길이 22,6cm 너비 8,6cm 높이 14,2cm 무게 710g
1969년 서안시 신성구(西安市 新城區) 서안진천(西安秦川) 기계공장에서 출토

Gilt Silver Coffin with Buddhist Relic

Silver | Tang Dynasty(618AD~907AD) | L 22,6cm W 8,6cm H 14,2cm Weight 710g
Excavated from Qinchuan Machinery Factory in Xincheng District, Xi'an in 1969

　뚜껑과 몸체로 구성된 은곽(銀槨)은 뒤에서 곧 소개할 도금동관(鍍金銅棺)과 한 세트이다. 장방형의 녹정(盝頂) 지붕 형식의 뚜껑과 직사각형에 가까운 몸체는 자모구(子母口)를 이루며 몸체 아랫부분은 2단으로 된 계단식 받침을 이루었다. 위가 작고 아래가 크며 한쪽이 조금 넓으면서도 높고 다른 한쪽이 상대적으로 좁으면서도 낮아 안정감을 더해 준다. 표면에 새긴 문양에는 금을 입혔다. 뚜껑 양쪽 측면에는 똑같이 꽃문양을 새겼다. 또한 사람의 머리에 새의 몸을 한 가릉빈가(伽陵頻伽)가 양쪽 측면에 각각 마주 보는 모습으로 새겨져 있다. 가릉빈가는 연꽃 한 송이를 들고 꽃이 흩날리는 하늘에서 춤을 추고 있다. 새의 꼬리는

층층이 위로 감긴 꽃잎 3엽으로 표현되었다. 뚜껑의 앞뒤 면에는 각각 활짝 핀 연꽃 한 송이를 새기고 가지와 잎으로 연꽃 둘레를 가득 채웠으며 가장자리에도 꽃을 둘렀다. 몸체 왼쪽은 열반경변도(涅槃經變圖)가 새겨져 있는데 중앙에는 화엽(花葉)무늬가 가득 새겨진 수미좌(須彌座) 위에서 열반(涅槃)하시는 석가모니의 모습이 담겨져 있다. 석가모니는 오른손으로 턱을 고이고 옆으로 누워 있으며 침대 앞에는 한 부인이 오른손으로 침대를 잡고 왼손으로 얼굴을 가리고 울고 있는 모습이다. 부인 뒤에는 한 승려가 부인을 부축하는 듯한 자세를 취하고 있다. 침대 뒤편에는 가사(袈裟)를 두른 제자가 왼손으로 석가모니의 발을 어루만지고 있으며 그 뒤에 다른 제자가 있다. 관의 양 측면에는 높은 육계(肉髻), 어깨에 닿을 듯한 귀를 가진 불상을 가운데에 배치하였는데 몸에는 가사를 두르고 연화좌(蓮花座) 위에 결가부좌(結跏趺座)를 하고 있다. 뒷면의 원형 광배(光背) 양측에는 각각 꽃 한 송이를 배치하였다. 우측면 아랫부분에는 잎무늬를 두르고 주위를 꽃으로 장식하였다. 관의 바닥에는 가운데에서 양측으로 겹겹이 펼쳐진 연잎을 새기고 계단식 받침에는 꽃과 호문문(壺門紋)을 둘렀다.

유금사리동관(鎏金舍利銅棺)

동(銅) | 당(唐) | 길이 13.7cm 너비 7.6cm 높이 8.7cm 무게 640g
1969년 서안시 신성구(西安市 新城區) 서안진천(西安秦川) 기계공장에서 출토

Gilt Bronze Coffin with Buddhist Relics

Copper | Tang Dynasty(618AD~907AD) | L 13.7cm W 7.6cm H 8.7cm Weight 640g
Excavated from Qinchuan Machinery Factory in Xincheng District, Xi'an in 1969

　표면에 전체적으로 금을 입힌 이 동관(銅棺)은 위에서 소개한 은곽(銀槨)과 한 세트이다. 뚜껑, 몸체, 관좌(棺座) 등 세 부분으로 구성되었다. 아치형 뚜껑은 앞부분이 넓으면서 높고 뒷부분이 좁으면서 낮다. 몸체는 직사각형에 가깝고 수면문(獸面紋)을 새긴 앞부분은 넓으면서 높은 아치형이고 뒷부분은 좁으면서 낮은 아치형이다. 몸체 아래의 각 모서리에 못을 두어 관을 관좌에 고정시켰다. 관좌는 앞부분이 크고 뒷부분이 작은 2단의 사다리꼴 모양이다. 아랫단에는 윗부분을 파도무늬로 장식한, 직사각형의 호문(壺門)이 투각(透刻)되어 있는데 양측에는 3개, 앞뒤에는 각각 1개가 배치되어 있다. 내벽을 주사(朱砂)로 칠한 관 안에는 형태가 불규칙적인 황색 사리 및 파손된 녹색 사리병 조각들이 있다. 이로부터 미루어 보아 녹색 병에 사리(舍利)를 담아 놓았음을 알 수 있다.

　금은기(金銀器) 그릇에 사리를 봉안하는 불교 풍습은 북위(北魏) 때 시작되었으며, 불교의 전파와 더불어 당대(唐代)에 와서는 더욱이 성행하였다. 특히 당 현종(唐玄宗) 연간 이후, 밀교(密敎)가 황실에서 절대적인 역할을 함으로써 이러한 풍속이 크게 성행했으며 송요(宋遼)시대까지도 금은기에 사리를 넣어 불탑에 봉안하는 풍속이 행하여졌다.

　사리(舍利)는 범어(梵語)의 음역(音譯)으로 석가불의 유골을 말하며 불교의 경전에서도 사리라고 부르는데 전자는 진신사리(眞身舍利)를 말한다. 불가서(佛家書)에서는 석가모니 사리는 쇄신사리(碎身舍利), 다보불(多寶佛)의 사리는 전신사리(全身舍利)로 보관하였다고 한다. 『위서(魏書)』「석로지(釋老志)」에서는 "부처님이 열반(涅槃)하자 향목으로 그 시체를 태우니 영골(靈骨)이 흩어져 알갱이 모양으로 되었는데 두드려도 부서지지 않고 태워도 그을지 않았다. 광명신(光明神)이 이를 보고 호인(胡人)의 언어로 사리라고 칭하였는데 제자들은 이를 보병(寶甁)에 넣어 봉안하고 정성을 보여 주기 위하여 수많은 향화(香花)를 재배하고 경모의 마음으로 궁우(宮宇)를 세워 탑이라고 하였다"는 기록이 있다. 한편『법원주림(法苑珠林)』「사리편(舍利篇)」에서는 "사리는 서역의 범어로 골신(骨身)이라 부르기도 하며 일반인의 유골과 분리하기 위하여 범어를 사용하였다. 사리는 하얀 골사리(骨舍利), 검은 발사리(髮舍利), 붉은 육사리(肉舍利) 등 세 가지로 나뉜다. 보살, 나한(羅漢) 사리도 위와 같은 세 가지로 나뉜다. 불사리(佛舍利)는 두드려도 부서지지 않으나 제자사리(弟子舍利)는 두드리면 부서진다"는 기록이 있다.

　진신사리(眞身舍利)를 '영골(靈骨)' 또는 '금골(金骨)'이라고도 한다. 사리가 없을 때에는 금은, 진주, 수정, 마노(瑪瑙), 호박, 유리 등으로 대체하거나 약초, 대나무 뿌리와 줄기, 옥수수 알갱이 등으로 대체할 수 있는데 이를 사리자(舍利子)라고 하며 불교의 경전에서는 법신사리(法身舍利)라고 한다.

'요주(姚州)' 금정(金鋌)

금(金) | 당(唐) 길이 14.2cm 너비 2.4cm 높이 0.7cm 무게 41.2g
1999년 서안시 신성구 서칠로(西安市 新城區 西七路) 서안중학교에서 출토

Gold Ingot with 'Yao Zhou' Inscription

Gold | Tang Dynasty(618AD~907AD) | L 14.2cm W 2.4cm H 0.7cm Weight 41.2g
Excavated from Xi'an Middle School in Xincheng District, Xi'an in 1999

　　직사각형의 황금색을 띠는 편평한 금정(金鋌)으로 표면이 그다지 매끄럽지 못하며 모가 뚜렷하지 않다. 금정 위에는 해서체(楷書體)로 "姚州貢金拾兩(요주에서 금 10냥을 공납함)"이라는 여섯 글자가 양각(陽刻)되어 있는데 당대(唐代)의 10전은 1냥이고 지금의 43g이다. 『당육전(唐六典)』에 따르면 "개원(開元) 9년, 도량형을 대소양제(大小兩制)로 규정하여 소 1자 2치는 대 1자, 소 3말은 대 1말, 소 3냥은 대 1냥으로 관민들은 일상생활에서 대제를 사용하고 종률(鍾律), 천문, 의약 등 영역에서는 소제를 사용하였다"는 기록이 있다. 이 금정은 오늘날 무게 단위로 계산하면 412g으로 당대 대제를 적용하여 만든 것으로 추정된다. 요주(姚州)는 당대 검남도(劍南道) 관할에 속하는데 현재의 운남성(云南省) 중서부 대리(大理), 초웅(楚雄), 곤명(昆明) 등 지역을 포괄하며 주치(州治)는 오늘의 운남 요안현(姚安縣) 성북(城北)에 있었다. 당현종(唐玄宗) 재위 기간(712~756년), 현재의 운남 서남부 및 미얀마 동북부에 위치한 남조국(南詔國)이 강대해지자 수차례 당군(唐軍)을 물리치고 요주를 점령하였다. 이로부터 요주에서 이 금정을 공납한 때는 고종 이후 현종 이전임을 추정할 수 있다.

　　당대의 황금 산지는 대부분 남방에 분포되어 있었고 호남 지역에 가장 많았다. 당대 번작(樊綽)의 『만서(蠻書)』「운남관내 제칠(云南管內 第七)」에는 "여수(麗水)에서 나는 부금(麩金)은 모래를 쳐서 얻은 것이다"라는 기록이 있다. 여수(麗水)는 장강(長江) 상류의 금사강(金沙江) 일대로 요주는 금사강 이남을 말한다.

　　금은정(金銀鋌)은 금은화폐의 일종이다. 정(鋌)이라는 명칭에 관한 기록은 『당육전(唐六典)』에 처음 나오는데 "견(絹)은 필(匹)을, 포(布)는 단(端)을, 면(綿)은 돈(屯)을, 사(絲)는 현(絢)을, 마(麻)는 려(線)를, 금은(金銀)은 정(鋌)을, 전(錢)은 관(貫)을 단위로 하였다"는 기록이 있다. 여태껏 발굴된 금정의 양은 비교적 적다. 1977년 4월, 서안시(西安市) 비림구(碑林區) 당(唐) 장안성(長安城) 동시(東市) 유적지에서 2점, 산서성(山西省) 평로현(平魯縣) 둔금구(屯金溝) 당대(唐代) 교장(窖藏)에서 82점이 출토되었다. 그중 명문이 새겨져 있는 것은 5점이다. 당대 은정(銀鋌)은 출토된 수량이 많은데 주로 장안, 낙양 지역에서 출토되었으며 간혹 기타 지역에서도 출토되었다. 당대 은정은 무게에 따라 50냥, 20냥, 10냥, 5냥으로 나뉘며 형태에 따라 호형(弧形)이거나 평평한 머리에 곧은 몸통을 가진 것, 평평한 머리에 잘록한 허리를 가진 것, 배 모양이나 뗏목 모양으로 된 것으로 나뉜다. 은정의 주조(鑄造)는 중앙주조와 지방주조로 나뉘는데 중앙에서 은정을 주조할 때, 보통 설명용 명문(銘文)을 새겨 넣었다. 지방에서 주조한 은정은 주로 납세품이나 진상품으로 사용되었는데 주조 목적 및 지점, 담당 관원 이름을 새겨 넣었다. 송대(宋代)에 와서는 백은(白銀) 화폐를 널리 사용하였는데 북송(北宋)의 은정은 평평한 머리와 잘록한 허리를 가진 머리가 밑부분보다 작은 것, 호형의 머리와 잘록한 허리에 가운데가 오목한 것, 둥근 머리와 잘록한 허리에 가운데가 볼록한 것 등 3가지 형태로 나뉘었다. 3가지 은정 표면에는 대부분 50냥이라 새겨져 있으나 실제 무게는 2,000g이며 모두 진상품에 속한다. 남송(南宋) 은정은 무게에 따라 몇 개 등급으로 나뉜다. 남송 초기에는 진상품으로 사용되는 은정을 50냥, 20냥으로 규정하였으나 후기에는 대·중·소 3등급에 따라 50냥, 25냥, 12냥 반으로 규정하였다. 그 밖에 주조 지점과 제련 성질에 따라 은정을 행재[行在, 행재는 황제의 임시거주지를 말함. 금이 북송을 멸하자 조구(趙構)가 임안(臨安)에서 남송을 세웠으나 도읍을 여전히 개봉(開封)으로 하고 임안을 행재로 칭하였음]은정과 지방은정 두 가지로 나뉘었다. 금대(金代)의 은정도 민간주조와 정부주조 2가지로 나뉜다. 비교적 간단한 민간주조에 비해 정부에서는 송대의 은정제도를 답습하여 호형의 머리와 잘록한 허리 형태의 은정을 주조하였다. 원대(元代)에 와서는 은정(銀鋌)을 은정(銀錠)이라고 고쳐 불렀으나 금대의 은정 형태를 답습하여 호형의 머리, 잘록한 허리에 앞면이 약간 오목하며 테두리에 여러 갈래의 사문(絲紋)을 두른 형태로 만들었으며 대부분 무게가 50냥이었다. 원말명초(元末明初)의 은정은 호형의 머리, 잘록한 허리, 양쪽에 날개가 달리고 머리가 밑부분보다 큰 새로운 형태로 탈바꿈하여 명청(明淸)시대 은정의 양식으로 정해졌다.

'증성원년(證聖元年)' 은정(銀鋌)

은(銀) | 당(唐) | 길이 23.3cm 너비 5.2cm 높이 2.1cm 무게 2,250g
1999년 서안시 신성구 서칠로(西安市 新城區 西七路) 서안중학교에서 출토

Silver Ingot with 'Zheng Sheng Yuan Nian' Inscription

Silver | Tang Dynasty(618AD~907AD) | L 23.3cm W 5.2cm H 2.1cm Weight 2,250g
Excavated from Xi'an Middle School in Xincheng District, Xi'an in 1999

　　은회색을 띠는 직사각형의 편평한 은정(銀鋌)이다. 모형주조법(模型鑄造法)으로 만들어진 은정은 위보다 아래가 넓은 편이다. 표면이 그다지 매끄럽지 않으며, 해서체(楷書體)로 "饒州銀五十兩, 證聖元年(요주은오십냥, 증성원년)"이란 글자가 새겨져 있다. 대제(大制)를 사용하여 무게를 측정하던 당대(唐代)의 은정 2개를 오늘의 무게단위로 계산하면 45g이다. '증성(證聖)'이란 두 글자는 당대 여황제 무측천(武則天)의 연호로 무측천 시기에 만들어진 것이며 증성원년은 695년이다. 요주는 당대 강남서도(江南西道) 관할하에 있었는데 오늘날 강서성(江西省) 동북부의 상요(上饒) 및 경덕진(景德鎭) 지역을 말하며 주치(州治)는 지금의 강서성(江西省) 파양현(鄱陽縣)에 있었다. 당덕종(唐德宗) 시기(780~805년), 은광을 일률적으로 관부에서 관리하고 개인이 채굴하는 것을 금지하였다. 당대 시기의 은광(銀鑛)은 대부분 남방에 분포하였는데 그중 요주 덕흥창[德興廠, 지금의 덕흥현 은산(銀山)]이 당대 최대 은산지(銀産地)였다. 이 은정은 당대 시기, 요주에서 조정에 바치던 진상품인 것으로 보인다.

'건부육년(乾符六年)' 은정(銀鋌)

은(銀) | 당(唐) | 길이 27.5cm 너비 7cm 높이 0.7cm 무게 1,625g
1977년 서안시 파교구 신축향 조원촌(西安市 灞橋區 新筑鄕 棗園村)에서 출토

Silver Ingot with 'Qian fu liu Nian' Inscription

Silver | Tang Dynasty(618AD~907AD) | L 27.5cm W 7cm H 0.7cm Weight 1,625g
Excavated from Zaoyuan Village Xinzhu County in Baqiao District, Xi'an in 1977

　　당대의 칭량 화폐로 중앙에서 주조한 것이다. 은으로 만든 은정(銀鋌)은 직사각형이며 정면에는 네 줄로 된 32글자, "乾符六年內庫別鑄重卌兩, 文思副使臣劉可濡, 文思使臣王彦圭, 內庫使臣王翺(건부 6년, 내고에 40냥 별주, 문사부사신 유가유, 문사사신 왕언규, 내고사신 왕고)"라는 명문이 새겨져 있다. 우측에는 "匠臣武敬榮(장신무경영)"이란 5글자가 새겨져 있다. '별주(別鑄)'는 채굴해 낸 은을 일정한 형태와 무게에 따라 주조하여 내고(內庫)에 보관하는 것을 말한다. 은정의 명문에는 '무게 40냥'이라 새겨졌는데 이는 당대 대제(大制)를 적용하여 측정한 것이며 당시의 1냥은 지금의 45g이다. 건부(乾符)는 당희종(唐僖宗) 이환(李儇)의 첫 번째 연호로 건부 6년은 879년이다. '내고', '문사원(文思院)'은 당대 장안(長安) 궁궐에서 황실과 조정에서 사용하는 금은그릇을 제작하는 기구로, 소부감(少府監) 관하의 중상(中尙), 좌상(左尙), 우상(右尙)으로 구성되었다. 각 기구에는 '금은작방원(金銀作坊院)'을 설치하였는데 그 중 중상서가 가장 크다. 그 밖에 문사원은 당선종(唐宣宗) 대중(大中) 8년(854년)에 설치되었는데 환관을 문사원사로 임명하여 금은서옥(金銀犀玉)과 같은 정교한 물품의 제작을 관리하도록 하였다. 내고는 대영고(大盈庫)를 말하며 당대 황실의 개인 창고로 황제의 개인용품을 보관하는 데 쓰였다. '문사부사(文思副使)', '문사사신(文思使臣)' 다음으로 '내고사(內庫使)'가 나오는데 이는 문사원(文思院)이 황실 전용 금은그릇을 제작하는 황실기구임을 말해 준다. 서안시문물보호고고학연구소에서 소장한 절지단화유금은타호(折枝團花鎏金銀唾壺)와 함께 출토된 이 은정은 표면에 확실한 주조시간 및 출토지점이 새겨져 있어 당대 화폐주조제도와 화폐발전사와 아울러 당대 후기 정치, 경제제도를 연구하는 데 있어서 중요한 의의를 갖고 있다.

'영남도(岭南道)' 진공은정(進貢銀鋌)

은(銀) | 당(唐) | 길이 27.7cm 너비 6.5cm 높이 1.2cm 무게 2,130g
1989년 서안시문물관리위원회(西安市文物管理委員會) 수집

Tribute Silver Ingot with 'Ling Nan Dao' Inscription

Silver | Tang Dynasty(618AD∼907AD) | L 27.7cm W 6.5cm H 1.2cm Weight 2,130g
Collected by Xi'an Culture Relic Administration Committee in 1989

직사각형의 은회색을 띠는 은정(銀鋌)이다. 정면에는 "阿達忽□頻陀沙等, 納元波斯伊娑郝, 銀壹鋌伍拾兩官秤, 銀青光祿大夫, 使持節, 都督廣州諸軍事, 廣州刺史兼禦史大夫, 充嶺南節度, □度營田五府經略觀察處置等副大使, 知節度事, 上柱國, 南陽縣開國子, 臣張伯□進, 嶺南監軍市舶使, 朝散大夫, 行內侍省內給事, 員外置同正員, 上柱國, 賜紫金魚袋, 臣劉楚江□(아달홀□빈타사 등 페르시아 상인들이 관평으로 측정할 때 하나에 50냥이 되는 은은 은청광록대부 · 사지절 · 도독광주제군사 · 광주자사겸어사대부 · 충령남절도 · □도영전오부경략관찰처치 등 부대사 · 지절도사 · 상주국 · 남양현개국자 등을 역임한 신하 장백□에게 바침. 영남감군시박사 · 조산대부 · 행내시성내급사 · 원외치동정원 · 상주국 · 사자금어대 등을 역임한 신하 유초강)"이라는 명문이 세로로 네 줄 새겨져 있다.

'영남(嶺南)'은 영남도(嶺南道)를 말한다. 당대(唐代)에는 전국을 10개 도로 나누었는데 영남도가 그중 하나이며 지금의 광동 · 광서 · 베트남 중북부를 관할했다. 최고 행정기구 소재지였던 광주에 대한 기록은 『신당서(新唐書)』「지리지(地理志)」에 나오는데, "영남도는 고대 양주(揚州) 남부지역으로 남해(南海) · 욱림(郁林) · 창오(蒼梧) · 주애(珠崖) · 담이(儋耳) · 교지(交趾) · 합포(合浦) · 구진(九眞) · 일남(日南) 등 군을 관할하였다"는 기록이 있다. 연주(連州) 연산군(連山郡) 계양(桂陽, 현재 광동성 연현(連縣))은 영남도 유일의 은산지로 해마다 조정에 은을 공납하였다. 시박사(市舶使)는 당대 중앙정부가 광주에 두었던 해외무역 관리기구이다. 당대에는 광주를 중심으로 동남아, 인도, 서아시아, 동아프리카 등 여러 지역과 해상무역이 활발히 진행되면서 조정에서는 광주에 시박사를 설치하고 대외무역사무를 관리하였다.

축요형은정(縮腰形銀鋌)

은(銀) | 당(唐) | 길이 20.1cm 너비 12.1cm 높이 7.2cm 무게 1,820g
1971년 서안시 비림구(西安市 碑林區) 서북공업대학(西北工業大學) 출토

Constricted Silver Ingot

Silver | Tang Dynasty(618AD∼907AD) | L 20.1cm W 12.1cm H 7.2cm Weight 1,820g
Excavated from Northwestern Polytechnical University in Beilin District, Xi'an in 1971

속이 빈 민무늬 은정(銀鋌)은 아치교 모양의 정면과 사다리꼴 모양의 측면 및 잘록한 허리를 가졌다. 표면이 매끈하지 않고 가장자리도 깔끔하게 처리되지 않았다. 전체적으로 은회색을 띠며 부분적으로 녹슨 것으로 보아 장기간 철제품과 함께 놓아둔 것으로 추정된다.

164

축요형은정(縮腰形銀鋌)

은(銀) | 당(唐) | 길이 19.5cm 높이 2.2cm 무게 2,000g
1973년 서안시 연호구(西安市 蓮湖區) 서안계기공장에서 출토

Constricted Silver Ingot

Silver | Tang Dynasty(618AD~907AD) | L 19.5cm H 2.2cm Weight 2,000g
Excavated from Xi'an Instrument and Meter Plant in Lianhu District, Xi'an in 1973

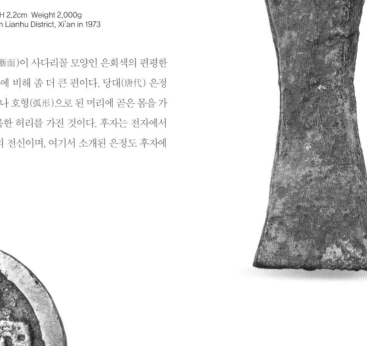

양끝이 곧고 허리가 잘록하며 횡단면(橫斷面)이 사다리꼴 모양인 은회색의 편평한 민무늬 은정(銀鋌)이다. 윗부분이 아랫부분에 비해 좀 더 큰 편이다. 당대(唐代) 은정은 두 가지 형태로 나뉜다. 하나는 평평하거나 호형(弧形)으로 된 머리에 곧은 몸을 가진 것이고, 다른 하나는 평평한 머리에 잘록한 허리를 가진 것이다. 후자는 전자에서 발전되어 온 것으로 송대(宋代) 은정 형태의 전신이며, 여기서 소개된 은정도 후자에 속한다.

165

'개원통보(開元通寶)' 금전(金錢)

금(金) | 당(唐) | 지름 2.52cm 무게 6.7g
1966년 서안시 신성구(西安市 新城區) 서안통신케이블공장에서 출토

Gold 'Kai Yuan Tong Bao' Coin

Gold | Tang Dynasty(618AD~907AD) | D 2.52cm Weight 6.7g
Excavated form Xi'an Cable Works in Xincheng District, Xi'an in 1966

당대(唐代)의 금화이다. 원형에 네모난 구멍이 있으며 내외곽으로 나뉜다. 정면에는 해서체(楷書體)로 된 '개원통보(開元通寶)' 4글자가 새겨져 있는데 그중 '元(원)'자 첫 획은 비교적 짧고 두 번째 획은 좌측에서 살짝 꺾으면서 시작된다. 뒷면의 네모난 구멍 윗부분에 새겨진 초승달무늬는 입을 벌린 쪽이 위를 향하였다. '개원통보'는 당고조(唐高祖) 무덕(武德) 4년(621년)에 주조되어 이당(李唐) 3백 년 동안 줄곧 사용되었으며, 당시의 저명한 서법가 구양순(歐陽詢)의 글씨를 사용했다. 오대십국(五代十國)시대의 남당(南唐, 937~975년)에서도 개원통보를 주조하였는데 화폐 윤곽 및 문자 풍격이 당대와 달랐다. 당대 금은전(金銀錢)은 공식적인 유통화폐가 아니었는데, 당률(唐律) 규정에 의하면, 사사로이 동전을 주조하면 엄격히 처벌하지만 금은전을 주조하면 책임을 묻지 않는다고 하였다. 따라서 조정에서도 금은전을 주조하여 궁정에서 유희를 하거나 상을 내리거나 아기를 목욕시킬 때(당대 시기, 아기가 태어난 후 셋째 날이나 만 한 달이 되었을 때 친척과 지인이 모여 아기를 목욕시켰다) 사용하였다. 조정의 영향하에 민간에서도 금은전을 주조하여 장신구로 사용하는 풍속이 생겼다.

금전(金錢)은 동전 양식에 따라 금으로 주조한 화폐로 원형에 네모난 구멍이 있다. 방공원전(方孔圓錢)은 한왕조(漢王朝) 때에 처음 생겨났으며 금오수(金五銖)라고 불렸다. 이후 오수전(五銖錢)은 700여 년 간 지속되었는데 사서에서는 오수전을 '금전'이라 적고 있다. 당대 초기에 이르러 개원통보가 오수전을 대체하고 이후 송(宋), 명(明), 청(淸) 등 왕조에서도 개원통보를 사용하였으며 청대(淸代) 말기에 와서는 서양의 기계를 이용한 동전제작기술이 중국에 전해지기도 하고 근대의 원형 금화가 생겨나기도 하였다. 역사적으로 황금화폐는 황제의 하사품, 지배계급의 축수품(祝壽品) 또는 하사품으로 사용되었다. 비록 송왕조(宋王朝) 때 지폐가 생겨나고 명왕조(明王朝) 때 백은(白銀) 화폐가 널리 유통되었으나 방공원전은 중국의 주요 화폐 형태로 널리 쓰였다.

유금동포수(鎏金銅鋪首)

은(銀) | 당(唐) | 지름 26.5cm 고리지름 20.6cm 무게 1,600g
1972년 서안시 신성구(西安市 新城區) 당(唐) 대명궁(大明宮) 유적지에서 출토

Gilt Bronze Animal Head Appliques

Silver | Tang Dynasty(618AD~907AD) | D 26.5cm Ring D 20.6cm Weight 1,600g
Excavated from the Ruin of Daming Palace in Xincheng District, Xi'an in 1972

원형 포수(鋪首) 2점이다. 수면문(獸面紋)을 주문양으로 하였
다. 두 눈을 부릅뜨고 눈살을 찡그린 흉악한 짐승이 입을 크게 벌
려 날카로운 이빨을 드러내고 혀를 말아 구리로 된 문고리를 문
형상이다. 짐승 머리의 뒷면에 있는 두 가닥으로 갈라진 못들은
문에 끼워넣기 위한 것인데 그 꼬리 부분은 가로로 꺾어 포수를
고정하고 있다.

추엽(鎚揲) 기법으로 만든 문양의 표면에 금을 입힌 이 포수는
당대 장안 대명궁(大明宮) 유적지에서 출토된 것으로 미루어 보아
궁전 대문에 달려 있었던 것으로 추측된다.

송원시대

宋元時代

Song & Yuan Dynasty Period

송원(宋元)시대

송대(宋代) 상품경제의 지속적인 발전과 더불어 각지에서는 금은기(金銀器) 제작업이 흥하였는데 위로는 황실종친, 아래로는 서민백성에 이르기까지 모두 금은그릇을 사용하였다. 송대 금은기는 당대(唐代) 금은기의 기초 위에서 부단한 혁신을 거쳐 자기만의 선명한 특색을 갖추었을 뿐만 아니라 상품성까지 갖추었는데 특히 은기(銀器)가 널리 유통되면서 금은그릇의 형태에 변화를 가져왔다. 송대 금은그릇은 무게가 가볍고 조형상 정교하며 참신하고 우아하면서 크기가 작다. 생동감이 있고 자연스러우며 소박하면서도 우아함이 묻어나는 문양들은 사회생활을 소재로 하였기에 사실적이면서 생활정취가 짙다. 당대 시기에 생겨난 이국적인 색채를 띠는 금은그릇은 송대에 와서 그 자취를 찾아볼 수 없었다. 이는 위진(魏晉) 때부터 시작된 금은기의 중국화 과정이 완성되었음을 나타낸다. 송대 금은기는 그릇의 전반적인 느낌에 따라 문양을 배치해 기물(器物)마다 문양이 다양했다. 추엽(錘揲)·참각(鏨刻)·투각(透刻)·용접(鎔接)·주조(鑄造) 등 기법을 사용함으로써 이중기법 효과를 선보였다. 금대(金代, 1115~1234년) 금은기는 발견된 것이 그리 많지 않으나 섬서(陝西) 임동(臨潼) 금대 가마터에서 출토된 금은기를 보면 금대와 송대 금은기의 풍격이 유사함을 알 수 있다. 원대(元代,1206~1368년) 금은기는 풍격상 송대의 것과 유사하지만 기물의 윤곽, 모서리가 보다 뚜렷이 표현되었을 뿐만 아니라 원조(圓彫)와 고부조(高浮彫) 기법도 사용하였다. 그 밖에 그릇과 장식품 외에도 진열품이 많아졌으며 문양이 화려하며 번잡한 추세로 나아갔다.

Song and Yuan Dynasty

In Song Dynasty, gold and silver industry was flourishing all over the country with the development of the commodity economy. People from all walks of life, up to the imperial family and down to the ordinary people, had extensive use of gold and silver utensils. Gold and silver wares in Song based on the gold and silver wares of Tang and innovated to form its own distinct characteristics in Song based on the gold and silver wares of Tang and innovated to form its own distinct characteristics. Gold and silver vessels of Song have already the characteristics of commodity, especially the silver wares has fully been to the market. Therefore the art designs of gold and silver have also changed accordingly. The gold and silver wares of Song usually possess small bodies which are delicately and exquisitely shaped, full of elegance and novelty. But, speaking of momentum, they might be light, thin, short and small. They mainly feature naturalness, vividness, plainness and elegance. Their prime subjects are from social life with highly realistic and rich validity Gold and silver wares of Tang emerged large quantities of objects with a strong exotic flavor which was rarely seen Song. It indicated that the gold and silver wares in Song Dynasty was based in the overall layout of the entire utensil. They would adopt multiple layouts to draw due to device. Techniques used in the craftsmanship included hammering, engraving, hollowing sculpturing, welding and casting, which were full of strong effect of sandwich technique. Few gold and silver wares of jin Dynasty(1115~1234A.D) have been found until now. However, from the excavations of style. Gold and silver wares in Yuan Dynasty(1206~1368A.D) share some similarities with those of Song, but utensils of Yuan have more prominent edges and corners. Techniques of full relief and high relief were employed in Yuan Besides utensils and ornaments of gold and silver, the number of stuffs increased. What's more, there was a magnificent complex decoration trend.

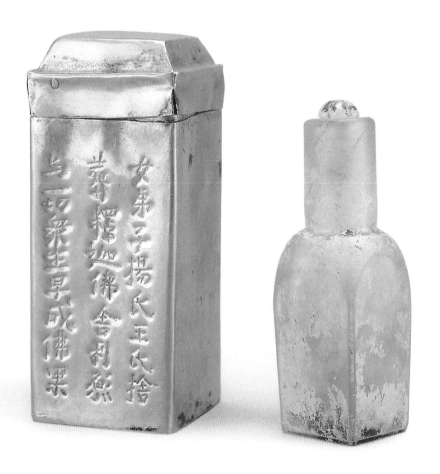

167

방형대개사리금합(方形帶蓋舍利金盒)

금(金) | 송(宋) | 길이 3.7cm 너비 3.7cm 높이 7.8cm 무게 106.4g
1969년 서안시(西安市) 제일중학교(第一中學校) 출토

Square Gold Lidded Case with Buddhist Relics

Gold | Song Dynasty(960AD~1279AD) | L 3.7cm W 3.7cm H 7.8cm Weight 106.4g
Excavated from the No. 1 Middle School of Xi'an in 1969

　사각기둥 형태의 민무늬 금합(金盒)이다. 장방형의 몸체와 녹정(盝頂) 지붕 형식의 뚜껑이 자모구(子母口)를 이룬다. 합 안에는 사리(舍利) 1과가 담긴 유리병 1개가 놓여 있다. 표면의 한 측면에는 "女弟子楊氏王氏捨葬釋迦佛舍利, 願與一切衆生早成佛果(여제자 양 씨와 왕 씨가 석가불의 사리를 얻어 부장하니 중생과 함께 하루빨리 성불하기를 비나이다)"라는 발원문이 새겨져 있다.

　이 사리합은 출토 시, 석관(石棺) 안에 놓여 있었다. 석관 뚜껑은 아치형이고 몸체는 직사각형에 가까우며 입구 부분은 평평하다. 낮은 침대 형태의 몸체와 관좌(棺座)는 서로 연결되어 앞부분이 크고 뒷부분이 작은 사다리꼴 모양을 이루었다. 바닥에는 투각한 직사각형의 호문(壺門)이 양측에 3개, 앞뒤에 2개가 배치되어 있으며 호문 사이에는 여의운문(如意雲紋)이 새겨져 있다. 뚜껑 안에는 고대 인도의 범문(梵文)이 가득 새겨져 있으며, 몸체 겉면에는 반부조로 사신(四神)이 새겨져 있다. 앞에는 주작(朱雀), 좌측에는 청룡, 우측에는 백호, 뒷면에는 현무(玄武)를 새겨 넣었다. 섬세하면서도 정연하게 표현된 문양에서는 석가모니불을 향한 공양자의 경건한 마음을 엿볼 수 있다.

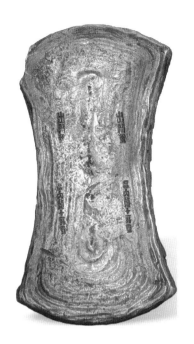

168

'사내황십일□호(思內黃十一□號)' 은정(銀鋌)

은(銀) | 남송(南宋) | 길이 12.7cm 너비 7cm 높이 1.5cm 무게 971g
1987년 서안시 장안구 (현) 풍서향(西安市 長安區 (縣) 灃西鄕) 출토

Silver Ingot

Silver | South Song Dynasty(1127AD~1279AD) | L 12.7cm W 7cm H 1.5cm Weight 971g
Excavated from Fengxi County Chang'an District, Xi'an in 1987

　　허리가 잘록하고 밑면이 윗면보다 작으며 긴지름 부분이 호형(弧形)인 은정(銀鋌)이다. 표면은 전체적으로 은회색을 띠며 평평하나 약간 오목한 데가 있다. 허리 양측의 가장자리와 가까운 부분에 각각 해서체(楷書體)로 "出門稅, 思內黃十一□號(출문세, 사내황십일□호)"라는 명문이 새겨져 있으며, 뒷면에는 크기가 서로 다른 벌집 모양의 작은 구멍이 가득한데 주조 시 생긴 흔적으로 보인다. '출문세(出門稅)'는 도장[戳記], '황십일(黃十一)'은 천자문으로 매긴 번호를 말한다. 남송(南宋) 후기, 유통의 필요에 따라 무게가 50냥, 25냥, 12냥반인 대·중·소 3개 등급의 은정이 생겨났다. 25냥을 지금의 무게 단위로 계산하면 914.2~1,000g에 해당하는데, 이 은정은 무게가 971g이므로 중간 등급에 속한다. 남송 은정의 주조지는 지방과 행재(行在)로 나뉜다. 행재는 각지에서 납부한 은정을 임안성(臨安城) 내 금은행(金銀行)에 명하여 용해시킨 다음, 새로 주조하는 역할을 한다. 쉽게 분별하기 위한 목적으로 은정의 각 모서리와 허리 양측에 도장을 찍는데 은의 순도, 은행 이름이나 '출문세'를 두 번 찍는 경우가 있다. 일부 천자문으로 번호를 매긴 것도 있다.

169

'유중전칭(劉仲典稱)' 은정(銀鋌)

은(銀) | 금(金) | 길이 14.5cm 높이 2.2cm 무게 2,000g
1972년 서안시문물관리위원회(西安市文物管理委員會) 수집

Silver Ingot with Characters of Weighted by Liu Zhongdian

Silver | Jin Dynasty(1115AD~1234AD) | H 2.2cm L 14.5cm Weight 2,000g
Collected by Xi'an Culture Relic Administration Committee in 1972

　　양쪽이 호형(弧形)이고 허리가 잘록한 은정(銀鋌)이다. 가장자리는 조금 볼록하고 가운데가 약간 오목하며, 뒷면에는 주조 시 생긴 벌집 모양의 흔적이 남아 있고 주변에는 파도무늬가 새겨져 있다. 앞면에는 "定准柒□□拾玖兩玖分, 行人史珏□□, 使司忠□, 劉仲典秤(정준칠□□19냥 9분, 행인 사규□□, 사사충□, 유중이 무게 측정을 맡음)"이란 글자가 새겨져 있다. 표면의 마모된 흔적을 보면 '정준(定准)' 두 글자는 다른 문자 위에 새긴 것이고, 다른 문자와 방향이 다를뿐더러 모호하게 보이는 '사사충□(使司忠□)' 네 글자는 먼저 새긴 글자로 보인다. 『구당서(舊唐書)』 「식화지(食貨志)」에 최초로 나오는 '행인(行人)'은 당대(唐代) 장안(長安)의 양식행회(糧食行會) 수령을 말하나, 송금(宋金)시대의 은정에 새겨진 행인은 일명 '은행인(銀行人)'이라고도 불리며 금은행회의 수령을 뜻한다. '사사(使司)'는 금대(金代)의 전운사사(轉運使司)·염사사(鹽使司)·권농사사(勸農使司)·국사사(鞠使司) 등 기구의 약칭으로 조정을 위해 세금을 거두는 직책을 담당한다. 그중 전운사사는 세금, 창고 출납 및 도량형의 척도를 가늠하고, 염사사는 각지의 염세(鹽稅)를 관장한다. 이 두 기구는 은정의 주조와 가장 밀접한 관계가 있다. 금대 은정은 민간주조와 정부주조로 구분된다. 양식이 간단한 민간주조 은정과 달리 정부주조 은정에는 흔히 주조기구·행인·보증인, 검증인의 이름 등이 새겨져 있다.

(1)

(2)

170

검형금이알(劍形金耳挖)

금(金) | 원(元) | 길이 (1) 15.8cm (2) 15.4cm 무게 (1) 10.5g (2) 8.8g
1974년 서안시 안탑구 등가파향 동등가파촌(西安市 雁塔區 等駕坡鄉 東等駕坡村) 출토

Gold Ear-picker in the Shape of a Sword

Gold | Yuan Dynasty(1206AD∼1368AD) | L (1) 15.8cm (2) 15.4cm Weight (1) 10.5g (2) 8.8g
Excavated from East Dengjiapo Village in Dengjiapo County Yanta District, Xi'an in 1974

검(劍) 모양의 귀이개이다. 자루 부분은 여러 줄의 철현문(凸絃紋)으로 자루와 가까운 몸체 부분은 파도무늬로 장식하였다. 귀이개는 귀지를 파내는 기구로 알이시자(挖耳匙子)·이알인(耳斡兒)·철료사(鐵了事)라고도 부른다. 숟가락 모양의 물건에 긴 자루가 달린 형태가 많으며 검 모양의 귀이개는 보기 드물다. 흔히 금속이나 뼈 등의 재료로 만들어진다. 원(元)나라는 중국 소수민족인 몽고족이 세운 왕조로 계급 갈등과 민족 갈등이 첨예하여 장기적인 불안 상태가 나타났다. 검 모양의 귀이개는 사용자의 성격, 나아가 길함과 평안함을 추구하는 당시 사람들의 염원을 반영해 준다.

171

호로문금잠(葫蘆紋金簪)

금(金) | 원(元) | 길이 11.7cm 무게 4.4g
1974년 서안시 안탑구 등가파향 동등가파촌(西安市 雁塔區 等駕坡鄉 東等駕坡村) 출토

Gold Hairpin with a Bottle Gourd

Gold | Yuan Dynasty(1206AD∼1368AD) | L 11.7cm Weight 4.4g
Excavated from East Dengjiapo Village in Dengjiapo County Yanta District, Xi'an in 1974

조롱박 장식이 달린 민무늬 금잠(金簪)이다. 원대(元代)에는 도교가 성행하였는데 의료에 쓰이는 조롱박은 도교 법기(法器) 가운데 하나였다. 조롱박 장식은 사람들의 생활에 미친 도교 사상의 영향을 반영하고 있다. 중국 민간에서 조롱박은 '복록(福祿)'을 뜻하기도 한다.

172

소화장편형금잠(小花長扁形金簪)

금(金) | 원(元) | 길이 13.9cm 무게 7.8g
1973년 서안시 장안구(현) 영소향 영가촌(西安市 長安區(縣) 靈沼鄉 英家村) 출토

Gold Long and Oblate Hairpin with Little Flower

Gold | Yuan Dynasty(1206AD~1368AD) | L 13.9cm Weight 7.8g
Excavated from Yingjia Village in Lingzhao County Chang'an Distrct, Xi'an in 1973

길고 가는 모양의 편평한 금잠(金簪)이다. 머리의 금사(金絲) 두 가닥은 서로 얽히면서 나가다가 끄트머리에서 갈라져 각각 모란 한 송이를 이루었다.

173

화판문금잠(花瓣紋金簪)

금(金) | 원(元) | 길이 13.2cm 무게 13.5g
1973년 서안시 장안구(현) 영소향 영가촌(西安市 長安區(縣) 靈沼鄉 英家村) 출토

Gold Hairpin with Petals

Gold | Yuan Dynasty(1206AD~1368AD) | L 13.2cm Weight 13.5g
Excavated from Yingjia Village in Lingzhao County Chang'an Distrct, Xi'an in 1973

금잠(金簪)은 두 가닥으로 되었는데 머리에는 서로 마주한 꽃잎, 끄트머리에는 격자무늬가 새겨져 있다.

174

전사소금잠(纏絲小金簪)

금(金) | 원(元) | 길이 7.33cm 무게 3g
1973년 서안시 장안구(현) 영소향 영가촌(西安市 長安區(縣) 靈沼鄕 英家村) 출토

Little Gold Hairpin with Winded Threads

Gold | Yuan Dynasty(1206AD∼1368AD) | L 7.33cm Weight 3g
Excavated from Yingjia Village in Lingzhao County Chang'an Distrct, Xi'an in 1973

　　민무늬 금잠(金簪)이다. 머리 부분의 금사(金絲) 두 가닥은 서로 얽힌 여러 개의 원
을 이루었다. 금실이 뻗어 나가는 부분에는 크기가 서로 다른 금합(金盒)이 이어져 있
는데 두 금합 안에는 원래 장식품을 상감했던 것으로 추측된다.

175

매화문금잠(梅花紋金簪)

금(金) | 원(元) | 길이 10cm 무게 9.12g
1974년 서안시 비림구 분항(西安市 碑林區 粉巷) 출토

Gold Hairpin with a Plum Blossom on the Top

Gold | Yuan Dynasty(1206AD~1368AD) | L 10cm Weight 9.12g
Excavated from Fenxiang Beilin District, Xi'an in 1974

활짝 핀 매화 한 송이가 장식된 원추형의 금잠(金簪)이다. 엄동설한(嚴冬雪寒)에도 꽃을 피워 추위와 맞서 싸우는 매화는 숭고한 정신의 상징이기도 하며, 꽃잎들은 기쁨 · 행복 · 장수 · 평화 · 순조로움 등 오복을 상징하기도 한다. 원(元)나라는 몽고족이 세운 왕조이다. 지배계급인 몽고 귀족들이 내부적으로 민족 억압정책을 실시하자 피지배계급이었던 한족들은 무장 등 여러 형태로 몽고 귀족 통치에 대한 불만과 불굴의 정신을 보여 주었다. 원대(元代)에 만들어진 이 금잠 역시 그러한 정신의 반영이다.

176

옥하엽금잠(玉荷葉金簪)

금(金) | 원(元) | 길이 12.5cm 무게 18.8g
1965년 서안시 안탑구 동하가촌(西安市 雁塔區 東何家村) 출토

Gold Hairpin with Jade Lotus Leaf

Gold | Yuan Dynasty(1206AD~1368AD) | L 12.5cm Weight 18.8g
Excavated from East Hejia Village Yanta District, Xi'an in 1965

민무늬 금잠(金簪)이다. 자루는 끄트머리가 원추 모양인 길고 가늘며 편평한 형태이다. 머리 부분은 가는 금사(金絲)를 꼬아 여러 개의 동그란 고리를 만든 뒤, 한쪽이 위로 말린 연잎 모양의 청옥(青玉)을 입혀 만들어진 것이다. 표면에는 가는 선을 음각함으로써 연잎의 잎맥을 표현하였다.

명청시대

明淸時代

명청(明淸)시대

명대(明代, 1368~1644년)는 중국 전통사회가 황혼을 맞이하는 시점이었다. 비록 사회경제가 지속적으로 발전하였지만 문화는 보수적인 경향이 있었다. 이러한 특징은 금은기(金銀器)의 조형 및 문양에서도 분명히 나타났다. 명대 금은기의 조형은, 원대(元代)와 비교할 때 별다른 변화가 없었으나 보석 상감기술이 널리 사용되었다. 풍격은 더욱더 화려하고 농염해졌으며 궁정 정취가 갈수록 짙어졌다. 용봉(龍鳳) 도안이나 형태가 주를 이루었으며 문양이 복잡해지면서 기물 전체에 꽃무늬를 새기기도 했다. 하지만 명대 금은기는 전반적으로 생기있고 고졸(古拙)한 원대 풍격에서 크게 벗어나지 못했다. 오늘날까지 전해지는 청대(淸代, 1616~1911년) 금은기는 상당수에 이르는데 풍격은 전통을 계승하는 한편 외래문화의 영향을 받아 이전보다 더욱 다채로웠다. 조형과 문양에서 고졸한 멋은 찾아볼 수 없었고 다양한 형태와 화려한 문양을 연출하였다. 청대 금은기 공예는 매우 복잡하다. 범주(范鑄) · 추엽(錘鍱) · 작주(炸珠) · 용접(鎔接) · 투각(透刻) · 겹사(掐絲) · 상감[鑲嵌] · 점취(点翠, 물총새의 깃을 넣어 만드는 공예) 외에도 기돌(起突) · 은기(隱起) · 음선(陰線) · 양선(陽線) · 투조(透彫) 등 다양한 기법을 사용하였다. 또한 복합공예도 매우 발달하였는데 금은기와 법랑(珐琅) · 주옥(珠玉) · 보석 등을 상호 결합하여 제작한 제품들이 대량으로 생겨났다.

Ming & Qing Dynasty

Ming Dynasty(1368~1644AD) was the beginning of decline of traditional Chinese society. While theeconomy continued to move forward at that time, cultural development became increasingly conservative, which was obviously presented by the shaping and decorative patterns of the gold and silver wares. Shapes of gold and silver wares in Ming changed little compared with those of Yuan Dynasty, but they extensively employed cameo incrustation technique. Their style became more and more gorgeous and bright-colored with stronger court flavor. Dragon and phoenix patterns or images occupied a very important position. Their decoration pattern tended to be much denser and denser, and usually gold and silver objects would be covered with decorative designs. However, in general, gold and silver wares of Ming till possessed the Yuan's style of vividness, simplicity, and unsophistication.

Lots of gold and silver wares of Qing Dynasty(1616~1911AD) passed down and remained popular. Gold and silver wares of Qing inherited the traditional style, and they were also influenced by exotic style, so they were more colorful compared with the former dynasties. Shapes and decorations were not simple and unsophisticated any more. They possessed a wide variety of shapes, and dense and magnificent ornamentations. Craftsmanship of gold and silver wares in Qing was very complicated, including, mold-casting, hammering, fried beads, welding, engraving, filigree, mosaic and kingfisher. In addition, other techniques were also employed. The composite technology was well developed at that time. A large number of productions of combining gold and silver wares and enamels, beads, jades and gemstones emerged.

177

봉화문금잠(鳳花紋金簪)

금(金) | 명(明) | 길이 15.1cm 무게 24.6g
1963년 서안시 비림구 사파촌(西安市 碑林區 沙坡村) 출토

Gold Hairpin with Phoenix and Flower

Gold | Ming Dynasty(1368AD~1644AD) | L 15.1cm Weight 24.6g
Excavated from Shapo Village Beilin District, Xi'an in 1963

순금(純金)으로 만든 잠(簪)의 머리에는 밧줄무늬를 두르고 그 안에 활짝 핀 해바라기 한 송이를 상감했다. 여러 방향으로 흩어진 해바라기 꽃잎에서는 부조화의 매력이 풍긴다. 머리와 몸체 사이는 화초로 장식하고 그 위에 작은 관상화(管狀花)를 배치하였는데 꽃잎 4개 사이로 꽃망울이 머리를 내밀고 있다. 봉황 한 마리가 풀숲 위에 내려앉았는데 주둥이를 작은 꽃 방향으로 하고 양쪽 날개는 살포시 모았으며 긴 꽁지 털은 아래로 내려뜨렸다.

178

봉화문금잠(鳳花紋金簪)

금(金) | 명(明) | 길이 15.5cm 무게 25g
1963년 서안시 비림구 사파촌(西安市 碑林區 沙坡村) 출토

Gold Hairpin with Phoenix and Flower

Gold | Ming Dynasty(1368AD~1644AD) | L 15.5cm Weight 25g
Excavated from Shapo Village Beilin District, Xi'an in 1963

순금(純金)으로 만든 잠(簪)의 머리 부분에는 작은 연주문(聯珠紋)을 두르고 그 위에 봉황무늬, 활짝 핀 해바라기와 초엽(草葉)무늬를 새겼다. 그 위에서는 봉황 한 마리가 노닐고 있는데 날개를 모으려는 자세를 하고 여러 가닥으로 된 긴 꽁지를 내려뜨린 것이 마치 장거리 비행 뒤에 잠깐 머물러 휴식을 취하는 듯싶다.

179

봉화문금잠(鳳花紋金簪)

금(金) | 명(明) | 길이 9.7cm 너비 5.2cm 무게 22g
1963년 서안시 비림구 사파촌(西安市 碑林區 沙坡村) 출토

Gold Hairpin with Phoenix and Flower

Gold | Ming Dynasty(1368AD~1644AD) | L 9.7cm W 5.2cm Weight 22g
Excavated from Shapo Village Beilin District, Xi'an in 1963

순금(純金)으로 만든 잠(簪)이다. 복숭아 모양의 머리에는 투각(透刻)한 봉황을 상감하고, 구름으로 그 주위를 장식하였다. 봉황은 날개를 펼치고 꽁지를 나풀거리며 하늘을 나는 형상이다.

180

봉화문금잠(鳳花紋金簪)

금(金) | 명(明) | 길이 14.8cm 무게 24.5g
1963년 서안시 비림구 사파촌(西安市 碑林區 沙坡村) 출토

Gold Hairpin with Phoenix and Flower

Gold | Ming Dynasty(1368AD~1644AD) | L 14.8cm Weight 24.5g
Excavated from Shapo Village Beilin District, Xi'an in 1963

순금(純金)으로 만든 잠(簪)이다. 머리에는 복숭아 모양의 판을 부착하고 그 위에 투각(透刻)한 봉황을 상감하였다. 봉황은 날개를 펼치고 둥실거리는 조각구름 속을 나는 모습으로 내려뜨린 긴 꽁지는 전지화(纏枝花)를 방불케 한다.

181

금망건(金網巾)

금(金) | 명(明) | 높이 4.7cm 지름 12.7cm 무게 52g
1973년 서안시 비림구(西安市 碑林區) 출토

Gold Hairnet

Gold | Ming Dynasty(1368AD∼1644AD) | H 4.7cm D 12.7cm Weight 52g
Excavated from Beilin District, Xi'an in 1973

가는 금사(金絲)를 엮어 만든 망건이다. 망건과 그 가장자리를 금실로 연결하였는데 가장자리에는 작은 구멍 4개가 배열되어 있다. 한쪽에는 세로로 원형방공전문(圓形方孔錢紋) 4개, 다른 한쪽에는 금실로 엮은 "福(복)" 자 도안을 배치하였다.

일명 '망건권인(網巾圈兒)', '망자(網子)'라고도 불리는 망건은 원래 도사들이 머리를 묶는 데 쓰였다. 구체적인 사용방법은, 망건으로 머리를 감싸고 머리 뒤에서 매듭짓는다. 명대(明代) 초기에 태조(太祖) 주원장(朱元璋)에 의해 중국 각지에 보급되었으며 그 뒤로 이와 같이 머리 묶는 방식이 오늘날까지 전해졌다.

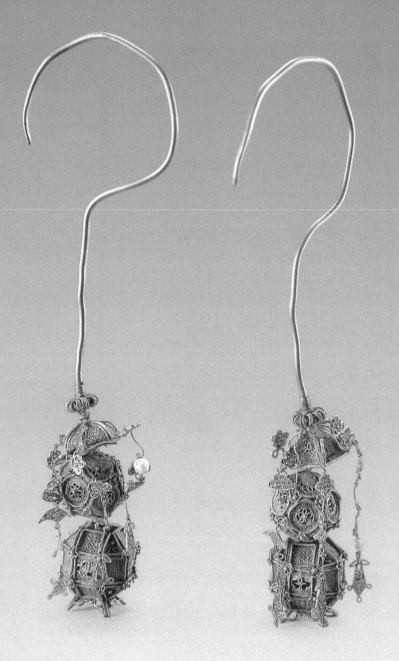

182

쌍층등롱형금이추(雙層燈籠形金耳墜)

금(金) | 명(明) | 길이 15.9cm 무게 14.8g
1973년 서안시 비림구(西安市 碑林區) 출토

Gold Earrings with Double Lanterns

Gold | Ming Dynasty(1368AD~1644AD) | L 15.9cm Weight 14.8g
Excavated from Beilin District, Xi'an in 1973

갈고리 모양의 고리와 휘감긴 금실로 엮은 육각형 투구 모양의 장식과 등롱(燈籠) 모양의 드리개로 구성된 금귀고리다. 여의권운문(如意卷雲紋) 여섯 송이로 장식된 모자 꼭대기로부터 금사(金絲) 여섯 가닥이 드리워져 있다. 모자 아래에는 등롱 모양의 드리개 2개가 있다. 위의 등롱은 원형 단화(團花) 12개로 장식되었다. 그 아래의 등롱은 이십사면체로 이루어져 있다. 가운데에는 창화[窗花, 창문을 장식하는 전지(剪紙)의 일종] 네 송이와 격자 4개가 번갈아 배열되어 있으며 아래위는 금사로 직조된 권운무늬로 장식하였다.

추자(墜子)라고도 불리는 귀고리는 여성들이 귓볼에 다는 장신구이다. 금은이나 옥석을 많이 사용하였고 일찍이 북조(北朝) 때에 나타났다. 오대(五代) 이전에 귀고리는 변방지역 및 중원으로 이주해 온 소수민족들 사이에서 유행하였으나 오대 이후에는 점차 한족 여성들이 애용하는 장신구가 되었다.

183

'수성원□(水盛原□)' 금잠(金簪)

금(金) | 청(淸) | 길이 7.2cm 무게 4.8g
1978년 서안시 장안구(현) 곽두진 신문촌(西安市 長安區(縣) 郭杜鎭 新文村) 출토

Gold Hairpin with Characters 'Shui Sheng Yuan □'

Gold | Qing Dynasty(1616AD~1911AD) | L 7.2cm Weight 4.8g
Excavated from Xinwen Village Guodu Town Chang'an District, Xi'an in 1978

금병(金甁)에 국화를 꽂은 모양의 장식이 달린 금잠(金簪)이다. 잎은 어자문(魚子紋)으로 장식하고 활짝 핀 국화 꽃잎에는 가는 선을 음각(陰刻)하여 잎맥을 표현하였다. 문양들은 투각(透刻)기법으로 만들었다. 금잠의 안쪽에는 해서체(楷書體)로 "水盛原□(수성원□)" 4글자가 새겨져 있다.

184

석장형금잠(錫杖形金簪)

금(金) | 청(淸) | 길이 12.2cm 무게 8.7g
1992년 서안시 안탑구 청룡(西安市 雁塔區 靑龍) 주택단지에서 출토

Buddhist Monk's Staff-shaped Gold Hairpin

Gold | Qing Dynasty(1616AD~1911AD) | L 12.2cm Weight 8.7g
Excavated from Qinglong Subdistrict Yanta District, Xi'an in 1992

　불교의 법기(法器)에 속하는 석장(錫杖) 모양의 장식이 달린 황금색 잠(簪)이다. 석장 모양의 장식은 앙련(仰蓮)과 복련(覆蓮)으로 이루어졌다. 두 연꽃에서 뻗어 나온 꽃실은 서로 연결되어 여섯 가닥으로 균일하게 배치되었다. 꽃실 위에는 금고리 12개가 달려 있는데 원래 장식품이 박혀 있었으나 떨어지고 없다.

　석장은 일명 지장(智杖)·덕장(德杖)·흘기라(吃弃羅)·명장(鳴杖)·성장(聲杖)이라 불리며 '석(錫)'이라 약칭한다. 승려들이 수행하거나 행각할 때 몸에 지니고 다니는 18물(物)의 하나이다. 18물은 양지(楊枝)·조두(澡豆)·삼의(三衣)·물병·향로·수건·여수낭(濾水囊)·칼·화수(火燧)·집게·승상(繩床)·경(經)·율(律)·불상 등을 포함한다. 당나라의 의정(義淨)이 쓴 『남해기귀내법전(南海寄歸內法傳)』 4권에는 "석장은 범어로 '흘기라(吃棄羅)'라고도 불리는데 '흘기라'는 들고 다닐 때 소리가 잘랑잘랑 난다는 뜻이다. 옛사람들은 이것을 석(錫)이라 옮겼으며 석(錫)에서 소리가 난다는 뜻에서 명장(鳴杖), 석장(錫杖)이라고도 불렀다. 고대 서역의 석장은 머리 부분에 2~3치가량의 철권(鐵捲)이 있고 그 아래에는 4~5손가락 길이의 촉이 있으며 장대는 나무로 되었다……밑부분에는 철로 된 둥글거나 편평한 고리를 달았는데 가장 짧은 지름은 엄지손가락만 하며 6개 혹은 8개를 안고(安股)에 꿴다. 그 밖에 동 방울은 임의로 단다"는 기록이 있다.

　현교(顯敎)와 밀교(密敎)에서 석장은 서로 다른 의미를 갖는다. 현교에서는 석장을 걸식하거나 해충을 막는 용도로 사용하는 반면에, 밀교에서는 석장을 지(地), 수(水), 화(火), 풍(風), 공(空)으로 이루어진 부처와 보살의 삼매야형(三昧耶形)으로 여겼다. 삼매야형은 부처와 보살의 내재적 증거이며 본원의 표지물이다. 흔히 네 가닥에 12개의 고리로 구성된 석장은 사체십이인연(四諦十二因緣)을 뜻한다. 이 금잠에 표현된 석장은 여섯 가닥에 12개의 고리로 구성되었으며 또한 장식품으로 사용되었다. 이는 청대(淸代)에 불교에 대한 일반 백성들의 관심은 형식에 있는 것이 아니라 정신적인 신앙에 있었음을 말해 준다.

불수형금잠(佛手形金簪)

금(金) | 청(淸) | 길이 15.5cm 무게 4.5g
1992년 서안시 안탑구 청룡(西安市 雁塔區 靑龍) 주택단지에서 출토

Gold Hairpin in the Shape of Buddha's Hand

Gold | Qing Dynasty(1616AD~1911AD) | L 15.5cm Weight 4.5g
Excavated from Qinglong Subdistrict Yanta District, Xi'an in 1992

　원추형의 금잠(金簪)이다. 머리에는 금사(金絲)를 엮어 만든 부처 손 모양의 장식
이 달려 있다. 여의(如意) 연꽃으로 손목 아래를 장식하고 한 가닥의 가는 금실을 손
등에 둘러 손바닥에서 나선형의 매듭을 지었다. 식지와 엄지로 불가(佛家) 법기(法
器)에 속하는, 금실로 엮은 작은 석장(錫杖)을 집었는데 석장 주위에 금고리가 드리
워져 있다. 중국 민간에서 부처의 손은 '복수(福壽)'라는 뜻도 내포한다.

축요형금편잠(縮腰形金扁簪)

금(金) | 청(淸) | 길이 9.8cm 무게 13.4g
1978년 서안시 장안구(현) 곽두진 신문촌(西安市 長安區 (縣) 郭杜鎭 新文村) 출토

Constricted Oblate Gold Hairpin

Gold | Qing Dynasty(1616AD~1911AD) | L 9.8cm Weight 13.4g
Excavated from Xinwen Village Guodu Town Chang'an District, Xi'an in 1978

　편평하고 허리가 잘록하며 양끝이 뾰족한 잠(簪)이다. 겉면 가장
자리에는 '回(회)' 자 무늬가 둘러져 있으며, 가운데에는 양끝을 가
로지르는 볼록선이 배치되어 있다. 안쪽 중심에는 해서체(楷書體)
로 "足金□立春(족금□입춘)" 5글자가 새겨져 있다.

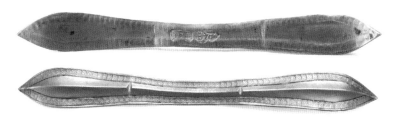

모단국화문축요형금편잠(牡丹菊花紋縮腰形金扁簪)

금(金) | 청(淸) | 길이 11.2cm 무게 35.5g
1976년 서안시 안탑구 어화채향 북침가교촌(西安市 雁塔區 魚化寨鄕 北沈家橋村) 출토

Constricted Oblate Gold Hairpin With Peony and Chrysanthemum Pattern

Gold | Qing Dynasty(1616AD~1911AD) | L 11.2cm Weight 35.5g
Excavated from North Shenjiaqiao Village in Yuhuazhai County Yanta District, Xi'an in 1976

허리가 잘록한 금잠(金簪)으로 능형(菱形)과 비슷한 안쪽 부분에는 각각 직사각형에 가까운 틀이 새겨져 있다. 한쪽 틀에는 전지(纏枝) 모양의 활짝 핀 모란 한 송이를 새겼는데 가지와 줄기가 구불구불하며 듬성듬성하게 분포된 잎들은 저마다 흩어졌다. 다른 한쪽 틀에는 꽃술을 두른 버들잎 모양의 꽃잎과 가느다란 가지와 잎으로 표현된 국화 한 송이가 새겨져 있다. 두 틀 모두 어자문(魚子紋)을 바탕에 시문(試紋)하였으며 틀의 바깥쪽에는 매화 반쪽을 배치하였다. 금잠 안쪽 면에는 해서체(楷書體)로 된 "德和(덕화)" 두 글자가 새겨져 있다. 끌로 조각한 문양들은 정교함이 묻어나는데 장인들의 뛰어난 솜씨를 엿볼 수 있다.

화초문축요형금편잠(花草紋縮腰形金扁簪)

금(金) | 청(淸) | 길이 6.99cm 무게 9g
1968년 서안시문물관리위원회(西安市文物管理委員會) 수집

Constricted Oblate Gold Hairpin with Flowers and Grass Pattern

Gold | Qing Dynasty(1616AD~1911AD) | L 6.99cm Weight 9g
Collected by Xi'an Culture Relic Administration Committee in 1968

편평하며 허리가 잘록한 금잠(金簪)이다. 양쪽이 넓고 가운데가 가늘며 표면은 조금 융기되었다. 양쪽 모두 형태가 똑같은 화초로 장식되었다. 가지와 잎은 가늘고 길며, 막 피어난 꽃이 달려 있다. 금잠 안쪽에는 해서체(楷書體)로 된 "原金(원금)" 두 글자가 새겨져 있다. 표면의 문양들은 모두 끌로 새겨 넣었다.

전지화문금이알(纏枝花紋金耳挖)

금(金) | 청(淸) | 길이 17.9cm 무게 14.2g
1974년 서안시 안탑구 등가파향 동등가파촌(西安市 雁塔區 等駕坡鄉 東等駕坡村) 출토

Gold Ear-picker with Crossed Branches

Gold | Qing Dynasty(1616AD~1911AD) | L 17.9cm Weight 14.2g
Excavated from East Dengjiapo Village in Dengjiapo County Yanta District, Xi'an in 1974

　단면(斷面)이 능형(菱形)인, 기다란 각뿔 모양의 장식이 달려 있는 귀이개
이다. 원뿔 모양 장식의 아랫부분에는 전지문(纏枝紋) 화초가 새겨져 있다. 단
면이 원형인 자루 가운데에는 타원형의 구체가 있으며 귀이개와 가까운 부분
에는 음현문(陰弦紋) 네 줄이 둘러져 있다.

능추형금이알(稜錐形金耳挖)

금(金) | 청(淸) | 길이 10.45cm 무게 5.5g
1975년 서안시 비림구(西安市 碑林區) 서안교통대학(西安交通大學) 출토

Pyramidal Gold Ear-picker

Gold | Qing Dynasty(1616AD~1911AD) | L 10.45cm Weight 5.5g
Excavated from Xi'an Jiaotong University in Beilin District, Xi'an in 1975

　귀이개 자루는 단면(斷面)이 능형(菱形)인 각뿔 모양이다.
귀이개와 가까운 부분에는 여러 가닥의 현문(弦紋)이 새겨져
있으며 나머지 부분에는 무늬가 없다.

191

'천덕(天德)' 금이환(金耳環)

금(金) | 청(淸) | 길이 7.2cm 무게 9.7g
1972년 서안시(西安市) 출토

Gold Earrings with Characters of 'Tian De'

Gold | Qing Dynasty(1616AD~1911AD) | L 7.2cm Weight 9.7g
Excavated from Xi'an in 1972

　　타원형의 넓은 고리에 박쥐 모양의 장식이 달린 귀고리이다. 여의(如意) 모양의 박쥐는 두 눈을 동그랗게 뜨고 날개를 펄럭이며 비상하는 모습이다. 귀고리 안쪽에는 "天德(천덕)" 두 글자가 새겨져 있다. '박쥐'는 다복을 의미하며 '여의'는 길상어(吉祥語)로 행복과 만사형통을 뜻한다. '천덕'은 당시의 은행[銀號] 명칭으로 추측된다.

192

'덕화(德和)', '족적(足赤)' 금이환(金耳環)

금(金) | 청(淸) | 지름 2.4cm 무게 12.4g
1976년 서안시 안탑구 어화채향 북침가교촌(西安市 雁塔區 魚化寨鄕 北沈家橋村) 출토

Gold Earrings of 'De He' and 'Zu Chi'

Gold | Qing Dynasty(1616AD~1911AD) | D 2.4cm Weight 12.4g
Excavated from North Shenjiaqiao Village in Yuhuazhai County Yanta District, Xi'an in 1976

　　여의운문(如意雲紋) 장식을 부착한 타원형의 귀고리이다. 외벽에는 활짝 핀 꽃잎과 버들잎 모양의 잎이 있는 화초 두 떨기를 역방향으로 새기고 바탕을 어자문으로 장식하였다. 안쪽에는 산저양문(鏟底陽文)으로 "德和(덕화)", "足赤(족적)" 4글자를 새겼다. '덕화'는 당시 은행의 명칭으로 추정된다. 일명 적금(赤金)이라 불리는 '족적'은 금의 순도가 비교적 높음을 나타내는데 보통 순도가 99.2% 이상이고 적황색을 띤다.

193

수면문금이환(獸面紋金耳環)

금(金) | 청(淸) | 지름 2.26cm | 무게 2.8g
1976년 서안시 안탑구 곡강향 서곡강지촌(西安市 雁塔區 曲江鄉 西曲江池村) 출토

Gold Earrings with Mask Motif

Gold | Qing Dynasty(1616AD~1911AD) | D 2.26cm | Weight 2.8g
Excavated from West Qujiangchi Village in Qujiang County Yanta District, Xi'an in 1976

타원형의 귀고리이다. 겉면에는 두 눈을 동그랗게 뜬, 날개를 펼치고 꼬리를 쫙 편
여의(如意) 모양의 박쥐를 새겨 넣었다. 날개는 어자문(魚子紋), 꼬리의 깃털은 음각
한 가는 선으로 표현하였다. 꼬리는 3각형에 가까운 모양이다. 나머지 부분에는 무늬
가 없다.

194

여의편복문금이환(如意蝙蝠紋金耳環)

금(金) | 청(淸) | 지름 3cm 무게 5.9g
1972년 서안시문물관리위원회(西安市文物管理委員會) 수집

Gold Earrings with Ruyi and Bat Patterns

Gold | Qing Dynasty(1616AD~1911AD) | D 3cm Weight 5.9g
Collected by Xi'an Culture Relic Administration Committee in 1972

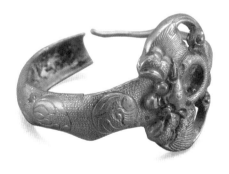

오목한 고리 모양의 귀고리이다. 세세한 어자문(魚子紋)을 바탕에 시문(試紋)하고
날개를 펄럭이는 박쥐 한 마리로 그 위를 장식하였다. 박쥐는 작은 눈을 동그랗게 뜨고
입을 뾰족하게 내밀었으며 두 귀를 늘어뜨렸다. 펼친 날개의 끄트머리는 여의(如意) 모
양을 이루며 머리 뒤에 동그란 고리가 부착되어 있다. 가운데가 오목하게 패인 것으로
보아 장식품을 상감했던 것으로 추측된다. 박쥐 아래에는 작은 원 5개가 음각되어 있
는데 그 안에는 마갈(摩羯), 부처의 손, 연잎 등 무늬가 새겨져 있다. 다복을 뜻하는 박
쥐 장식에서는 행복한 생활에 대한 동경과 추구를 엿볼 수 있다. 범어(梵語)로 '아나룻
다'라고 하는 '여의'는 법구(法具)의 하나이다. 손가락 모양의 머리가 있고 한 자쯤의
자루가 달려 있다. 법회나 설법 때에 법사가 손에 드는 물건으로 사용되기도 하고 가려
운 데를 긁는 도구로 쓰이기도 하여 사람의 뜻대로 사용할 수 있다는 데서 이름이 유래
되었다. 남북조(南北朝)시대에 스님들은 설법할 때 늘 여의를 손에 들었다.

195

'수(壽)'자편복문금이환(字蝙蝠紋金耳環)

금(金) | 청(淸) | 지름 3.24cm 무게 8.7g
1976년 서안시 비림구(西安市 碑林區) 서안교통대학(西安交通大學) 출토

Gold Earrings with 'Shou' Character and Bat pattern

Gold | Qing Dynasty(1616AD~1911AD) | D 3.24cm Weight 8.7g
Excavated from Xi'an Jiaotong University in Beilin District, Xi'an in 1976

　고리띠 모양의 귀고리이다. 겉면 정중앙에는 "壽(수)"자가 새겨져 있고 그 양측에는 서로 마주한 박쥐가 배치되어 있다. 글자와 박쥐는 모두 투각(透刻)하였다. 편평한 고리의 양쪽 가장자리에는 각각 석문(席紋) 한 줄을 두르고 안쪽 두 줄무늬 사이에는 띠 모양의 장식도안을 새겼다. 가는 고리에는 비취(翡翠)로 만든 옥벽(玉璧) 모양의 청옥(靑玉) 하나가 부착되어 있다. 발음이 비슷한 '복(蝠)'과 '복(福)'은 모두 행복과 장수를 뜻한다. '박쥐'는 길상어(吉祥語)로서 원말명초(元末明初)에 생겨나 명청(明淸) 시기 각종 기물의 장식에 쓰였다.

196

'□성(□盛)' 금이환(金耳環)

금(金) | 청(淸) | 지름 2.7cm 무게 14.1g
1976년 서안시 신성구(西安市 新城區) 팔부장(八府莊) 출토

Gold Earrings with Characters '□ Sheng'

Gold | Qing Dynasty(1616AD~1911AD) | D 2.7cm Weight 14.1g
Excavated from Bafuzhuang Village Yanta District, Xi'an in 1976

　비취(翡翠)로 만든 옥벽(玉璧) 모양의 청옥(靑玉) 하나를 부착한 타원형의 귀고리이다. 겉면 앞부분은 여의형(如意形) 화염(火焰)무늬로 되었는데 세 가닥의 어자문(魚子紋)으로 그 안쪽을 가득 채웠다. 투각(透刻)된 화염무늬는 삼각형에 가깝다. 아래쪽 가장자리에는 현문(弦紋) 두 줄이 음각되어 있으며 고리 안쪽에는 해서체(楷書體)로 된 "□盛(□성)" 두 글자가 새겨져 있다.

197

'만(卍)'자편복문금이환(字蝙蝠紋金耳環)

금(金) | 청(淸) | 지름 4.6cm 무게 14g
1966년 서안시 안탑구(西安市 雁塔區) 섬서화학화공학교에서 출토

Gold Eardrops with Bat and 卍 Patterns

Gold | Qing Dynasty(1616AD~1911AD) | D 4.6cm Weight 14g
Excavated from Shaanxi Chemical Engineering institute in Yanta District, Xi'an in 1966

　박쥐 장식이 달린 편평한 고리 모양의 귀고리이다. 박쥐는 머리가 아래를 향하는데 눈이 볼록하고 입이 뾰족하게 나왔으며 작은 귀가 뒤로 말렸다. 양쪽 날개는 활짝 펼쳐진 모습이다. 귀고리 안쪽에는 "瑞蘭(서란)" 두 글자가 새겨져 있다.

198

어장문금이환(魚腸紋金耳環)

금(金) | 청(淸) | 지름 3.09cm 무게 6.1g
1966년 서안시 함녕로(西安市 咸宁路) 출토

Gold Earrings in Fish Intestine Pattern

Gold | Qing Dynasty(1616AD~1911AD) | D 3.09cm Weight 6.1g
Excavated from Xianning road, Xi'an in 1966

　편평하며 동그란 형태의 귀고리이다. 고리 부분에는 어자문(魚子紋)을 바탕에 시문(試紋)하고 꽃가지에 달린 매화 다섯 송이를 새겼다. 앞부분에는 어장문(魚腸紋)을 투각하고 가는 사선으로 그 표면을 장식하였다. 안쪽에는 해서체(楷書體)로 된 "□□足赤(□□족적)" 4글자가 새겨져 있다. 금어(金魚)는 불교의 8개 보물 가운데 하나로 영원한 행복, 매화 다섯 송이는 오복[五福, 수(壽)·부(富)·강녕(康寧)·유호덕(攸好德)·고종명(考終命)]을 뜻한다.

호두형양보석금계지 (虎頭形鑲寶石金戒指)

금(金) | 청(淸) | 지름 2.5cm 무게 16g
1977년 서안시 안탑구 장팔구향(西安市 雁塔區 丈八溝鄕) 동도원(東桃園) 출토

Tiger-head-shaped Gold Ring Inlaid with Precious Stones

Gold | Qing Dynasty(1616AD~1911AD) D 2.5cm Weight 16g
Excavated from East Taoyuan Village in zhangbagou County Yanta District, Xi'an in 1977

　서로 반대 방향으로 놓인, 두 호랑이 머리 모양의 장식이 달린 반지이다. 호랑이 입에서는 가락지의 고리가 뻗어 나왔으며 머리에는 표면이 평평한 송석(松石)이 상감되어 있다. 송석 표면에는 동물이 음각되어 있다.

　일명 '약지(約指)', '수기(手記)'라고도 불리는 반지는, 손가락에 끼는 작은 고리로 신석기시대에 생겨났다. 흔히 금, 은으로 만들며 보석을 박아 넣기도 한다. 초기에는 장식용으로 사용되다 계급사회에 들어서면서 황제와 황후의 합방 여부를 알리는 표식이 되기도 하였다. 그 후 사랑의 증표가 되어 오늘날까지 전해졌다. 수천 년 동안 용도의 제약으로 그다지 형식상의 변화가 없었는데 주로 고리 표면에 장식을 더하거나 조각 장식하거나 보석 등을 상감할 뿐이었다. 양한(兩漢)시대에는 보석을 박아 넣은 반지가 보편적이었다. 진대(晉代, 265~420년) 이후에는 반지에 각종 무늬를 새기고 너비를 늘리는 한편 보석을 박아 넣기도 하였다. 명청(明淸)시대에 와서는 보석의 크기와 등급에 따라 반지의 가치를 규정하였다.

양보석금화식계지 (鑲寶石金花飾戒指)

금(金) | 청(淸) | 지름 2.1cm 무게 18.5g
1968년 서안시 안탑구 곡강향 서곡강지촌(西安市 雁塔區 曲江鄕 西曲江池村) 출토

Gold Floral Ring with Inlaid Precious Stones

Gold | Qing Dynasty(1616AD~1911AD) | D 2.1cm Weight 18.5g
Excavated from West Qujiangchi Village in Qujiang County Yanta District, Xi'an in 1968

　넓고 편평한 고리에 꽃 장식이 달린 금반지이다. 여덟 꽃잎 형상으로 중심의 청옥을 상감한 둥근 틀 1개와 외곽의 백옥을 상감한 동그란 틀 8개로 이루어졌다. 백옥 가운데에 구멍이 나 있으며 두 틀 사이와 테두리에는 금구슬 장식이 있다. 위쪽 양측에는 꽃을 사이에 두고 날개를 펼친 박쥐무늬가 배치되어 있다. 날개 앞부분에는 원형방공전문(圓形方孔錢紋)이 새겨져 있으며 날개와 등에는 잎맥을 표현한 가는 선이 음각되어 있다.

201

유금첩화은탁(鎏金貼花銀鐲)

은(銀) | 청(淸) | 지름 6.7cm 무게 100.3g
1974년 서안시문물관리위원회(西安市文物管理委員會) 수집

Gilt Silver Bracelets with Applique

Silver | Qing Dynasty(1616AD~1911AD) | D 6.7cm Weight 100.3g
Collected by Xi'an Culture Relic Administration Committee in 1974

원형 팔찌 두 점이다. 표면의 문양은 서로 같은데 각각 사발 · 대바구니 · 원보(元寶, 화폐의 일종) · 집호(執壺) 모양의 꽃바구니 장식 4개가 부착되어 있다. 바구니 속에는 촘촘한 가지와 잎에 활짝 핀 꽃이 달린 화초 한 다발이 꽂혀 있다. 표면에는 전체적으로 금을 입혔다. 꽃바구니에 꽂혀 있는 꽃은 부귀영화를 가리켜 청(淸) 옹정(雍正) 연간(1723~1735년)에 많이 사용되었다.

팔찌는 일명 약환(約環)이라고도 불린다. 팔에 착용하는 장신구로 신석기시대 중기에 생겨났다. 초기에는 동물의 뼈 · 이빨 · 돌 · 고령토 · 옥 등 재료로 만들어졌으며 관(管)이나 고리모양 또는 반원 2개를 조합한 형태였다. 상주(商周)시대부터 춘추전국(春秋戰國)시대까지 옥으로 만든 팔찌가 주를 이루었는데 상주시대에는 금속 팔찌도 만들어졌다. 양한(兩漢) 이후에는 금속 재질이 주를 이루었다. 팔찌는 원래 남녀 모두 사용하였으나 점차 여성용 장신구로 변화되었으며 형태는 변화가 거의 없고 표면의 장식이 점점 더 다양해졌다. 금은 재질로 만든 팔찌는 역대 여성들이 즐겨 착용하는 장신구이며 재부(財富)의 상징이기도 하다.

202

유엽형은탁(柳葉形銀鐲)

은(銀) | 청(淸) | 길이 6.07cm 7.48cm 너비 2.58cm 무게 79g
1974년 서안시문물관리위원회(西安市文物管理委員會) 수집

Silver Bracelets in shape of willow Leaf

Silver | Qing Dynasty(1616AD~1911AD) | L 6.07cm 7.48cm W 2.58cm Weight 79g
Collected by Xi'an Culture Relic Administration Committee in 1974

은팔찌 두 점이다. 은백색을 띠는 팔찌는 여러 군데가 녹슬어 있다. 가운데가 넓고 양쪽 끝으로 가면서 점차 좁아진다. 겉면에는 띠가 3개 있는데 양옆이 위로 들리고 가운데가 볼록하며 그 사이가 오목하다. 팔찌를 펼쳐 놓으면 버들잎과 흡사하다. 양쪽에는 은사(銀絲)가 감겨져 있으며 끄트머리에는 동그란 구멍이 있다. 무늬 없는 안쪽은 흰빛이 감돈다. 제작기법이 간단하지만 양식이 독특하다.

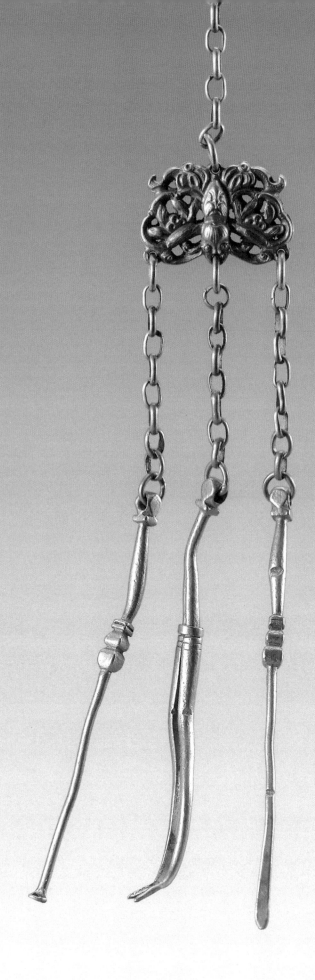

203

금삼수(金三需)

금(金) | 청(淸) | 길이 31.7cm 무게 51.2g
1978년 서안시 장안구(현) 곽두진 신문촌(西安市 長安區(현) 郭杜鎮 新文村) 출토

Three Gold Necessities

Gold | Qing Dynasty(1616AD~1911AD) | L 31.7cm Weight 51.2g
Excavated from Xinwen Village Guodu Town Chang'an District, Xi'an in 1978

일명 금삼사인(金三事兒)이라고도 불리는 금삼수(金三需)는 복식용품이다. 꼭대기에는 사슬 모양의 금고리가 배치되어 있고 그 아래에는 투각(透刻)된 크고 작은 나비 2마리가 연결되어 있다. 모두 날개를 펼친 모습이다. 작은 나비의 양쪽 날개에 달렸던 물건은 떨어지고 없다. 작은 나비의 입에서 뻗어 나온 금사슬은 아래쪽의 큰 나비와 연결되어 있다. 큰 나비의 머리와 양쪽 날개로부터 금사슬이 드리워졌는데 각각 귀이개, 족집게, 따개가 걸려 있다. 3가지 필수품이라 하면 일반적으로 이쑤시개, 귀이개와 같은 물건을 가리킨다. 이러한 것들은 생활용품에만 국한되지 않고 장식품으로도 사용되었다.

204

은불상(銀佛像)

은(銀) | 청(淸) | 길이 6.45cm 너비 4.9cm 무게 9.1g
1963년 서안시 비림구 사파촌(西安市 碑林區 沙坡村) 출토

Silver Buddha Statue

Silver | Qing Dynasty(1616AD~1911AD) | L 6.45cm W 4.9cm Weight 9.1g
Excavated from Shapo Village Beilin District, Xi'an in 1963

불상은 넓적한 얼굴, 큰 귀, 오똑한 코, 작은 입을 가졌고 두 눈은 지그시 감고 있다. 양손을 포개어 다리 위에 놓았는데 왼손 위에 얹은 오른손으로 손바닥이 위를 향하게 하여 선정인(禪定印)을 짓고 양손으로 물건을 받쳐 들었다. 몸에 가사(袈裟)를 두르고 결가부좌(結跏趺座)를 하고 연화좌(蓮花座) 위에 앉아 있는 모습이 매우 장엄하다. 2단의 연화좌 사이에는 가는 연주문(聯珠紋)의 띠가 있다. 불신(佛身) 주위는 각양각색의 꽃으로 꾸미고 테두리는 톱니무늬와 불꽃무늬를 조합한 광배(光背)로 장식되었다. 문양은 새기거나 두드리는 공예기법으로 만들어졌다. 송대(宋代) 이후, 불교가 날로 쇠퇴함에 따라 성리학이 점차 전반적인 사회사상에 영향을 미쳤고 사람들은 전처럼 불교를 숭상하지 않았다. 도시 상업의 번영과 더불어 사람들의 의식은 날로 현실적으로 변했다. 이로써 불상은 세속화되었고 수량 또한 적어졌으며 단지 사람들이 정신적 평안을 얻기 위한 용도로 존재하였다.

'서안성영흥경(西安省永興慶)' 등 은정(銀錠)

은(銀) | 청(淸) |
(1) 길이 3.66cm 너비 2.23cm 높이 1.71cm 무게 224g
(2) 길이 4.81cm 너비 3.42cm 높이 2.2cm 무게 194g
(3) 길이 4.87cm 너비 3.53cm 높이 2.46cm 무게 156g
(4) 길이 4.83cm 너비 3.65cm 높이 2.33cm 무게 224g
1963년 서안시문물관리위원회(西安市文物管理委員會) 수집

Silver Ingots with Charactors of 'Xi'an Sheng Yongxingqing

Silver | Qing Dynasty(1616AD~1911AD) |
(1) L 3.66cm W 2.23cm H 1.71cm Weight 70g
(2) L 4.81cm W 3.42cm H 2.2cm Weight 194g
(3) L 4.87cm W 3.53cm H 2.46cm Weight 156g
(4) L 4.83cm W 3.65cm H 2.33cm Weight 224g
Collected by Xi'an Culture Relic Administer Committee in 1963

은백색을 띠는 은정(銀錠) 4점이다. (1) 정면은 허리가 잘록한 모양이고 오목하다. 측면은 사다리꼴 모양이고 밑굽이 평평하다. 정면 정중앙에는 동그랗게 파인 부분이 있는데 해서체(楷書體)로 "喜喜(희희)"자가 양각되어 있다. (2) 표면이 매끈하다. 정면에서 보면 허리가 잘록한 모양이고 측면에서 보면 위가 넓고 아래가 좁은 사다리꼴 모양이다. 정중앙에는 직사각형의 세로로 파인 부분이 있는데 "晉泰銀號(진태은호)" 4글자가 세로로 음각되어 있다. (3) 정면이 타원형에 가깝고 오목하며 벽은 호형(弧形)이고 밑굽이 둥글다. 정면 중앙 사각형으로 파인 부분에는 "涇陽萬年(경양만년)" 4글자가 양각되어 있다. (4) 표면이 울퉁불퉁하다. 정면은 타원형에 가깝고 외측 면은 호형이며 밑면은 타원형이다. 정면에는 해서체(楷書體)로 3자씩 두 줄로 '서안성영흥경(西安省永興慶)'이란 글자가 세로로 음각되어 있다. 청대(淸代)에는 백은으로 계산하는 세금제도를 실시하였으며, 청대 초기 섬서(陝西) 서안(西安)에서는 공납에만 순은을 사용하고 일상생활에서는 순도가 낮은 은을 사용하였다. 청대 말기, 섬서에서 유통한 순은의 주조기구는 관청주조와 민간주조로 나뉘었다. 관청에서는 지정은(地丁銀), 이금은(厘金銀) 등을 주조하였다. 서안부(西安府) 지역 각 현에서 유통한 순금의 표면에는 '西安省永興慶(서안성영흥경)' 6글자가 새겨진 인장이 찍혀 있는데 '성(省)'은 성 소재지를 말한다. '경양만년'은 경양현(涇陽縣)에서 주조한 것이고 '진태은호(晉泰銀號)'는 청대 말기 산서성(山西省) 해주관(解州官) 진태은호 은행에서 발행한 은정이다. 이러한 것들은 은 순도가 비교적 낮았다.

은정(銀錠)은 원명청(元明淸)시대에 유통된 은의 일종이다. 원대(元代) 초기에는 은정(銀鋌)을 은정(銀錠)이라 개칭하였다. 이때의 은정은 무게가 50냥이고 호형의 머리에 허리가 잘록하며 정면이 약간 오목하며 여러 가닥의 견사(絹絲) 무늬가 둘러져 있는 것을 지칭한다. 원대 시기, 관청에서는 주조한 은정 표면에 백은의 원산지·용도·무게·주조연대·담당관원·장인 이름 등 내용을 새겨 넣음으로써 주조기구와 유통 지역을 밝혔다. 명대(明代) 은정은 두 가지 형태로 나뉜다. 하나는 둥근 머리와 잘록한 허리를 가진 정면과 밑굽의 크기가 같은 것이고 다른 하나는 호형의 머리와 잘록한 허리에 날개가 달려 있는 정면이 밑굽보다 큰 것이다. 은정은 크기의 구분이 있는데 50냥의 큰 은정과 30·20·10·5냥의 작은 은정으로 나뉜다. 큰 은정에는 명문·출처·무게·담당관원·장인 이름 등 많은 내용이 새겨져 있으나 작은 은정에는 단지 주(州), 현(縣)과 장인 이름만 새겨져 있다. 명대 후기에는 명문(銘文)을 새기는 것이 보편적이었으며 무게·순도·장인 이름·은행 이름을 새겨 넣었다. 청대에는 타원형 은정이 주를 이루었는바, 바깥의 측면은 호형이고 밑굽은 타원형이었다. 관청에서는 세금으로 거두어들이는 백은의 순도에 대해 명확히 규정하였다. 청대 초기에는 정부에서 직접 은정을 녹이는 관은장(官銀匠)을 지정하기도 하였다. 건륭(乾隆) 원년에는 각 주와 현에서 관할 구역의 은 장인들한테 이름이 새겨진 인장을 발급하도록 규정하여 납세자들이 필요에 따라 부스러기 은전을 녹여 새로 주조할 수 있도록 하였다. 당시 은정의 표면에는 주, 현 및 장인의 이름이 찍혀 있었다.

(1)

(2)

(3)

(4)

'백하리금(白河厘金)', '삼수지정(三水地丁)' 등 이금은(厘金銀), 지정은(地丁銀)

은(銀) | 청(淸) | 길이 4.8cm 너비 3.66cm 높이 2.5cm 개당 무게 151g
1977년 서안시 비림구 우의서로(西安市 碑林區 友誼西路) 소안탑보관소(小雁塔保管所) 출토

Silver ingots with charactors of `Ba ihe Li jin` and `San shui Di ding`

Silver | Qing Dynasty(1616AD~1911AD) | L 4,8cm W 3,66cm H 2,5cm Weight 151g for each
Excavated from the Custody of Xiaoyanta in West Youyi Road Beilin District, Xi'an in 1977

은회색을 띠는 은정(銀錠) 36점이다. 거꾸로 된 깔때기 모양으로 정면은 타원형이고 측면은 호형(弧形)이며 밑굽은 둥글다. 부분적으로 허리가 잘록한 것도 있다. 대부분 오목하며 주조 시의 흔적도 보인다. 오목한 밑바닥에는 지문(指紋)이 그대로 남아 있다. 정중앙의 정사각형 안에는 2자씩 두 줄로 된 "白河厘金(백하리금)", "三水地丁(삼수지정)"과 같은 명문이 새겨져 있다. 지금의 섬서성(陝西省) 백하현(白河縣) 일대에 위치한 백하(白河)는 하남(河南)·섬서·호북(湖北) 세 성의 접경으로 진(秦, 섬서성 약칭), 예(豫, 하남성 약칭), 악(鄂, 호북성 약칭) 간의 교통 요로이다. 삼수(三水)는 지금의 섬서성 순읍현(旬邑縣)을 말한다. 이 밖에 '壬子韓城任軒(임자한성임헌)', '辛亥年咸陽劉永(신해년함양유영)'과 같이 6글자나 7글자로 된 것도 있다. 이처럼 흔히 주조연대, 주조자의 원적지 및 이름, 은정의 용도 등을 새겨 넣었다.

이금은(厘金銀)은 청왕조(淸王朝) 때 조세로 사용된 화폐의 일종이다. 청 함풍(咸豊) 3년(1853년) 홍수전(洪秀全)을 대표로 한 태평천국(太平天國) 농민봉기를 진압하기 위하여 형부시랑(刑部侍郎) 뇌이성(雷以誠)은 양주(揚州)에서 소득의 1%를 세율로 하여 행상(行商)에게 통과세(通過稅)를 거두어들이고 좌상(坐商)에게 거래세를 거두어들였다. 청선종(淸宣宗) 함풍(咸豊) 8년(1858년) 섬서성에서도 이를 본떠 일상용품에 대해서도 세금을 거두어들였으며 세율을 2~3% 올렸다. 흔히 무게가 5냥인 이금은을 사용하였다. 지정은(地丁銀)도 청왕조 조세의 일종이다. 청왕조에서는 "16살이 된 성년 남자는 병역에 참가하거나 은전을 지불한다"라고 규정하였다. 토지세는 소유한 토지면적 및 등급에 따라 거두었다. 청성조(淸聖祖) 강희(康熙) 51년(1712년)에는 "가족원이 늘어나도 세를 늘리지 않는다"는 영을 반포하였다. 옹정(雍正) 초기 각 성에 영을 내려 정년의 남자에게 부과되는 조세를 지무(地畝)로 합하여 세를 같이 납부하게 하거나 징수하였는데 둘을 합하여 '지정(地丁)'이라고 하였다. 지정은은 무게가 약 4냥 좌우이고 순도가 비교적 높다.

207

‘기산이정(岐山李正)’ 은정(銀錠)

은(銀) | 청(淸) | 길이 4.55cm 너비 3.9cm 높이 2.25cm 밑지름 2.38×2cm 무게 182g
1979년 서안시 장안구 (현) 쌍정향 보현촌(西安市 長安區 (縣) 雙井鄕 普賢村) 수집

Silver Ingot with Charactors of ˙Qi Shan Li Zheng˙

Silver | Qing Dynasty(1616AD~1911AD) | L 4.55cm W 3.9cm H 2.25cm Bottom D 2.38×2cm
Weight 182g
Collected by Puxian Village Yijing County Chang'an District, Xi'an in 1979

청왕조(淸王朝) 때 섬서(陝西)에서 유통했던 이금은(厘金銀)이다. 표면은 전체적으로 은회색을 띤다. 정면은 타원형이고 양 끝이 위로 살짝 들려 있으며 가운데가 약간 오목하다. 정중앙에는 정사각형의 파인 부분이 있는데 해서체(楷書體)로 된 "岐山李正(기산이정)" 4글자가 새겨져 있다. 벽은 호형(弧形)이고 밑굽은 타원형이며 자른 흔적이 있다. 기산(岐山)은 지금의 섬서성 기산현을 말한다. 이정(李正)은 청대(淸代)에 섬서성 기산현에 거주한 은장인(銀匠人)의 이름인 것으로 추정된다.

208

‘합양이무(合陽李茂)’ 은정(銀錠)

은(銀) | 청(淸) | 길이 4.65cm 너비 3.7cm 높이 2.5cm 밑지름 2.36×1.88cm 무게 151g
1979년 서안시 장안구(현) 쌍정향 보현촌(西安市 長安區 (縣) 雙井鄕 普賢村) 수집

Silver Ingot with Charactors of
˙He Yang Li Mao˙

Silver | Qing Dynasty(1616AD~1911AD) | L 4.65cm W 3.7cm H 2.5cm
Bottom D 2.36×1.88cm Weight 151g
Collected by Puxian Village Yijing County Chang'an District, Xi'an in 1979

청왕조(淸王朝) 때 섬서(陝西) 일대에서 유통한 이금은(厘金銀)이다. 정면과 밑굽은 타원형이고 벽은 호형(弧形)이다. 안쪽의 깊게 파인 부분에는 거푸집으로 찍어낸 정사각형의 틀이 있는데 해서체(楷書體)로 된 "合陽李茂(합양이무)" 4글자가 새겨져 있다. 은회색을 띠는 표면에는 주조 시 생긴 흔적이 그대로 남아 있다. 합양(合陽)은 지금의 섬서성(陝西省) 합양현(合陽縣)을 말한다. 이무(李茂)는 청대(淸代)에 섬서성 합양현에 거주한 은장인(銀匠人)의 이름으로 추측된다.

209

은동자(銀童子)

은(銀) | 청(淸) | 높이 4.7cm 무게 6.5g
1977년 서안시문물관리위원회(西安市文物管理委員會) 수집

Silver Boy

Silver | Qing Dynasty(1616AD~1911AD) | H 4.7cm Weight 6.5g
Collected by Xi'an Culture Relic Administration Committee in 1977

속이 빈 은으로 만든 동자(童子) 형상이다. 동자는 온몸이 토실토실한데 머리에는 곰의 귀 모양 모자를 썼다. 온 얼굴에는 웃음꽃이 활짝 피어 있다. 이마에는 자그마한 점이 있고 두 눈은 커다랗게 떴으며 입꼬리가 살짝 올라간 동시에 볼우물 두 개가 옴폭 파였다. 두 손을 가슴 앞에 얹고 배꼽을 드러내었다. 두 다리로는 오른발을 왼발 위에 얹은, 앉은 자세를 취하였다.

동자는 앞뒤 부분을 용접하여 만든 것이다. 정수리와 발아래에 구멍이 있는데 정수리 쪽 작은 구멍에는 파손된 가느다란 은사슬이 연결되어 있다. 이로 볼 때 은동자가 기물(器物)의 장식물로 사용되었음을 알 수 있다.

210

'북평(北平)' 금탁(金鐲)

금(金) | 민국(民國) | 긴지름 6.6cm 짧은지름 5.8cm 무게 37.5g
1988년 서안시 남소항(西安市 南小巷) 출토

'Bei Ping' Gold Bracelet

Gold | Republic of China(1912AD~1949AD) | D 5.8~6.6cm Weight 37.5g
Excavated from Nanxiaoxiang in Xi'an in 1988

황금색을 띠는 원형에 가까운 팔찌로 단면(斷面)이 반원 모양이다. 평면에 가까운 안쪽에는 직사각형의 오목면 4개가 주조되어 있다. 그 위에는 각각 해서체(楷書體)로 "北平(북평)", "中原(중원)", "加煉(가련)", "足赤(족적)" 등 8글자가 새겨져 있다. '북평' 자 오른쪽 위에는 오각성(五角星)이 배치되어 있다. 금팔찌의 양 끝은 공 모양으로 되었으며 서로 맞닿지 않은 특이한 형태이다. '북평'은 지명으로 오늘날의 북경(北京)을 말하는데 명청(明淸)시대에는 경사순천부(京師順天府)라 일컬었다. 1928년, 국민당 정부는 북경을 북평이라 개칭하고 하북성에 귀속시켰다.

211

'패(貝)'자(字) 명문금조(銘文金條)

금(金) | 민국(民國) | 길이 1.94cm 너비 1.16cm 두께 0.4cm 무게 15.6g
1982년 서안시(西安市) 문물상점(文物商店)으로부터 넘겨받음

Gold Bar with 'Bei' Inscription

Gold | Republic of China(1912AD~1949AD) | L 1.94cm W 1.16cm Thickness 0.4cm Weight 15.6g
Transferred by Xi'an Culture Relic Shop in 1982

순금(純金)으로 만든 막대 모양의 금괴다. 정면의 중심과 가까운 부분에는 왕망(王莽) 시기의 산폐(鏟幣) 도안이 있다. 가운데 세로줄 왼쪽에는 "패(貝)" 자의 이체(異體)를 새기고 오른쪽에는 기호를 새겼다. 뒷면에는 "S40644", "成色(성색, 금의 함량) 9800", "市兩(시냥) 500" 등 글자가 가로 세 줄로 새겨져 있다. 1931년 만주사변(滿洲事變) 이후, 일본군은 중국 동북 3성을 점령하고 뒤이어 상해사변(上海事變)을 일으킴과 동시에 장성(長城)의 여러 요새를 공격하였다. 일제의 침입과 더불어 중화(中華)는 멸망의 위기에 처하게 되었으며 항전(抗戰)을 위해 1935년 국민당(國民黨) 정부는 법폐정책(法幣政

策)을 실시하였다. 규정에 의하면 황금은 모두 국가은행을 통하여 법폐로 바꾸어야 하며 황금은 시장매매를 금지하고 정부가 단독으로 매입하도록 하였다. 중일전쟁에 이르러 미국정부는 중경(重慶)에 있던 중국정부에 5억 달러의 차관을 제공하고 황금을 매입하게 하였다. 1945년 국민당 정부는 중경 중앙화폐 주조공장에 명하여 금괴를 주조하여 대출을 갚으려 했는데 1946년 1월 말에 이르러 무게가 2돈~100냥 사이인 금괴를 모두 4,273,376개(총 무게 1,443,987.158냥)를 주조하였다. 이 금괴도 그중 하나인 것으로 추정된다.

The Spring and Autumn & Warring States Period

1 Crouching Hollowed-out Golden Tiger with Backward Head

The crouching tiger is hollowed out with a backward head, a large stiffing mouth, a wide nose, a pair of large hollow eyes, a pair of up-rolling ears and an up-rolling long tail. The tiger, serving as the ornament of a certain utensil, is decorated with pearl grains and curly cloud grains.

2 Gold Tiger Amulet

This is the left part of the tiger amulet. The golden crouching tiger has an up-rising head, large eyes and ears, an opened mouth with bared teeth, bending legs and an up-rolling tail. The patterns are carved with the combination of intaglio and rilievi. The tiger belly is half raised and half cupped. From the corresponding convexity and concave proportion with length, width and depth, the assumption of the opposite structure of the other half could be made. According to the ancient Chinese military operation system, the emperor kept the right half of the commander's token, while the other half was taken by the general. To send an army of over fifty soldiers to the front battle, the general should inform the emperor by reuniting the separated token. Thus, this token belongs to a front-battle general.

This golden tiger amulet is fairly rare. Despite its small shape, the tiger amulet is delicately made with vivid carving and unique sculpting. As a precious material to the research on the commander's-token system in the Warring States Period, it is of great artistic and historical values.

3 Gilt Silver Belt Hook

It is a unicorn with a large mouth, a wide nose, protruding round eyes and long ears. There is a deity animal at its belly, whose open mouth holds the neck of the former animal. The deity animal has sharp tusks and feather-like decorations on both sides. The original inlay contained in the oblong hole on its head is lost. There are two pairs of ox horns, with the small back-rolling ones in cord pattern and the big forward-rolling ones in the shape of knot, with long concaves on their sides, and a piece of green jade wafer in between, fixed by the protruding part at the horn root. At the back of the horns, there are sharp-edged concaves in the middle, with round trace on both sides, which are assumed to be the break-off gold-inlays. An accipiter sits on the above, with a hooked beak, round eyes, whose inlayed jade breaks off. The elongate horns on the eyebrows are connected with the hook with its end. The protruding edges of the concave between the horns face upward. The accipiter has up-holding wings and up-standing legs with two sharp claws on the each paw. The original jade inlayed on the semicircle hollow hole between the paws is now lost. A pair of spiral ox horns is decorated above the accipiter horns, with a round wafer jade in between. The jade is fixed with a nail in its center between the concave sides.  There is a square hole at the end. A hat-shaped column button is at the center of the hook back, with a seal character "heart". With basso-relievo animal faces and accipiter, this hook and the gilt copper hook with shell-inlay are typical gold and silver wares in the Northern prairie of the Warring States Period.

Belt Hook or "Hook" in short, was used in ancient China to fasten the waist belt or hang various accouterments. It is elongate with one end bending as a hook and a round button on its back. The earliest hook was used by Northern nomadic peoples. Till the Spring and Autumn Period, hook had been used in the central plain, primarily on the armours and then for the nobles. In Warring States Period and Qin-Han Period, hook prevailed with various shapes, i.e. waterfowl, lute, long card, animal face, spoon, fox, tiger, deer, dragon, and fish etc. After The Three Kingdoms, belt hook was replaced by DaiJue, an annular buckle, while belt hook hadn't disappeared in people's life until early Qing Dynasty.

This belt hook is gilded in its front. Gilding, as one of the traditional technics of metalworking, was born in Warring States Period. Gilt involves the following process. First, hammer or cut the gold. And then melt it with mercury in the proportion of 1:7 under the temperature of 400℃. After cooling, it turns into mud-alike solid. People often call it as "Gold Mud". Then the gold-paste layer is paved on the surface of utensil. Heat the utensil with smokeless carbon to vaporize the mercury. Thus, the gold remains on the utensil surface. In Spring and Autumn Period and Warring States Period, pure gold ware were fairly common, while the silver ones were quite rare, for the dissociative gold is easy to be found and used, while silver coexists with other minerals as compound, which is difficult to be found and abstracted. Therefore, this unearthed gilt silver belt hook is of great significance for the research of scientific and technological history in Spring and Autumn Period and Warring States Period.

4 Gilt Hook with Shell-inlay

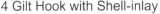

This gilt hook with shell-inlay is in the shape of bending stick, wide and flat, with groove on its back. On the animal head hook, there is a wide mouth, a slightly up-rolling wide nose with little nostrils on each side, eyes with black beads inlayed, long protruding eyebrows and long horns above the eyebrows. The horns extend to the thin and long neck with the end rolling, with concave on its surface. There is a groove between the neck and chest. A rightward open short jacket is on its chest, with an up-side-down heart shell in the center of the chest. The shell is fixed by the foot-like sticks on both sides. Its tail up-rolling in a circle fixes the above shell. There is an oval shell in the center. For the animal head at the end, there is a slightly open wide mouth, a wide nose with two protruding edges on the nose-bridge, eyes with black beads inlayed, protruding wide eyebrows and a pair of long horns above them. The horns are inward-rolling at the end, with an oblong shell in between. The nose is protruding in the front face and concave in the back. There are belt-shaped decorations on both faces to fix the underneath shell inwardly and downwardly, with a protruding decoration fixing the oval shell. On the back of the belt hook, there is deadwood remains in the groove, with hat-shaped column button in the middle. A seemingly reversed seal character "Left" is on the button and a character "Nothing" below the button.

5 Silver-gilded Lute-shaped Belt Hook

The lute-shaped hook is small and thick. The hook is in the shape of animal head. The head, horns on the hook head and animal legs on the hook body are in silver-inlay pattern. The short, thick, and protruding button on the hook back is backward, with silver-inlay whorl pattern. Because of the beautiful natural color and luster, gold and silver decorations enable the copper-ware to be magnificent. Besides, the natural tractility of gold and silver enables the gold-inlay and silver-inlay technics to be realized. This technics was born in the late Spring and Autumn Period, with its development in Warring States Period, meeting its maturity in West Han Dynasty. In the Spring and Autumn period and Warring States period, the process of this technics was as following: firstly, make protruding patterns on the copper-ware mold. After the casting of bronze-ware, inlay purl into the grooves. Then polish the surface till smoothness. Gold-inlay ware was among the first of all the works. In the mid-Warring States Period, there were silver-inlay and gold-and silver-inlay ware. The emerging of those ware was closely related to the social background. At that time, with the decline of Zhou's central power, the expansion of the individual enfeoffment states, the development of the social economy and the enlargement of the noble class, the demand for the luxury ware increased accordingly. In addition, due to the limitation of the mining, the gold-inlay or silver-inlay ware could save much more materials than those of pure gold or silver. That's why gold-inlay or silver-inlay wares were thriving in the Spring and Autumn Period and Warring States Period and gradually dropped off after Western Han Dynasty.

6 Silver-gilded Belt Hook with Geometre Patterns

The belt hook is in the shape of cambered column. The hook head is in the shape of an animal head. There is an oblate button on the hook back. The hook is decorated with geometry silver-inlay patterns, with roe patterns in the spaces.

7 Silver-gilded Lute-shaped Belt Hook with Geometry Patterns

The hook is in the shape of cambered lute, with deformed hook head and an oblate button on its back. There are gold-and-silver-inlay patterns on the front face. The patterns are divided into two parts, with distorted geometry patterns and flower patterns on each part.

8 Silver-gilded Hornless-dragon-shaped Belt Hook with Cicada Patterns

The hook is in the shape of cambered column of a hornless dragon. The backward dragon's head forms a hook. There is a round button at its back. Five wide string patterns equally distribute on the hook surface, with a set of reverse variant cicada pattern on each string. The patterns are chiseled, with silver inlayed. In Warring States Period and Qin-Han Period, Taoism was widely spread. Cicada was mysteriously treated by the alchemist as an auspicious insect, by their rebirth ability after exuviation Thus, human body was metaphorized into carapace, and after the death of the body, human spirit could get rebirth. The silver-inlay cicada patterns on this hook are the reflection of this immortal thinking.

9 Silver-gilded Belt Hook with Animal Moiré

The hook is in the shape of cambered column of a hornless dragon. On one end, the backward dragon head forms a hook. The dragon body bends into a natural arc, with a round button at its back to connect the strap. The hook is decorated with silver-inlay curling moiré, between which there are silver-inlay roe-patterns, symbolizing the dragon scute.

10 Ancient Ying's Gold Coin

It is an inverted trapezoidal oblong, with hollow on top. One side has cut marks while the other three sides are outlined with "Ying Yuan" cut in intaglio. The bottom is not flat because of the cast traces left behind. "Ying Yuan" is the gold coin of Chu kingdom in the Warring States period, and it is the earliest gold coins that have ever been founded. "Ying" is the capital of Chu kingdom in Spring and Autumn period. Ancient Ying's gold coins were popular in Chu kingdom at Spring and Autumn period, so most of its engraved characters are related with the cities in Chu. The Chu's capital Ying produced the most Ying ancient coins. It was often used as a largess instead of money.

In the Spring and Autumn period, Chu kingdom is the famous gold producing area. In "the Chapter On Currencies by Guan Zhong", there are such descriptions: "Chu has plenty of gold, just like Ru and Han.

"Ru"means Ru River which started in Funiu Mountain in the west of Henan province. Han River is full of alluvial gold deposit. "Han" refers to Han river, originated in Ninqiang County of Shaanxi Province, east longitude in southern Shaanxi Hanzhong, Ankang, Running through Hubei, into the Yantze River in Wuhan. In Qing Dynasty, Ru and Han is famous for its Production of gold.

This gold discus made in Chu Kingdom in Warring States Period have various shapes, square with extrados, oblong and round etc.. Most of the coins were unearthed from Hubei, Hunan, Henan, Anhui, Jiangsu and South Shandong, in middle and lower reaches of the Yangtze River and lower reach of the Yellow River, with some other from Guan Zhong Area in Shaanxi. The complete coin weights about half a kilogram. Among the known 60 seal patterns, there is Ying Yuan, Chen Yuan, Ge Yuan, Lu Jin, Shao Zhen and Zhuan Yuan, in the order of the amount. "Yuan" means exchange, and later becomes a unit of weight. Some of the rest words are the place names, while "Lu Jin" and "Shao Zhen" mean refined. When being used, it was often cut into blocks in different sizes, whose value depends on the weight. It was used from an unknown time to early West Han period. In West Han Dynasty, there were many copies used as funeral objects.

Qin & Han Dynasty

11 Silver-inlay Belt Hook with Cicada Patterns

The hook is in the shape of cambered column of a hornless dragon. The backward dragon head forms a hook. There is a round button at its back. The hook is decorated with two sets of opposite silver-inlay cicada patterns, between which there are silver-inlay roe-patterns.

12 Silver-inlay Rammer

The rammer is in the shape of quadrate column. The surface is divided into two parts by the thin protruding strings in wide space, with different silver-inlay phoenix patterns. The overall shape is graceful with the feathers floating as if flying. Gold-inlay or silver-inlay were emerged in late Spring and Autumn Period, and developed in Warring States Period, with more gold-inlay works than silver-inlay ones. This silver-inlay rammer is beautifully patterned, which is the representative of all then silver-inlay works.

Rammer is the accessory of long-rod weapons, at the end of a handle. When placing the weapons, ancient soldiers usually stick them on the shelf, with the end-side-down. Thus metal rammer could protect the wood or bamboo rod.

13 Silver-inlay Annular Vehicle Decoration

This pair of vehicle decoration is in the shape of oblate annularity. The surface is decorated with silver-inlay geometry curling moire. Between the pair of string patterns, there are geometry flowing moire. The patterns in both sides of the vehicle decoration are same, chiseled with silver-inlay.

14 Silver-inlay Turtledove-shaped Cap of Dagger Handle

The cap of dagger handle is in the shape of a turtledove. The turtledove is in the position of laying, looking backward with long tail holding together. The silver-inlay on the surface serves as the feather, which vivifies the sculpting. The pedestal is a cuboid tube, which could fix the handle. There are eleven characters-"finished in the year of 23, 38 " intaglioed on the inner side of the pedestal. On the top of the dagger handle, the cap could protect the wood or bamboo handle of the weapon, together with the metal protection on the other end of the handle.

15 Gold-and-silver-inlay Bucked-shaped Vehicle Decoration

It is in the shape of bucked, with gibbosity edge at one end. Each pair is arranged in the opposite position, with four distort cicada patterns. The cicada is big in head and small in body, in the shape of triangle. The patterns are chiseled, with gold-and-silver-inlay cicada eyes and wings. The outline is smooth with strength.

16 Hollow Golden Bead

The fine-gold-ball is joined by 12 golden rings, with each ring as a surface of the ball. Five sets of hollow golden beads are welded in the spaces, with four for each set. This hollow bead is similar with the ones unearthed from Emperor Qi Tomb of Western Han, Zibo, Shandong, and No.4013 Eastern Han Tomb, Longshenggang, Xianlielu, Guangzhou, which is manufactured by the technics of welding golden bead. This technics was originally emerged in Western Asia and Southern Europe, and came to China in Western Han Dynasty. The process is cutting gold or silver sheet into filaments, and agglomerating the filaments into granule by heating. After cooling, it could be ranged and welded. This hollow bead is unique in shape, which is a typical work from Western Asia and Southern Europe in Han Dynasty. In Qin-Han Period, Western Roman Empire reined a territory around the Mediterranean, including Western Asia, Southern Europe and Northern Africa. (Established by Augustus in 27BC, the Roman Empire was divided into Western Roman Empire and Eastern Roman Empire in 395. The former collapsed in 476, and the latter in 1453.) In the Pre-Qin Period, there was no record of the communication between China and those areas. In period of Emperor Hanwu, the Silk Road was built by Zhang Qian to connect China and the West, when the trade on the road became thriving. Chinese silks and china, which became the luxury goods for the Roman ruling class, were transported to Roman Empire through West Region and Central Asia. Meanwhile, their gold and silver wares and other goods were transported to China as well. This hollow bead is an important evidence of the trade between China and Roman Empire.

17 Gold-and-silver-inlay Pot with Goulian Moiré

This is a pot with slightly square body. It has a square and short spout, a deep and plump body and a square pedestal. There is no obvious dividing line between shoulder and abdomen. A pair of ring-handle is on the upper abdomen. At the bottom of its abdomen, there are inscription with 19 Chinese characters"March 20···Jin", "Private Official···Six..." and "eighteen and half buckets". Its cubage is 35.4 liter. The overall gold-and-silver-inlay Goulian moiré is different in different parts. There is a circle of Goulian moire decorated on the edge. Opposite-angle Goulian moiré is decorated on each side of the four arrises. On the neck and the abdomen, there are larger patterns of inclined grid Goulian moiré in symmetry. There are symmetric geometry patterns around the pedestal. The patterns of this pot are smartly designed in symmetric layout, which is a practical art. Together with this delicate pot, there were copper lamps, copper censers and cooper flat pan unearthed from South Shang Lin Parkland site in Han's Chang'an, which indicates that this pot is an imperial ware in West Han Dynasty.

18 Gilt Phoenix Drinking Vessel

Zhong, a kind of drinking vessel, consists of a lid and a body. This gilt vessel's lid and body could be closely connected. The lid is protruding with a phoenix-shaped button in the middle. The phoenix stands with up-rising head and tail, a bead in the mouth and wings gathering backward. The outline is vividly smooth. The vessel has a wide mouth, a narrow neck and a plump abdomen. There is a pair of symmetrical Chinese doorknocker with ring-handle on the upper abdomen. Its square pedestal, edge, shoulder and abdomen are slightly protruding with wide string patterns. Ancient Chinese believed that gold and silver tableware could prolong their life or even enable them to be immortal. The wish of being immortal could date back to the repeated records of"long live"in The Book of Songs in Zhou Dynasty. In Qin Dynasty, this wish was even stronger that it was associated with gold by those mysterious Taoists. In the period of Hanwu Emperor, Li Shaojun, the alchemist, preached that"Cinnabar could be alchemized into gold. By using the golden tableware, people would live long and meet the immortal in the fairy land Penglai, so as to be immortal themselves."The thriving of gold and silver wares in Tang Dynasty was influenced by this health-preserving view. This gilt copper drinking vessel belongs to the gold and silver tableware.

This gilt copper drinking vessel was unearthed from the wing-room of a grand long-path-single-roomed Han Tomb. There was another similar vessel with same fabrication and size, 17 bronze-ware including copper cooking vessel and copper pot, five cocoon-shaped pottery pot and 101 pieces of jade unearthed from this tomb. According to the tomb fabrication and those funeral-wares, this is a vassal's tomb in Wenjing Period of Western Han Dynasty, and the gilt copper drinking vessel is an imperial ware.

19 Gilt Goat-shaped Lamp

This is a gilt lighting in the shape of a lying goat. The goat has an up-rising head, forward-looking eyes, bending horns, back-kneeing front legs, forward-bending back legs, a plump body and a short tail. The hollow abdomen is for the storage of lamp oil. Its back could be parted from its body, which was done by the button behind the head and on the buttocks. The back could be up-lifted and put on the heat, forming a concave oval tray. In the tray, there is a small flowing path to hold the wick and lead the lamp oil back to the abdomen after black-out. By resetting the back, the lamp regains its shape as a vividly sedate goat. Because of the similar sound of "goat" and "lucky" in Chinese, goat is a symbol of luck to Han people, e.g. the inscription on bronze-ware. This gilt goat-shaped lamp is artistically practical. A similar lamp was unearthed from Zhongshan King Liusheng's Tomb, Mancheng, Hebei, which indicates that this type of copper lamp is for the vassals only.

20 Gold Discuses

The gold discuses are in the shape of round cakes, with a slightly protruding upper-surface and a concave bottom. There are marks of"V"and"千"(Chinese character, meaning thousand), and inscriptions of"lucky"and"Yang Cheng"in regular script. These discuses are also called persimmon-shaped discuses, or golden cake-shaped discuses, some of which are carved with"Lingzhi", the similar sound for"Kylin toe". This indicates that this type of gold disuses can be categorized into Kylin-toe-shaped coin. U-shaped discuses and Kylin-toe-shaped discuses are the first class coin in largess and large-scale trade. The average weight of these discuses is 247g, with the maximum being 254.4g and the minimum being 227.6g. Most of the discuses are countermarked, and some are sculpted with characters, including nouns, numerals, locations, surnames and compound words, and signs, including V, U and S. It is die-casted. These discuses were originally buried into three piles in a number of 219. The disordered burying indicates that these discuses were buried in a hurry.

In the early West Han Dynasty, because of the Peasant Revolt in the late Qin Dynasty, the country was in poverty. After Wen-Jing Regime, a series of currency reforms gradually turned the country into prosperity. At that time, quare-holed copper circular discus was the main currency. Besides, white deerskin coins and gold discus were served in tribute, largess and large-scale trade. In the late West Han Dynasty, Wang Mang, Han Yuan Emperor's nephew, wrested the political power and established Xi Dynasty. The power was soon retaken by the imperial clansman of West Han Dynasty because of Wang's improper policies. Thus, these gold discus could be founded after Wen-Jing Regime in West Han Dynasty (179BC- 141BC), and be buried before Wang Mang's Xin Dynasty (9AD- 23AD).

21 Gilt Silver Phoenix Weight

These four gilt silver weights are in same fabrication and size. The lying phoenix is licking its back feather with a backward head. Its wings are slightly up-flapping. The tail feathers unfold on the ground. It has forward bending claws, a Ruyi-shaped crest, a short sharp beak, slight open eyes. There is a silver chaplet around its neck, besides the wings and tail are alternate with gold and silver, other parts are gilded.

Weight is multi-functioned. In Han Dynasty, sleeve weight was a u-shaped utensil putting inside the cuff of the dead as funerary object. Canopy weight was put on the four corners of the canopy in the tomb. Before Tang Dynasty, it was a convention for people to sit on the mats. Thus, weights were needed to keep the mat neat. Compared with the simple weights used by the common people, the ones used by the upper class were extremely luxurious, in copper, gilt copper, or gold-and-silver-inlay copper. These four gilt silver phoenix weights are the reflection of the luxurious life of the upper class. After heyday of Tang Dynasty, tables and chairs, the high-legged furniture gradually replaced weights in people's daily life.

22 Gilt Silver-inlay Crouching-tiger-shaped Weight

The four tiger-shaped weights are same in fabrication and size. The crouching tiger has a backward head, whose mandible is on the hip, a large mouth and a wide nose, slightly opened eyes and backward ears. With its claws holding together as an arc, strong long tail inward bending beside the belly, the tiger is in drowsiness. A thin intaglio outline extends from nose to the head till the back, then reaching the hip. Its mouth, nose, eyebrows, beards, elbow hairs and the outline of its dapples are carved in intaglio. These four tiger-shaped gilt silver-inlay weights are naturally and magnificently alternated with gold and silver. (The process of the silver-inlay technics is as following, carve the shallow groove of the pattern on the tiger surface, press the silver in the groove, and then polish.) Lead could be filled in from the hole at the center of the bottom to add its weight. The shape of tiger symbolizes exorcisement and evil avoiding.

23 Weights of Fighting Tiger and Bear

These two gilt weights are same in shape and size. They are solid with flat bottom in the shape of fighting tiger and bear. The fierce tiger has wide opened eyes and erect ears, pining the bear with its front claws, with its left back leg standing, right leg stepping the bear's ear and biting the bear's belly. The bear was painfully wailing under the tiger, with a front claw tightly holding the tiger's right ear, the other claw holding its body and right back claw kicking the tiger's shoulder, desperately struggling. Tiger's ferocity forms strong contrast against the bear's clumsiness. Tiger's bread, eyebrows and bear's hair are carved in short lines, vividly setting off the fierce tiger and the frighten bear and the cliff-hanging scene.

24 Gilt Chinese Door-knocker with Ring-handle

The gilt Chinese door-knocker is in the shape of an animal face. On the face, there is a triangle nose, slightly protruding eyes, up-rising long eyebrows and one claw at each side. On the hook under its nose, there is a copper ring-handle. The hair is curled in vortex, ferociously.

According to Chinese myth, Fushou is one of dragon's nine sons. Due to its quietness and responsibility, it is often placed on the door and other utensils as the guardian or the handle. From Warring States Period till now, Fushou is always a good choice for door-knocker, serving the need of both knocking, revealing identity and exorcising. These two gilt door-knockers are delicately made. Unearthed from Chang'an, the capital of West Han, this magnificent utensil is an imperial one.

25 Kylin-toe-shaped Coin and U-shaped Coin

Both U-shaped coin and Kylin toe coin are currency in Han Dynasty. The U-shaped coin is in the shape of a hollow horse hoof, with a concave oval bottom. Among its fastigiated vertical surfaces, the front is the highest, with the side ones gradually reducing and the back only half height of the front. There is a hole at the coin back. The kylin-toe-shaped coin has a round front surface, a hollow back, and fastigiated vertical surfaces. The round animal-hoof-shaped coin has a small top surface and a big bottom. There were gold discus before Han Dynasty. In 95BC, the western holy horse and southern Kylin in Emperor Hanwu's dream were considered to be auspicious signs. In fact, the holy horse, whose sweat is bloody-like, is originated in Da Yuan of the West Region, (Xinjiang, China and central Asia). Kylin was an imaginary animal created by then popular Taoism. Then Emperor Wu remolded coins into U-shape and Kylin-toe-shape, as the largess to the vassals. In West Han Dynasty, copper coins were the main currency, and gold coins served as largess.

Gold and silver were the first precious metals that come to people's life. In Yin-Shang Period, Chinese gold and silver process technics were mature. In Spring and Autumn Period, gold discus began to be in currency. Till Warring States Period, gold as currency was in a considerable amount in the Central Plain states, the Southern state, Chu and between merchants and nobles. After the unification of China in Qin Dynasty, gold discus were only for the upper class, which was the same in Han Dynasty. In Xin Period, more than 700,000-Jin of gold was stored in national treasury. After Wei-Jin Period, gold was still the measure of value and means of storage, while its function of means of circulation was replaced by silver. In Tang Dynasty, gold and silver continued to serve their functions. However, under a silver standard monetary system, gold was more of a means of storage. In the mid-Ming Dynasty, with the development of commodity economy, silver was major in currency.

26 Golden Seal with Character Wang Jing

On the pedestal of this golden seal, there is a tortoise. On its up-rising head, there is a protruding nose, an open mouth and a pair of open eyes. On its protruding back shell, there are hexagon patterns, with linked-pearl patterns in and around the hexagons. Its feet are decorated with dot patterns. This seal is delicately made; with realistically exaggerate sculpting, making form show the tortoise's spirit. At the bottom of the seal, Wang Jing, these two Chinese characters are intaglioed in an exquisite and vigorous manner.

Seal is a kind of conventional voucher used by ancient feudal officials, individuals and religious events. The seal materials are various, including gold, silver, copper, lead, iron, jade, amber, stone, wood, bone, horn, tooth, pottery and colored glaze. Gold is among the earliest seal materials. According to Han's official seal system, jade seal with dragon button, was exclusive to emperor and empress. For the nobles, as vassals, princes, ancient prime minister, military general and allegiance-pledging minority leaders, their seals were made of gold, with tortoise or camel button. The low rank officers should use silver-tortoise-button seal. The even lower rank officers with should use copper seal with common button. Vassal and lower officers' seals were called Yin, and generals' seals were called Zhang (badge). This seal system was used from Qin-Han Period to Sui-Tang Period. After Song Dynasty, besides the jade seal for the emperor, other officers' seal were all made of copper, which reflected the then administrative system and hierarchical system.

Besides the official seal, there are private seals, which are various in material and type and equal in rank. For thousand years, from official to private seals, among the various materials, copper is the major choice. Different sizes, button types, seal shapes and seal scripts enable seals to be dynamic and charming.

According to the seal system since Han Dynasty and chirography, this golden seal belongs to a vassal named Jing in Xin Period. As the official or private identity mark, seal is also the embodiment of power and class. This golden seal indicates the superior social status of its owner. It is a precious treasure among relics in Xin Period.

27 Golden Kitchen Range

This is a golden kitchen range model. The originally partial enchased turquoises have now peeled. The oval-shaped model consists of an oven door, an oven chamber, a flat top, kettle and chimney. The kettle is placed on the flat top, with kettleful millets. Around the flat top, there are wirying swirl band patterns and arc patterns. On the right corner of the flat top, there is a spun gold entwined chimney. There were originally two turquoises enchased on both sides of the kettle, which had peeled with only traces left. On the arc-shaped front face, there is a turquoise, below which there is a square oven door, which is the entrance of firewood. S-shaped patterns with spun gold and beads and arc-shaped patterns are decorated around the oven door as well as the other three faces of the oven. Constant flowing cloud patterns are popular in Han Dynasty. There is an oval ash container under the oven. Seal characters "Ri Li (lucky everyday)" are carved at the oven bottom. Millets are made by the technics of welding golden beads.

Kitchen range is the major tool used in people's daily life for cooking. According to an ancient Chinese book, kitchen range is the food-creator. The earliest kitchen range was found in Yang Shao culture, which is in Neolithic period. As funerary objects, kitchen ranges were mainly found in Qin-Han period to

the Northern dynasties, especially in Han dynasties, with pottery and copper kitchen range and seldom golden one. In Western Han Dynasty, most of the kitchen ranges were in plain surface with one fire eye. During mid-Eastern Han Dynasty, there were three to four fire eyes in each funeral kitchen range, with carved cookers and food on the surface. As for its shape, round kitchen range was popular before the mid-Eastern Han Dynasty, while the square one was typical in late Easter Han Dynasty. Piety was the ruling moral of Han Dynasty, luxurious burial was popular under the idea of "treating the dead equally with the alive". In Han tombs, pottery kitchen range models were common, while the golden one was rare, which indicated the noble status of its owner. Taoism was popular in Warring States and Qin-Han period, which believed that by eating golden elixir, people could be immortal. According to people's knowledge at that time, gold is the most stable metal which is acid/alkali-resistant and corrosion resistant. Thus, after being eaten, its qualities could be transferred to people, who then could receive eternal life. In History of Nan Dynasty Biography of Tao Hongjing, there is a paragraph recording the event of Tao making elixir and paying in tribute to the emperor. This kitchen range is the image of elixir-making range and the millet symbolizes the golden elixir. This small utensil is vividly made with delicate craftsmanship, magnificent decoration, complicated technics and inscription. It is of great scientific research and artistic value.

28 Gilt Eagle-shaped Goblet

These two gilt eagle-shaped goblets are same in fabrication, size and weight. On its upright head, its eyes and coronal are enchased with colored glazes and turquoises, and its beak is hook-shaped. There are also hooks at its back neck, as if the erect neck feather of an angry eagle; on its chest, enchased with vortex turquoises, as if a hunting falcon; and at other four spots enchased with turquoises, as if eagle heads. There is a wide string pattern near the handle-installing hole. At the bottom, there is a flat hole with other fixing holes beside it. These two eagle-shaped goblets in a whole are like a group of eagles, and also geometric structure with connect hooks. They are the combination of abstract and symbol, revealing a sense of dread.

The goblet is a handle-protecting accessory of the weapon. Refinement, mold, melt casting, enchasing and gilt are applied in this pair of utensils. This pair of utensils is finely made, smartly designed, precisely constructed, with superb shape, which might be the accessory of guard-wears for the imperial family or upper class officials.

Wei-Jin and North-South Dynasty

29 Gilt Copper Sitting Buddha

The gilt Buddha is sitting with a plump face, a wide forehead, smiling eyes and a high bowl-shaped bun on the head. He wears a round-necked cassock covering both shoulders; with the neckwear extending from right should till the chest to the back of his left shoulder. His hands fold together with the centre of the palm being inby, left hand inside and right hand outside, making the mudra of meditation. On a front-squared-back-rounded pedestal decorated with geometric and diamond patterns, the Buddha sits in meditation. The two holes on the back of his head are for the use of fixing the back lights. A line of Kharosthi is on the back of the pedestal, saying "presented by Zhi Meng, this statue gives regards to Fu Si Tuo Jia Hui Yue, descendant of Mo lie Jia." Fu Si Tuo Jia Hui Yue was the descendant of the distinguished family Mo lie Jia in Great Y ü eh-chin.

The mudra of meditation is one of the gestures of Buddha. According to Buddhism, different gestures of the Buddha are called mudra, which are also different in meaning. This statue's gesture is to put both hands in front of the abdomen, with the palm being upwards. Cover the left hand with the right hand, with the tip of thumb being connect. This gesture means meditation, calming the mind. Sitting in meditation is one of the most common sitting postures, which is considered to be the steadiest one. This common posture could prevent fatigue while keep an upright mind. As a vital part of Buddhist culture, Buddha statue came to China along with the spread of Buddhism, which is the object for its believer to sacrifice and pray. Bronze statue was originated in India, which was sacrificed in the palace or the temple. In China, the earliest Buddha statue was found in 67AD, Yong Ping 10th year of Han Ming Emperor Liu Zhuang. Emperor Ming once asked craftsmen to carve Buddha statues and place them in Qing Liang Tai and Guang Wu Emperor Liu Xiu's Xian Jie Mausoleum. At first, bronze Buddha statues were called golden statues, and later, golden copper statues. It was popular in South-North Dynasty to Tang Dynasty. Most of the statues were gilded, which were also known as gilt folds Buddha.

30 Gilt Statues of One Buddha and Two Bodhisattvas

The Buddha wears high bun, with a plump face, a wide forehead, a square cheek, a pair of downward looking eyes and an uprising mouth, smiling. He wears a double-necked drooping cassock covering both shoulders with a kasaya inside, and a long dress. His gesture is the mudra of supreme generosity, with hands naturally downward extending, figures downward pointing and palms being outward, which

means the Buddha could fulfill his believers' wishes. Thus gesture is often combined with the Abhaya Mudra. This Buddha stands bare-footedly on a lotus pedestal, whose bottom open with a platform. There are assistant Bodhisattvas standing on each side with tendril cornet on the head, silk on the shoulder and long dress. They put the palms together standing on the lotus pedestal bare-footedly. The out circle of the boat-shaped back board is carved with blaze patterns, in which sits an alternative Buddha, with round back light behind him. "The Buddha's disciple—Wang De is offering a figure of the god is carved at the back. The Buddha is gilded.

31 Gilt Standing Buddha

The upright Buddha is gilded, with a spiral-patterned high bun on the head. On the plumply comely face, there is a wide forehead, earlobes extending to the shoulders, uplifting eyebrows, downward looking eyes and uprising mouth. The jovially sedate expression reveals his kindness. He wears a round-necked cassock covering his shoulders and a long dress. His right arm bends upward from the elbow with the palm being outward and five figures holding together and unbending upwardly. This Abhaya Mudra's gesture shows Buddha's benevolence to his believers, comforting their fear, which is the origin of this gesture's name. His left arm slightly lifts upward from the elbow with palm being outward, thumb bending toward the palm center and other four fingers downward pointing, which is the mudra of supreme generosity. He stands bare-footedly.

This statue has wide shoulders and a strong body. The costuming of the cassock is light and clings to the body, revealing his legs. The dense veins are in round and protruding rope-shaped patterns. This is the basic feature of Gandhara statues-strong stereoscopic impression of the realistic pleat, which is also the pattern of the cloth.

32 Gilt Standing Buddha Statue

This Buddha has a plump face with short beard. He wears a high coronet and an open-necked and wide-sleeved gown, with a round-necked long dress inside and a belt on the waist. Standing on the lotus pedestal, his hands are in front of the chest holding a cimelia. The branches of lotus join with the pedestal, as if the blooming lotus holding the upright Buddha. There is a peach-leaf-shaped back board behind his shoulders, whose patterns are divided into two layers. The outer layer is decorated with flame patterns and oval lotus patterns on the inner layer. The Buddha is shaped with a mold, the detailed patterns being chiseled. This Buddha is the upper class god of Taoism. Except the statue itself, the back board, the lotus and the branches are all Buddhist objects, which are derived from the imitation of Buddhist technique.

In Jin and South-North period, Buddhism, introduced from Tian Zhu in West Region (now known as India), began to popular in China. Meanwhile, domestic religion Taoism was increasingly influential. To compete with each other, they debated furiously on Chinese and NonChinese, feudal ethics, national power and economy. Buddhism was introduced with rigorous system info, while it is the weak point for Taoism. Thus, the latter often stayed in the disadvantageous position in their conflicts. However, they also introjected with each other on philosophic theory, ceremony, method and even theogony. In North Dynasty, their inosculations were only simple imitation. After early Tang period, there were real inosculations in terms of sculpture, architecture and philosophic theory.

33 Gilt Sykyamuni Statues Built in the 5th Year of Tian He

The Sykyamuni is standing and has a high bun, spiral hair, wears a round neck through shoulder robe and a long dress. he looks plump with slight comeliness, with bending eyebrows extends to straight nose, eyes half-opened, nose and mouth slightly upward tweaking. His extraordinarily pleasant and peaceful expression looks very kind-hearted. His left arm rises like a right angle, with palm outward and Finger peg-leg to make a gesture of wishes. He stands barefoot on the up-side-down lotus throne. A beast-faced man squats in front with arms holding a disc with aromatherapy in it. On each side of the beast-faced man, a long mane Custodian Lion shows its teeth like a roar, with Hind leg squatting, one leg hanging before one leg lands and tail up erecting. On the root, there is a "xuan" shaped four-foot square bed, with boat-shaped hollowed-out backlight, burning flame decorative patterns around and bead patterns combined with blossom patterns. The four-foot square bed has eight rows vow texts on its back: "in the fifth year of Tian He, Biqiuni Ma Faxian built a figure of Sakyamuni for parents and Buddhism members to pray. Gilt Quintana. Biqiuni is the name of a male lay Buddhist, and Ma Faxian is a name.

Sakyamuni is also called as Gautama Bouddha. He is the son of Suddhodana , who is the king of Kapilavastu in the late sixth century BC in ancient Indian. In his manhood, he left his home, started za-zen and finally became a Buddha. People address him Sakyamuni respectfully (meaning the saint of Sakya). After his death, he is regarded as the supreme god of Buddhism. Sakyamuni has seating, lying and standing statuary. The standing statuary is that Sakyamuni stands on the lotus throne, and wears a Sengzhizhi and a gown, with a through coat outer wear. His right hand gesture means braveness, and right hand gesture means wishes. All these represent the Sakyamuni's marching propagandizing and liberation of all beings. Tian He is the period of King Yuwen Yong of North Chou Dynasty. The fifth year of Tian He is 570 A.D. The statue is exquisite, quintana gilt, clinquant, and also well-preserved, so it is a precious works of art.

34 Golden Tablet Decorated with Goat Head

These four golden tablets are same in fabrication, size and weight, used as decoration. The tablet is peach-shaped, with intaglio string patterns around the edge. There are two goat heads decorated in the tablet, whose chins keeping close to each other and facing the same direction. The goats have straight noses, tightly closed mouths, round eyes, backward ears and huge horns, which extend from the ear, circling the ears and bending forward. It is strongly characterized with northern prairie culture. The patterns are made by mould pressing, with strong stereoscopic impression. There are two holes on each margin of the tablet, for the use of fixing. Thus, these four tablets could be the decoration of the clothes or some utensils. Jin, South and North dynasties (265AD-589AD), were the turmoil period when the five northern minorities caused in Central China. Northern China north of Qin Mountain and Huai River, including Guanzhong area in Shaanxi, was reined by minorities as Hun, Xianbei, Jie, Di and Qiang. In this period, a large number of minorities came to the Central Plain. Half of the millions of populations in Shaanxi were the minorities. The 300-year-rein of the minorities left in Guanzhong area many sites and relics marked with ethnic features. These four golden tablets with goat head are part of the heritage.

35 Golden Coin with the Bust of East Roman Empire's Theodosius II

These two gold discus are Solidus, the currency used after East Roman Empire's Constantinus Magnus' currency reformation. (East Roman Empire is also known as the Byzantine Empire 395AD-1453AD.)There are image and inscription on both sides of the coin. On the obverse side, there is the bust of the East Roman Empire's Theodosius II with his head turning leftward. He wears helmet with beads hanging down the cheek from both side of the coronet. The emperor wears a piece of cross-necked loricae and a battle gown, with the outline of the loricae and the battle gown decorated by bead patterns. He holds a gavelock in his right hand, lifting his right shoulder and the gavelock point extending to the left temples. Around the bust, there are Latin inscription, sayingDNTH∧TTA and SIVSPPAVI, which is short forD(ominus)N(oster)TH∧TTASVPSPP(ius)F(elix)AV, meaning Our lord, Theodosius, devout and happy emperor. The other side of the coin is carved with the goddess of victory, with a pair of wings on her back. She holds a long cross in her right hand, beside which is a eight-arista-star. Her left hand is placed under her belly. Latin letters VCTORIA andaAVGGG∧ extend around the goddess. Under the feet, there is CONOB, i.e.CON(Stantinople)OB(Signata), which means casfed in Constantinople. (Constantinople is the capital of East Roman Empire, also known as Byzantine. It is now known as Istanbul, the current capital of Turkey.)The layout of emperor and goddess being on the same coin simultaneously indicates the equality of emperor and God in ancient Rome.

The trade between China and the West can date back to the ancient time. The Silk Road increases the bilateral trade. In the period of Three Kingdoms, Jin, Southern and Northern Dynasties, there were constant wars in Northern China. Although the social economy was destroyed, the bilateral economic trade continued. Tang Dynasty reaches the peak of ancient China, with flourishing state power and developed economy. A large amount of Chinese goods were transferred from Central Asia, West Asia and North Africa reigned by Arab Empire to East Roman Empire east to Mediterranean on the Silk Road. This golden coin witnesses that period of history. At present, this kind of coin is often found in the mouth of the dead, e.g. the coins in Tang Heruo Tomb, Xi'an Xianyang Airport in 1988, and the coins in North Zhou(557AD-581AD) Kangye Tomb, Jingshang, Weiyang, Xi'an in 2003. These coins were put in the mouth of the dead as the fenural objects. It was the convention in Northern China to put an object in the mouth of the dead.Before the Spring and Autumn period, cooked food was most common in the mouth of the dead. In the Qin-Han Dynasty, with the spread of early Taoism, the desire of being immortal was expanded in people's mind. Gold is considered to be erosion-resistant and jade is believed to be of spirituality. Thus by wearing and eating gold or jade, such as mouth jade, jade burial suit and gold discus, people could gain their spirituality.

36 Golden Coin with the Bust of East Roman Empire's Leo I

This round golden coin is Solidus, the currency used in East Roman Empire's Leo I period (457AD-474AD). On the obverse side, there is the bust of the emperor with his head turning leftward. He wears a feather-decorated helmet with a pair of tassels behind the head and beads hanging down the cheek from both side of the coronet. The emperor wears a loricae and a battle gown, with the loricae wearing chest exposed from the battle gown. He holds a shield in his left hand, covering his left shoulder. Around the bust, there are Latin inscription starting from his right hand, spreading clockwise and parting at the coronet feather. The two-set-fifteen-letter-inscription is "NIVSTINVSPP UG". The other side of the coin is carved with the goddess of victory, who stands obversely, with her body slightly turning leftward. She wears high coronet, long dress, with a pair of wings on her back. She holds a long cross in her left hand, below which is a six-arista-star. (Cross is the symbol of Christianity. Orthodox Church, a branch of Christianity was then state religion of East Roman Empire.) Her right hand holds a bamboo-joint-shaped crosier. Latin letters"VICTORIA" and"AAUGGG?" extend around the goddess. "VICTORIA"means goddess of victory. "AUG" is short for Augustus, meaning sacrosanctity, which is the honorific title given to the empire-creator Octavian by the senate in 27BC. The following emperors all inherited this honorific title. The constant three Gs indicate the number with the last one the 4th Greek character on the alphabet, meaning the 4th mint out of the ten mints in Constantinople. The sentence could be translated as "The saint's goddess of victory, the 4th mint." Under the feet, there is"CONOB", i.e."CON (Stantinople) OB (Signata) ", which means casted in Constantinople. The corresponding period in China was Wencheng Emperor to Xiaowen Emperor Period in Northern Wei Dynasty.

Solidus is East Roman Empire's currency. In 1st cen. BC, Roman Empire used Aureus, a kind of coin equals 1/40 of gold pound (7.7-8.4 grams). Till 4th cen. AD, Constantinus I Magnus reformed the currency to lighter gold discus, called Solidus, or Nomisma, which weighs 1/72 pound (about 4.4-4.54 grams). This is the beginning of the independent development of Roman Empire's currency system. This golden coin had been used till the end of East Roman Empire in 1453 with only weight alteration in different periods.

Sui & Tang Dynasty

37 Gilt Standing Hollowed-out Avalokitesvara Statue

This Bodhisattva stands bare-footedly. He wears an anadem with the belt extending along the arm to the wrists, a chaplet with bells and a piece of cloth over the shoulders and extending to the pedestal. He bares his upper body, with only a long thin dress from the navel. His right arm hangs with a kalasa in the hand. His left arm bends from the elbow with a whisk in the hand. He stands bare-footedly on the High Sumeru, under which is a four-legged square couch. There is a leaf-shaped back board above his shoulders, with an alternative Buddha sitting on a lotus petal on the top.

This infinitely merciful Avalokitesara has various terms. He has 33 different avatars and can save people from 12 disasters. He protests the principle of save people from disasters in spite of their status. Thus he is regarded as the infinitely merciful Bodhisattva. It is said that he sermonizes the way in Putuo Mountain. He was born in Feb.19th in lunisolar calendar. His Ereignen Day was on Jun. 19th in lunisolar calendar and Nirvana in Feb. 19th. According to the early sutra, Avalokitesara is the brother of Mah ā sth ā mapr ā pta. The former is willing to cultivate him so as to give relief and help to all mortal beings. These brothers assist Amitabha, and together are called "three holies in the West". According to Buddhists, Avalokitesara has achieved the realm of Buddha in terms of religion, merits and virtues. Thus his believers hold he will relief them from trouble when hearing the voices. That is the origin of his name. In early Tang Dynasty, to avoid the similar sound of Avalokitesara and Emperor Li Shimin, his name was changed into "Guanyin". The early image of Avalokitesara was a male. Later, it was transferred and till Yuan Dynasty, it was fixed as a young personable female. Avalokitesara is often known as standing or sitting on the white lotus pedestal in white dress, with a Kalasa in the hand. By sprinkling the amrita, he reliefs the mortal beings.

38 Gilt Amitabha Statue Made by Dong Qin

This set of statues consists of a high-legged couch, a Buddha, two Bodhisattvas, two Nryanas, a censer, a four-legged square couch and two squatting lions. Sitting in meditation on the middle-concaved lotus pedestal, which is located on the back center of the high-legged couch, Amitabha slightly pitches his upper body. His right arm bends upward from the elbow with the palm being outward. His left arm lifts upward from the elbow with fingers stretching out and palm being outward, which is the combination of Abhaya Mudra and mudra of supreme generosity. Wearing a high spiral bun, he has a plump face, on which the eyebrows and moustache are inked and the red trace could be noticed on his lips. He wears a cassock baring his right shoulder, with an asam! khya inside, revealing his muscles. The pleats on the clothes are simple and liquid. On the peach-shaped back board behind his head, there are lotus patterns surrounded by the flame patters. Two assistant Bodhisattvas wear high coronets, with the coronet belts extending till the knees. They are slim and slender-waisted, with the upper body naked. They wear chaplets with bells, bead necklaces, armlets, and double-bar bracelets. A piece of long cloth extends from the shoulders to the abdomen, bending around the arms and naturally hanging down. The long dress extends below the ankles. They stand bare-footedly on the lotus pedestal, with lotus-petal-shaped back board behind their heads. The right assistant Bodhisattva bends his right arm upward with a lotus bud in the hand. He bends the left arm in front of the chest, with fingers stretching and palm being downward. The left assistant Bodhisattva naturally hangs his right arm with a lotus bud in the hand. He lifts the left arm with a bead being hold by the thumb and forefinger. There are two upper-body-naked Nryanas stand bare-footedly in front of the Bodhisattvas, with burly muscles and protruding abdomens. On their heads, there are large noses and mouths, angry eyes and coronets with belt hanging down from both sides. They wear belts on the shoulders extending to the ground, chaplets and bead necklace. There is a round back board behind their heads, with lotus petal patterns. The

Nryanas on the right stands in the position of holding a sword in the right hand, with left arm slightly lifting and palm being downward as if pressing the sharp end of the sword. The one on the left rises his right arm protecting the chest, with left arm slightly lifting and hand half holding as if holding a Vajra. There is a censer clustered by lotus in the center, which is labouredly held by a naked pygmy. The sculpting is vivid. There is a pair of lions squatting in front of the couch. The strong lions squat with the inclined front legs. The Amitabha statue, the lotus pedestal, the high-legged couch and other accessories are all casted separately and tenoned, which could be disconnected. On the right side, the edge of the back and legs of the high-legged couch, there carved vow and eulogy in 118 characters. The inscription is " on July 15th of the fourth year of my majesty, general Ningyuan, county magistrate WuQiang as well as official Dong made this Buddha in great respect. It is mainly worshiped for the Saddarma of my majesty, parents, brothers and sisters as well as my wives. Firstly, life is not easy to spend and the only way to overcoming these obstacles is to take a big cart. Secondly, the Buddha sit into a lotus seat and save my life in different shapes; thirdly, I should think about the karma and concern about the common people, so as to get away from worries; fourthly, I hope everyone understand this and leave this human world together." This magnificent gilt statue is finely made and well preserved.

The year of Kai Huang is the reign title of Yang Jian, Emperor Sui Wen. The 4th year of Kai Huang is in 584AD. In the late North Dynasty, Emperor Zhou Wu, Wen Yong carried out the policy of Buddhism persecuting in the year of Jian De (572AD-578AD), because of the overwhelming power of Buddhism and the decreasing financial revenue. After Yang Jian replaced Zhou of North Dynasty by Sui Dynasty, he advocated Buddhism to win the support of the Buddhists. Thus, it was popular for the public to cast Buddha statues. This set of gilt Buddha statues is the reflection of the society in that period of time. Meanwhile,the complete inscription and reign title play an important role in the research of archaeological period and iconology.

39 Gilt Copper Standing Buddha Statue

This Buddha statue has a high bun, a properly plump face, a wide forehead, a square cheek, shoulder-attached earlobe and bowed eyebrows, smiling. He wears a round-necked cassock covering both shoulders and a long dress. His right arm lift from the elbow, with the palm being outward and fingers stretching upward, which is Abhaya Mudra. His left arm hangs with palm being rightward, the thumb slightly bending inward and other four fingers pointing downward, which is mudra of supreme generosity. He stands bare-footedly on a round pedestal, which is placed on a four-high-legged couch. From the proportion of human body, this Buddha has a slightly bigger head. His square face, strong body and short legs reveal the characteristic of Sui statue, which is derived from North Zhou Dynasty.

40 Gilt Standing Hollowed-out Avalokitesvara Statue

This Bodhisattva wears a high anadem with the belt hanging along the arm, a piece of cloth over the shoulders, bending around the arms and extending to the pedestal and a chaplet around the neck. He bares his upper body, with only a long thin dress from the navel. His right arm hangs with a kalasa in the hand. His left arm lifts from the elbow with an object in the hand. He stands bare-footedly on the lotus pedestal, under which is a four-legged square couch. There is a boat-shaped back board above his shoulders, with protruding flame patterns and an alternative Buddha sitting on a lotus petal on the top.

41 Little Silver Kettle

The silver kettle has a restrained and concave edge. Its abdomen is divided by a narrow protruding arris. The upper part is slightly bowed, with a circuit of three-lined intaglio string pattern near the edge. The other part gradually reaches to the flat bottom. The shape is not neat. This kettle is in the color of brassy.

Kettle is the cook-ware, most of which have round edge, bowed abdomen, thin side and surrounding bottom. It was born in the early Neolithic era. In the book of "Lihan Wenjia", it recorded that human distinguish themselves by making fire by drilling wood and cook the unripe so as to avoid diarrhea. According to the book of " The Ancient History",kettle was made by Huang Di. Kettle was derived from an ancient cook-ware,whose food experienced the process of shortening and disappearing. In Warring States Period, there was kettle that has surrounded bottom, round abdomen, restrained and down-turned edge. In Han Dynasty, kettle,rice-steaming utensils and basins were fixed. At this time, kettle was divided into two parts from the abdomen,with the upper part like a bowl and the rest like a flat-edged basin. These two parts were connected by rivets. The earliest kettles were made of pottery. In Shang-Zhou period, there were pottery kettles and copper kettles. According to Mencius—Teng Wen Gong, kettles and rice-steaming utensils were used by the civilians. In Han period, copper kettles were commonly used. After Sui-Tang period, kettle was replaced by boiler. In spite of the different shapes, kettle served the same function in all dynasties. In Spring and Autumn period, kettle was used as measure of containers. A kettle equals six Dous four litre, two Hus,or three Hus. (A Hu equals 10 or 5 litres.) Before mid-Tang, especially in early Tang period, the manufacture of gold and silver wares was monopolized by the central government and the imperial family. Craftsmen inherited the skill generation

after generation. However, the number of advanced craftsmen decreased due to the chaos in the late Sui Dynasty. Thus the works became coarse due to the decreased technics and smelting technology. Before Tang Dynasty, most gold and silver wares were decorations for appreciation and collection without much practical function. Till Tang Dynasty, there were practical utensils. This small silver kettle is a funeral object without much practical function.

42 Silver Bowl with Plain Surface

This silvery grey bowlhas a slightly wide edge, a deep and slightly bowed abdomen, a bugle-shaped short square pedestal with wide and thick edge. The brassy bowl has plain surface.

Bowl is a kind of table-ware, used for food filling, tea drinking and wine drinking. For most bowls, there is an open mouth, a bowed abdomen, and a squared or round pedestal. There are mainly pottery bowls but seldom golden or silver ones, which are used by the upper-class of the ruling class. Bowls were born in Neolithic age. The bronze bowls in Shang-Zhou period were similar to the current ones. In Jin period, celadon bowls were commonly used. Under the influence of Buddhism, there were many lotus-petal-pattern bowls. From early to the heyday of Tang period, white porcelain bowls boomed and golden and silver bowls were widely used by the imperial court and upper class officials. The main patterns on the bowls were flower, phoenix, mandarin duck, fish and dove. In late Tang period, bowls were various in shapes as lotus leaf, crabapple and sunflower petal. In Ming-Qing period, there were more shapes with dragon, phoenix, pine, bamboo, plum-blossom and other flowers as the propitious patterns.

This silver bowl has a deep abdomen, with a wide and thick square pedestal, which is different from the shape in the period of late Sui to early Tang. In early Tang period, gold and silver wares were still in the phase of imitation. As for bowl, its shape in early Tang period was a small cup with square edge, deep abdomen and flat round pedestal. In the late Tang period, the bowls had bugle-shaped edge, outward inclined abdomen and narrow pedestal with a big hole in the center. In the late Tang to Five dynasties (907AD-960AD), the pedestal became ring-shaped with the edge in the shape of lotus leaf, crabapple and sunflower petal. The abdomen has slightly rolling outline.

43 Silver Bowl with Deep Belly and Plain surface

This plain-surfaced silver gray bowl has an open edge, a deep abdomen, bowed side, a gradually adducted abdomen, a round bottom and a short square outward pedestal. Unearthed from the imperial forbidden garden of Tang Dynasty, this bowl is large in size, belonging to the imperial ware in early Tang period, which could be concluded from the development track of bowls.

44 Small Silver Bowl with plain surface

This plain-surfaced bowl has an open edge, bowed side, a round bottom, with a short spout on the edge.

45 Eight-petaled Silver Bowl with Enwinding Branches

This shallow bowl is in the shape of a eight-petaled sunflower, with the side slightly bowed and adducting into a multi-arris bugle-shaped short square pedestal. The eight concave lines on the out surface form raised arris in the inner surface. On the inner surface of this eight-petaled bowl, there is one symmetric plant on each line. On the top of the plant, there is a three-petaled flower with a round and two pointed petals, and the end of these plants connecting into an octagon. There is a double bead-pattern on the inner bottom, among which there are eight honeysuckle blooms, so as the patterns on the outer surface. The pedestal is composed by big beads. The ware were taken into shape by thump, with the patterns being chiseled and gilded.

Honeysuckle is a plant that doesn't fade in winter. Honeysuckle pattern was one of the most important patterns introduced from the West, which was widely used in Wei-Jin-South-and-North period. In Tang Dynasty, this pattern consisted of three to five half-sized leafs. When used in decoration, two opposite leafs roll to each other or leafs enwind the branch rolling symmetrically. Linked-pearl pattern consists of consecutive circles or beads, usually carved on the edge, the bottom and the arris. As the major pattern of gold and silver wares, linked-pearl pattern existed throughout Tang Dynasty with bigger beads before the mid-8th cen. And smaller beads after mid-8th cen.

The honeysuckle patterns on this silver bowl are same with the golden cup with handle unearthed from Tang gold-and-silver-work cache in He Jia Cun, Xi'an, Shannxi. It is the silver work in centre Asia's Sugda, in Tang Dynasty, before mid-8th cen.

46 Silver Bowl with Patterns of a Mandarin Duck and a Swan Goose in the Branches of Flowers

This silver bowl has a large edge and a shallow abdomen, in the shape of a plate. In the center of the bowl, there is a male mandarin duck and a swan goose frolicking in the peonies. The mandarin raises its head and unfolds wings ready to fly, as if looking for its partner. The swan goose bends its neck around the branches, with beak holding a flower, flapping the wings to fly. The peonies and these two birds are harmoniously combined. In both surfaces there chiseled six branches of flowers in double layer with the back covered by leafs. On the edge there are chiseled gilded patterns in transformed leafs. On the silver utensil, the shining gold reveals the magnificent quality of Tang people. At the bottom of the bowl, there inked two Chinese characters "Zhao Yi". It's common to find ink on the Tang utensils, which are the name of the owner and date. It is speculated that this was inked by a person surnamed Zhao.

Chiseling is a technics of decorating the utensil surface after its molding, which was born in late Spring and Autumn period and was popular after Warring States period. By beating the utensil surface with tools, craftsmen chisel the utensil with different patterns. After the technics of thump was applied on gold and silver wares, chiseling was the main processing means of decorating the detailed patterns. Branch pattern is a kind of pattern that takes a part of certain plant as the decorative patterns, with realistic flower heads, buds and leafs. The branches are separated and the flowers form cluster. It was popular from the early 8th cen. To the late 9th cen.. Leaf patters consist of leafs. It was born in the mid-8th cen. and was popular in 9th cen.. The pattern of double-layer branches of flowers was popular in mid-8th cen.. This silver bowl is a mid-Tang period work.

47 Petal-shaped Gilt Silver Bowl with Mandarin Duck

This silvery grey bowl is in the shape of four pedals. It has an open edge, bowed side with four arrises extending from the indentations. On the inner edge, there are superposing petal patterns. Under the plain inner surface, there are pedal patterns on the bottom. In the gilt branches of flowers, there is a pair of strolling mandarin ducks. One bends its head looking forward, and the other turns backward its head in sedateness. On the outer surface, each of the four parts is decorated with a tuft of blooming flowers with petals being layer upon layer, forming four clusters. Between each two clusters, there is a tuft of gilt flowers on the top and the bottom respectively. The original square pedestal is now deformed. On the outer bottom, there carved regular script of three Chinese characters "Servant Kang's Tribute". This silver bowl is the tribute from a local official named Kang to the imperial court.

Patel pattern was born in mid-8th cen. and was popular on various utensils in 9th cen.. Pattern of cluster of flowers was popular after the mid-8th cen.. According to the literature and data from archaeological excavations, it was prevailing for the local officials to pay tribute to the imperial court. In the early and heyday of Tang period, the tributes were wrought gold and silver and in the middle and late Tang period. Thus, this utensil is a mid-8th cen. gold and silver work.

48 Silver Bowl with Pattern of Swan Goose and Cluster Flowers

This round bowl has a wide edge, a bowed abdomen and a flat bottom. The surface is divided into four parts by the inward convex arrises. On the edge were made curling cloud lines. There is an oval cluster of flowers in each part, which has large leaf and is flourishing. On the bottom, there is lotus leafs, which are rolling as if flowing in the wind. In the center, there are two swan gooses with unfold wings and stretching necks looking at each other. The outer surface is plain. There is the jointing trace at the bottom, which may be the peeling square pedestal. The patterns are chiseled and the surface is gilded. The pattern of cluster of flowers is the decorative pattern of an uncertain round flower. On gold and silver wares, this pattern is the front view image and overlook image of a blooming flower, extending from the central layer to the outer layers. Compared with Baoxiang Flowers, the former is a realistic flower, being popular in the mid-8th cen.. The pattern on the edge of every curling cloud lines being in a oval was popular after mid-8th cen.

Silver bowl with multi-petal patterns was born in 6th BC in countries around Mediterranean and ancient Persia's Achaemenid Dynasty (558BC-330BC), and was popular in centre Asia and West Asia since after. In Sugda (now known as the valley of Amu and Syr Darya in Center Asia), silver bowl is featured in undulate multi-petal patterns on the inner surface from 5th cen. to 6th cen.. In the early 7th cen., this multi-petal-patterned silver bowl was introduced to China and soon became popular, whose petals at first, however, didn't extend to the edge. In the late 7th cen., this kind of bowl was domestically adopted, with decreasing number and increasing size of petals. After 8th cen., the petals extended to the edge. The cluster of flowers, lotus leafs and swan goose on this silver bowl are traditional Chinese patterns. Its shape differs greatly from Sugda's silver bowl, which is domesticated. From its patterns, it could be concluded that this silver bowl was made in early mid-Tang period.

49 Silver Bowl with Guava Patterns

This silver bowl has a wide edge, a bowed abdomen and round bottom. It is shaped by hammering with gilt patterns. Its inner patterns could be divided into three parts. At the bottom, there is a round pattern composed by three large leafs and three blooming flowers, with four guavas at the center. On the inner surface, there are five sets of cluster of flowers composed by guava and flowers, with equal distance in between. On the edge, there are leaf patterns with large leaf, smooth outlines and plump layout. The outer surface is plain. This pattern was popular from the grand Tang to mid-Tang and till late Tang period. Thus, this bowl was made in mid-Tang or late Tang period.

50 Silver Bowl with Butterfly Patterns

This bowl has a restrained edge, slightly slanting abdomen and a small flat bottom. There are wide string patterns on the inner edge and four butterflies intaglioed on the inner surface with a flower between each pair. There are two circles of wide string patterns near the bottom with incomplete crabapple patterns in between. There is a flying butterfly carved at the bottom. The patterns are gilded and the outer surface is plain. This bowl is a great piece of work in late Tang period.

51 Silver Plate with Patterns of a Swan Goose and Branches of Flowers

This plate has an open edge, a bowed abdomen and a round bottom. There is cloud pattern around the edge. On the inner surface of the plate, there are six sets of branches of peonies distributed with equal distance in between. At the center of the bottom, there are patterns of large leaf and branches of peonies. Among the flourishing leafs and the blooming peonies, there is a flying swan goose, who raise its tail high with shining eyes and feathers on the neck, back and chest flowing in the wind. The outer surface is plain with five Chinese characters "eleven Liang Two Fen" at the center of the bottom. The utensil is made by gilt, flower chiseling and thump. The patterns are chiseled.

Thump is one of the technics of gold and silver work making, by forging the unprocessed or smelted gold and silver, according to their quality of soft and ductibility, so as to form the wanted shape for the further process. Thump was originally introduced from West Asia to China in the late South–North period, which was prevailing in Tang Dynasty.

The chiseled and gilt flowers and birds and magnificently plump. The overall layout of the patterns is smart and clear.

52 A Tribute of Silver Plate with Double-fish Pattern and Plants by Li Mian

This plate has a wide open edge and a shallow bowed abdomen. At the center of the plate, there are circles composed by honeysuckle leafs, with a pair of fishes swimming within. There are branches of flowers decorated in and around the honeysuckle circle with chiseled pearls within. The utensil is thumped, by hammering the outline of the patterns, chiseling the details and gilt. On the outer bottom, there is inscription "Chaoyi Official, Shichi position, Commander of Hongzhou area, governor of Hongzhou area, Mid–level inspector, in charge of the military affairs of Western Jiangnan, purple golden fish token bestowed, Li Mian is called to come in". Hong state is now known as Nanchang in Jiangxi Province. According to Xin Tang Shu, Li Mian was the vizir in Su Zhong, Dai Zong and De Zong periods from Sep. 764AD to Apr. 767AD. He was praised as the embodiment of rectitude, austerity and loyalty. Even though, he paid tribute to the imperial court during his term, which reveals the corruption in the mid–Tang period. The vice of local officials paying tribute to the emperor began in Gao Zong and Empress Wu period and was popular in Xuan Zong period. In mid–Tang and late Tang period, due to opposition to the splittism, central government's revenue decreased badly. Besides, because of the corruption of official administration, the trend of local officials paying tribute for a promotion increased.

Fish pattern is common on the gold and silver wares in Tang Dynasty. In ancient China, the relationship between fish and water is symbolized as the harmonious relation between the emperor and his ministers and the ministers' loyalty to his lord.

After mid–Tang Dynasty, economy was badly destroyed by the constant wars in the North, while economy developed well and handicraft and commercial industries were flourishing in the South under the stable condition. The economic center moved southeastward after the blooming of Yang Zhou (today known as Yang Zhou, Jiang Su) and Yi Zhou (today known as Cheng Du, Si Chuan). The situation of gold and silver wares being monopolized by the central government and imperial family in early Tang period was broke with the large–scale exploitation of southern bullion mines. The former monopoly was broke by the local feudal officials and private handicraftsmen. Thus, the manufacture of gold and silver wares was done by the central government, local feudal officials and private handicraftsmen, which was particularly obvious in the Southeast. This tribute from Li Mian was made by the local feudal officials in Hong Zhou in Tang Dynasty.

53 Petal-shaped Gold-inlay Silver Plate with Patterns of Flowers and Birds

This is a round plate with flat fold edge, vertical side and flat bottom. There are five protruding arrises dividing the inner surface into five petals. The outer surface is plain. There are three different patterns on the inner surface. On the edge and the protruding arrises, there are leaf patterns, dividing the inner surface into five parts, in which there are two birds flying. The front bird turns its head backward with the one behind chasing. There is a branch of plum–blossom between the birds. The plum is surrounded by three out–stretching leafs. There are five clusters of flowers chiseled at the bottom. Each cluster is surrounded by leaf patterns with three flowers in the middle and three pedals on each flower. Between the bottom and the side, there are branches, under which there are trusses of plant dividing the periphery of the bottom into five parts. On each part, there is a cluster of flowers. At the center of the bottom, there are two phoenixes holding a ribbon with the mouths together, circling. The phoenixes extend their wings, with the long tails flowing in the air. The patterns are chiseled and the surface is gilded.

Phoenix is a holy bird in ancient Chinese myth, symbolizing auspicious. On the gold and silver wares in Tang Dynasty, the early phoenix pattern is a single phoenix, with the pair appearing in the middle and late Tang period. Ribbon pattern is plant-shaped belt knotting together. Two birds with a ribbon symbolizes blessedness, longevity and auspicious. Ribbon patterns on the gold and silver wares in Tang Dynasty was popular in the late 9th cen.

Most ancient Chinese plates are round. After Empress Wu in Tang Dynasty, under the influence of Sugda culture, traditional Chinese plate with multi-petal patterns were gradually popular, which are called sunflower-petal-shaped silver plate. In the grand Tang, there is a single animal pattern in most of the sunflower-petal-shaped silver plates, revealing its Sugda style. After the grand Tang, the style is domesticated, with wide turning-over on the edge and animal and plant patterns at the center of the plate, which is of great difference from Sugda's style of narrow edge.

54 Crabapple-shaped Silver Plate with the Pattern of Figures and a Dancing Crane

This crabapple-shaped plate has a wide edge with the pedestal peeled off. On the left of the plate, there is a recluse sitting on the ground, with a Gu Qin on the knee and playing. He wears a cross-necked loose gown, with wide belts. The recluse stares at the Guqin, with the hair tied. There is a boy assisting behind him, holding a wand and listening attentively to the music. A crane is dancing towards the recluse by flapping the wings. There is a pile of stone at each corner, with a branch of hemerocallis filling the spaces. There are rhombus patterns and Ruyi cloud head around in two circles, with guava, peach and branches of flowers on the edge. The patterns are combined with thump and chiseling.

The recluse, boy and Guqin, together with the crane, guava, peach and branches of flowers form this dulcet picture. In ancient China, Guqin, chess, calligraphy and painting were considered as the tools of cultivating people's morality. In traditional Chinese patterns, peach is a symbol of health and longevity; pine, wind, moon, cloud and crane are the reflection of freedom and unconstraint. In the early Tang Dynasty, under the influence of profoundly open-minded social fashion, people's living attitude was also tolerate, enterprising and confident. They enjoyed their life and were always ready for the coming challenges. During and after An-shi Rebellion (755AD-763AD), the unstable political system broke people's dream and their happy life. Afterward, with the transfer from Tang culture to Song culture, traditional Chinese culture gradually transferred from the extroverted to introverted. Scholar-bureaucrats began to pursue negative retiracy, with the aesthetical taste transferring from flippancy to steady, pursuing the chasteness and refine.

55 Petal-shaped Protruding Silver Plate

These two round silver gray plates are shallow, with wide and flat fold edge, shallow bowed abdomens and flat bottoms. There is a stem of plant at the bottom, with four plum-blossoms. The five-petaled large one on the branch is blooming at the center. The rest are in buds, with gilting surface. The silver plate is made by mould impacting. The protruding while smooth plant patterns on the inner surface are gilded. The patterns are chiseled after gilt. The corresponding outer surface is sunken in plain. There is no trace of processing, which is originally an accessory enchased on another utensil.

56 Silver Plate with Protruding Flowers

This shallow round plate has flat fold edge, a shallow bowed abdomen, with a Baoxian Flower on the bottom. The big flowers are thumped. The rest are in buds, with the patterns thumped and the surface being gilded. The outer surface is plain. This silver plate with protruding flowers were unearthed from the same location with the former two silver works, at the center of the pool, Qu Jiang site, Qu Jiang Chi village, South of Xi'an. Qu Jiang located in the Southeast of Chang'an in Tang Dynasty. In the Qin-Han period, this was the imperial garden. In Tang Dynasty, this was a renowned tourist attraction, where candidates who passed the imperial exams would hold a banquet. These three silver plates probably fell into the center of Qu Jiang at the banquet.

57 Small Silver Plate with a High Pedestal

This plate has an open edge, a shallow slanting abdomen, a flat bottom and a bugle-shaped high pedestal with thinner top and thicker bottom. The gilt on the utensil has now peeled off.

Plate is the water container or food filler in pottery, gold, silver and copper etc.. Plate was born in the early Shang Dynasty, with round abdomen, square pedestal and without ears. There often decorated patterns of tortoise and fish on the inner surface and bird casted on the edge. From West Zhou to Spring and Autumn period, most of the plates have accessory ears, square pedestal or tri-pedestal and stream. In Warring States period, some plates were in the shape of oblong, some had wide lip and round bottom and some was earless. In South and North period, celadon plate was popular. With the influence of Buddhism, celadon plate with lotus patterns was prevailing. Afterward, most plates were made in pottery with other only few plates made in other materials. In Sui and mid-Tang period, the shape of the plates was exotic in style, due to the unprecedented political, economic and cultural exchanges. After An-shi Rebellion, although the bilateral exchange continued, Chinese culture turned to be more inward self-examination. Thus, daily-ware including plate were dominated by Chinese traditional culture. After Five dynasties, both in terms of shape and decoration were domesticated. In Song Yuan Ming Qing period, the types and decorations on the plate were more various, when emerging displayed plate and plate rack.

This small high-pedestaled plate is similar with the porcelain high-pedestaled plate in Sui Dynasty, belonging to the imitation of porcelain works, which indicates that gold and silver wares in Tang Dynasty were sill not an independent branch of utensils.

58 Eight-petaled Long Silver Cup with Sassanian Style

This plain-surfaced utensil is in the shape of an eight-petaled oval, with deep body. The pedals are in symmetry, with the curves concaved into the utensil. The curves on both sides don't extend to the bottom, as transverse delamination petals. The square pedestal has peeled off.

This silver long cup has obvious multi-arrises with lost oval square pedestal, which is of Sassanian style. Crabapple-shaped silver cup is also known as multi-petal long cup, which was popular in Iran Altiplano from 3rd cen. to mid 8th cen., characterized in its oval shape and multi-petal side. At this period of time, Iran Altiplano was under the reign of Sassanian Dynasty (226AD-624AD). That's why this long cup is also called multi-petal Sassanian style cup. In the late 4th cen., its making technics was introduced into China, with eight-petal and twelve-petal, whose petals are distinctly protruding. In the late 7th cen., multi-petal long cup was domesticated with less distinctly protruding petals and slight undulation. After the mid-8th cen., the pedals became smooth. And the curves evolved from the edge-to-bottom style to vertical-division style, with only four pedals. The former geometric pedals transferred into realistic plant style. The artistic design is completely domesticated.

59 Oval Silver Cup with Single Ring

This silvery grey cup is in the shape of oval. This plain-surfaced cup has an open edge, a bowed abdomen and a flat bottom, with the edge and the bottom in the shape of an oval. The bottom is flat. There is a ring-handle at the side.

60 Silver Bowl

This silver gray bowl has a wide edge, a deep bowed abdomen and a round bottom in plain surface. Bowl is a kind of food-container, born in Neolithic period and made of pottery. After entering the civilized society, there were also copper and iron bowls. In the early East Han Dynasty, together with Buddhism, Buddhist ritual instruments were also introduced in China. Because the alms-bowl was similar with Chinese bowl in shape, it was named after its Sanskrit name patra. Most bowls were made of pottery or iron with few jade, agate, gold and silver ones.

61 Silver Cup with Plum-blossom Patterns

This silvery grey cup is round in shape. It has a cover with a protruding hunch in the center and a six-petal plum-blossom. There is an umbrella-shaped handle. The cover has wide edge, with a circle of up-side-down bugle-shaped button in the inner side. The body has an open edge, a deep bowed abdomen and a bugle-shaped square pedestal.

62 Silver Cup with Thin Middle

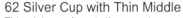
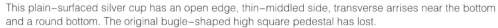

This plain-surfaced silver cup has an open edge, thin-middled side, transverse arrises near the bottom and a round bottom. The original bugle-shaped high square pedestal has lost.

The shape of this silver cup is different from other cups in the grand Tang, but similar with the pottery bowl, high-pedestaled cup and high-pedestaled plate in late-Sui and early Tang period, which is closely related to the sculpting style and eating manner at that time. In early Tang period, people were used to sitting on the ground, with short legged table. Thus, the shape of cup should adapt the living manner and environment. As a holding utensil, thin-middled utensil could satisfy people's visual need by its stability, plump shape, and up-rising spirit. After the year Tian Bao in Xuan Zong period (742AD-756AD), there were high legged table and chairs, which brought a series of changes in table-ware. The abdomen of bowls and cups became slightly bowed, for the comfort of visual need.

63 Small Silver Cup with High Pedestal

This silver cup is in the color of brassy, with plain surface. The utensil has an open edge, thin upper abdomen, plump lower abdomen, a flat bottom and a short square pedestal. The inner surface of the pedestal is bugle-shaped. In China, high pedestal cup was born in Warring States period, with square edge or wide edge, vertical side, canister-shaped deep abdomen, a round bottom and bugle-shaped high square pedestal. This utensil is different from Chinese traditional high pedestal cup, but similar with the one from East Roan Empire and North coast of Black Sea of European in 6th cen. AD. Thus this cup is an imitation of East Roman Empire's craftwork.

64 Eight-Petaled and Single-handled Silver Cup with Maiden Hunting Patterns

This silver cup has narrow flat fold edge, eight-petal-shaped side, linked-pearl lips, and a bowed abdomen. Eight concave lines divide the side into eight protruding petals, with eight transverse lotus petals holding the cup at the bottom. The square pedestal has lost. The ring handle is decorated with ball-shaped beads, with Ruyi Cloud head-alike finger mat in the shape of triangle, reaching the level of the edge. There is a fancy-horned deer patter chiseled on the circle of the finger mat. Below the handle, there is a hook joined on the body. The lower part of the body is the transverse lotus pedal, between which there are willow branches. Four pedals are carved with men hunting patterns, the other four pedals are carved with maidens hunting patterns, with these two patterns alternate with each other. There is pattern of fishes and lucky animal swimming in the sea, chiseled in the center of the bottom. The silver cup was thumpted, with the roe pattern being chiseled and gilded. This utensil is beautiful in pattern and exquisite in technics, which is the rare treasure in Tang Dynasty.

Deer is considered as a kindly pure animal in ancient time. Deer pattern was mainly used on table ware in Tang's gold and silver wares. It is related with the literary quotation of Lu Ming Banquet. The system of selecting talents by imperial examination was started in Sui Dynasty. In Tang Dynasty, after the candidates passed the examination, at the banquet, they should sing the first chapter of Lu Ming in The Book of Songs, which was thus called Lu Ming banquet. Thus, the craftsmen pined their best wishes on the deer patter.

Silver works with handle and in the shape of multi-pedal was introduced from the Center Asia's Sugda in the early Tang period with the increasing trade exchange between the East and the West. From 7th cen. to the early 8th cen. these silver works were with handle and finger mat with head portrait, in the shape of eight pedals and jar. After the mid-8th cen. the shape transferred to canister and round-bottomed bowl, from tall and thin into short and thick, with caliber gradually larger than its height. This is because Sugda utensil was greatly influenced by Chinese culture.

65 Oval-shaped Gilt Silver Cup with Dragon Pattern

This oval-shaped cup has a wide edge and a plump abdomen. Its edge is a anomaly eight-petaled oval. The inner surface is well-regulatedly divided by four transverse bend protruding arrises into five parts. The upper opposite parts are sea with rolling billows with mountains dotted between the billows. On the middle opposite parts, there are mysterious mountains, lotus and plants patterns on the roe-patterned grounding. On the lower part, two dragon-headed-and fish-bodied animals are playing a lotus in the rolling billows. The outer surface is divided by four concave arrises into five parts. The upper opposite parts are carved with a spotted deer and a lion running among the mountains. On the middle opposite parts, there is a pair of symmetrical lanes with a lotus in between, each holding a ribbon flying in the sky. On the lower part, a pair of symmetrical dancing girls with a oval in between, wearing cross-necked and narrow-sleeved dress, dancing in the cluster of plants, with belts flying in the air.   The square pedestal has peeled with an oval trace. On the remained part, there are patterns of branches of large leafs and flowers. This silver long cup is mould casted, with the patterns chiseled and thumped. The utensil is of strong Sassanian (ancient Iran) and Persian style, while the paintings are in the traditionally Chinese style. Two cranes with a ribbon symbolizes blessedness, longevity and auspicious, due to the similar sound of ribbon and longevity in Chinese characters.

66 Crabapple- shaped Silver Cup with Cetacean Pattern

This silver cup has a slightly open edge, a bowed abdomen and a round bottom, with the square pedestal lost. The edge and the abdomen are in the shape of an oval. The body and the inner surface are chiseled with realistic lotus leafs. The edge is equally divided into four parts by its longest and shortest diameters. Each part has a half lotus leaf, with its edge stretching to the bottom and osculating with another leaf's edge. The nervation is detailed and fluency. In the middle of the cup's inside, there is a double Capricorn surrounding a fireball in the bottom. The shape and the patterns are made by thump. The patterns are chiseled. The inner surface is gilded and the outer surface is plain. The realistic lotus leafs have detailed veins with lotus, being popular in the late 9th cen.. Capricorn is a long-nosed, sharp-teethed and fish-tailed animal in ancient Indian Buddhism. It is also called Makara, which is called whale in China. In the bood of "Xuanying's Pronunciation and Meaning", it says: " Magha fish, or Capricorn fish, is the king of the fish." It is considered to be the essence of the river and the root of life. As a traditional pattern in ancient Indian, it was often found on the ancient Indian sculptures, especially in the paintings and the pylons in fane architecture. As Buddhism introduced into China, Capricorn was also found on the grottos, gold and silver wares. In traditional Chinese gold and silver wares, it was found in the late Tang period. Bow-abdomened and round-bottomed long cup is the development of Sassanian long silver cup in China, which is deeper with a high bugle-shaped pedestal and smooth rolling lotus leaf patterns. This silver cup is the combination of Chinese, Indian and Sassanian culture, which is the production of the exchange of their politics, economy and culture.

67 Crabapple-shaped Silver Cup with Chinese Oriole and Flowers

This cup has a slightly open edge and slightly bowed side with contracted slant. Both of the body and the square pedestal are in the shape of crabapple. It is thumped with the neat gilded patterns and roe-

patterns as the grounding. The lotus petals in the center of the cup form an oval, with five Ru Yi cloud patterns within. Among the Ru Yi cloud patterns, there are two swan gooses flying, with one stretching its neck looking forward, and the other looking backward. In the middle of the inner surface, there is a circle of Ru Yi cloud patterns. There are deformed crabapple pattern on the inner edge. On the outer surface, there are flourishing branches of flowers, with a Chinese oriole on each petal. At the ends of short diameter, the Chinese orioles have just landed, looking forward and flapping the wings. The Chinese orioles at the ends of long diameter hold together the wings, looking backward, as if walking among the flowers. Each Chinese oriole is in different manners with vivid expressions. There is a circle of lotus patterns on the top and the bottom edge and wave pattern around the square pedestal. The patterns are richly delicate.

68 Crabapple-shaped Silver Cup with Phoenix Patterns

This silver cup has a wide slightly folded edge, deep and slightly bowed abdomen, a flat bottom and high square pedestal. This gilt crabapple-shaped utensil is thumped, with patterns chiseled. There is a circle of petal patterns on the inner edge. The inner side of abdomen is equally divided into four parts by four arrises, with a large bunch of flowers in each part. The inner bottom is in the shape of an oval, with a circle of petal patterns and plant patterns within. Two phoenixes are flying among the plants. The outer surface is plain.

69 Plain-surfaced and Crabapple-shaped Silver Cup with "Ge Er" Inscription

This crabapple-shaped silver cup has an open four-petaled edge, with arrises below each petal indentation. Below the round bottom, the square crabapple-shaped pedestal has lost. The utensil is plain-surfaced. On the outer bottom, regular script "Ge Er" is chiseled.

70 Plain-surfaced Silver Spoon

These are two spoons.
(1) The long handle of the silver spoon is flat and slightly bended, with one end wider than the other. The narrower end is connected to the spoon. The spoon body is slightly bended, with oval concave.
(2) The long handle of the silver spoon is slightly bended, with one end as square and the other triangle. The flat wider end is connected to the slightly bended spoon body. The other end is an oval concave.

71 Long-handled Silver Spoon with Goose Head

This long-handled silver spoon has an oval concave body. The end of the long handle is in the shape of a goose head. The other end of the handle is smooth-surfaced. Near the goose head, there is an arris and two wave-shaped bends. There is a flat beak, a high nose and a pair of small round eyes in its face.

72 Silver Spoon with Duck Head

This silvery grey spoon has an oval concave body and a slightly bended long handle. At the end near the body, both sides are flat. The other end is bowed-surfaced in one side and flat-surfaced in another. The end is in the shape of a duck head, with a long beak, a high nose and a pair of small eyes. The patterns are in intaglio.

73 Plain-surfaced Silver Spoon with a Long Handle

This silvery grey spoon has a flat and bend long handle. The handle is wide near the spoon body, and contracts into a triangle in the middle, with an arris in the centre of the other end. The body is in the shape of a concave oval. The spoon is plain-surfaced. At the end of the long handle, there are two intaglio Chinese characters in regular script "Ji Cai".

74 Plain-surfaced Silver Chopsticks

The thin and long silvery grey chopsticks are in the shape of poles without patterns. One end is thicker than the other, in the shape of duck beak.
With various terms, chopsticks got the name in Ming Dynasty. As a kind of table-ware, chopsticks ar used to catch food. In the grand Tang, the ruling class pursued a luxurious life so as to show their unparalleled noble status. Thus, gold and silver table-ware with practical functions came to be popular. According to "the Anecdotes in the period of Kaiyuan and Tianbao", in Xuan Zong period, premier Song Jing got a pair of chopsticks as a largess on a spring banquet. In the early Tang period, gold and silver chopsticks were short, and later in the grand Tang and after, the length increased, with some 30 centimeters in max.

75 Small Silver Basin with Round Bottom

This basin has a brassy surface, with square edge, a shallow bowed abdomen and a round bottom. It is plain-surfaced.

Basin is a kind of water container. In ancient sacrifices, it was used to contain blood. Later, it was used as washing ware. Most of the basins are made of pottery and bronze, with few golden and silver ones. Basin was born in Shang–Zhou period. After Han Dynasty, iron basins were gradually popular.

76 Small Silver Basin with Flat Bottom

This basin is in brassy. It has an open edge, flat fold edge, a slightly bowed abdomen and a flat bottom. It is plain–surfaced.

77 Silver Basin with Patterns of Flower, Bird and Butterfly

This silver basin has an open edge, a slanting vertical abdomen and a flat bottom. The edge is slightly folded. The basin is in the shape of a five–petaled sunflower, with a circle of flowing leaf patterns chiseled around the surface. There is a wide string pattern connecting the edge and the abdomen. The abdomen is divided by five protruding arrises into five parts, with gilt butterfly chiseled on the arrises. There is a grass on the lower part. In each middle part, there is a bunch of blooming flowers with a bird rest within. There are two wide string patterns connect the abdomen and the bottom, with lotus chiseled in the spaces alternate with each other. On the inner bottom, there are branches of flowers with two phoenixes flying within. The outer surface is divided into five parts with five grooves, with a lotus leaf in the middle of each part. Besides the gilt patterns, the rest are plain–surfaced.

78 Silver Ladle

This silvery grey ladle has several copper rusts. It is in the shape of square round. It has a bowed abdomen and a flat bottom. There is a handle at the edge. The surface is in the shape of bending crabapple. There is a spout in the shape of a duck beak at the middle bottom from the abdomen. There is a square carved in the inner bottom. Out of the double–lined comb pattern frame, there is one intaglio lotus from each side, with clouds between the lotuses. At the center of the square, there is a Taiji pattern, with four lotuses equally distributed around. This is a pattern combined with Buddhism and Taoism.

Ladle is a wash–ware. It was popular from Shang–Zhou period to Han Dynasty. It is in the shape of a long cup with spout at one end and sometimes a handle at the other end. Some of the ladles have pedestals. It is made of copper, pottery, gold and silver.

Taiji pattern is one of the main symbols of Taoism. Taiji means that all the creatures in the world are from the combination of Yin and Yang. According to On Taiji Pattern, written by Zhou Dunyi in Song Dynasty, is says: "Wuji is just Taiji. Taiji's movement creates Yang and the movement's utmost turns to be stillness, which creates Yin. Stillness's utmost turns to be movement. The changes of Yang and Yin create water, fire, wood, metal and earth. These five essences create the four seasons. The combination of Yin and Yang create the world infinitely". Grown in the mud, lotus remains clear in its nature, which is the symbol of Buddhism. Born in the early East Han Dynasty, Taoism is Chinese domestic religion. Born in ancient India, Buddhism was introduced into China form the land and the sea in the early East Han Dynasty. The dispute has never stopped between these two religions since their encounter. After the mid–Tang Dynasty, Confucianism, Taoism and Buddhism gradually came into confluence.

79 Six-edged Gold-inlay Silver Jar with Wide Edge and Branches of Flowers Patterns

This silvery grey jar has a wide edge, thin neck and a slightly plum abdomen. The square pedestal has deformed. There is a wide string pattern below the edge and the neck, with six lines equally dividing the space into six parts. There is a small flower chiseled in each part. There is a string pattern on both the upper and the lower part of the abdomen with six lines equally dividing the space into six parts. There are two bunches of in each part, with a knot connected below. Near the bottom, there is a circle of branches of flowers. The patterns are chiseled and the surface is gilded.

80 Silver Case with"Da Tang" Inscription

This flat round silver case's cover and body could be closely connected. There are two circles of protruding string patterns decorated on the cover, with the edge slanting folded into vertical. The case has square edge and vertical side. There is a shallow arris outside the connecting line of the edge and the side, for the use of holding the cover. The lower part of the side is inward bowed. On the flat bottom, there is intaglio regular script "Da Tang" at the center.

81 Plain-surfaced Silver Basin

The bottom of the silver basin is round. It has a slightly small edge, a shallow bowed abdomen and a flat bottom. It is plain–surfaced. There are partial remaining of wrapping clothes at the bottom.

82 Silver Case with a Cover

This silver case is in the shape of flat round. Its cover and body could be closely connected. The cover protrudes with a hole at the top center. The original handle has lost. There is a circle of intaglio string

decorated around the cover. The case has a small edge, a plump abdomen and a small flat bottom. There are two circles of intaglio strings decorated around the edge.

83 Small Silver Case with Round Bottom
The cover of this case has lost. The case has an open edge, a shallow bowed abdomen and a round bottom. There is a circle of intaglio string pattern decorated in and around the edge. The center of the bottom is in the shape of a saucer, who is round with the center protruding as a shallow plate. There are two circles of intaglio string patterns around the inner bottom. The silver case is in the color of brassy, with cooper rust, which should be the alloy of copper and silver.

84 Plain-surfaced Silver Rouge Case
 This silvery grey case is round. Its cover and body could be closely connected. The cover protrudes. The case has a vertical side and a round bottom. It is plain-surfaced.

85 Plain-surfaced Silver Puff Case
This round silvery grey case is plain-surfaced. Its cover protrudes with the edge folding downward. The cover and the body could be closely connected. The case has vertical side and a round bottom. The original silk powder puff in the case has deteriorated.

86 Gold Rouge Case in the Shape of Petals

Shaped with eight curves, the box has a snap button and a crowning lid and a crowning bottom of the same pattern. Patterns on the surface of the lid are decorated in dual structure, with eight peach-shaped honeysuckle cockades, whose tips point outwards in a radial type, in the center and eight peach-shaped cockades, whose tips point inwards to the center, in the outer field. The between is decorated with pattern of Ruyi winded by branches. Three little flowers are engraved in every curve on the brims of the lid and the bottom, both of which share the same emblazonry. The modeling and the layout of pattern of the petal-shaped rouge box is similar to the Peach-shaped Cockade Silver Box with Eight Curves housed in White Crane Art Gallery in Japan. The two boxes are contemporary products. Vessels in shapes of water-caltrop flowers and sunflowers mainly emerged in the turn of the 7th century and 8th century and they became popular from and after the mid 8th century.

87 Round Silver Puff Case with Pairs of Birds

This flat round puff case's cover can be closely connected with the body, with roe-pattern as the grounding. It is chiseled with flowers and birds. There is a pair of bird sitting shoulder to shoulder on the cover. Another pair flies with flower holding in their mouths with branches of flowers around. At the bottom, a pair of birds flies with mouths holding flowers. This utensil is of the vigorous spring scenery.
Case has the largest number in Tang's gold and silver wares with various types. In different times, the shape of the case differed. Round footless silver case was popular before mid-8th cen.. In the early Tang period, it has plain surface, while in the grand Tang , the patters on the surface increased.

88 Small Round Silver Case with a Pair of Playing Monkeys

This round case's cover can be closely connected with the body. Both of the bottom and the cover is slightly up-bowed in the middle. The utensil is with roe-pattern grounding. The cover and the body have different patterns. There is a large-leafed tree chiseled on the bottom and the cover with shade extending to the ground and branches bending with each other. There is a pair of monkeys under the tree. The space is filled with petals. The side is decorated with cirrus clouds lines. These two monkeys sit in a face to face way on the cover. On the bottom, one monkey is climbing the tree and the other is to climb. This is a traditional pattern with good wishes.

89 Gold-decorated Silver Case in the Shape of Petals

The orthostomous silver case is in silver gray and shaped like petals. On the outside belly is stamped with four dents, which separate the mouth rim and the upper belly in the pattern of four connected arcs. It had a foot ring which is incomplete now. One side of the case mouth has riveted a little handle, opposite to which there is a damaged hinge that enables the lid to open and close freely, and which also serves as a fastening when the case is closed. The inner side is plain, while the outside wall is carved four piles of floral clusters that form a circle with a design pattern of grass leaves filling around the flowers. The lower belly is hammered and folded a circle of in sharp-tip and arch-shape petals, whose stem veins are high-visible, and whose bellowing part is a circle of united pearl motif. Its bottom is plain. From its modeling, clustering flower shapes and decoration of united pearl motif, it is can be concluded that the case was made after the mid 8th century.

90 Silver Cases Engraved with Figures from Seven Countries
It is a set of three silver cases, including an outer one in the shape of hexapetalous splay, a middle one

having a parrot pattern and a begonia-shaped ring foot and an inner one with tortoise shell pattern, in which there are two crystal beads and a brown olivary agate bead in the inner case. In the shape of hexapetalous splay, the outer case has a rising surface, an inserting mouth, a flat bottom and a high foot in the shape of splay.

In the center of the lid surface, it is carved hexagonal pattern, whose sections are surrounded by ovate specifications. In the hexagonal pattern, there is an elephant rider, in front of who is a worshipper carrying things on the head, and behind who is an umbrella holder. On the right of the elephant, which is equipped with a set of saddle and saddle blanket, stands a man, and on its left is an accompanying person, and there is another man who is sitting on the ground casually. In front of the worshipper is a titled inscription of Seven Countries of Duguan , whose center is inscribed "Kunlun Kingdom" with two Chinese characters carrying the meaning of future below.

From the right of the Kunlun Kingdom, there are countries and regions in clockwise order as follows: Brahmin States, Tufan States, Shale, Koryo, Country of Baituokou and Country of Wuman. In the area of Brahmin States, there stands a Buddhist monk who is wearing a kasaya and holding a staff on the left, and two men on the right who are gesturing like inquiring. In the middle, there is square bottle with a little mouth on the ground. Inside the bottle mouth is a spark-like radiation. On the left is the inscription of the country's name and right is two Chinese characters "orally granted". In the area of Tufan States, there are two men driving a stout and strong ox whose four hoofs are galloping. The inscription is on the upper left side. In the area of Shale, there are two men carrying a knife each on the right, and two men on the left with one standing respectfully and the other pulling the bow. The inscription is in the very middle. In the area of Koryo, the venerable is sitting cross-legged on the left, and four men are standing around him. Two bird feathers are inserted in the head of each of them. They are all wearing long clothes with bag-sleeves. Two Chinese characters carrying the meaning of Koryo is inscribed in the very center. In the area of Baituomen, there is an old man sitting on the futon on the left and a boy offering gifts on the right. The inscription is in the very center. In the area of Wuman, there are two venerable men stepping forward on the left and three men welcoming guests on the right. They are all wearing a long dress and a loose gore. On their heads there are bag horns. The inscription is on the right. With the vine scroll as background, the upper and lower parts of the case mouth are carved with twelve Chinese zodiac signs, each of which has an inscription, saying Zi Shi is midnight in the period of the day from 11 p.m. to 1 a.m., Chou Shi is the period of the day from 1 a.m. to 3 a.m. when cocks are crowing, Yan Shi is the period of the day from 3 a.m. to 5 a.m. when people stop talking, Mao Shi is the period of the day from 5 a.m. to 7 a.m. when the sun rises, Chen Shi is the period of the day from 7 a.m. to 9 a.m. when people have breakfast, Si Shi is the period of the day from 9 a.m. to 11 a.m. when it's getting close to noon, Wu Shi is the period of the day from 11 a.m. to 1 p.m. when it is noon, Wei Shi is the period of the day from 1 p.m. to 3 p.m. when people are sleepy, Shen Shi is the period of the day from 3 p.m. to 5 p.m. when people have supper, You Shi is the period of the day from 5 p.m. to 7 p.m. when the sun sets, Xu Shi is the period of the day from 1 p.m. to 3 p.m. when dusk falls, and Hai Shi is the period of the day from 1 p.m. to 3 p.m. when people go to bed. The middle case has a rising lid surface, an inserting mouth which is in the shape of Begonia, a flat bottom and a splay-shaped ring foot. In the very middle of the lid surface is a pair of parrots flying in opposite directions. Biting flower branches, the parrots are dancing in the air. The background is set with patterns of interlocking branches and floral scrolls. Its edge is a circle of rising lotus petals. The mouth of the case is decorated with patterns of interlocking branches and floral scrolls, and its rim is also a circle of rising lotus petals. Over the case mouth is a design of··· The small case is like a turtle back, which has a highly rising surface and a flat bottom. Only the surface is carved with a tortoise shell pattern, while the rest is plain. There are two crystal pearls and a brown olivary agate bead in it. This set of silver cases is appealing in design and delicate in carving, with a unique range of decorative patterns from flowers and birds to mankind. It is beyond a boutique among the silver wares in Tang Dynasty, but a reflection of the grand occasions of cultural communication between China and foreign countries in Tang Dynasty, which is seen from the modeling of figures and their nationalities.

Human serving as decorative themes is a unique feature of gold and silver wares in Tang Dynasty. Contents concerning hunters, musicians and palace maids and so on appeared mainly before the mid 8th century, while those concerning with people stories and amusements mainly date back to the post mid 8th century. This set of cases is made by ninth-century country of Nan Zhao (748 A.D.-937 A.D.) where is Yunnan Province located now. They are similar to the Petal-shaped Silver Case Carved with pattern of Two Lions, which is a post ninth century production and has been housed by Famen Temple Museum in Fufeng County, Shaanxi Province since 1980s, and the Tian Sijv Petal-shaped Silver Case with Double Phonixes Pattern, which is preserved by Lantian County Bureau of Cultural Relics in Shaanxi Province, in terms of modeling and design. They are made during the period from 847 A.D. to 873 A.D. At that time, Tang's nation power was weakening, while Nanzhao's nation power was rich and powerful. Nanzhao unceasingly invaded in all directions, and Tang army was defeated several times to lose large tracts of land, so Nanzhao was becoming more and more arrogant and scornful of Tang Dynasty. The seven countries carved on the case were originally Tang's vassal states, but they appeared on the silver case made by Nanzhao, indicating Naozhao's madcap desire to conspire to snatch Tang's vassal states.

91 Five-carved Silver Case in the Pattern of Double Phoenixes with Ribbon

The body of the silver is oblate and round and has five curves. The lid and the bottom are inserting together. The surface of the lid and bottom is rising. A circle of natural shape of raised string separates the emblazonry on the lid surface into an inner area and an outer one. The inner area is decorated a round design of double phoenixes biting four ribbons. Space between the double phoenixes and the ribbons is filled a trailer pattern. The outer area is the shape of petals with five carves, each of which has the same emblazonry within. The main pattern is a pair of flying swan geese, which is filled with trailer and honeysuckle pattern. The brim and case mouth are decorated with seriate design consisting of mandarin ducks and trailers. The whole emblazonry on the case body is alternatively filled by fish roe crackle. The main emblazonry is pressed by a mould ware, while the fish roe crackle is carved, but the entire surface is gilt with gold. On the outer side of the bottom is carved four lines in Chinese characters "It is an oblation from envoy Tian Sijv to the inner palace. It was made in November 15th, 866 A. D. It weighs fifteen liang, five qian and one zi."

In Tang Dynasty, only in the official workshops will men with an official position participate in the working process. From the official organization of "inner palace" and one's formal name of "envoy", this silver case can only be made by central feudal officials or royal workshops in Tang Dynasty, namely Institution of Gold and Silver Workshop or Wensi Institution. The habit of carving inscriptions on the gold and silver wares can date back to mid 8th century and thereafter. It is might because the manufacture of gold and silver wares before Tang Dynasty was monopolized by central feudal government. In the late Tang Dynasty, local official and private gold and silver workshops emerged, so the gold and silver wares were carved with inscriptions to identify their manufacturing organizations. Together with this silver case, there are other wares excavated, including three silver ingots, one silver plate with parrot and clustered flowers pattern, one plain silver bowl in five-petal-shape, one large silver bowl lid with broken branches and floral, one silver bowl in eight-petal shape with four ribbons pattern, two cloud pattern cases in pattern of parrots and grapes, one silver key and three silver chopsticks. In addition, there are some silver ornaments and horse gears and so on. Broken branches and floral take a major part in this group of silver wares, and the ribbon pattern takes as the second, which reflect the ruling classes' wish to pray for longevity. This group of silver wares was buried in a mass, indicating that they were buried in a hurry especially when they were buried with the horse gears. The late Tang Dynasty is a period often at war, so this group of silver wares might hurriedly buried by their owners when they retreated.

92 Gilt Silver Spittoon in Floral Pattern

The spittoon has an upper part serving as a plate mouth which is connected with the belly by the thin neck, and a lower part which has a plump belly, a flat bottom and a short ring foot. The mouth, the body, and the foot are divided into four petaloid parts, while the plate mouth is carved with triple emblazonry: the first one is an eight-petalled lotus flower in the spittoon mouth; the second one is four oblate twin flowers growing on one stalk and each petal is decorated with a triangle branch-broken flower and a tawny day lily, whose stems twine and flowers blossom toward different directions to form a variegated floral pattern; the third one is a circle of disguised rising lotus petals. The outer belly wall has four groups of branch-broken flowers, each of which has two flowers twining together with a blossoming centered flower surrounded by a circle of leaves to form a variegated floral pattern. In the variegated floral pattern, there are triangle branch-broken flowers. The parts carved with flowers are all gilt.

Spittoons used for gargling and spitting were widely used in Qin and Han Dynasty. Ancient people usually put them on the tables or beds. Spittoons belonging to emperors and aristocrats are mainly made of gold, silver and jades, while those of ordinary people are made of ceramics. Their shapes are like a plate mouth, a narrow neck, a plump belly, a flat bottom and a short ring foot.

Spittoons are daily used items in Tang Dynasty, and they are mainly made of ceramics and few are made of gold and silver. This spittoon is hammered and folded to form its shape and the whole body is well proportioned. It was excavated from the working field in Zaoyan Village, together with the silver ingot of 879 A. D. which is collected by Xi'an Institution of Historical Relics Preservation and Archeology. It is also identical with the Silver Plain Spittoon excavated from the "Shuiqiu" Tomb in Linwan County, Zhengjiang Province. The Silver Plain Spittoon was made in the late Tang Dynasty. They are all top-notch artistic works in silver wares made in Tang Dynasty in the late ninth century.

93 Silver Saucer in Pattern of Composite Flowers

Made of silver, the saucer has a shallow round shape, a curving belly, within which there are four evenly distributed Design of Composite Flowers s. The inner bottom is raised like a shallow plate, while the outer is plain and has a splay-shaped ring foot and a flat bottom. Its modeling is shaped by panel beating, and the emblazonry of Design of Composite Flowers s are hammered and folded. The surface of the saucer is gilt. Being a unique decoration pattern in Tang Dynasty, Baoxiang emblazonry is originally a stylized Buddhism decorative pattern, which originates from lotus flowers. The composing method of a Design of Composite Flowers is to put the image materials like blossoms, buds, receptacles and leaves in forms of symmetric radiation in four or multi-directions to organize multi-leveled floral designs to show the whole plane of the flowers. So Design of Composite Flowers s belongs to pictured flowers.

The saucer, also known as teacup boat and teacup holder, is like a shallow plate, and it has a small ring foot. The teacup is placed in the sunken center. In that case, it can prevent the teacup from leaning and the tea from overflowing. The saucer is one of the tea set matching to the cup. Saucers came into being in Jin Dynasty, and became popular in Tang Dynasty due to the exceedingly prevalent trend of tea drinking in Tang Dynasty.

94 Silver Bottle with a Narrow Neck

In silvery grey, it has a wide-open mouth, a narrow and long neck, a deep and plump belly and a splay-shaped short ring foot. The lower part of its long neck is welded to the belly. The welded part forms a frustum of a pyramid.

A Bottle is the container used to draw water or to hold and contain liquid. It came in to being in Neolithic Age. Deduced from the relevant ceramics and carved stones of Buddhism, which are excavated in the contemporary archaeological process, this long-neck bottle was popular in the northern part of China from Northern Dynasties to Grand Tang Dynasty.

95 Silver Tongue Scraper

It is silvery grey and in an arch form. The two ends are slightly thinner and in the shape of square, while the middle is a little broader. The handle close to the ear spoon and the little knife is decorated with two raised string patterns respectively. One side of the long handle is flat, while the other side has a ridge in the middle. One end of the handle is the ear spoon, and the other end is in the shape of a slightly whittled knife.

Tongue scrapers are used to remove the filth. They appeared in the last years of Western Han Dynasty. They were mainly made from bamboo and wood. There are some made from gold, silver and bronze, but rarely seen. Tongue scrapers gradually became distinct in the late years of Northern Song Dynasty when toothbrushes were made.

96 Silver Lampstand

This lampstand consists of three parts: two stories of lamp plates and a stand. The upper lamp plate is smaller than the lower one. The lamp plates have a flat bottom, a shallow belly, a vertical wall, and a slightly outward rolling brim. Both of the plates have a round hole in their center, and the plates are put on the stand throughout the hole. Between the hole and the outer edge is decorated with a circle of filament string pattern cut in intaglio. The stand is shaped in the way that it is can be taken by hand. It is hollow, and its middle part is slender, like knotty bamboo joints, at each of which is decorated with a circle of string pattern cut in intaglio. The upper part of the stand is like a pipe, under which there is a prominent circle of shallow frustum of a pyramid to hold the small lamp plate; the lower part is like an overturned bell, the center of which has a circle of shallow frustum of a pyramid to hold the big plate. The ridge of the bell outward extends enough to form a ring foot. The entire lampstand is brassy, and parts of it have coppery rust.

97 Gilt Hollowed-out Silver Censer Ball with Double Bees and Floral Pattern

The silver censer ball is a container for burning incense of Tang Dynasty. It is shaped by panel beating, and the entire ball is hollow out, and some parts of the emblazonry are gilt. The ball consists of two hemispheres that are fastened together. The upper hemisphere serves as the lid, while the lower serves as the body. One side of the fastened part is a double-bee-shaped hinge, while the other side is installed a hook, which enables the lid to open or close. On the top of the lid is installed a ring button, which is interlinked by a lotus-bud-shaped connection that attached to a silver chain. The lid surface is carved six groups of clustered floral. The group of clustered floral on the lid top has four carved bees, while other groups have only two. The hollow out parts are in the shape of broad leaves. The upper hemisphere and the lower hemisphere have symmetrical emblazonry. The brims at the jointing part of the lid and the body are carved a circle of creeping pattern. There are two balance rings inside the censer ball. The incense container is riveted to the inner ring by minor axis. The outer ring is also riveted to the inner ring and the censer body by minor axis. When the censer is rolling, the inner ring and the outer ring will also roll. Because the incense container's center of gravity is downward, the container can hold the balance so that the ashes or the sparks will not overflow. In that case, the ball can be put in the sleeves or bedclothes. Rolling but still firing, the censer is also called Censer in Quilt. Females in Tang Dynasty liked wearing censor balls. On one hand, they can be used to burn incense to perfume clothes. On the other hand, they can be used as waist accessories. In addition, this kind of censer is all used in Buddhism activities in the religious occasions, which might be concerned with avoiding evil spirits and warding off calamities. The archaeological materials show that, the censer ball remained popular throughout the entire Tang Dynasty.

The censer ball is also known as Gold Ball or Gold & Silver Incense Ball.

This censer ball is ingenious in manufacture and exquisite workmanship, which show the craftsmen's superb metalwork and excellent capacities in machinery manufacturing.

98 Gilt Five-footed Bronze Coil Base with Winged Beast Pattern

The coil base is a component of musical instruments used in a Buddhist. The entire coil base is gilt. It has a wide-open mouth and a flat bottom. The coil base surface is carved five layers of variegated patterns. In the center of the surface, there are two flying beasts with wings that are monstrous, bizarre and majestic like lions and tigers. The beasts have raised eyes, huge noses, broad ears and long beards. Long wings spreading and big tails swinging, they are biting long flowing scud together. The flying beasts are carved turgidly, and their wings and tails compose of flowers and leaves, which overspread the coil base center. The second layer is branch-crossed lotus in sinuated pattern. The third layer is tortoiseshell fine pattern with carved flowers. The forth layer is decorated by a circle of branch-crossed lotus with big leaves, within whose center there are four mandarin ducks. Some of the ducks are standing on the branches and leaves. Some are tuning their hands intending to fly. Some are playing, clapping. In various postures, they are vivid and lively. The fifth layer is the coil base edge, which is decorated with a circle of leaves pattern. The emblazonry of the entire coil base has the fish roe crackle as the background. Five flowing-cloud-shaped feet are evenly distributed under the coil base bottom. The tip of the foot is outward like a cloud cluster floating in the air. There are five lotus-leaf-shaped animal head appliqué holding rings, which hang five tassels in a ribbon pattern. The plate is riveted to the feet and the animal head appliqué in a well-defined and solid type. The carved emblazonry and the surface's golden light set each other off wonderfully, seeming palatial.

The modeling of this gilt bronze coil base is similar to the coil base of Gold-Coated Five-foot Silver Sandalwood Burner with Tortoise and Lotus Pattern, excavated from the underground palace of Famen Temple in Fufeng County, Shaanxi Province. They also share a common function, serving as the censer stands. The coil base's workmanship is superior among the gilt bronze craft at that time. This gilt bronze coil base is quite exquisite in terms of craft making, modeling, and emblazonry and so on. It is unearthed in the Xi'an Railway Station square, the Eastern Palace of Taiji Imperial City, where the imperial family used to live in Tang Dynasty. Therefore, this gilt bronze coil base might be one of the loyal family's tributes, which was used when they had Buddhism activities.

99 Octagonal Silver Mirror Shell with Hunting Patterns

This is an accessory to a bronze mirror. It is made of silver and is silvery grey. It is in the shape of eight petals and its surface is carved with hunting patterns. It also has a clustered floral shaped round button. There is an inner emblazonry and an outer one. The inner emblazonry consists of two groups of hunting patterns: one is about two men are hunting a running goat on the back of a galloping horse, with one man attaching the arrow to the bow forwards while the other attaching the arrow to the bow backwards; the other group is about two men are hunting a running boar on the back of a galloping horse with one man attaching the arrow to the bow forward while the other attaching the arrow to the bow backwards. The rest space is decorated with running hares, spotted deer, around which branches of flowers are interspersed. The outer emblazonry is carved on the edge of the eight petals with four as a group. In each group, the following patterns are distributed alternately: two little swallows are chirping oppositely to a bunch of flowers; white cloud is twisting in the mountains and flowers are clustering. The edge of the mirror shell is carved with cirrus cloud pattern, while the entire shell is carved with fish roe pattern as background. All the emblazonry is hammered and folded out. Gold and silver mirror shells are the major workmanship of bronze mirrors in Tang Dynasty. Their production method is to paste the silver or gold plate to the mirror's back, and then to hammer and fold out a variety of decorative patterns. Patterns of this silver mirror shell are densely and orderly laid out. It is a competitive product among the silver decoration of Grand Tang Dynasty.

100 Gold-plated Mirror with Auspicious Animals and Flower Branches

In the shape of eight-petalled water-caltrop flower pattern, the mirror is pasted with a gold shell on its back. The gold plate is hammered and folded out emblema anaglyph patterns. In the raised center, there a button, which is decorated with a pair of rear-end beasts. A circle of raised ridge divides the shell surface into two areas. The inner area is decorated with eight beasts and the branch-interlocked trailer pattern. In front of the face of each beast, there is a ring. The auspicious beasts gesture differently, such as walking, bending over, lying and jumping, like they are intending to play and climb up the tree. The branch-interlocked trailer pattern of the inner area overspread the raised ridge to the outer area. The trailers blossom in the eight water-caltrop flower petals. The flower branches in each petal are separated but still connected. In every petal, there is a four-leaf bud pointing to the center of the water-caltrop flower. On the both sides of each petal, there hang grapes, below which there are two birds biting the branch and pecking the seeds. Birds in each petal are different from one another. With the shape border of the inner mirror edge is carved with branch-broken flowers. Grape pattern carved in the bronze mirror of Tang Dynasty is the product of cultural communication between eastern and western worlds. Grape pattern originated from Ancient Greeks' worship toward Wine Gold Dionysus, also named Bacchus, who is the guardian of grape growing industry and grape brewing industry, and who is one of the most popular gods with Ancient Greek and Ancient Roma ordinary people. In the sculptures and paintings of Ancient Greek and Ancient Roma, Dionysus always showed up with grape leaves and fruits. After 4th century, Eastern Roman Empire inherited the ancient western artistic traditions. With the development of western and eastern trades, grape pattern was introduced into China in the early years of Tang Dynasty, and mixed with Chinese auspicious animals to decorate the bronze mirror. Bronze mirror with grape patterns came in reign of Li Zhi, Emperor Gaozong of Tang, became popular in the reign of Empress Wu Zetian of Tang, and gradually died away after Emperor Xuanzong of Tang.

The body of this gold-shelled mirror is thick and heavy. The gold plate is fine in texture, smooth in surface and exquisite in processing. Even the pinfeather on birds' wings can be recognized. From the grape pattern featuring over-ridged branches decoration, this Gold-plated Mirror with Auspicious Animals and Flower Branches was made in the late years of Tang Dynasty.

101 Octagonal Silver Lock

The lock is a silvery grey padlock. The lock hook is like a sword handle, inserting into the hollow octagonal-prism-shaped lock body. The body surface is decorated with four wide belt patterns, each of which is decorated with two circles of filament string pattern cut in intaglio. Three flowers hang on the lock hook with the middle one having a long stem. The blossoming middle flower is hollow like the shape of three petals. Flowers of both sides are in the shape of the calyx and receptacle of a persimmon, and they are put to the three rivets on the back of the lock.

102 Gold Hairpin with Phoenix and Peony Filigrees

The entire hairpin is made of deep colored gold and its body is long and oblate. The tipped end is like an oblate awl, and the pommel is welded an oval gold plaque, on which is welded a bunch of flowers in grass leaves pattern and a phoenix, whose wings are spreading and tail floating in the air, flying above a cluster of peonies.

Hairpin is used to pin the hair. It is also known as hair clasp or hair pin. It came into being in Neolithic Age.

The gold and silver hairpins in Tang Dynasty are more complicated than those made before Tang Dynasty. They have many shapes, like flowers, dragon and phoenix, trees, mountains and rivers, and even human images. Beside gold and silver, they are made of other precious materials like hawksbill turtles and azure stones. This gold hairpin is decorated with a phoenix and peonies, which imply wealth, rank, and prosperity in traditional Chinese emblazonry. Both of them show up on this gold hairpin, indicating people's pursuit of wealth, rank and safety on one hand, and symbolizing people's mental outlook of making progress in an active way in Grand Tang Dynasty.

103 Gilt Silver Hairpins with Chrysanthemum Pattern in the Shape of Shield

There are two of them. The first one is oblate and flat strip, and it is gilt all over. The pommel is in the shape of a shield, with the shape border of whose fringe carved a circle of line cut in intaglio. The inner side is carved with a bunch of chrysanthemums cut in intaglio on the background of the fish roe patter. The branches and leaves of the chrysanthemums are disheveled. The second one shares the same shape with the first, but the emblazonry on the shield-shaped pommel is too rusted to be recognized.

104 Gilt Silver Hairpins with Peony Pattern in the Shape of Shield

Both two of them are made of silver. In the shape of shield, their entire surface is gilt and carved with a peony in full bloom. The peony is surrounded by twining branches and leaves, close but not chaotic. These two oblate hairpins are made in peculiar shape and symmetrical layout. Their surface is made in the production processes, like carving, polishing, gilding and so on. These two oblate hairpins share the same modeling and emblazonry.

105 Silver Hairpins with Flowers and Grass

They are silvery grey and gilt on the surface. The first one is oblate and flat. Close to the pommel is spiral-shaped. The pommel is oblate and flat, and it is carved with three clustered lotus in full bloom. The second one is oblate and flat. The part close to the pommel is spiral-shaped. The pommel is oblate and flat, like a willow leaf, whose ridge is in link-arc shape. The inner part is carved with the leaf pattern of three branches as a single entity. The dense leaf veins stretch from center to the leaf margin.

106 Silver Hairpin with Phoenix Pattern

The hairpin body is oblate and flat. Its head is in the shape of gingko leaf, whose edge is fretwork. In the middle of the leaf, there is a bunch of flowing cloud floating in the air. In the cloud, there is a phoenix with a high crest and long eyes. Soaring into the vast sky, its head feather is floating backward, and its wings are spreading synchronically, and its flower-like tail is floating with the wind. The hairpin bottom is carved with pearl pattern. The entire body is gilt.

107 Gold Hairpin with a Silver Ingot

The entire hairpin is made of deep colored gold, and it has two plies which are even and fine long strip. The pommel is connected with two trapezoidal silver ingots with plump belly. The two ingots are connected by the by-sides and the connecting part is bending upwards. Each of the unconnected side is linked with a plain hairpin.

108 Plain Gold Hairpin

The entire hairpin is made of deep colored gold, and it has two plies which are even and long strip. The section is circular. The connecting part to the pommel is like herringbone. It has a plain surface.

109 Plain Gold Hairpin

The entire hairpin is made of deep colored gold, and it has two plies which are even and long strip. The section is circular. The connecting part to the pommel is like herringbone. It has a plain surface.

110 Gold Hairpin with an Arced Head

The top end is arc, both sides of which are sharpened long round poles that function inserting into hair. The entire gold hairpin is plain without any emblazonry.

111 Silver Hairpin with Double Leaves Pattern

The hairpin has two plies, which are thin long strips. Section of each ply is circular. The pommel is connected with a little underbrush, whose leaves are binding up layer upon layer. Two petals put forth on the top of the underbrush. The venations of grass leaves and petals are all carved. The hairpin surface is gilt.

112 Silver Hairpins with Flowers and Birds Pattern

There are eight of them.

(1)The first one's pommel is in the shape of gingko leaf, plain without any emblazonry.

(2)The second one is oblate and in the shape of two-armed fork. There are two two-armed forks stretching from the center to two opposite sides. One of the fork serves as the handle, where is carved with grass leaves pattern formed by interphase semi-rings. Nipple nails are distributed between the connecting parts of the semi-rings.

(3)The third silver hairpin is oblate, thin, and long strip. The pommel is in the shape of Asiatic plantain ear, above which two peacocks are flying.

(4)The hairpin body has two arms. The pommel is carved in the shape of sunflower, whose petals are blossoming. There are two threads of silver on the sunflower, like floating in the air.

(5)The pommel is a long triangular with three uneven sides. Its surface is hollow with cirrus cloud pattern decorated in the center. There is a little swallow flying in every cirrus cloud.

(6)The pommel root is carved in the pattern of banana leaf, in which a large group of clustered flower in pattern of trailers twining branches. The space between leaves and branches are hollow.

(7)The pommel is divided into two petals of oblate and flat branches and leaves which twine at first and then separate. The tip of the petal develops to two or three petals. Ridge of every leaf is carved a circle of line cut in intaglio. Blossoming lotus fills the inner part of the petal. There are two in each, alternatively arranged.

(8)The hairpin is oblate and flat. The hairpin head is in the shape of double leaves, between which a pair of phoenix with long tails is carved. On its surface, it is carved layer-upon-layer flowing cloud. On each cloud flies a skylark, which has sharp beak and round eyes. The skylark is spreading its wings synchronically, dragging its long tail, and flying freely.

113 Silver Hairpins

They are silvery white and have grey silver rust on them.

(1)One has two plies, whose section is circular. It is plain and its pommel is in the shape of Chinese character "Pin".

(2)It has two oblate and flat plies. A silver fork consisting of two twined plies stretches in the middle of the silver hairpin. The two plies twine twice and then separate to form a pommel. Every ply is decorated with feather pattern. The handle tip is triangular.

114 Silver Hairpin in Capricorn Pattern

The surface of the silver hairpin is gilt. The hairpin pole is broken. The hairpin head is in the shape of petals, among which there are two lotuses. Above the lotuses, there is a Capricorn sucking a round ball. The Capricorn bends its tail upwards like jumping. Capricorn is a traditional emblazonry in India's manufacture craft. In Sui and Tang Dynasty, Capricorn pattern as a propitious emblazonry became quite prevalent with Buddhism flourishing in China.

115 Silver in Hairpins Pomegranate Blossom Pattern

The hairpin pole is broken. The pommel of the hairpin pole has fruited a pomegranate among the flowers and leaves. The pomegranate has two branches of flowers and leaves, whose leaf levers are comparatively long. The flowers and leaves are hollow interlocking flowers, above which the skylark is flying with spreading wings. The entire hairpin is gilt.

116 Gold Pearl Buttons

There are two of them. The gold pearl buttons are round and hollow. The surrounding part is made by a circle of hammered and folded gold plaque. Their centers are raised. In the buttons, there is a crystal dead in each of them. There are three oval notches. Their bottoms are flat with two holes, through which two thin spun gold stretch out to fasten the pearl buttons.

117 Gold Flower Comb

Its body is meniscate and hollow. Originally, it was embed with a wood comb. The decorative pattern is made by welding the wire inlay on the meniscate gold plate. The wire inlay is embedded with the same emblazonry on both sides with a plum blossom in the middle of each. Beside the plum blossom, there is a mandarin duck on each side. Plum-blossom and water-drop patterns fill the space in between. All the emblazonry is made by weaving thin spun gold and gold plates. Used to be inlaid in the comb, the kallaite were surrounded by a circle of contact pearls, but it fell off.

118 Hollow-out Gold Flower Comb

The middle part of the gold comb is made of wood. It is in the shape of sawtooth. Majority of the comb teeth are broken. Both sides of the comb are decorated by the pattern of gold flowers and leaves which are made by hammered and folded thin spun gold. The two sides are same in pattern that their petals and leaves are hollow and there are two juxtaposed plum blossoms in the middle. The two plum blossoms have two leaves both on the left and on the right. There are inlaid things on the branches and leaves, but most of them fell off and only one kallaite left on one of the leaf. The kallaite surface is carved with thin lines cut in intaglio to stand for venations. There is a circle of little holes, which might be used to thread and fasten the gold flowers on both sides.

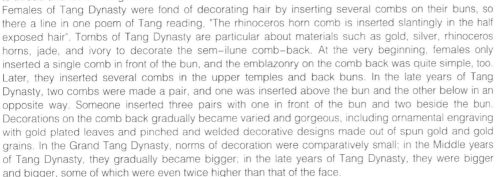

Females of Tang Dynasty were fond of decorating hair by inserting several combs on their buns, so there a line in one poem of Tang reading, "The rhinoceros horn comb is inserted slantingly in the half exposed hair". Tombs of Tang Dynasty are particular about materials such as gold, silver, rhinoceros horns, jade, and ivory to decorate the sem-ilune comb-back. At the very beginning, females only inserted a single comb in front of the bun, and the emblazonry on the comb back was quite simple, too. Later, they inserted several combs in the upper temples and back buns. In the late years of Tang Dynasty, two combs were made a pair, and one was inserted above the bun and the other below in an opposite way. Someone inserted three pairs with one in front of the bun and two beside the bun. Decorations on the comb back gradually became varied and gorgeous, including ornamental engraving with gold plated leaves and pinched and welded decorative designs made out of spun gold and gold grains. In the Grand Tang Dynasty, norms of decoration were comparatively small; in the Middle years of Tang Dynasty, they gradually became bigger; in the late years of Tang Dynasty, they were bigger and bigger, some of which were even twice higher than that of the face.

119 Silver Armlet in the Pattern of Willow Leaf

The armlet is silvery grey. It is a unclosed oblate ring. In the middle of outer side, there is raised edge connecting the two ends which are thinner compared to the middle in a gradual way. The two ends are twined by several cycles of filamentary silver to the end tip where the filamentary silver forms a little ring. The outer of the filamentary silver ends are gyrate, which the inner part is plain and oblate. The entire body bends like a willow leaf.

Armlets are decorations that females wear on their arms. They were introduced to the mainland through the western regions in Western Han Dynasty. At the very beginning, they were rings. In the Jin Dynasties, some armlets' size was adjustable and some were twined into several cycles with a minimum of three and a maximum of ten. In the early Sui Dynasty, armlets were worn on the arms. When it came to Grand Tang and thereafter, armlets were gradually moved down and became wristlets. After Tang Dynasty, most armlets had breaches and they were wide in the middle and narrow at the ends. Their workmanship included gold inlaid with jade, gold inlaid with precious stones and gold and silver mould pressing patterns. Their modeling included the shapes of beads string, twisted wire, pigtail, ring and bamboo joint. Some of them were carved with dragon heads at the two ends.

120 Gilt Silver Armlets with Flying Apsaras Pattern

There two of them. Their bodies are in the shape of willow leaf. Both of them are made of silver, and their surfaces are gilt. In the middle of the leaf shape, there is a raised edge which separates the willow leaf into two parts. Each part is carved a flying Apsaras high up in the air, whose arms are stretching in front of her body, and whose hands are holding something. Gilt Silver Armlets in Flying Apsaras Pattern employ a method of hammering and folding. Flying Apsaras, also known as "Flying celestial nymphs",

are family dependants of senior gods. In the Buddhism pictures, flying celestial nymphs have thousands of gestures. Flying high up in the air, their images are very beautiful. Using flying celestial nymphs as decorations indicates that mysterious estrangement between human beings and gods before Tang Dynasty has been eliminated. The artistic conception of a happy life in religion is one of human beings' spiritual ballasts.

121 Gold Hair Ornaments in the Pattern of"Jin Kuang Bao Dian"

There are two of them, both of which are hair ornaments in the pattern of "Jin Kuang Bao Dian". There are two kinds: one is in the shape of butterfly and the other one is in the shape of phoenix. The hair ornament in the shape of butterfly consist of two "S" shaped rolling lotus patterns which are formed in a horizontally eudipleural way. Its image is like a flying butterfly soaring to great heights. The two rolling lotuses are welded to the goldleaf by the connecting part, while the other part is hollow. The lotus branches and leaves are decorated with fine gold pearl pattern, while the blossoms and inner leaf parts have hollow frame made of thin spun gold strips. In the frame, it is inlaid various jade of all colors. The hair ornament in the shape of phoenix consists of several rolling lotus pattern which assumes the emanative phoenix feathers. The making methods of branches, flowers and petals are the same with those of hair ornament in the shape of butterfly. Most of the inlaid jades fell off. These two hair ornaments in the pattern of "Jin Kuang Bao Dian" employ several complex working procedures, including hammering & folding, wire inlaying, pearl frying, welding, openwork, turned engraving, inlaying and polishing. They are exquisite and excellent in craftsmanship and magnificent in style, which indicate craftsmen's superb skills in Grand Tang Dynasty.

These two ornaments in "Jin Kuang Bao Dian" pattern were excavated from the Xianzhu Jinxiang Tomb of Tang. Xianzhu Jinxiang was the third daughter of Prince Teng who is the twenty-second Emperor Gaozu, Li Yuan, of Tang. She was born in the second year of Yong Hui in the reign of Emperor Gaozong of Tang (651), and died in the Kaiyuan in the reign of Emperor Xuanzong of Tang. She enjoyed a seventy-one-year life. Xianzhu Jinxiang lived in the Grand Tang Dynasty, and she was an imperial clan of Li family who ruled the Tang. In that case, she possessed a distinguished social position, so her funeral objects are generous and rich. These two hair ornaments were what the Xianzhu Jinxiang used to wear.

Ancient Chinese females paid great attention to their prettification and ornamentation. They started to wear flowers on their head in very early. To use gold and silver jewelry to adorn was popular all the time. In Grand Tang Dynasty, females advocated high buns and wearing flowers in the hair became common practice. Females from the upper class favored artificial gold flowers, which were known Jin Dian. When Jin Dian was inlaid with jades, it would be called Bao Dian. Ancient females' hair ornaments are used to adorn, but also to symbolize one's identity and status. In the Sui Shu • Etiquette 6, it is written that, the Empress has four grades of dress. She has twelve hair ornaments in the form of jewelry Dian; the three concubines have nine; others like Gongfuren, Xianzhu, Erpinming have eight. The number becomes less when the female's social position becomes lower. (The lower position, the less.). Tang inherited systems from Sui Dynasty, so Xianzhu Jinxiang was Erpingaoming Lady whose hair ornaments should be eight.

122 Gold Hair Ornament with Trailers

Gold flowers have a leaf-shape pattern and a clustered-flower-shaped pattern. The leaf-shaped flower consists of twisted branch-crossed lotuses, and its shape likes a flower leaf. The clustered flower pattern also consists of twisted branch-crossed lotuses, and its shape likes a ring. The ornament is composed of branches, leaves and blossoms. There used to have inlaid round and peach-shaped jades which fell off. There are a lot of round hole in the branches, leaves and blossoms.

The gold trailer flower ornament plate has six types:

Ⅰ.The first type is oval. Its diameter is 7cm to 5.5cm. Its center has crossed round leaves distributed four directions. Four flowers surround the leaves, and in and out the flower heart, there is a circle of flower leaves. Originally, there are inlaid jades which fell off between the center and the flowers. Among the flower leaves, there are eight holes which are used to decorate thumbtacks. There were inlaid jades on the leaves, too.

Ⅱ.The second type is a spray of branch-broken flowers. It is 8cm in length, and 4.5 in width. As a spray of flowers, its stem threads the blossoms, branches and leaves. On the spray, there are five flowers blossoming towards left. Four of the five flowers were inlaid with jades which fell off.

Ⅲ.The third type is also a spray of branch-broken flowers. It is a spray of flowers. Its stem threads the blossoms, branches and leaves. On the spray, there are five flowers blossoming towards left. Four of the five flowers were inlaid with jades which fell off.

Ⅳ.The forth type is a spray of branch-broken flowers with little leaves. It is 3cm in length. It is a spray of flowers. On its stem grow plenty of little leaves. Originally, there are inlaid jades which fell off on each little leaf, leaving hole on them.

Ⅴ.The fifth type is a spray of branch-broken flowers with big leaves. It is 3.5cm in length. It is a spray of flowers. On its stem grows plenty of big leaves. Originally, there are inlaid jades which fell off on each big leaf, leaving hole on them.

Ⅵ.The sixth type is plum flower-shaped ornament. It is 6 in length. On the stem grows plum flowers.

123 Gold Lindens

There are two gold lindens, which are composed of a trunk, brunches, flowers and leaves. There are flowers and leaves covering the big and small branches. There are also burls on the trunks around which a vine is twining from the bottom up. The root is exposed at the trunk bottom of every linden. The flowers on the tree were originally inlaid kallaites. Gold trees with green flowers and strong trunk with gentle vine are particularly gorgeous and dazzlingly eye-catching, producing a feeling of being massive and rigorous. On the trunks, roots and part of the leaves, there are holes which are used to thread thumbtacks. In that case, the two lindens ought to be accessories to some utensil. The making of the two lindens are made in good taste, proportion and density.

Lindens are trees originally grew in the regions of southern Asia. They are evergreen trees. Their leaves are egg-shaped, their trunks are yellow and white, and their receptacles are slightly global, where the flowers hide in. Their fruits are oblate and become dark purple when they are ripe. The fruit seeds can be used as prayer beads, so Buddhists always use the linden seeds to make prayer beads. It was said that it was under the linden tree that Siddhartha Gautama the founder of Buddhism contemplated and awoke to attain Buddhahood. Therefore, on the aspect of Buddhists, lindens are consciousness trees and reason trees and they are the symbol of Buddhism. The production and distribution of these lindens indicate that Buddhism was blended into China in Tang Dynasty, and it became a part that would affect the cultural accumulation in the life of the upper. These two lindens are made by hammering and folding, and they have inlaid kallaites. They are beautiful natural and vivid in modeling, indicating that craftsmen of Tang were superbly skillful.

124 Gilt Walking Dragon

The entire walking dragon is gilt. It gestures walking. Left legs are backward, while right ones forward. Its mouth is sharp, opening to show the teeth. Its tongue is long and rolling. It has a single horn and its ears stand. Curls on its head are backward. Its back ridge is in the shape of serration. Its long tail is trailing with its end rolling up. The entire body is engraved fish scales. Its legs are long with three toes. It is muscular, strong, energetic and powerful, and its looks and manners are dignified, showing that it is high-spirited and confident. It shows a vigorous vitality and flourishing vigor. Dragons are imaginative animals. Embodying most of Chinese national characteristics, the dragon pattern is one of the most widely used and most vigorous materials in Chinese traditional emblazonry. In Tang Dynasty, dragons are not exclusive to imperial families. So the engraving of this walking dragon was made by the artists who cast it based on the animals in reality and employed high skills and accurate body cutting skills. This lively and lifelike gilt walking dragon mainly shows the aesthetes in Grand Tang Dynasty.

125 Gold Phoenix

There are three of them, who share the same modeling and decoration method. The gold Feng intend to fly with its two wings stretching and its two feet stepping on the ground. It heads high comb and its long floss floating backwards. It has short beak and phoenix eyes, eyeing to the front. It neck crooks, its chest straightens, and its tail rolls. Every bunch of tail feathers is in the shape of crossed branches and leaves. It lays over and over until to a clump of buds and flower leaves at the top. Originally, there were inlaid kallaites on its chest, belly and flying feathers. Its wings, tail and feet act in a harmonious way, highly dynamic. The momentary action of the gold Feng's intending to raise high into the air was grasped and vividly engraved. Its comb, wings, tail end and feet all have a hole, which is used for fixing thumbtacks. These three gold Luan and Feng are excavated together with the maintained Gold Dragon and Gold Duck, so it might be an accessory to the gold decoration plate of some utensil. The gold Feng's shape is full and round, which are the two characteristics of Feng in Tang Dynasty. Feng is a symbol of mysterious spirit at that time. "Feng and Huang are the best among birds with feathers". Feng symbolizes lofty and honor, so it represents the empress and concubines. Feng is also one of the four direction showing sprites in ancient China, and it stands for the south and summer.

126 Gold Dragon

The dragon is running high up in the air. It has a long head and a single horn, which is rolling backwards. It has big eyes and wide mouth. There are three tufts of beards under its eyes and ears. Its two fore limbs are stretching out like buck-jumping. Its paw has three toes. Its body is straight, while its neck and back curl, forming taper angles. Its long tail is straight and the twig is rolling. Its back limbs are squatting. Its paws are sharp. The entire dragon scales are distinct and fine. The whole shape is strong, vigorous and powerful. Part under the body is hollow and inlaid kallaites. On the dragon's horn, three paws and tail, there is a hole, which is used to thread thumbtacks. Therefore, this gold dragon might be one accessory to some utensil. As one of the four direction showing sprites in ancient China, the dragon stands for the east and the spring.

127 Leaf-shaped Gold-Quinto Ornament with Inlaid Kallaites

There two of them. The spike has a irregular leaf-shaped gold frame, whose edge is decorated with a circle of Lianzhu pattern. It is inlaid with kallaites and carved with shallow carving layers of lotus leaves. Those leaves blossom and those lotus flowers flower. A couple of mandarin ducks are swimming among the leaves and flowers.

128 Gold Ducks

There are two gold ducks, which are the same in terms of shaping and decorating method. The duck has a long beak and a crooked neck. It intends to fly with two spreading wings and two feet stepping on the ground. It eyes to the front, and it trails tail backwards, forming the shape of Ruyi cloud head. Originally, there were inlaid kallaites on its chest, belly and flying feathers. On one of its wings and the end of its tail, there is a little hole, inside which there is a thumbtack functioning fixation. This gold duck is one accessory to some utensil.

129 Peach-shaped Gold Ornament

The gold ornament's appearance is like a peach. Around its edge is a circle of tiny united pearl motif. Next to its edge are inlaid two gold plaques with the shape border. On the gold plaques there are little round case-shaped ornament in united pearl motif. In the center of the peach, there is a six-petalled plum flower which is surrounded and protected by leaf patterns. The plum flower is hollow. The pearl pattern serves as the background. Originally, there are inlaid precious stones on the plum flower and the leaf pattern, but they fell off. On the back is a rectangle handle.

130 Heart-shaped Gold Flower Ornament

With a heart-shaped form, this ornament's center is decorated with a plum flower pattern which is hammered and folded out, and there are flower leaves above and below the plum flower pattern. Around the edge is a circle of Lianzhu Pattern, and the rest part is decorated with pearl pattern as background. There used to have inlaid precious stones in the plum flowers and Lianzhu pattern, but they fell off now.

131 Fan-shaped Gold Flower Ornament

The outer shape is like an expanding fold fan, only half remained. The flower leaves pattern fills the middle area; a circle of Lianzhu pattern decorates the edge, while the pearl pattern adorns the rest area as the background. There were inlaid precious stones on the flower leaves and Lianzhu pattern, but they dropped off. On the back are line engraved with honeysuckle pattern and pearl pattern serving as the back ground.

132 Gold Hinge

t is one of the components of boxes and baskets. It consists of two gold-plate curlicues. There is a hollow-out peach-shaped pattern, two cloud-shaped patterns and five holes, which are used for binding, on each plate of the hinge. The two plates are riveted by a spindle to form a hinge. The riveting technique is a great invention in gold and silver ware techniques in Tang Dynasty. The riveting of gold and silver wares is to hole little holes on the union piece and the main part, and then drift bolts through the holes. This method is always employed when making small pieces of artifacts. This shows that there were simple machine tools at that time.

133 Silver Hinge

It is one of the components of boxes and baskets.It is made of silver.It consists of two silver pieces. Each of them has an arc shape on one side and a riveted ring on the other side.On the its back, there are three cap-shaped silver nails for binding.The two pieces are riveted by a by a spindle to form a hinge.

134 Gilt Silver Chain Lock with a Bronze Dragon Head

The chain is weaved by silver filaments. There are dragon-head-shaped locks on the end of the silver chain. The dragon heads are made of copper and their surfaces are gilt. The dragon head has a single horn, a long mouth, big eyes, sharp teeth, big ears, long beards, and an up-rolling nose. It is biting a round ring serving as the lock catch. The dragon head is welded to the chain. Modeling of this chain is quite similar to that of the necklace worn by the gilt gold Bodhisattva, and they also share the similar proportion, so they might belong to religious articles. It is supposed that it was worn by monks or kulapatis. The purpose of wearing it is to worship Buddha and to protect and maintain the Buddha dharma.

Buddhism advocates to find happiness out of bitterness, it requests Buddhists to be resigned to the status quo and willing to stand all the bitterness. This Gilt Silver Chain Lock with a Bronze Dragon Head belongs to adorning wares of the monks and kulapatis. It is exquisitely made and the materials are expensive. This reflects the social economic development level and the development degree of the Buddhism cloisters in Tang Dynasty.

135 Gold Jaw Holder

The plain jaw holder is made of thin gold plates by hammering and folding. The entire shape is oval. The holder is oval and concave in the middle. It is spherical and used to hold a person's jaw. The left and the right side of the jaw holder have oblate long arc handles which are used to set the jaw holder. It is a funerary object. Funerary objects are objects that put on the decedents or in their coffins and buried together with the corpses. The purposes that ancient people used gold as funerary objects are as follows: first, the ancient people believed that corpses would not become rotten if they were wrapped in gold. Chemical compositions of gold are steady, and it will not easily react with other metals, so it lasts forever. Using gold to wrap corpses will prevent corpses from rotten. Second, gold and silver are precious metals. Only people with high social status could use them as food vessels and funerary objects. So using gold and silver wares is a symbol of the tomb owner's social status.

This jaw holder is similar to the jaw holder of the gold mask in the Shi Daode's Tomb, which's made in the third year of Yifeng (675) in the reign of Emperor Gaozong of Tang and excavated in Guyuan County, Ningxia Hui Autonomous Region in 1999 in term of modeling. The ancestors of Shi Daode were men from Shi Country among the nine surnames of Zhaowu (Sogdian) in Middle Asia in Tang Dynasty. His ancestors moved to the inner land in Southern and Northern Dynasties. At the same time, they brought with them the funerary habits of the nine surnames of Zhaowu in Middle Asia. From the gold coin in Shi Daoshi's mouth and the design of round animal in the gold, this mask shows that their funeral concepts are related to the Zoroastrianism that Suteren believed. Zoroastrianism was created by Zoroaster, Persian in the 5th century BCE, and was popular in Persian and countries in Middle Asia. King of Ancient Persian Empire, Darius I ade it the state religion. It worships the supreme God, Ahura Mazda, who stands for light and happiness. It makes fire as the symbol of light. It stipulates that worshipping the holy fire is its major ritual, so it is also called Mazdaism. Its fundamental characteristic is publicizing the concept of universal struggling between good and evil, light and dark, which affected the formation of Christian in era of Roma Empire. It was introduced to China in Wei-Jin and the Northern and Southern Dynasties by Sogdian of Middle Asia, and it was called Zoroastrianism or Mazdaism.

From this, this gold jaw holder reflected the funeral customs that Sogdian kept when they moved to the northwestern regions of China from Northern Dynasty to Tang Dynasty.

136 Gilt Bronze Western Tri-saints Statue

The statue consists of a sunflower-shaped high hollow stand, a Chinese flowering crab-apple-shaped socket, a flower receptacle, a Buddha, two and bodhisattvas. Western tri-saints are Amitabha who leads beings toward Sukhavati, Kwan-yin who is the left costa servant, and Mahasthamaprapta who is the right costa servant. They three together are called Western Tri-saints, and also known as Three Statues of Amitabha. Amitabha has a high meat bun, big ears and a moderate round physiognomy. He also has curved brows and beautiful eyes. There are two silkworm section-shaped lines around his neck. He wears a 2-way collar kasaya, and inside the kasaya is a holy shirt . He wears a pair of long pantskirt. His right arm bends upwards at the elbow, and his five fingers are straight up, and the palm is outward and applied Abhaya Mudra. His left arm hangs down, and the palm is inward and placed on the left knee and applied KrissSword which is also known as Earth-touching Sign. It is to put the hands on the knees, and the fingers touch the ground to defeat the evils. The soles of the feet are upward and they bend in front of the belly and sit cross-legged on the round base. The edge of his cloth covers the round base. The left costa servant Kwan-yin wears an ornate crown of the Buddha, whose bands hang down to the shoulders. His ears also hang down to the shoulders. He has a moderate round physiognomy. He also has curved brows and beautiful eyes. His nose bridge is high. There are two silkworm section-shaped lines around his neck, which is decorated with two pearl and jade necklaces with rings. On his right shoulder, there is a slant long pearl and jade necklace. He wears bracelets. He bares upper body, and wears a long dress from the navel. He is the Amitabha who leads people to the Western Paradise. A long scarf goes around his arms and then hangs down. His right arm bends upwards, holding a sallow, while his left arm hangs down, carrying a white vase. He sits cross-legged on the round base, which a sheet of clothing on the top. The right costa servant Mahasthamaprapta wears an ornate crown whose bends hang down to the shoulders. His neck is decorated with two pearl and jade necklaces. His left shoulder has a slant long pearl and jade necklace, and he wears bracelets. He has a moderate round physiognomy, and his ears hang down to the shoulders. He also has curved brows and beautiful eyes. There are two silkworm section-shaped lines around his neck. He bares upper body, and wears a long dress from the navel. His left arm bends up and holds a vase-shaped item, while his right arm hangs down and carries a lotus. He sits cross-legged on the base which has a sheet of clothing on its top. The Tri-saints all have a hollow halo each. The halo is surrounded by burning fire pattern, within which is decorated with lotus branches, lotus petals and rhombic and checkered patterns. The bases they sit on are lotus flowers on the same branch. Under the branch is a petal-shaped high bed.

Amitabha is a name of the Buddhist, and one of the four Buddhists in four directions. The four Buddhists are: Akahobhya in the East Land of Happiness, Ratnasambhababuddha in the South Land of Delight, Amitabha in the West Land of Elysium and Amoghasiddhi in the North Land of Lotus. Amitabha is the hierarch of the Western Paradise. It is said that one can regain life in bliss even if he says the courtesy name of Amitabha. Amitabha has a lot of courtesy names, such as Amitayus Buddha, Escorts Buddha, Buddha of Wisdom Light, and Buddha of Happiness Light. He is the major belief object of the Pure Land. Mahasthamaprepta is also a name of Bodhisattva. In Buddhism, wherever he is, the world will be shocked. He is powerful and influential to extinguish disasters of all kinds. His out-looking is quite like a

female. He has a big meat bun on the top of his head, and on the bun there is a precious vase, containing light. His right hand always holds a heliotrope and his left hand poses Fear-not Sign with great sympathy. It is also said that, he can empower the ones in the hell and drive them out of their miseries. He is embodiment of wisdom, so he is worshipped by people together with Kwan-yin the embodiment of mercy.

137 Gilt Standing Buddha Statue

The Buddha is standing. He wears a high arango hat, on which there are three lotus buds, and in front of which there is a transformed Buddha. The two sides of the precious silk fabrics hang down. He has a round square physiognomy with smiles. He also has curved brows and beautiful eyes. There are two silkworm section-shaped lines around his neck with a chaplet and pearl and jade necklaces. The pearl and jade necklaces are decorated with round flowers at the part in front of his belly and their ends hang down to the sides of his feet. He wears a long skirt and stands on the round base with bare feet. Under the base is placed an overturned lotus-shaped base. The waistband behind hangs a ring knots. There is a tenon behind, which is used to fix the halo that is round and has two divided areas. The outer area is carved with braches-crossed leaves, while the inner area has multicoated relief sculptures in the shape of lotus leaves, up which is decorated three directional floriation. The center is a round raised shape, around which is carved a circle of lotus petals. On the lotus petals, there are square cloud-shaped scarf band. At the five knots, there are engraved a relief. The entire statue is gilt.

138 Gilt Standing Devaraja Statue

Devaraja is one of the Guardian Deity—Four Lords. His hair stands straight like a burning flame and he stares with raised eye-brows. His naked upper body is covered with a long scarf. He wears a long skirt with a girdle. He is muscular. His left arm is hanging down with the palm downwards and the five fingers pointing to the left. His right arm uplifts and holds a vajra. He stands on a base which has an overturned lotus-shaped below and an upward lotus-shaped above with bare feet. Upper the shoulders there is a round halo. Guardian Deities are the gods that protect the Buddhism and its worshipper. Vajra is said the hardest weapon in Buddhism, and it can destroy everything, so it is one of the musical instruments used in a Buddhist mass.

139 Gilt Standing Buddha

The Buddha is standing. He has a high topknot, a plump face, thin eye-brows, beautiful eyes, a high nose bridge and big ears. He wears a kasaya on the left shoulder, and a thin and transparent long skirt. His right arm bends upwards at the elbow with the palm facing out and five fingers upwards, posing a gesture symbolizing medication on emptiness. His left arm is hanging down, and his left hand holds a pearl. He stands on the base which has an overturned lotus-shaped below and an upward lotus-shaped above with bare feet. Under the base is an octagonal high-profile with four stories.

140 Gilt Sitting Buddha Statue

The Buddha has a high topknot, a moderate and radius face, thin eyebrows, slightly closed eyes, and a big micro-sipping mouth. His ears hang down to the shoulders, and there are silk lines around his neck. He wears a collar drooping kasaya, and the tie crosses the right shoulder and the front belly then hangs on the back of the left shoulder. He wears a holy shirt under the kasaya and a long skirt with a waistband, which ties a knot in front of the left part of the belly. The hem of the skirt covers the base. He bends his right arm up at the elbow with the palm facing out, holding a withy with five broken fingers. His left arm places on his left lap with the palm upward. Five fingers of the left hand extend straight posing. Mudra of teaching is a gesture which is made by twirling the thumb with the middle finger, the forefinger, or the ring finger, and the rest naturally spread. This gesture symbolizes the Buddha is teaching the Buddhism. His legs hang down, full-lotus posture on the broken base. His bare feet are stepping on two lotus blossoms.

141 Gilt Standing Bodhisattva Statue

The Buddha has a wavelike mound of flesh. His face is square and round, and eyebrows are thin. His eyes are slightly open and look down. His nose bridge is high and straight, his ears are big and his neck is short. His facial expressions are solemn and grand. He wears a kasaya baring the right shoulder. He gestures a hero posture on the overturned girdled lotus Xu Mi base, which has a compress on the top, hanging down. Over and below the overturned lotus base, there is an octagonal stylobate with two stories. Upper part of the girdle is covered by the compress. His right arm uplifts at the elbow with the palm facing outwards and fingers closing together, gesturing meditation on emptiness. His left palm is inward, and fingers spread straight and place on the left knee, gesturing a KrissSword posture. Behind his back there is an oblate tenson which has a hole. It is might be used to fix the halo. This Buddha is exquisitely and skillful made, especially the compress on the girdled pedestal. The waves of the compress are carved with rich feeling of texture.

142 Gilt Tri-Bodhisattva Sitting Statue

The three Bodhisattvas all wear crowns, chaplets, armlets and bracelets. Their upper bodies are all naked, and they wear long skirts. Their right arm uplifts at the elbow with items in hand. Their left arm places on the left knee. His right leg hangs down, while the left one is on the lotus base, posing playfully. The three Bodhisattvas sit on a round base each. The three bases are placed on a rectangular bed. They have a petal-shaped halo on each of their shoulders and each halo is carved with flame pattern cut in intaglio. Halos of the two Bodhisattvas on the right have a sitting Buddha on the top, while the halo of the Bodhisattva on the left is broken.

143 Gilt Sitting Kwan-yin Bodhisattva Statue

Kwan-yin Bodhisattva wears a crown of Buddha, and the crown bands hang down along the sides of both arms. His upper body is naked and one of his shoulders is covered with a pearl and jade necklace. He also wears a long skirt, a necklace, armlets, and bracelets. His right arm uplifts at the elbow with the palm facing outwards and fingers pointing to the upper right. His left hand places on his left leg. His right leg hangs down and steps on a sub-lotus, while his left leg overlaps on the right one, gesturing a hero posture on a base which has an overturned lotus-shaped below and an upward lotus-shaped above with bare feet, and the bottom edge presents octagonal. Under the base, there is a rectangular bed. This statue has an oval face, beautiful features, raised chest, and obvious female features, and his manners are peaceful and serene. His head slightly lowers, looking down, which makes people feel he is worshipful and affable.

144 Gilt Hollowed-out Sitting Bodhisattva Statue

The za-zening Bodhisattva is all gilt with a high blossom crown on hair, and its belts sag to shoulder which has a long scarf on it. The scarf ends hang on the seat. His necklace incised with a thread of collar. The buddaha wears a light fitted dress. His right arm sags, with hand on the right knee, and left arm ascending with a treasure in his hand. His left bending leg is in front of his bingy and his right barefoot leg is trampling on a lotus throne. The throne is covered with dressing towel on top and has a four feet square bed below. Behind the Bodhisattva, there is a hollowed-out backlight peach ornament with flame pattern around. On the top and two sides, two Bodhisattvas are on the flourishing lotus.

145 Gilt Standing Buddha Statue

The Bodhisattva statue is standing. He wears a high crown, whose bands surpass the shoulders and hang down to the ground. His upper body is naked and he wears a thin and light long skirt fitting his body well. He also wears a waistband which knots a cockade in front of the belly. His shoulders are covered with long scarves, which hang along the arms down to the both sides of the Xu Mi Zuo. He has a plum face, thin and arched eyebrows, and square cheeks. He wears bracelets. His left arm hangs down, and his left hand carryings a white vase. His right arm bends upwards at the elbow with a horsetail whisk. With his writhed body, he stands on the oval lotus-like girdled Xu Mi pedestal, under which there is an octagonal high-profile with four stories. There is a square tenon behind the Bodhisattva to fix the halo.

146 Gilt Sitting Buddha Statue

The Buddha statue has a polished high mound of flesh, a moderately plum face, a broad forehead, a square face, big ears, thin eyebrows, a short neck and slightly opened eyes looking down. He is wearing a thin and light kasaya fitting to him with his right shoulder exposed. He sits on the overturned girdled lotus Xu Mi pedestal with a hero posture. On the top of the pedestal is covered with a compress, which hangs down and forms the inverted "Mountain" word. Under the pedestal there a two-story octagonal stylobate. His right arm uplifts at the elbow with a broken hand. His left hand palm is inward and his left hand places on the left knee with fingers point downwards straightly, gesturing a KrissSword posture. Behind his back there is an oblate tenson which has a hole. It is might be used to fix the halo. The proportion of this statue is appropriate, and it is exquisitely made. The lines of the clothes are smooth, and the approaches are realistic. It also has a strong secular atmosphere. The image and manners are quite like those of the real life characters of dignitaries. This is the characteristic of the Buddha statues in Tang Dynasty.

147 Gilt Sitting Buddha Statue

The Buddha statue is sitting. He has a spiral high mound of flesh, a plump face, thin eyebrows connecting to the nose bridge, lightly opened eyes, and a high and straight nose bridge. His mouth upturns, smiling. His facial expressions are dignified and solemn. He wears a double collar hanging on through the shoulder-style coat, and a holy shirt inside. He also wears a pair of trousers, sitting on the overturned girdled lotus Xu Mi pedestal, gesturing a hero posture. On the top of the pedestal is covered with a compress, which hangs down and forms the inverted "Mountain" word. The lowest story is an oval base. His right arm uplifts at the elbow with the palm facing outwards and fingers closing together, gesturing meditation on emptiness. His left palm is inward, and fingers spread straight and place on the left knee. Behind his back there is an oblate tenson which has a hole. It is might be used to fix the halo. The Buddha statue is exquisite in making, plump in shaping, and realistic in technique. His attitude is modest and simple with a strong secular atmosphere, reflecting the real life at that time.

148 Gilt Sitting Buddha Statue

The Buddha statue is sitting. He has a wavelike mound of flesh, in the center of which there is a nipple-like nail. His head is lowering slightly. He has an oval face, ears hanging down to the shoulders and a square forehead. He has delicate features. His eyes slightly open and look down. His mouth upturns, smiling. There are two lines on his neck. He wears a double collar hanging on through the shoulder-style coat, and a long skirt. His right arm uplifts at the elbow with the palm facing outwards and fingers closing together, gesturing meditation on emptiness. His left palm is upward and places on the left knee. He is sitting with a hero posture. The statue is plump in face making, delicate in look portraying, and implicit in facial expressions, appearing vivid and vibrant.

149 Gilt Standing Buddhist Arhat Statue

The Buddhist arhat is standing. He has a bare head, a round face, a square forehead, thick eyebrows and big ears. He is smiling. He wears a high-necked kaftan inside and a kasaya outside. He cups his fist in the other hand before the chest. He stands on a round pedestal, under which there are three short feet. The entire expression is moderate, friendly and easy-going.It was gilt but most of the gilding fell off.

150 Standing Kwan-yin Bodhisattva Statue

The Bodhisattva is standing. He wears a crown, whose bands float on the pedestal. He has a plump face, arched eyebrows, and thin eyes. He is smiling gently. On his shoulders, there is a boat-shaped hollow halo, which has a sitting Buddha on the top. His body twists to the right, posturing naturally. The upper body is naked. He wears a light-yarn long skirt. His left arm hangs down, and his left hand carryings a white vase. His right arm bends upwards at the elbow with a horsetail whisk. With his writhed body, he stands on the oval lotus-like girdled Xu Mi pedestal, under which there is a square bed with four feet. The chest of the Bodhisattva rises, full of female features. His posture is gentle and beautiful and his facial expressions are moderate and glad, showing the female's graceful body. The subtle and moving outline of the entire body is full of ups and downs. The soft and light skirt material shows the abundant energy of the smooth skin and plump body.

151 Gilt Buddhist Provider

The provider has a topknot and a round face. He wears a double collar hanging on through the shoulder-style coat with wide sleeves. He also wears a long skirt with a waistband. He stands on the upward lotus pedestal, under which there are branch and leaf patterns. His right arm rises at the elbow, holding a treasure bead in the hand. His left arm rises at the elbow with the palm upward and fingers slightly curving.

152 Gilt Sitting Buddha Statue

The Buddha statue has a high mound of flesh, a plump face, thin eyebrows, thin eyes which are slightly closed like concentrating on thinking. There are two silk lines around his neck. His right arm uplifts at the elbow with the palm facing outwards and five fingers extending straight, gesturing meditation on emptiness. His left palm is inward, and fingers spread straight and place on the left knee, gesturing a KrissSword posture. He wears a double collar hanging on through the shoulder-style coat, and a holy shirt inside. The collar edge is decorated with wavelike pattern, and the belly is decorated with rhombic and checkered patterns. He is on the overturned girdled lotus pedestal in a hero posture. Up the girdle is covered by the hanging down compress and kasaya. Under the girdle is a two-story five-round-petal-shaped pedestal, and the lowest story is an oval base which has a oblate square tenon with a hole on both sides. The tenon might be used to fix the statue. On his back there is a oblate square tenon, which is broken, to fix the halo. The statue body is plump and stocky, graceful and generous, which show his vividness and vitality. It also presents his open mind and detachment of the inner spirit. The carved lines of the clothes are smooth, reaching an unprecedented maturement and perfection, so it is a classical production of Grand Tang Dynasty.

153 Gilt Standing Kwan-yin Bodhisattva Statue

The Bodhisattva is standing and he is gilt all over. He wears a high flower crown, which has an aquarius in the front. The two sides of the precious silk fabrics float down naturally along the outside of the arm. His face is plump. He wears a necklace and a silk scarf on the shoulder. His upper body is naked. His left arm hangs down, and his left hand carryings a white vase. His right arm bends upwards at the elbow with a horsetail whisk. There are pearl and jade necklaces on his body from the left shoulder to the front of his calves. He wears a light and thin long skirt fitting his body well. He stands on the oval lotus-like girdled Xu Mi pedestal with bare feet. This statue has graceful and beautiful facial features, and quiet and harmonious manners. The proportion of the body is appropriate. The body is slightly bent

"S" shape. His posture is vigorous and graceful, and stances are mild and moving. The beauty of gentle outlines and rhythmic aromas are fully presented in term of artistic modeling. It has the beauty to move and touch people.

154 Gilt Hollow-out Sitting Kwan-yin Bodhisattva Statue

The Bodhisattva wears a crown on the head, nothing on the upper body and a light and thin long skirt fitting to his body. He also wears a necklace. A long scarf covers his shoulder, crosses his arm and hangs down to the bottom of the pedestal. His right arm is hanging down on the right knee with the palm facing downwards, while his left arm uplifts at the elbow, holding a horsetail whisk. His left leg bends in front of the belly and his right leg hangs down and steps on the round pedestal with a barefoot. He is on the overturned girdled lotus Xu Mi pedestal in a hero posture. On the pedestal there is a compress, and under the pedestal is a square bed with four feet. Above his shoulders there a plain and boat-shaped halo which has a decoration of a transformed Buddha on the top.

155 Gilt Standing Kwan-yin Bodhisattva Statue

The Kwan-yin Bodhisattva wears an ornate high Corolla, which has a transformed Buddha in the middle. The bands of the Corolla flow down to the shoulders, which are covered by a long scarf. The upper naked body is obliquely hung a pearl and jade necklace. He wears a fitting draggle-tail with a waistband. He also wears a necklace of beads as well as a chaplet and bracelets. The right shoulder is covered with a pearl and jade necklace which hangs down to the knee. His face shape is round and square, his forehead is broad, his eyes are beautiful and eyebrows are thin. He smiles gently. There is a silk line around his neck. His right arm uplifts at the elbow with broken hands, and his left arm broken, too. He stands on the overturned girdled lotus pedestal with barefoot. Under the pedestal there is a high octagonal stylobate. Behind his head there is a tenon used to fix the halo.

156 Gilt Standing Kwan-yin Bodhisattva Statue

The Bodhisattva wears a crown, whose bands hand over the forearms, with a transformed Buddha. The half naked statue is covered with the embroidered cape hanging on the shoulders and a long skimpy soft skirt at the bottom. He is wearing a necklace and a long pearl ornament hanging over the left ankle. Her right arm forward with forearms upward is holding a horsetail whisk, while her left arm is hanging down with a pure vase . With her writhed body she stands barefoot on the oval lotus-liked girdled Sumeru pedestal, under which there are two tenons to fix the statues.

157 Gilt Silver Coffin with Buddhist Relic

This one and the following gilt bronze coffin make a set. This silver consists of a lid and a body. The lid is a long lu roof, and the body is a cuboid. The lid and the body are inserted together. Under the body is a base stand with two flights of steps. One end is higher and wider than the other. The upper part is small while the lower part is big and both of them have contractures. The entire coffin is engraved with emblazonry, on the top of which is gilt. On the top are five braches-crossed flowers. Emblazonry both on the left and the right are the same, a Kalavinka bird who has a human head and a bird body. The bird's both hands hold a lotus. Its long tail is in the shape of three flower leaves, rolling upwards layer by layer. There are plenty of flowers in the sky. There is a lotus in front and at the back of the lid. The lotus is fully surrounded by leaves. The edge of the lid is carved with a circle of braches-crossed flowers. On the body is engraved with the picture of Nirvana Sutra Change. In the middle of the picture is engraved with Xu Mizuo with plenty of flower leaves pattern. The upper part of the picture tells the situation when Sakyamuni was reaching the state of Nirvana. Sakyamuni is lying on the side. His head is on his bent right arm. In front of the bed is a woman, who places her right hand on the bed and covers her face with her left hand, crying. Behind the woman is a Buddhist monk. Behind the bed is a disciple who wears a kasaya. His left hand is touching Sakyamuni's feet. There is another disciple closely behind the first one. On the right side of the coffin is decorated with a circle of leaf petal pattern at the bottom part. Surrounding the leaf-petal pattern is engraved with branches-crossed flowers. The front side is a Buddha, who has a high meat bun, twofold ears. The Buddha is wearing a kasaya, posing hero posture, on the lotus base with a round halo. On both sides of the round halo are decorated with a bunch of flowers. The back side is the same. The bottom edge of the coffin is engraved with overlapped lotus petals extending towards both sides. Around the flight of steps is carved with braches-crossed pattern and pot door pattern.

158 Gilt Bronze Coffin with Buddhist Relics

This Gilt Bronze Coffin with Buddhist Relic and the former Gilt Silver Coffin with Buddhist Relic are a set. The entire coffin is gilt. The bronze coffin consists of a coffin lid, a coffin room and a coffin base. The lid is raised, and its front part is high and wide, while its back part is narrow and short. The coffin room is a slant cubiod, the front room is high raised and wide with a carved beast face and the back room arch is narrow and short. Each of the four corners of the coffin room's bottom has a dowel, inserting into the four corners of the coffin bed. The coffin base is trapezoid-shaped with a big front and a small back. It has two flights of steps. The bottom layer has three hollow rectangular pot doors on both sides and one

on the front as well as the back. The pot doors are decorated with wave pattern. Inner wall of the coffin is painted with cinnabar. There is a green bottle of Buddhist relics. The green bottle was broken, and inside it there are some irregular yellow Buddhist relics. The custom of enshrining and worshipping Buddhism Relics in gold and silver wares dated back to the Northern Wei Dynasty. With the extensive popularity of Buddhism, this trend became more and more intensified when it came to the Tang Dynasty, especially when it was the time after the reign of Emperor Xuanzong of Tang. Buddhism doctrines took absolute advantages in the belief of the imperial Dynasty. This trend was the most popular until Song and Liao Dynasties when they still kept the custom of keeping the Buddhism relic in gold and silver wares. Buddhism relics refer to the Buddhist corpse bone left after incineration. In addition, Buddhism classics are also called Buddhism relics, but the former one refers to Mami relics. In some Buddhism books, it is said that relics of Sakyamuni Buddha are broken body relics, while relics of Treasure Buddha refer to the whole body relics. Wei Shu · Tonnochy Release says, after the Buddhist died, burn his body with scented wood; his bones are broken like grains which can not be hit down or burnt. Some of them have light and experiences so they are called Buddhist relics. His pupils gathered them and worshipped them in a precious bottle, and put fragrant flowers and show respects toward them. The constructions built to put the relics are call pagodas. "Fa Yuan Zhu Lin · Saria Articles" says: "Saria means bones in Sanskrit. This name is used to separate the holy monks' bones from the ordinary. There are three types of Saria: the Buddhist bone relics which are white, the Buddhist hair relic which is black and the Buddhist flesh relics which is red. There are three kinds of Buddha and Buddhist arhat. If there are relics of a Buddha, they can not be hit broken. If they are relics of Buddha's pupil, they would be hit broken. The Saria are also known as holy bones or gold bones. If they are the inanimate bones, they can be replaced by gold, silver, pearls, crystals, agates, ambers and even glass. They can also be replaced by medical herbs, bamboo's roots, corn grains. They are called Sariputra. The classics of Buddhism are called Dharma–body relics.

159 Gold Ingot with"Yao Zhou"Inscription

The ingot is golden yellow, oblate and rectangular. The surface is uneven, and edges and corners are not clear. There are six characters in regular script "Yao Zhou Gong Jin Shi Liang" cut in relief. The carry of currency in Tang Dynasty is ten qian for one liang, equal to 43g. According to the Weights and Measures Act in Tang Liu Dian in 721 A.D, "Length, capacity and weight have two units, one big and one small. One chi and two cun of small chi equals to one big chi. Three small dou is one big dou. Three small liang is one big liang. " Officials and ordinary people often used the big unit system in daily life and used the small unit system in adjusting the bell tune, astronomy and medicine. This gold ingot weighs 41.2g, so it should be made according to the big liang system. Yaozhou was in the region of Jiannandao of Tang Dynasty, which is now the area of Dali, Chuxiong, and Kunming in middle and western part of Yunnan Provintce. Zhouzhi is in the north of the Yao'an County, Shaanxi Province. When it was in the reign of Emperor of Xuanzong of Tang, Nanzhao Country which was in the southwest of Yunnan and the northeast of Burma became more and more powerful. It defeated Tang army several times and Yaozhu was occupied by it. In that case, this gold ingot as a tribute was paid by Yaozhou during the time after Emperor of Gaozong and before Emperor of Xuanzong.

Tang's gold production mainly distributed in the south, and to the most in Hunan Province. On the production in Yunnan, Fan Zhuo's works– "About Man" , chapter seven of Yunnan says, "Gold comes from Li Water and sands replaces it." Here Li water refers to Jinsha River, the upper reaches of Yangtze River. Yaozhou was in the south of Jinsha River.

Gold and silver ingots are one of gold and silver currencies. The name of ingot first appeared in Tang Liu Dian, "tough silk is measured by pi, cloth by duan, cotton by tun, silk by xun, linen by li, gold and silver by ding, money by guan." The discovery of gold ingots is rare. In April, 1977, two gold ingots were excavated in the Eastern Market of Chang'an City of Tang in Beilin District, Xi'an City, and eight–two in Tang cache in Tunjingou, Pinglu County, Shanxi Province. Five of the eight–two are engraved with inscriptions. There are more silver ingots of Tang excavated mainly in Chang'an and Luoyang and less in other areas. In accordance with different weights, silver ingots of Tang can be divided into four categories: fifty liang, forty liang, ten liang, five liang. According to their shapes and modeling, they can be divided into three categories: the one with straight body, flat or arc head; the girdled one with flat head; the boat–shaped one or the raft–shaped one.

The casting of silver ingots has two types: one cast by the central government and one by the local government. The former one is always noted by inscriptions and the tribute silver ingots cast by the local government to the central will be inscribed the casting aim, location and the handling officials. The later one is always cast to pay taxes and tributes to the court. In Song Dynasties, silver ingots were more widely used than before. Ingots of Northern Song have three shapes and modeling: one has flat head, slightly girdled waist, and a surface which is bigger than the bottom; one has an arc head, girdled waist, and slight raised center; one has a round head, girdled waist, and slightly raised center. Most of these three types of silver ingots are noted fifty liang, equal to 2kg. They are sacrifices to the court from the local government.

Ingots of Southern Song can be divided into several grades according to their weights. In the early years of Southern Song, the sacrificed ingots have two grades of fifty liang and twenty liang. Later, there were three grades: the large one of fifty liang, medium one of twenty–five liang, and small one of twelve liang. According to the casting location and casting nature, they can be divided into HangZai ingots' and local ingots. Ingots of Jin Dynasty have nongovernmental cast ingots and governmental ones. The former ones were comparatively simple. The later ones inherited the silver ingots system of Song Dynasties, employing an arc head and a girdled waist. The name of silver ingots was replaced by silver ingot in Yuan Dynasty. However, their shape and modeling inherited those in Jin Dynasty, employing an arc head, girdled waist, and slightly sunken front side. There usually have several line patterns around the ingots. Usually, one will weigh fifty liang. In the late years of Yuan Dynasty and the early years of Ming Dynasty, the shape and modeling of silver ingots gradually changed into new ones of an arc head, girdled waist, upturning two wings, and bigger face that is larger than the bottom. The new shape was the fixed mode of casting silver ingots in Ming and Qing Dynasty.

160 Silver Ingot with"Zheng Sheng Yuan Nian"Inscription

In silvery grey, the silver ingot has an oblate and rectangular body with a small upper part and a big lower part. The surface is uneven and engraved in regular script of "50 liang of Raozhou district, in the first year of Zhengsheng". "Zhengsheng" were created in the reign of Empress of Wu Zetian. Liang belonged to the big liang system of Tang, and every liang equals to 45g.This silver ingot was cast in a mold. Zhengsheng is the title of empress'reign of 695 A. D. Raozhou was administered by Xidao in the south of the River. It covers the areas of Shangrao and Jingde Zhen in the northeast part of Jiangxi Province. Zhouzhi is Poyang County in Jiangxi Province. In the reign of Emperor of Dezong of Tang (780–––805),silve mines were reverted to official business, and private mining was strongly prohibited. Most of the silver mines of Tang were in the south. Among them, Dexingchang in Raozhou (now Yinshan in Dexing County) was the biggest. This silver ingot belongs to the tributes that Raozhou paid to the court.

161 Silver Ingot with"Qian Fu Liu Nian"Inscription

It was the weighing currency of Tang and cast by Tang central government. Made of silver, the ingot has a cuboid body. The front side is engraved with four lines and thirty–two characters. On the right side, there are five engraved characters "Craftsman Wu Jingteng". "Casting classification" means to recast the gathered silver ingots in accordance with shapes and weights, and then store them in the Privy Purse. Every liang equals to 45g, so it belongs to the big liang system. "Qian Fu" is the first titile of Li Huang, Emperor of Zongli of Tang's reign. The six year of Qian Fu is 879. "Privy Purse" and "Wen Si Yuan" were the agencies that made and provided gold and silver wares to the imperial family and the court in Chang'an of Tang, and they had Zhongshang, Zuoshang and Youshang under the Shaofu's investigation. Zhongshang was the biggest one in the "Gold and Silver Workshop" under every bureau. "Wen Si Yuan" was established in 854 and governed by eunuchs, who were in charge of making gold, silver, rhinoceros horns, and jades wares. "Privy Purse", also known as "Da Ying Ku", was the private store to store private stuff of the emperor. This silver ingot was excavated with the Gilt Silver Spittoon housed by Xi'an Institution of Historical Relics Preservation and Archeology. It has specific cast time and excavation site, which has great significance on the studies of coin casting system and currency development as well as the political and economic systems.

162 Tribute Silver Ingot with"Ling Nan Dao"Inscription

In silvery grey, it is cuboid, and its front side is inscribed with regular script, "fifty liang each ingot officially, Yinqing Guanglu official, military official, inspecting the military affairs of Gunagzhou area, governor and inspector of Guangzhou area, inspector of Chongling, commander, Kaiguo of Nanyang county, Zhang Bo offers", "Sea Affairs official of Lingnan area, position of Wensan, commander, purple golden fish token bestowed, Liu Chujiang" .
"Ling Nan" is Lingnandao. In Tang Dynasty, the whole nation was divided into ten Dao, and Liangnandao was one of them and its administered area covered Guangdong Province, Guangxi Province and the middle and north part of Vietnam. The highest administrative agency was located in Guangzhou. In New Tang · Geography: Lingnandao was in the south of ancient Yangzhou and was in charge of Nanhai, Yulin, Cangwu, Zhuya, Zhan'er, Jiaozhi, Hepu, Jiuzhen and Ri'nan in Han Dynasty. Lingnan was rich in silver, and every year it would pay silver tributes to the court. However, it had only one silver mine, which was located Guiyang, Lianshan, Lianzhou (now Lian County, Guangdong Province). Maritime Trade was the central government oversea trade and management agency in Guangzhou. The oversea trade in Tang was well developed. Trades between China and Southeast Asia, Indian Subcontinent, West Asia and East African countries all took place in Guangzhou, so Tang Government set a Maritime Trade in Guangzhou to charge oversea trade affairs.

163 Constricted Silver Ingot

It is constricted and plain. The front side is like a bridge arch, and the side is like a trapezoid. It is hollow and its surface is unsmooth and the edge is uneven. The entire ingot is silvery grey and some part is rust. That might be because it has been kept together with iron.

164 Constricted Silver Ingot

In silvery grey, it is oblate and constricted with one big flat upper end and one small flat lower end. Its section is trapezoidal. The entire ingot is plain. There were two shapes of silver ingot in Tang Dynasty. One had a straight body and a flat or an arc head. The other had a constricted waist and a flat head. Being pioneer of silver ingot shaping in Song, the he later evolved from the former. This one belongs to the later shape.

165 Gold "Kai Yuan Tong Bao" Coin

It is the coin of Tang Dynasty. It has a round shape and a square hole in the center. On the front side there are four characters "Kai Yuan Tong Bao" in the regular script. The first stroke of "Yuan" is short and the second rises toward left. On the back there a crescent pattern, which opens up. "Kai Yuan Tong Bao" was cast in 621 A.D. It is said that the four characters were written by then famous calligrapher Ouyang Xun. It has been being made throughout Dynasty, as well as in the Southern Tang (937~975A.D.) in the period of Five Dynasties and Ten Kingdoms, but the style of profiles and characters were quite different from that in Tang Dynasty. Gold and silver coins in Tang Dynasty were not the official currency in circulation. It was formulated in the Tang laws that private copper coin making would be seriously punished and but private gold and silver coin making will not be investigated. The court also cast gold and silver coins which were mainly used to play games, treats, wash children (three days or a month after the baby was born, friends and relatives would get together to wash the baby) and so on. Under the influence of the court, the habit of making gold and silver coins as accessories began to emerge among the people.

Gold coins are coins cast in accordance with the style of copper coins. They have a round profile and a round hole in the center. The earliest coins were made in Han Dynasty, called Gold Wuzhu. From then on, in the seven hundred years history of Wuzhu coin, gold wuzhu appeared from time to time, and they were called "Gold Coin" in history until Tang Dynasty when they were replaced by gold Kai Yuan Tong Bao coins. Later, gold Tong Bao coins have been cast several times in Song, Ming and Qing Dynasty. In the late years of Qing Dynasty, the western technique of machine made round coins was introduced to China, so the modern silver coins appeared. In the history, round coins with square holes have long been the mainstream of the money system. Paper money appeared in Song Dynasty. Silver as money entered in to the circulation domain in a wide range in Ming Dynasty. However, gold coins have always been the rewards from the King and birthday gifts within the ruling class.

166 Gilt Bronze Animal Head Appliqués

There are two of them and all of the head appliqués are round sheets. The main pattern is animal mask. The animal opens its eyes and knits its brows, his mouth widely opens to show its sharp teeth, and his tongue rolls and hangs a bronze ring. Its facial expressions are very ferocious. His back is a split rivet, which is used to be inserted into the door wall. The tail end of the rivet is horizontal folded to fix the head appliqués.

The animal appliqué is hammered folded, and the surfaces are gilt. It was unearthed within the Tang Chang'an Daming Palace Site. It should be one component on the gate of some palace.

Song & Yuan Dynasty

167 Square Gold Lidded Case with Buddhist Relics

The gold case is square column and plain all over. The case lid is a lu roof, which is inserted to the case body. A glass bottle with a grain of Buddhist relic is in the case. One side of the case in engraved the inscription of one's wish speaking, "Your female worshippers Ms Yang and Ms Wang buried cased Sakyamuni Buddha relic in the hope that all beings will reach the spiritual state of an immortal by practicing Buddhism".

This gold square column was placed in a stone coffin when it was excavated. The lid of the stone coffin is arch, and the coffin room is oblique rectangular with a flat mouth. The coffin base and coffin room make a unity, forming a trapezium which has a big front and a small back like a short bed. The bottom has three hollow rectangular pot doors on both sides, and two in the front and two at the back. Between the pot doors is engraved ruyi cloud pattern. The inner side of the lid is carved with Ancient Indian Sanskrit. The four outer sides of the coffin room have demirelief of four gods, each of which has a Scarlet Bird in the front, a Green Dragon on the left, a White Tiger on the right, and a Black Tortoise at the back. The pattern carving is neat and fine, showing the worshipper's extreme devout feeling to Sakyamuni Buddha.

168 Silver Ingot

In silvery grey, the ingot is constricted and its bottom is smaller than the surface. The two ends of the long diameter are arch. Its surface is slight sunken and has casting marks. Margins to the left and the right side at the waist are vertically engraved inscriptions in regular script, "outdoor tax, Sinei Gold No. 11□". Its back is covered with honeycomb holes of various sizes, which are the casting marks. "Outdoor tax" is the stamp, and "Gold No.11" is the order number complied with the Thousand Character Classic. In the late years of Southern Song Dynasty, there were three grades of silver ingots of large, medium, and small size because of circulation: fifty liang, twenty liang, and twelve-five and a half liang. Twenty-five liang is 914.2g to 1000g, so this ingot is a medium size. Silver ingots of Southern Song Dynasty have two types: the local made one and the imperial made one. The imperial made ingots were from contribution all over the country. The imperial agency ordered that all gold and silver shops in Lin'an should melt the ingots and recast them. There were stamps on the four corners and two waist sides. Silver fineness and number of the casting shop would be tamped twice as well as the "outdoor tax". The aim of doing so is make it easy to recognize. Some ingots would use Thousand Character Classic to mark and order them.

169 Silver Ingot with Characters of "Weighted by Liu Zhongdian"
The two ends of the ingot are arch, and it is girdled. Its edge of the surface is slightly raised, while the center is sunken. There are honeycomb traces left when casting on the back which has wave patterns around the margin. The front side was engraved with characters. Its surface has rubbing traces. Two characters of "Ding Zhun" were re-engraved on other characters. There are four vague characters in an opposite direction. It is obvious that these four characters were carved first and then removed and re-carved. The phrase "Guild People" was first seen in Old Tang Book · Food and Money, meaning the food guild leaders in the Western and Eastern Market in Tang Chang'an. In Song and Jin Dynasty, guild people described in the inscriptions on silver ingots refer to the ringleaders of the gold and silver guild. They were also known as "Silver Guild People". "Shi Si" is short for the agencies like Transportation Shi Si, Salt Shi Si, Agriculture Shi Si, and so on in Jin Dynasty, and their function were to collect taxes for the court. The Transportation Shi Si was in charge of "collecting taxes, warehouse cashier, and weighting measure systems". Salt Shi Si was in charge of collecting salt taxes. The Transportation and Salt Shi Si had the closest relationship with silver ingot casting. There were non-governmental cast ingots and governmental cast ones in Jin Dynasty. Ingots cast by the non-governmental workshops were simple, and the one cast by the government had names of their casting agencies, guild people, guarantees, and examiners.

170 Gold Ear-picker in the Shape of a Sword
Sword-shaped, the ear-picker has several raised line design on the handle and water ripples on the body close to the handle. The handler holder forms the ear-picker. The ear-picker is a clean tool for human beings, and it also has other names. Its shape always has a long handle and a spoon on the other end. Most of them were made of metal and bones. Sword-shaped ear-picker was rarely seen. Yuan Dynasty was established by Mongol minor ethnic group in China's history. At that time, class and ethnic conflicts were quite sharp and the society was in long-term unrest. The sword-shaped ear-picker reflected the personality of its user to some extent and also reflected people's expectation of luck and safety.

171 Gold Hairpin with a Bottle Gourd
The entire hairpin is plain. One end of it is a little gold bottle gourd. In Yuan Dynasty, Taoism was quite popular, and the bottle gourd was medical item and also one of the musical instruments used in a Taoist mass. To use bottle gourd as ornament reflected that Taoism influenced people's life style and customs. The bottle gourd has the implication of fortune and prosperity.

172 Gold Long and Oblate Hairpin with Little Flower
The gold hairpin is an oblate strip. The pommel has two plies of spun gold which tangle together and then separate at the top to form a peony respectively.

173 Gold Hairpin with Petals
The gold hairpin has two plies which were cast two blossoming petals respectively close to the handle. The top was engraved cellular pattern.

174 Little Gold Hairpin with Winded Threads
The gold hairpin is plain, and two threads of spun gold spread from its handle wind several rings which are tangled together. The two spun gold are connected by a big gold case and a small one at their ends. The two cases might have some inlaid ornaments but they fall off.

175 Gold Hairpin with a Plum Blossom on the Top
As a pyramidal, the hairpin is decorated with a plum blossom at the pommel. A plum blossom, usually having five petals, is the symbol of people's purchase of five blessings: joy, happiness, longevity, peace,

and smoothness. Plum blossoms blossom in the winter, defying frost and braving snow, so they are the symbols of a noble character. Yuan Dynasty was established by Mongol minor ethnic group. Mongolian aristocrats, as the ruling class domestically practiced national oppression. Han people as the oppressed group took up arms against the Mongolian on one hand, and they expressed their dissatisfaction with Mongolian aristocrats' ruling and their noble sentiments of unwillingness to fall on their knees in surrender.

176 Gold Hairpin with Jade Lotus Leaf

The hairpin handle is an oblate strip and the tip is a pyramidal. It is plain, and the pommel, having several rings tangled by thin spun gold, is put on a lotus-leaf-shaped gray jade. One corner of the leaf rolls upwards. It surface is engraved thin lines cut in intaglio to present the venations of the lotus leaf.

Ming & Qing Dynasty

177 Gold Hairpin with Phoenix and Flower

The entire hairpin is made of deep colored gold. Its pommel edge is carved rope figure, which has a blooming sunflower on the surface. The sunflower petals bloom dispersedly in picturesque disorder. Below the sunflower, there is a on a bunch of flowers and plants whose branches and leaves are messy. On the top of the flowers and plants, there is a tubulous with four petals. There are buds spread from the petals. A phoenix is flying over the underbrush. Its beak is pointing to the tubulous, its wings slightly collect and its long tail feathers roll and draw backwards.

178 Gold Hairpin with Phoenix and Flower

The entire hairpin is made of deep colored gold. Its pommel edge is carved fine and tiny pearl string patterns and felt with a phoenix and a blooming sunflower. The phoenix is lying over a bunch of grass-leaf-shaped flowers, and its wings tend to collect, its long tail has several wisps and its feathers extend backwards. It seems that the phoenix just finished its long journey and is contemporarily resting on the flowers and plants.

179 Gold Hairpin with Phoenix and Flower

The entire hairpin is made of deep colored gold. The peach-shaped pommel is inlaid with a hollow phoenix, which is flying high to the sky with spreading wings and fluttering feathers. Around the phoenix, there are several clouds floating.

180 Gold Hairpin with Phoenix and Flower

The entire hairpin is made of deep colored gold. The peach-shaped pommel is inlaid with a hollow phoenix, which is flying with spreading wings. Its long tail flutters backwards like cross-braches pattern. It flies high into the sky and clouds float around it.

181 Gold Hairnet

It is weaved with thin spun gold. The hairnet and its outer edge are connected by spun gold. Four holes are evenly distributed on the outer edge. On one side of the hairnet is vertically arranged with four coin (round out edge with a square hole in the center) patterns. On the opposite side is decorated with a character design "blessing" twisted by spun gold.

Hairnet, also known as "Caul scarves" or "Net", used to be the hairdo of Taoist. Use the hairnet to wrap and fix the hair first, and then tie the end of the hairnet. In the early years of Ming Dynasty, Emperor Taizu of Ming, Zhu Yuanzhang popularized hairnets all over the country. From then on, this way of doing hair remains popular until now.

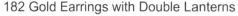

182 Gold Earrings with Double Lanterns

As gold ear ornaments, the earrings have hook pommels, which have hexagonal cap-shaped ornaments weaved by rolling-cloud spun gold. The caps are decorated with six ruyi-rolling-clouds, below which hang six spun gold spikes. Below the caps there are two lanterns-like ornaments. The lanterns are composed of twelve ornate round clustered flowers, under which there is an eight-sided lantern made of square spun gold check. Four window decorations and four checks are alternatively and evenly distributed. They are all made of rolling-clouds squares.

Earrings, also known as eardrops, are one of female ornaments, referring to dropping ornaments on the earrings. Most of them are made of gold, silver and jades, which can be moved. The earliest earrings appeared in the period of Northern Dynasty. Before Five Dynasties, earrings were quite popular in the border areas and among the ethnic minorities that moved to the Mainland. After Five Dynasties, earrings were accepted by Han People, and became one of the major ornaments for Han females.

183 Gold Hairpin with Characters "Shui ShengYuan□"

The gold hairpin is shaped like a bunch of chrysanthemum, inserting into a gold vase that has fish roe pattern on its surface. The chrysanthemum is blooming, and its petals are carved venations cut in intaglio. The pattern is hollow. The body part is cast four characters "Shui Sheng Yuan □" in regular script.

184 Gold Hairpin in Shape of Buddhist Monk's Staff

The entire staff is golden yellow, and the pommel is in the shape of Buddhist monk's staff. The upper is an upward lotus, while the bottom is an overturned lotus. The two lotuses are connected by the six lotus filaments. The six spun gold hang with twelve gold rings which has ornaments but they fell off.

Buddhist monk's staff also has other names. It is one of the eighteen personal necessities when Buddhist monks practice Buddhism and wander for religious purpose. Those necessities include a poplar branch, bath beans, three clothing, water bottle, censer, towel, a water-filtering sac, a knife, a fire beacon, tweezers, a rope bed, Buddhism books and statues. Tang · Yi Jing's works "the Story about Sending Buddhism from South Sea"says, "Tin staff means sound in Sanskrit. Ancient people translated it into tin for its sound. The tin staff in the western countries has a iron curl which has 2 or 3 cun, the pipe installed below has a length of 4 or 5 fingers, and a iron ring is made under the pipe which might be round or flat···".Exoteric and Tantra gave different meanings to the Buddhist monk's staff. Exoteric used Buddhist monk's staff to beg for food and drive away worms, while Tantra looked Buddhist monk's staff as Samaya form, he five most important Buddha and Bodhisattva. Samaya form is the icon of Buddhist and Bodhisattva's ultimate willing. The Buddhist monk's staff differentiates by the multi-plies and multi-rings.Usually,it has four plies and twelve rings, indicating four truths and twelve principal and secondary causes. This one, having six plies and twelve rings, appeared as an ornament, showing that in Qing Dynasty people paid attention to Buddhism on the spiritual belief rather than its form.

185 Gold Hairpin in the Shape of Buddha's Hand

The hairpin is pyramid, and its pommel is twined by spun gold and forms a Buddha's hand. Under the wrist is decorated with ruyi lotus. The back of hand is twined with a thin spun gold, the two ends of which are connected by a spiral at the palm. The index finger and the thumb pick up a Buddhist monk's staff, which is a pole twined by spun gold. Gold rings hangs on the Buddhist monk's staff. The Buddha's hand has the implication of happiness and longevity.

186 Constricted Oblate Gold Hairpin

The hairpin is constricted with two sharp ends. The outer edge is carved a circle of "Hui" characters. A raised line design goes through from one end to the other one. The inner side is cast five characters of "Pure gold, □ Spring Commencement " in regular script.

187 Constricted Oblate Gold Hairpin with Peony and Chrysanthemum Pattern

This gold hairpin is constricted, and its two ends are like diamonds which have a rectangular frame respectively that has the fish roe pattern as the background. One side is decorated with a bunch of branch-crossed peony. The branch is crossed and twined and leaves are thinly disordered. There is a peony blossom on the branch. The other end is decorated with a bunch of chrysanthemum. The branch is thin and there is a chrysanthemum on it and its petals which are like willow leaves surround the flower center. Half plum is one each side of the rectangular frame. Inner the frame there are two carved characters "De He" in regular script. All ornamentations are engraved and they are fine, possessing superb artistic skills.

188 Constricted Oblate Gold Hairpin with Flowers and Grass Pattern

The hairpin is constricted with two broader ends and a thinner middle. Its surface is slightly raised. The two ends are decorated with the same thin flower and grass. There is a little blooming flower on the leaves. The venations are quite obvious. The inner side is carved with two characters in regular script. Patterns all over the body are carved.

189 Gold Ear-picker with Crossed Branches

The ear-picker is a long strip and in the shape of pyramidal. The section is rhombic. Its pommel is carved with a bunch of flowers and grass in branch-crossed pattern. Section close to the handle is round. The middle part is an ellipsoid. There are four circles of line pattern cut in intaglio close to the picker.

190 Pyramidal Gold Ear-picker

Its handle is pyramidal. Close to the picker, there are carved several string pattern, and the rest part is plain.

191 Gold Earrings with Characters of "Tian De"

The earrings consist of bats and wide oblate rings. The bats are shaped like Ruyi. Their eyes are widely open and they are flying with spreading. The inner side is carved two characters of "Tian De". Bats have implications of multi-happiness and matching one's wishes, so they are used as auspicious terms, indicating happiness and smoothness. "Tian De" might be the name of the private banking house.

192 Gold Earrings of "De He" and "Zu Chi"

The earrings are oblate and round with Ruyi cloud pattern. The outer side makes fish roe pattern as the background, on which there are engraved two clusters of flowers and grass in different directions. Their leaves are like willow leaves, and the petals are blooming. The inner side is engraved with four characters "De He" and "Zu Chi" on the shoveled bottom. "De He" was the name of a private banking house. "Zu Chi" means deep-colored gold, indicating that the gold enjoys a higher purity of gold and it is helvolus. It's purity is generally more than 99.2%.

193 Gold Earrings with Ruyi and Bat Patterns

The earrings are fluted and round. There is fine and tiny fish roe pattern as background, on which there is a flying bat that has a prominent mouth, widely opened eyes and unfolded wings. Wing tips are in the shape of Ruyi. There is a raised ring at the back of its head whose center is sunken, which might be because there was inlaid ornament, but they fell off. Below the bats, there are five rings, each of which has patterns like Capricorn, Buddha's hand and lotus petals. Bats have the implication of multi-happiness, presenting its owner's desire for a better life and the pursuit of happiness. Ruyi is one of Buddhist's staffs. It is called "Anuruddha" in Sanskrit. The end of the long handle is in the shape of fingers that can be used to scratch where it itches, so it can satisfy human beings' needs, and then it is called Ruyi. In Southern and Northern Dynasty, Buddhists always held a Ruyi when they were preaching.

194 Gold Earrings with Mask Motif

They are oblate and the outer side is engraved Ruyi-shaped bat pattern. The bat opens its eyes widely, spreads its wings and draws its tail backwards. Its wings are decorated with fish roe pattern. Its tail feathers are engraved by thin lines cut in intaglio. The rest part is plain. The entire shape is like a triangle.

195 Gold Earrings with "Shou" Character and Bat Pattern

They are zonal. In the middle of the outer side has a character "Shou" whose two sides are decorated with two oppositely flying bats. The character "Shou" and the "bat" pattern are all carved. There is a matt pattern in the outer side and the oblate rings at the lower part of the earrings. In the matt pattern, there are decorations between the two line designs as well as a green jade pendant, which is of jade quality and in the shape of Disc (bi). "Bat" is homophonic with "Fortune" in Chinese, means double fortunes and longevity. Bats as propitious words appeared in the late years of Yuan and in the early years of Ming, and large numbers of them were seen in various objects as ornaments in Ming and Qing Dynasty.

196 Gold Earrings with Characters "□Sheng"

They are oblate, and the front part of their outer sides is cast with Ruyi shaped flame pattern. There are three fish roe designs decorate the inner edge of the flame pattern which is hollow. The entire shape is like a triangle. Edges of the lower part are decorated with two circles of string patterns cut in intaglio. The inner side is cast with two characters "□Sheng" in regular script. Each earring has a green jade pendant, which is of jade quality and in the shape of Disc (bi).

197 Gold Earrings with "卍"Character and Bat Patterns

They are oblate and each is decorated with a bat in the front. The bat's head is downward, and it has a sharp mouth and prominent eyes. Its ears turn backwards and its wings spread. The inner side is engraved with two characters "Rui Lan".

198 Gold Earrings in Fish Intestine Pattern

The earrings are circular and their edges are oblate. Inner side of each ring makes fish roe pattern as the background, on which five fine and tiny plum on the same branch blossoms are engraved. The front part is hollow out fish intestine pattern, on which cord pattern is decorated. The inner side is engraved with four characters "□□Pure Gold" in regular script. Fish intestine is one of Buddhism's eight treasures, carrying the meaning of boundless happiness. Five plum blossoms imply five fortunes.

199 Tiger-head-shaped Gold Ring Inlaid Precious Stones

The ring consists of two bifarious tiger heads and the ring comes out from the mouths of the two tigers. The two tiger heads are inlaid with rammel ring surface which is flat and carved an animal cut in intaglio. The ring, also known as finger ring, is a ling ring on the finger. They are made of gold and silver and

beginning, they were popular ornaments. After they were brought to the class society, they became symbols used by concubines as being called to sleep with the emperor and taboos. Because of usage constraints, for thousands of years, rings had little change in forms, mainly adding ornaments or carvings or inlays. In the Eastern and Western Dynasty, most gold rings had inlaid precious stones. After Jin Dynasty (265–420 A.D.), rings were carved with pattern and they became broader and some of them had inlaid precious stones. In Ming and Qing Dynasty, the luxury level of a ring would be determined by its diamond size and precious stone grade.

200 Gold Floral Ring Inlaid Precious Stones

The entire ring is deep colored gold, and it is wide and oblate. The middle part is wider and is decorated with a gold flower which consists of one ring frame in the center and eight small ring frames outside. Within the center ring frame is inlaid a green jade, and in the eight small round ring frames are inlaid eight small gold beads. There is a decorative bat on each side of the flower. The bat heads to the flower and spreads its wings which have coin (round with square hole in center) patterns on both sides. Arteries and veins on its wings and back are carved with thin line cut in intaglio.

201 Gilt Silver Bracelets with Appliqué

In the shape of ring, the bracelets have the same emblazonry and four pasted baskets that have bale handles. Shapes of the four baskets are bowl, bamboo basket, ingot and pitcher. In every basket, there is a bunch of blooming flowers and leafy plants that are gilt. With the implication of a basket of richness and honor, basket flower arrangement was usually seen from the Emperor Yongzheng of Qing Dynasty from 1723 to 1735 A.D.

Bracelets are ornaments around one's wrist, and they appeared in the Middle Neolithic. At the very beginning, most of them were made of animal bones, animal teeth, stones, pottery or jades. Their shapes included circular tube, traffic circle, and mosaic made of two semi-circular rings. From Shang and Zhou Dynasty to the Spring and Autumn and the Warring States Periods, the bracelet materials were mainly jades. There were metal bracelets appeared in Shang and Zhou Dynasty. Originally, bracelets were worn both by men and women, but later they were ornaments only for women. There was little change in shape and modeling throughout dynasties, but the decorations on them were becoming richer and richer. Bracelets made of silver are popular among women, for they symbolize fortune at the same time.

202 Silver Bracelets in Shape of Willow Leaf

In silvery white, the two bracelets are wide in the middle and narrow at the two ends. The outer side of them has three raised edges, which consist of a rising middle one and two rolling other ones, forming two sinks. They are in shape of willow leaves when they are extended. Their ends are twined with filamentary silver to form a hole at the tip. Several parts have rust. The inner side is plain. In a unique style, the bracelets are simply made.

203 Three Gold Necessities

They are dressing ornaments and they are also known as Three Gold Things. On the top is a gold ring, connected with a small and a big wing-spreading butterfly that are hollow. Items connected to the small butterfly's wings were lost and a big butterfly was connected to the small one by a gold chain. Three necessities, ear-picker, eyebrow-picker, opener, are connected to the big butterfly's head and two wings respectively. Usually, three necessities refer to toothpick, ear-picker and so on, which are mainly used as living equipments. At the same time, they can be used as ornaments.

204 Silver Buddha Statue

The Buddha statue has a square face, big ears, a hump nose and a small mouth and his eyes close slightly. His hands are on his legs, and right hand is in his left hand with the palms upward, posing Dhyana-mrdra. He wears a kasaya, gestures a hero posture on the lotus pedestal. His facial expressions are serious and solemn. The lotus pedestal under the statue has two stories which are separated by a string of fine and tiny linked pearl pattern. The Buddha statue is surrounded by flowers. The halo is decorated with hackle mark and flame pattern. The entire emblazonry is carved out. After Song Dynasty, Buddhism was increasingly declining, while New-Confucianism was gradually permeating into the whole social ideology system, so people did not rely heavily upon worshipping Buddha any more. With the city business prosperity, social ideology tended to be realistic. Buddhist statues were becoming more and more secularized, and there are less and less of them in number. They only existed as spiritual ballasts.

205 Silver Ingots with Charactors of "Xi'an Sheng Yongxingqing"

The four ingots are all silvery white. (1) The front side is approximately oval, its outer side is curved, and its bottom is also oval. The surface is uneven and is vertically carved two lines with three characters of each in regular script in intaglio. (2) Its front side is constricted. When looked from side face, it is like a

big end up trapezoid. Its surface is smooth and there is a vertical rectangle on the shoveled face in its center. Within the rectangle, there are four vertically cast characters "Jin Tai Private Banking House" that cut in intaglio. (3) Its surface is approximately oval and notched. The outer side is an arc wall, and the bottom is ring. There are four cast characters in the shoveled square in the center of the front surface. The characters are regular scripts and cut in relief. (4) Its front side is constricted and notched. Its side faces are like trapezoids. The bottom is flat. There is a cast character "Xi" in the shoveled circle in the center of the front surface. The character is regular script and cut in relief. In Qing Dynasty, taxes were paid by silver. In the early years of Qing Dynasty, Xi'an, Shanxi paid boundary taxes by pure silver. Silver used in daily life was not pure enough. In the late years of Qing Dynasty, there is government-cast pure silver and non-government-cast pure silver in circulation of Shaanxi.

Silver ingots were one of the circulating silver in Yuan, Ming and Qing Dynasty. In the early years of Yuan, the name changed and they especially referred to ingots of fifty liang. They usually had an arc head, a constricted waist, and a slightly sunken front surface. There were several wire patterns. In Yuan Dynasty, if ingots were governmentally cast, they would be carved with where they were from and where they would go. Some contents might include the origin, function, and weight, date of casting, handling officials and craftsmen and so on. In Ming Dynasty, there were two types of silver ingots. One has a round head, tight constricted waist, and bottom and front surface of the same size. The other one has an arc head and a constricted waist. Its surrounding rose and turned outwards and its front surface was bigger than its bottom. Silver ingots have a big size and a small size. The big size refers to the fifty liang ingots, while the small size refers to ingots of thirty liang, twenty liang, ten liang, and five liang. There were usually carved inscriptions on the big-size ingots, indicating their origins, weights, handling officials and craftsmen's names. However, small-size ingots only had the names of Zhou or Xian and craftsmen. In the late years of Ming, inscriptions were hit out and they only stated the ingots' weight, purity, and the names of the craftsmen and the silver houses. In Qing Dynasty, their shapes were mainly oval. The outer side was arc and the bottom was oval. The government had required purity of the silver for tax-paying. The silver casting craftsmen should be appointed by the Qing government. In 1736, it was formulated in prevision that every Xian in every Zhou should distribute countermark to every silversmith in their administration, and that tax-payers could go to the silversmith to casting the scattered silver at their will and the recast ingots would have the countermarks of the Zhou, Xian and the silversmith.

206 Silver Ingots with characters of"Baihe Lijin"and"Sanshui Diding"

There are thirty of them and they are all silver grey. The front surface is oval. Some of them are constricted. The side face is arc and the bottom is circular, like an overturned Chinese peck. Most of them are notched on the front surface which has casting marks. On the bottom of the socket there are finger prints; in the center is a hit out square which has inscriptions of lines and two characters of each, such as, "Baihe Likin Silver" and "Sanshui Land Silver". Haihe, Baihe County in Shaanxi, is located in border region of Henan, Shaanxi and Hubei Province and it is the vital communication line of Shaanxi, Henan and Hubei Province. Sanshui is Xunyi County in Shaanxi Province. Some inscriptions may include six or seven words, such as "Renxuan, Hancheng city in the year of Renzi", "Liuyong, Xianyang city in the year of Xinhai". Most of them would be cast with year of casting, native place and name of the casting craftsman, and their functions.

Likin silver was one of the taxes in Qing Dynasty. In 1853, in order to suppress down the Taiping Uprising led by Hong Xiuquan, assistant minister of Board of Punishments Lei Yicheng assessed a passing tax on the itinerant traders and a trading tax on the tradesmen in Yangzhou. The tax rate was one out off one hundred. In 1858, Shaanxi replicated the tax system of Yangzhou. Later, Likin also included articles of daily use, and the tax rate increased to two or three out of one hundred. The likin silver usually weighed five liang. Land silver was also one of taxes in Qing Dynasty. It was formulated in prevision that "males are adults when they turn sixteen, so they have to fulfill poll service or they can pay silver money. Land tax would be collected in accordance with the farm sizes and grades. In 1712, it was formulated in prevision that, "the born one will not pay tax". In 1722, it was ordered that every province should put poll tax into farmland tax, which was called "farmland tax". The farmland silver ingot weigh about four liang, and it usually enjoys a high purity.

207 Silver Ingot with Characters of"Qi Shan Li Zheng"

It is the likin silver used in Shaanxi, Qing Dynasty. It is silvery grey. The two ends are slightly upward, while the center is slightly sunken. Four imprinted characters "Qi Shan Li Zheng" in the regular script are in the square stamping back in the center. It has an arc wall, and an oval bottom which has cutting marks. Qi Shan is the Qishan County in Shaanxi Province, while Li Zheng was a famous silversmith in Qishan, Shaanxi, Province of Qing Dynasty.

208 Silver Ingot with Characters of"He Yang Li Mao"

It is the likin silver used in Shaanxi, Qing Dynasty. It is silvery grey. The front is oval with deep socket and casting marks. Four imprinted characters "He Yang Li Mao" in the regular script are in the square stamping back in the center. It has an arc wall, and the back is oval. He Yang is the Heyang County in Shaanxi Province, while Li Mao was a famous silversmith in Heyang, Shaanxi, Province of Qing Dynasty.

209 Silver Boy

It is made of silver, and hollow. The boy is sitting. He is fat, wearing a flower-trimmed bonnet with two bear ears. With big opened eyes, his cheeks dimple upon the upturned mouth as he smiles. There is a dot in the middle of his forehead. He holds hands in the chest, and the navel exposes. He is sitting with his right foot stepping on the left one.

The boy is composed by welding the front part and the back part. There is a hole in the top of the head as well as in the bottom. The hole on the head is tied to a broken silver chain, so it is supposed that this silver boy is one decoration on some item.

210 "Bei Ping" Gold Bracelet

In golden yellow, it is nearly around, while the cross-section is semi-circular. The inner side is almost flat and cast with four rectangular concaves, each of which has two characters in the regular script consequently: "Bei Ping", "Zhong Yuan", "Jia Lian", and "Zu Shi" that are engraved in the shoveled bottom. The upper right side of "Bei Ping" has a five-pointed star. The two ends of the gold bracelet are spherical and unclosed. "Bei Ping" is a geographical name, standing for Beijing. It was called Capital Shuntian in Ming and Qing Dynasties. Then in 1928, it was changed into Beijing by the National Government and merged into Hebei Province.

211 Gold Bar with "Bei" Inscription

Bing cubiod, the gold bar is deep colored gold. In the center of the front, there is a shovel money picture of Xinmang Dynasty. In the center of the shovel money picture, there is a vertical line, which has a variant of "Bei" on the left and a symbol on the right. On the back of the bar, there are three lines in turn: "S40644", "purity of gold 9800", "liang 500". In 1931, after "9·18" incident, the Japanese imperialists invaded and occupied three northeastern provinces of China. Then they made "1·28 incident" in Shanghai, while attacking the fortresses along the Great Wall. Japanese invaded China step by step, pushing Chinese nation to a critical moment of national subjugation and racial extinction. To meet the war needs of resistance, National Government issued Legal Money Policy to require that those who hold gold should exchange the gold for legal money with the National Bank, and also require that gold should be collected by the governments and marketing be prohibited. In the late years of China's War of Resistance against Japan, American Government loaned 500 million U.S. dollars to Chinese Government in Chongqing for the purchase of gold. In 1945, national government ordered the Chongqing Central Mint to fusion cast gold bars and to cash gold certificate savings certificates. By January in 1946, Chongqing Central Mint had fusion cast 4273.376 thousand gold bars, weighing 1 443 987.158 liang, of various sizes from two qian to one hundred liang. This gold bar is one of them.

시안(西安, 長安)은 중화문명의 중요한 발원지로 상주(商周)시대에서 한당(漢唐)시대에 이르기까지 줄곧 금은기 (金銀器) 제작 중심지였다. 반세기 이래로 이곳에서 대량의 고대 금은기가 출토되었는데 그 종류 및 변화, 발전이 상 당히 체계적이었다. 이 금은기들은 직접적이면서도 정확하게 고대 시안의 역사를 반영하고 있다. 하루빨리 이 진귀 한 고대 금은기를 독자들에게 선보이고 시안은 물론 중국 내 인문과학 연구에 새로운 자료를 제공하기 위해 시안시 문물국 쑨푸시(孫福喜) 박사가 『西安文物精華(시안문물정화)-金銀器(금은기)』를 기획하고 펴내게 되었다. 본서는 시안 지역에서 출토된 전형적 · 대표적인 금은기 200여 점을 수록하였다.

본서는 쑨푸시 박사가 책임기획자로 양홍이(楊宏毅)가 함께 체계를 잡고 문물 해설을 집필했다. 도편은 왕바오 핑(王保平), 교정은 자시아오얀(賈曉燕), 리시핑(李喜萍), 자오시리(趙希利), 왕러칭(王樂慶)이 책임졌다. 왕창치(王長 啓)는 편찬과정에 모든 금은기의 이름, 시대구분 등 많은 의견을 내주셨으며 전언 부분도 써주셨다. 시안시문물국의 시앙더(向德), 지앙시아오콴(姜曉泉), 탕시광(唐世廣), 타이야친(邰亞秦) 등도 본서의 출판에 힘을 보태었다.

본서는 쑨푸시 박사가 최종 심사하였다. 세계도서출판시안공사(世界圖書出版西安公司) 우훙차이(武宏才), 판신 (樊鑫)도 본서의 출판에 여러모로 도움을 주었다. 이 자리를 빌려 모든 분들께 감사드린다.

2011년 11월

엮은이